W9-CEC-023

Evaluating Correctional
and Community Settings

RUDOLF H. MOOS

EVALUATING CORRECTIONAL AND COMMUNITY SETTINGS

A WILEY- INTERSCIENCE PUBLICATION

JOHN WILEY & SONS, New York ● London ● Sydney ● Toronto

Copyright © 1975 by John Wiley & Sons, Inc.

All rights reserved. Published simultaneously in Canada.

Library of Congress Cataloging in Publication Data:
Moos, Rudolf H   1934-
    Evaluating correctional and community settings.

    "A Wiley-Interscience publication."
    Includes bibliographies and index.
    1. Corrections. 2. Corrections—Evaluation.
I.   Title.
HV9275.M66   364.6   74-30267
ISBN 0-471-61502-1

Printed in the United States of America

10 9 8 7 6 5 4 3 2 1

To

PAUL MOOS

(1863–1952)

Author—critic—iconoclast

Preface

This book is a continuing statement of our work in the Social Ecology Laboratory at Stanford University and the Palo Alto Veterans Administration Hospital. My first book, *Evaluating Treatment Environments: A Social Ecological Approach*, presented the development of methods by which the social environments of psychiatric treatment programs can be systematically assessed and changed. Conceptually similar but empirically independent work on correctional and community settings is reported in this book.

Although the book is complete in itself, many of the issues have parallels in psychiatric treatment programs and are also discussed, sometimes from a slightly different perspective, in *Evaluating Treatment Environments*. Specific chapter references to the relevant portions of *Evaluating Treatment Environments* are included for the interested reader. My attempt has been to minimize overlap between the two books but still to include enough detail to permit this book to stand as an entirely independent contribution. The extensive empirical data presented here are of course totally new.

The Book in Brief. This book discusses the development and utility of new methods for evaluating the social environments of institutionally based correctional programs, community-based correctional programs, families, and military companies. Part I presents an overview of our

vii

concepts. Parts II and III focus on the assessment and evaluation of institutionally based correctional programs. Part IV focuses on the generalization of the work to community settings (i.e., community-based correctional programs, families, and military companies). Part V summarizes the empirical work and discusses the broader implications of the concept of social climate.

Chapter 1 presents the rationale and methods for characterizing social and organizational climates. The relevance of these concepts to correctional programs is described, and we identify three basic categories of dimensions—Relationship dimensions, Personal Growth dimensions, and System Maintenance and System Change dimensions—which characterize a wide variety of social environments.

In Chapter 2 we discuss the theoretical rationale and the methodology involved in constructing a technique, the Correctional Institutions Environment Scale (CIES), which assesses nine dimensions of the social climates of correctional programs. A rapid practical method for repeated assessments of correctional programs is presented, as is a method for assessing and comparing resident, staff, and correctional administrators' values regarding ideal or optimum correctional programs.

Chapter 3 uses extensive normative samples of more than 100 juvenile and 90 adult correctional programs to describe current conditions in correctional facilities of different types. Certain important comparisons are made—for example, juvenile halls with ranches and camps, male with female prisons, and juvenile with adult programs. Resident and staff ideas about ideal correctional environments are discussed, as are the enormous differences between actual and optimum programs. The relationship between the social environment and other dimensions characterizing correctional programs (e.g., size and staffing) is discussed.

Chapter 4 deals with the practical utility of measuring social environments and presents both clinical CIES profile interpretations and a paradigm for using CIES data for teaching and social change purposes. The range of correctional environments is illustrated by detailed profile examples of different types of correctional programs. The utility of the CIES for program description, for understanding institutional dynamics, and for program consultation is illustrated.

The analysis in Chapter 5 indicates that both correctional and psychiatric programs may be classified into six essentially similar categories: Therapeutic Community, Relationship-oriented, Action-oriented, Insight-oriented, Control-oriented, and Disturbed Behavior programs. The six types are described, and implications for differential treatment procedures are drawn.

Part III discusses the use of the CIES in program comparisons and evaluations. Chapter 6 is a detailed discussion of a correctional program evaluation study in which the CIES was a measure of the social environment. Two large correctional institutions were investigated; one used transactional analysis as its major treatment approach, whereas the other used a behaviorally oriented reinforcement approach. The two programs are described and their respective social environments contrasted. Descriptions of individual living unit programs illustrate the wide variations to be found within transactional and behavioral treatment approaches.

Chapter 7 discusses work in which the differential impact of correctional programs was assessed. The impact of correctional programs is treated in relation to resident morale and self-esteem, to modes of adaptation and coping, to behavioral rating and personality test changes and, finally, to parole outcome. A perceived climate index linking parole outcome to program social climate is derived. Implications for objective evaluations comparing correctional programs are drawn.

Chapter 8 covers a portion of an extensive project using the CIES in experimental group homes and camps administered by the New York State Division for Youth. The main focus is on the effects of the social environment and of personality variables in accounting for the differential impact of correctional programs, particularly absconding. The work suggests that the CIES may be useful in predicting which residents will run away or abscond from correctional programs.

Chapter 9 deals with several aspects of program congruence and incongruence: (1) the degree of resident–staff congruence and its implication for correctional programs; (2) the accuracy of individual perceptions of the correctional environment, and the extent to which residents who perceive the environment deviantly react deviantly to it; (3) the relation of different indices of person–environment congruence to the amount of rule-breaking and troublemaking behavior.

Part IV presents some applications of this work to three different community settings. Chapter 10 discusses current and future trends in community-based correctional programs, such as halfway houses, group homes, and residential community centers. A project that used an adapted observer form of the CIES to measure the social environments of community group homes is discussed. Our analysis indicates that community programs may also be conveniently categorized into six major types, which are conceptually analogous to the six major types discussed in Chapter 5.

Chapter 11 reviews some work on the relationship between delinquency and the family milieu, discusses studies that emphasize the importance of the family environment in influencing program outcome, and presents the development of a scale, the Family Environment Scale (FES), which systematically assesses 10 salient dimensions of family climate. Some preliminary empirical work on this scale is presented.

Chapter 12 focuses on the social climates of military companies. The relationship between company environment, negative or distressful affect, sick call, and military test performance scores is discussed. Two perceived climate indices, which are highly related to company test performance and sick call rates, respectively, are derived. The role of positive perceptions and expectations in enhancing adaptation to military life is anlayzed. Contrasting clinical case histories of the adaptation of enlisted men to basic training are used as examples.

Part V summarizes the empirical work and its implications. In Chapter 13, an overview of the results, we consider the practical utility of the social climate concept and of the Social Climate Scales, and briefly review broadly convergent data suggesting tentative conclusions about the impact of social environments. Some conceptual and methodological issues of recurring importance in this work are addressed.

RUDOLF H. MOOS

Social Ecology Laboratory
Department of Psychiatry and Behavioral Sciences
Stanford University Medical Center
and Veterans Administration Hospital
Palo Alto, California
March 1975

Acknowledgments

The research was generously supported in part by NIMH Grants MH 16026, MH 8304, and MH 16461; in part by NIAAA Grant AA 00498; and in part by Veterans Administration Research Project MRIS 5817-01. Portions of the work were conducted under a subcontract from the National Council of Crime and Delinquency to the Social Ecology Laboratory.

The data on correctional programs were collected with the collaboration and assistance of individuals too numerous to mention. Most notably, Gordon Adams, Marilyn Cohen, Karl Schonborn, and Edison Trickett participated in the initial data collection on juvenile correctional programs. Jean Otto, Charles Petty, Robert Shelton, Penny Smail, and Paul Sommers coordinated the second phase of data collection on juvenile programs. Carl Jesness and Robert Wedge generously assisted and collaborated with us in the studies at Karl Holton and O. H. Close (Chapter 6), and William Megathlin and Ernst Wenk assisted in the collection and analysis of portions of the data on adult correctional facilities.

The data on families (Chapter 11) were collected with the assistance of Rick Bliss, Paul Insel, Stewart Kiritz, Steve Lynn, Charles Petty, Richard Price, Penny Smail, and Paul Sommers. The work on military companies (Chapter 12) was done in collaboration with Harris Clemes.

Jim Stein and Bill Lake coordinated the initial computer analyses. Marguerite Kaufmann and Robert Shelton coordinated most of the detailed and extensive computer analyses during the middle phases of the project. Bernice Van Dort handled the data analysis during the final phase of the project. During the last two years of the project Paul Sommers importantly facilitated all aspects of the work.

Susanne Flynn helped organize the myriad secretarial and editorial details. She and Louise Doherty typed and organized each of the various drafts of this book.

Carl Jesness and Saleem Shah read and competently criticized an earlier draft of the book. Their comments caused me some consternation, but were instrumental in helping me to improve and clarify several chapters. Saleem Shah and George Weber, of the Center for the Study of Crime and Delinquency, assisted me in obtaining funding for the final revision and extensive data analyses on the Correctional Institutions Environment Scale.

My wife Bernice contributed to the compilation of the data and to various statistical and computer analyses throughout the long life of the project. She was also responsible for all the analyses on the Family Environment Scale (Chapter 11). Karen and Kevin used an earlier draft of this book as a model for writing their own books, and thereby facilitated my work. Would that I had finished this book as quickly and efficiently as they finished theirs!

R.H.M.

Contents

Tables

Figures

PART ONE

Overview

CHAPTER ONE

Social Climate:
The "Personality"
of the Environment

Social Climate: The "Personality" of the Environment

The Social Climate Perspective.   Human environments have significant impacts on human functioning. The environments of correctional programs are thought to have significant impacts on their members. It is therefore imperative that we understand different methods by which environments can be described and by which these descriptions can be related to human behavior. Six major ways in which human environments have been related to human functioning have recently been identified (Moos, 1973). These are (1) ecological dimensions, which include geographical, meteorological, architectural, and physical design variables; (2) behavior settings, which are units characterized by ecological and behavioral properties; (3) dimensions of organizational structure, such as size and staffing; (4) dimensions identifying the collective characteristics of the people in an environment; (5) variables relevant to the functional or reinforcement analyses of environments; and (6) dimensions related to the psychosocial characteristics and social climates of environments.

The measurement of social climate is one of the principal means of characterizing human environments. This chapter presents a rationale for the measurement of social climate, briefly describes the development of a related series of Social Climate Scales, and discusses similar underlying patterns that characterize a wide diversity of social milieus. Some evidence illustrating the importance of social setting influences on behavior is reviewed, with particular reference to examples from correctional environments and implications for correctional practice.

The social climate perspective assumes that environments have unique "personalities," just like people. Personality tests assess personality traits or needs and provide information about the characteristic ways in which people behave. Social environments can be similarly portrayed with a great deal of accuracy and detail. Some people are more supportive than others. Likewise, some social environments are more supportive than others. Some people feel a strong need to control others. Similarly, some social environments are extremely rigid, autocratic, and controlling. Order, clarity, and structure are important to many people. Correspondingly, many social environments strongly emphasize order, clarity, and control.

Almost everyone intuitively believes that the social environment or social climate has a significant impact on the people functioning in it. For example, many people feel that the current social climate in the United States fosters aggressive and criminal behavior. One can cogently argue that every institution in our society is attempting to set up social environments that will maximize certain directions of personal growth and development. Families, social groups, business organizations, secondary schools, colleges and universities, military companies, psychiatric treatment programs, correctional institutions, and communes all arrange social environmental conditions that they hope will maximize "desirable" behaviors (and minimize "undesirable" ones). There is of course great disagreement about what effects should be maximized and what social environmental conditions maximize them.

The Lester and Mitchell Families.   Consider two families living in physically similar homes on the same block of a middle-income suburban area. Each has four immediate family members: mother, father, teenaged son, and teenaged daughter. At first glance these two families appear similar, but this impression changes radically when information about the social environment or the "personality" of the families is provided.

The Lester family has a strong sense of belonging and togetherness. The members get along well together, have a good deal of fun as a family unit, and are involved in and proud of their family. Family members help and support one another and are able to talk together about their personal problems and uncertainties. The Lesters feel relaxed and confortable at home. They show warmth and physical affection toward one another. Laughter, spontaneous discussions, silly horseplay, and spur-of-the-moment activities are frequent. Each of the Lesters is actively involved in hobbies, sports, and other recreational activities. A visitor sees tennis rackets, fishing gear, baseball gloves, and other sports equipment around the house. The Lesters often go to movies, and they participate in sports events, camping and hiking. Friends are always at the house, joining in for dinner or an activity.

The Lesters also emphasize a moral and religious orientation. They attend church regularly. The Bible is often read and discussed in their home, although it is not taken literally. Prayers are said before meals. The family often talks about the religious meaning of Christmas, Easter, and other holidays. Moral and ethical issues are openly discussed and debated, with the express purpose of defining a practical and useful set of ethical standards for each individual. Family members respect others who have high moral and ethical principles and try to emulate them.

Our second family has a quite different social environment or "personality." The Mitchell family is extremely well organized. Each family member has certain chores or duties at home, and each follows a fairly regular daily schedule. Neatness and orderliness are paramount virtues. Family activities are carefully planned. The household runs on the principle of "a place for everything, and everything in its place." Dishes are usually done immediately after eating, being on time is considered to be crucially important and financial planning, budgeting, and allowances are handled with extreme care. There is a high degree of clarity and consistency in this family. People say what they mean, and everyone knows exactly what is expected of him. The family has explicit rules (e.g., the amount of allowances and the number of nights out for each child), which are generally mutually agreed on. Each family member has defined responsibilities around the home. There is very little confusion, changing of minds, and spur-of-the-moment activity in this family. Thus the Mitchell family is highly predictable. The family has a set of rules that must be followed. Father is the head of the household, but he and his wife usually agree on all important matters anyway.

The Mitchells set very high goals for themselves. Each of them feels that it is important to be the best at whatever he does. Getting ahead in life is essential, and school grades and promotions are often discussed. Self-improvement is a cardinal virtue, and everyone strives to do things just a bit better next time. The family believes in competition and tries hard to succeed. Perhaps its motto is: "If a job is worth doing, it's worth doing well." Intellectual and cultural activities are also strongly emphasized. The Mitchells frequently read books and magazines and have intellectual discussions about political and social issues. They go to lectures, plays, and concerts and actively participate in artistic and other craft endeavors. Classical music, art, and literature are emphasized—father plays the violin and mother the piano. Often all the Mitchells read a book and discuss it over the dinner table or in the evening.

The Lester and Mitchell families clearly have very different "personalities." The adolescent children in these families will probably develop quite differently. They are likely to engage in different activities and to have different values; later they are likely to organize their own families in very different ways. In our terms, the Lester family is characterized by involvement, cohesion, belonging, and mutual support; by open, spontaneous, expressive activity; and by active recreational pursuits and an emphasis on moral, ethical, and religious development. This family does not particularly stress achievement or intellectual and cultural pursuits, nor does it value order and regularity or a careful and clear structuring of family activities and rules.

The Mitchell family stands in sharp contrast. They strongly emphasize order, organization, and neatness, clarity of expectations, and consistency and strictness of rules and procedures. The Mitchells are oriented toward academic achievement and success and toward a broad intellectual and cultural education. But success is not to be bought at any price; the emphasis is on achievement through inner control, excellence and competence. The Mitchells are not heavily involved in recreational activities and they consider organized religion to be largely irrelevant to their everyday life. Although the family has a certain degree of cohesion, family members tend to do their jobs routinely. The emphasis is somewhat more on competition among family members than on support, and there is relatively little careless joking and spontaneity.

This example of two contrasting families is intended to convey the concept and probable impact of social climate. Two families that superficially appear similar may be quite different. One family was not "doing better" than the other. Parents and children in both families were active, successful in their chosen pursuits, and generally satisfied with their family lives. The example simply indicates the range of widely divergent family styles and climates.

Describing Social Environments. Pace (1962) has illustrated the importance of the social climate of a college or university. Colleges have their own special atmosphere and establish their own particular image. However, only certain information about a college is commonly available. It is easy to find out the size of a college, whether it is coeducational, where it is located, when it was founded, what degrees it offers, whether it is public or private, religious or nonsectarian, what it costs, and so on. Pace points out that having learned the answers to all these questions, one really knows very little that is important about a college.

> Suppose one asked the same kinds of questions about a prospective college student: What is his height and weight, sex, residence, age, vocational goal, religious affiliation and his family income. Knowing all these things one is still left in ignorance about what kind of a person the prospective student really is. The important knowledge concerns his aptitudes and interests, his motivations and emotional and social maturity. In short the crucial knowledge concerns his personality. So, too, with a college the crucial knowledge concerns its overall atmosphere or characteristics, the kinds of things that are rewarded, encouraged, emphasized, the style of life which is valued in the community and is most visibly expressed and felt. (p. 45)

Popular and professional writers have attempted to capture the "personalities" of different social environments. Almost every biography and autobiography discusses the essential elements of the family environment that was presumably responsible for the outstanding achievements of its subject. For example, Bertrand Russell describes his grandmother's intense concern for his welfare, which "gave me that feeling of safety that children need" (Russell, 1967, p. 18). Russell states that his grandmother had an important impact on him, "her fearlessness, her public spirit, her contempt for convention and her indifference to the opinion of the majority have always seemed good to me and have impressed themselves upon me as worthy of imitation" (p. 18). Russell also describes how his brother tutored him in Euclid, which was "one of the great events of my life, as dazzling as first love. I had not imagined that there was anything so delicious in the world" (pp. 37–38).

Mahatma Gandhi was exposed to a different set of environmental influences, which must have been important in his later life. Both his father and grandfather were known to be men "of principle." Gandhi describes his father as "incorruptible, truthful and brave" and as having a "reputation for strict impartiality" (Fischer, 1962, p. 21). Gandhi described his mother as deeply religious and saintly. She often made arduous vows and fasted for long periods of time. Once she vowed not to eat unless the sun appeared. Gandhi and his sister and brothers watched for the sun, and when it shone through the clouds they rushed into the house and announced that their mother could now eat. But her vow required her to see the sun for herself, and so she went outdoors, and by then the sun was hidden again. "That does not matter," she cheerfully comforted her children, "God does not want me to eat today"

(Fischer, 1962, p. 22). These examples underscore the importance of early family environment on later development.

Naturalistic "case study" accounts have been written of contrasting college and university cultures. For example, Riesman and Jencks (1962) have presented informative accounts of the characteristics of several colleges and universities (e.g., the University of Massachusetts, Boston College, and Michigan State University). Bushnell (1962) has described the student culture at Vassar College, and Hughes, Becker, and Geer (1962) have identified the unique culture of one medical school environment. In *Death at an Early Age* Jonathan Kozol (1967) vividly described the destructive impact on the hearts and minds of Black children of the physical and social environments in the Boston public schools. Compelling narratives of the impact of positive and negative psychiatric treatment programs have come from many writers (e.g., Greenberg, 1964; Kesey, 1962; Ward, 1946).

Thus biographers, sociologists, anthropologists, physicians, and popular novelists have described social environments in exhaustive detail. Their reasons for doing so have varied. Their feelings about the impact of different social environments have also varied. But they all agree on one central point: that the social climate within which an individual functions may have an important impact on his attitudes and moods, his behavior, his health and overall sense of well-being, and his social, personal, and intellectual development.

Social Setting Influences on Behavior.   People vary their behavior substantially in different social settings. Some cogent empirical evidence of this is related to the current "generality–specificity" controversy in personality theory and assessment. Until recently personality research and theory was largely concerned with person variables or traits. Individual differences were typically conceived to be relatively static dimensions. However, those who attempted to measure personality traits usually found that the validity coefficients of their measures were quite limited; that is, the proportion of variance attributable to consistent differences among people was rarely higher than 25% (Mischel, 1968).

One of the most widely quoted series of studies bearing on this problem was conducted by Hartshorne and May (1928), who concluded that conflict between honest and deceitful behavior was specific to each situation and that one could not generalize about a subject's honesty from a few samples of his behavior. They suggested that consistency of behavior from one situation to another was due to similarities in the situations, not to a consistent personality trait in people. The correlations between the cheating tests utilized were too low, the investigators believed, to provide evidence of a unified character trait of honesty or deceitfulness. This conclusion about honesty has been upheld by some (Allinsmith, 1960) and vigorously challenged by others (e.g., Burton, 1963).

The issue of whether the person or the situation accounts for the major source of behavioral variance has recently aroused considerable controversy. Hunt (1965) labels it a "pseudo question." He states that "behavioral variance is due primarily to neither persons nor situations . . . it is neither the individual differences among subjects per se nor the variations among situations per se that produce the variations in behavior. It is, rather, the interactions among these which are important" (pp. 82, 83). Endler and Hunt (1966, 1968) found that about 30% of the variance in hostility and anxiety could be attributed to various person, setting, and mode of response interactions. They conclude that "the fact that such a substantial portion of the total variance comes from interactions confirms the suggestion that personality description might be improved by emphasizing what kinds of responses individuals make, with what intensity in various kinds of situations" (1966, p. 336). Recent exchanges regarding these issues can be found in Alker (1972), Bem (1972), and Endler (1973). The most important conclusion is that both social settings and person-by-setting interactions consistently account for substantial portions of the variance in a wide range of individual behaviors.

Two of our studies provide specific examples of the importance of the interpersonal setting in psychotherapy. In one study each of four therapists saw each of four patients in counterbalanced order for one brief psychotherapeutic interview. Each of five variables (total activity, percentage of feeling words, percentage of action words, number of questions, and number of reinforcements) was scored separately for each patient and each therapist. Both therapist and patient behaviors were determined by the therapist, by the patient, and by the particular patient by therapist interaction. Interestingly, therapists showed more variation in their behavior with different patients than patients showed in their behavior with different therapists. The results thus indicated that most of the therapists' behaviors in therapy were not the result of either a "behavioral trait" or a consistently applied "therapeutic technique" but, rather, were determined to an important extent by the situation or by the patient (Moos and Clemes, 1967).

For example, the variable of "talkativeness" is generally considered to be a personality trait. Thus it should show consistent (across settings) individual differences—an individual who is relatively talkative in one setting should also be relatively talkative in a variety of other settings.

If this were not the case, the status of "talkativeness" as a personality trait would be open to doubt. Consistent differences among therapists on the variable of "talkativeness," even though statistically significant, contributed only about 15% of the total variance. These results indicate that the interpersonal setting the therapist is in (i.e., which patient he is talking with) may contribute as much to the amount he talks as does his "trait" of "talkativeness." Therapists may differ consistently from one another in the amount they talk; however, they also consistently talk to some patients more than they do to others.

This result was basically replicated in a second study (Moos and MacIntosh, 1970), in which we measured a conceptually more important variable—the degree of empathy the therapist expressed toward the patient. The results were surprising. Almost 30% of the variance in therapist empathy was accounted for by the specific patient the therapist was seeing. Another 15% was accounted for by the patient–therapist interaction effect. Little if any of the variance was attributed to consistent differences among therapists. In an earlier study, Van der Veen (1964) had found somewhat similar results; that is, 55% of the variance in therapist empathy was related to the patient, to the interview, to the particular section of the interview, and to various first-, second- and third-order interactions. These results indicate that therapists are not necessarily consistent in the amount of accurate empathy they show across a small sample of patients. The patient (i.e., the interpersonal setting) is an important determinant of the actual amount of therapist empathy recorded. Other studies have come to similar conclusions regarding the importance of the setting in influencing individual behavior (e.g., Moos, 1968, 1969). The systematic assessment of social environments is important precisely because people do vary their behavior in accordance with the characteristics of their social and physical setting.

The Prediction "Sound Barrier". The failure to systematically include environmental and setting variables in understanding behavior has limited the accuracy of prediction. For example, attitude, background, and personality characteristics have been studied extensively to identify the characteristics of men who cannot give effective service in the military because of personality problems and/or medical and psychiatric disabilities. Glass et al. (1956a, 1956b) studied psychiatrists' predictions of the military effectiveness of army recruits. Each of 505 men was interviewed by a psychiatrist during the early weeks of training. These evaluations were compared against the subsequent performance of the men in combat and noncombat assignments. The psychiatrists failed to identify men who were later unable to perform their military assignments. Neither the evaluations as a whole nor the component ratings of family history,

socioeconomic status, religious influences, and so on, foretold poor military performance. The authors attribute predictive failures mainly to the inability of the psychiatrist to take account of the situational and emotional circumstances in which the men would meet their future assignments. Wichlacz, Del Jones, and Stayer (1972) reached similar conclusions about the inability of psychiatrists to predict potential failures in future military assignments from psychiatric interviews.

The past 50 years of the use of personality and other background characteristics to predict the performance of military personnel has been reviewed by Nelson (1971). Effective predictions of task proficiency have been hindered by the relative inadequacy of on-the-job work criteria, which are necessary to improve selection and training procedures. Predictions of emotional adjustment have been limited because the personality or life history characteristics associated with good performance vary significantly depending on the population being studied and the environmental context within which the performance is to take place.

For example, Nelson points out the necessity for assessing the personal qualities of leaders in terms of the specific situational task and interpersonal process requirements inherent in the leadership process. He concludes that

> greater effort is required to identify attributes and measure functional relationships over time between man and his social/organizational environment and between man and his physical/biological environment if more efficient predictions of performance effectiveness are to be achieved . . . transactional and ecological analyses must be increased in studying man and his environment be it social or physical. Improved classification methods for measuring environmental parameters, human characteristics sensitive to those parameters and dimensions of transaction reflective of both reactive and proactive efforts of human coping with environments are needed. (pp. 111–112)

Arthur (1971) reviewed personnel prediction studies in military organizations and reached similar conclusions. Many of the studies Arthur reviewed demonstrated that the predictive validity of psychological tests and other background characteristics varies over different adjustment and performance criteria and in different subject populations. Arthur posited a "sound barrier" effect, since "no matter how much information about the individual one adds to the predictive equation, one cannc bring the correlation coefficient between individual characteristics ar prediction criteria much above about .40. This is a good correlatⁱ but obviously leaves an enormous amount of variance unaccounted ᶠ (p. 544).

Attempts must be made to systematically quantify different aˢ

of the social and physical environment and to combine these organizational and institutional characteristics with individual personality, attitude, and background variables, to increase predictability. Research indicates that better predictions of performance require the assessment of the environment in which the performance is to take place and recognition of the connection between the relevant environmental characteristics and the relevant performance variables. These conclusions hold as well for predicting the outcome of correctional programs on individual delinquents as for predicting indices of military performance.

Predicting Violence and Aggression.   The practical implications of the work just described may be illustrated by considering the problem of predicting violent and aggressive behavior. Two recent reviews of this area have concluded that background and personality characteristics of individuals are poor predictors of violent behavior (Megargee, 1970; Monahan, 1973). Why is this so? Monahan offers several reasons, including lack of corrective feedback (i.e., the legal or mental health official who makes the predictions seldom learns of his errors) and differential consequences to the predictor (i.e., underprediction means that a freed inmate may commit a violent act, thereby arousing intense community anger and pressure, etc.). The perspective discussed previously suggests another set of reasons. Environmental and social setting influences are themselves important determinants of aggression. This implies that to adequately predict individual aggressive behavior, one must know something about the environment in which the individual is functioning.

For example, there is substantial evidence that various attitudinal and behavioral indices of anger, hostility, and aggression vary considerably over different settings, even for the same individuals. Endler and Hunt (1968) found that consistent individual differences accounted for between 15 and 20% of the variance in hostility, as measured by a questionnaire. Setting differences accounted for between 4 and 8%, and various interactions (e.g., subjects by situations) accounted for approximately 30%. This and similar work indicates that there is an upper limit to the accuracy of predicting aggressive behavior from knowledge of the individual alone.

Many environmental characteristics have an impact on the determination of individual and group aggressive behavior. For example, different types of behavior setting differentially elicit aggressive or hostile behavior. Rausch, Dittman, and Taylor (1959) found that changes in hostility in hyperaggressive children were setting specific. One child showed a marked reduction in hostile responses toward adults in a structured group setting, where another child showed these changes mainly during

meal times. Gump, Schoggen, and Redl (1957) observed children in camp settings and found that the quality of interaction of the same boys in swimming and craft settings differed quite markedly. Asserting, blocking, and attacking behaviors were significantly higher in the swimming setting, whereas helping reactions were higher in craft settings.

Another relevant example is that of the "interpersonal reflex" (Leary, 1957) or "behavioral reciprocity" (Rausch et al., 1959). Aggression begets aggression, and the proportion of hostile actions "sent" by an individual often parallels the proportion he "receives." Purcell and Brady (1964) found that the interpersonal response of affection was preceded by .the interpersonal stimulus of affection 80% of the time. It was preceded by the interpersonal stimulus of aggression 0% of the time.

In a particularly relevant study, Couch (1970) found that the response of interpersonal hostility was more highly related to the immediately preceding behavior input than it was to a broad combination of personal background predictors. Thus knowledge of the immediately preceding interpersonal stimulus was the best predictor of interpersonal hostility. This finding should give pause to all of us who attempt to make predictions from personality and background factors alone.

Milgram (1964) has shown that subjects who are not usually aggressive can be made to behave very aggressively under experimenter and group pressure encouragement. Kurt Lewin and his associates (Lewin et al., 1939) demonstrated that the leadership climate of a group (e.g., authoritarian vs. democratic) markedly affected the amount of aggressive behavior shown by the same boys in different settings. Finally, the potential effects on aggressive behavior of both positive and negative reinforcement procedures (including imitation and modeling) are well known (Bandura, 1969). Bandura and Walters (1959) have illustrated the specificity of aggressive behavior in their finding that parents who punished aggression in the home but simultaneously modeled aggressive behavior and encouraged it in their sons' relationships with peers, produced boys who were not aggressive at home but were markedly aggressive at school.

Thus evidence indicates that behavior settings, social and organizational climate, reinforcement variables, and so on, all have important impacts on aggressive and violent behavior. Similar analyses may be carried out, and similar conclusions probably hold for many other categories of behavior (e.g., behaviors that are relevant to the prediction of parole success). This analysis in no way minimizes the importance of individual dispositions. It is obvious that some individuals are more prone than others to express aggressive and violent behaviors. In addition, individual dispositions may have their effects in interaction with environmental conditions. But the importance of this work can hardly

be overemphasized, particularly in its implications for both behavior prediction and behavior change. Knowledge of the probable behavioral and
attitudinal impacts of different environmental arrangements is at least
as central an issue for corrections as is knowledge about traditional personality theory and psychotherapeutic and other treatment modalities.
In this connection, Monahan (1973) calls for an entirely new perspective
on the prediction and prevention of violence. He suggests that we attempt to identify and modify *situations* conducive to violence in addition
to our usual attempts to identify violence-prone persons and to modify
their behavior.

Describing Correctional Environments.   For Goffman (1966), correctional facilities are one type of total institution. Total institutions are
distinguished by their all-encompassing character, often symbolized by
barriers to social intercourse with the world outside—locked doors,
barbed wire, cliffs, water, forests, or moors. According to Goffman, a
total institution breaks down the barriers normally found between the
basic spheres of life (work, play, and sleep) in various ways: (1) All
aspects of life are conducted in the same place and under the same
authority. (2) Each phase of daily activity is carried on by a large group,
all of whose members are treated alike. (3) All aspects are formally
scheduled by a body of officials. (4) Contents of all enforced activities
are seen as part of an overall plan designed to fulfill the goals of the
institution.

Total institutions strip their inhabitants of extrainstitutional roles by
exchanging their personal clothing for institutional garments, by removing authority to do even the simplest things on individual initiative,
and by insulting, degrading, and depriving people both mentally and
physically. This process of "stripping" or mortification necessitates a personal reorganization of each person, which takes place around the rules,
and privilege and punishment systems. Associated with this reorganization is the development of a sub- or counterculture that includes a special slang, fraternization, and shared knowledge about specially available deals, gimmicks, or privileges. Personal reorganization and adaptation may follow general patterns, such as situational withdrawal, intransi-
gence, conversion, or "playing it cool."

Cressey (1965) takes a somewhat more differentiated view in relating
the organizational patterns of prisons to influences in society, and the
behavior of staff and inmates to influences in the prison's environment.
Four basic attitudes of society toward control of crime are distinguished:

(1) desire for retribution, (2) desire that suffering be inflicted on apprehended criminals as a deterrent to potential criminals, (3) protection of society from criminals, (4) reduction of crime rates by changing the behavior of criminals. Various correctional interest groups representing combinations of these attitudes impinge on the domain of prison management: inmate leaders, politicians, humanitarian groups, higher prison administration, and guard organizations. Resolution of the differences in these attitudes and interests results in a management policy that may be treatment-oriented or punitive–custodial.

Patterns of authority, communication, and decision making are based on the management policy. Authority in punitive–custodial prisons is based on rank and incumbency. In treatment institutions authority is presumably based on technical competencies. Communication in punitive–custodial prisons is downward but not upward; decisions are made at the top whenever possible. Treatment-oriented facilities maximize the autonomy of staff members and encourage extensive communication among staff members to facilitate treatment of inmates.

Patterns of organization are also determined by management policy and are important in that they influence the behavior of staff towards inmates. Cressey says:

> Many traits exhibited by individual staff members in correctional organizations might well be the properties of the organization, not of the person in question. . . . One should not ask . . . why sadistic men get into institutional work; he should ask what organizational conditions are present in the prison to produce conduct defined as sadistic. (p. 1034)

Similar claims could of course be made for the influence of prison environments on inmate behavior. For example, fights among inmates may not be caused by aggressive personalities nor homosexual acts by a disease of the inmates. Both types of behavior may be seen in part as the result of the organizational conditions prevailing in the prison (i.e., its social environment).

Correctional environments have been described most poignantly by persons who participated in them as inmates and later wrote anthropological or literary descriptions of them. An outstanding example of this type of work is *Ruhleben* by J. Davidson Ketchum (1965). Ruhleben was an institution created on a former horse racing track to house British subjects interned in Germany during World War I. Ketchum, a sociologist, describes the physical facilities (horse barns, with six men assigned to each stall), as well as the development of the social relations and institutions during the 4 years of the camp's existence. The study documents the ability of prisoners to create their own subculture, which facilitated their adjustment to prison life.

An example of this subculture was the creation at Ruhleben of a civilian administrative structure, headed by barracks captains. This structure managed all internal affairs of the camp during the years of internment, including finding sleeping places for new internees and negotiating complaints with the German officers who nominally ran the camp. The result of the quick growth of a prisoner-run government in the camp was the appearance of order and routine. The food was insufficient, and the horse stalls were miserably cold and cramped throughout the internment. Social conditions were so altered by the new "government" that 240 new internees, brought in 3 weeks after the first batch of 4000, found roll calls run by prisoners, meal fetching and work details working smoothly, recreational and religious activities organized by inmates, a prisoner barracks captain to assign them a sleeping place, and a prisoner-policeman to inform them about smoking rules and staying in line at the canteen. This situation caused one German-born internee to remark, "You Englishmen set to work as if you were founding a new colony" (p. 29–30).

Alexander Solzhenitsyn has provided a literary example of life in a prison camp. *One Day in the Life of Ivan Denisovich* describes life in a Siberian work camp during the 1950s. Ivan Denisovich, an inmate in this camp, is followed for one complete day as he eats breakfast and steals food in the mess hall, works as a mason in subzero weather, does favors for other prisoners in exchange for gifts of food, smuggles a knife blade into camp, and falls asleep with an unusually full stomach. In the course of Ivan's day every major institution of the camp is encountered.

One such institution is the work detail. Ivan's work gang was constructing a concrete block wall on the second floor of a future guard tower in the middle of a Siberian snow storm. The gang was run by one of the prisoners who acts as a foreman, directing some of the gang to steal fuel for a stove, others to build a stove, some to carry hod, and just 4 out of about 20 men to lay blocks on the wall. All the gang members worked at a very fast pace under the direction of their fellow prisoner, but the illegal stove, with its stolen fuel helped them to stay reasonably dry and warm. Had a guard been running the gang, there would have been no stove, less work, and frostbite among the men. In this case the prisoner subculture facilitated the work goals of the prison staff although certainly not their goals in the areas of discipline and control over prisoners.

An example of a prisoner's personal perceptions of a prison environment is provided by Nathan Leopold (1958):

My new home was eight feet long, four feet wide, and about seven feet high. The floor and ceiling were of stone; the walls, also of stone, were painted. There was a narrow double-deck bunk of iron slats containing mattresses and pillow, a rough rectangular wooden stool, a small tin shelf in one corner, a mirror and an unshaded fifty-watt electric light on one wall, and a tin bucket with a cover to care for bodily wastes . . . soon a line of convicts began to file by. Most of the men stared curiously into my cell as they passed. After a moment I heard the cell doors all along the gallery being opened and then slammed shut and the sharp crash of a long metal bar, extending the whole length of the gallery, being shot home as the automatic lock was pushed into place. A moment later a keeper appeared, placing his key into each individual lock and locking each separate cell. This operation he accomplished with amazing rapidity, never wasting a motion. *(p. 88)

Leopold describes another period in his life in prison as follows:

The next four years, from 1932 to 1936, were, in many ways, the best I have known in prison. Not only for me personally, but for the institution in general. If the two or three years before the riot were the Wild West days, this period could be called the Golden Age. Hobbies flourished among the men; discipline was at its least stringent. For example, there was yard every day now instead of once a week, and the men were permitted to go to the yard any time they were not actually working. Rules like the one requiring lines to march in strict military cadence were relaxed or not enforced. There was a general spirit of informality. So marked was this that when one of the judges of the Criminal Court of Chicago visited the institution he described it as the "Stateville Country Club," a designation that didn't help much, but one which, while not entirely accurate, still had some element of truth. The garden plots were going full blast; athletics of all kinds were encouraged. There were handball courts all around the prison, and everywhere you could see fellows, dressed only in shorts and shoes, engaged in hot games. Naturally, everyone was sun-tanned. Sun-bathing became a hobby; there was a place behind Cell House C, for instance, where a group gathered. From after supper until time for lock-up there must have been thirty or forty men out there every afternoon soaking up the sun. They started modestly enough, taking off their shirts. Soon the undershirts followed, then the pants. Eventually a few hardy spirits began to peel to the altogether.

*From the book *Life Plus Ninety-Nine Years* by Nathan F. Leopold, Jr. Copyright © 1957, 1958 by Nathan F. Leopold, Jr. Used by permission of Doubleday & Company, Inc.

I remember one day when Captain Seton rode up on his horse and made a couple of fellows put their shorts back on, there was grumbling: "What does he think this is? Russia?"* (p. 219).

Not only do prison environments have distinct personalities, but as Nathan Leopold so aptly conveys, the distinctive feel of the environment may change from time to time as officials and policies change, relax, or tighten.

Thus a broad range of naturalistic descriptions of life in correctional facilities exists. The importance of the social environment or social climate is emphasized in almost every case. But thus far no standard techniques for systematically identifying or assessing the relevant variables have been developed.

Measuring Social Climate.   How can the "blooming, buzzing, confusion" of a natural social environment be adequately assessed? Many procedures have been developed. For example, Withall (1949) developed a Social Emotional Climate Index for categorizing teachers' statements in seven areas (e.g., approval, disapproval, advice, clarification). Withall observed a group of seventh grade students in social science, English, science, and mathematics class sessions. The differences among the classroom climates created by the different teachers were substantial. There was some variation in the day-to-day climate in each classroom, but there was an overall consistency in the atmosphere that a teacher created in her classroom over a period of time. For example, one teacher often punished or disapproved of student behavior (about 25% of her remarks were coded in this category), and she limited students' choices of action and controlled the classroom situation. Withall concluded that the students had to cope with quite different psychological climates as they went from class to class.

In a different approach, Simpson (1963) defined the "social weather" as the overall social treatment a particular individual receives (e.g., some people may "give him the cold shoulder," whereas others may "treat him like a king"). Simpson developed scales for rating nine aspects of social weather (e.g., acceptance–rejection, affectionateness–hostility, approval–criticism). This technique has not been extensively used, but Simpson found that the social weather of six preschool children differed from that of six school children, even in similar behavior settings.

*From the book *Life Plus Ninety-Nine Years* by Nathan F. Leopold, Jr. Copyright © 1957, 1958 by Nathan F. Leopold, Jr. Used by permission of Doubleday & Company, Inc.

The Concept of Environmental Press. The construction of social climate scales for the more systematic assessment of the differences among social environments has mushroomed in the past 10 to 15 years. Much of the recent empirical work in this area derives directly or indirectly from the contributions of Henry Murray (1938), who first conceptualized the dual process of personal needs and environmental press. Murray suggested that individuals have specific needs (e.g., needs for achievement, for affiliation, for autonomy, for order). The strength of these needs characterizes "personality." The concept of need represents the significant internal or personal determinants of behavior, but Murray pointed out that this "leaves out the *nature of the environment,* a serious omission" (p. 116).

Murray classified environments in terms of the benefits (satisfactions) and harms (frustration, dissatisfactions) they provide. He formulated the concept of press, which represents the significant external or environmental determinants of behavior. He selected the term *press* to designate a directional tendency in an object or situation which facilitates or impedes the efforts of an individual to attain a particular goal. He concluded that:

> One can profitably analyze an environment, a social group or an institution from the point of view of what press it applies or offers to the individuals that live within or belong to it. . . . furthermore human beings in general or in particular can be studied from the standpoint of what beneficial press are available to them and what harmful press they customarily encounter. (p. 120)

Thus Murray suggested that individuals have certain needs, the strength of which characterizes their "personality." The environment has certain "press," which potentially satisfies or frustrates these needs. Murray presented various categories of environmental press (e.g., friendship, affiliation, dominance, order, coercion, lack of support, rejection, aggression), and his overall model for studying behavior consisted of the interaction between personality needs and environmental press.

Pace and Stern (1958) further developed the concept of environmental press by applying the logic of "perceived climate" to the study of "atmosphere" at colleges and universities. They constructed the College Characteristics Index (CCI), which measures the global college environment by having students act as reporters. Specifically, students were asked to answer true or false to items covering a wide range of topics about their college (student–faculty relationships, rules and regulations, classroom methods and facilities, etc.). This approach suggests that the

consensus of students characterizing their college environment constitutes a measure of environmental climate, which supposedly exerts a
directional influence on their behavior. Our own work basically follows
this logic, as does the work of many other investigators (e.g., Findikyan
and Sells, 1966; Halpin and Croft, 1963; Stern, 1970; Walberg, 1969).

Stern (1970) remarks that descriptions of environmental press are
based on inferred continuity and consistency in otherwise discrete events.
For example, if residents in a correctional program are assigned specific
duties, if they must follow prearranged schedules, if they are liable to
be restricted or transferred for not adhering to program policies, if obey-
ing staff is crucial, it is likely that the program emphasizes staff control.
The development of submissive responses by the residents is probably
encouraged. It is these conditions which establish the climate or atmosphere of a program.

Underlying Patterns of Social Environments.   The idea that vastly different social environments can be characterized by common or similar
dimensions can serve as a framework for understanding the work reported in this book. My colleagues and I have completed work in nine
different types of social milieu: (1) hospital-based psychiatric treatment
programs, (2) community-based psychiatric treatment programs, (3) correctional institutions for adult and juvenile offenders, (4) military basic
training companies, (5) university student living groups (e.g., dormitories, fraternities, and sororities), (6) junior high and high school classrooms, (7) social, task-oriented, and psychotherapeutic groups, (8) industrial or work milieus, and (9) families (Moos, 1974a).

We have developed different Social Climate Scales for each environment. Each of the dimensions (subscales) on each of the nine Social Climate Scales has been empirically derived from independent data obtained from respondents in that particular environment. Chapter 2 provides an example by detailing the empirical procedures used in the
development of the Correctional Institutions Environment Scale (CIES).
Common categories of dimensions have emerged from studies of these
environments. These dimensions are useful in characterizing the social
and organizational climates of a variety of groups and institutions. There
are three broad categories: Relationship dimensions, Personal Development or Personal Growth dimensions, and System Maintenance and System Change dimensions.

1. *Relationship dimensions* identify the nature and intensity of personal
relationships in an environment. They assess the extent to which people

are involved in an environment, the extent to which they support and help one another, and the extent of spontaneity and free and open expression among them. The basic dimensions are very similar in all nine environments studied, as shown in Table 1.1. Involvement in families reflects the extent to which family members actively participate in and are emotionally concerned with the family (e.g., sense of belonging and togetherness). Involvement in a university living group reflects the degree of commitment to the house and residents and the amount of social interaction and feeling of friendship. Involvement in a classroom measures the attentiveness of students to class activities and their participation in discussions. Involvement in a correctional program measures how active and energetic residents are in the day-to-day functioning of the program (e.g., pride in the program, feelings of group spirit, and general enthusiasm).

The degree of Support present in an environment is particularly important, and each of the environments studied has at least one Support dimension. For example, Emotional Support in student living groups reflects the manifest concern for others in the group, efforts to aid one another with academic and personal problems, and an emphasis on open and honest communication. Support in a correctional program measures the extent to which residents are encouraged to be helpful and supportive toward one another and the extent to which staff are supportive toward residents. Peer Cohesion and Staff Support in a work milieu measure the supportiveness of workers to one another and of management to workers. Peer Cohesion and Officer Support in military companies assess the degree of friendship and communication among enlisted men and between officers and enlisted men, and the degree to which officers attempt to help and encourage enlisted men.

A separate relationship dimension of Expressiveness or Spontaneity, which is identified in some environments, is not separately identified in all environments for two reasons. First, certain environments (e.g., military companies) differ so little in Expressiveness that this dimension simply does not discriminate among them. Second, Expressiveness is sometimes very highly related to one of the other relationship dimensions (e.g., to Emotional Support in university living groups and to both Peer Cohesion and Staff Support in work milieus). Thus there are three basic *Relationship* dimensions which characterize the nine environments: Involvement, Support and Expressiveness.

2. *Personal Development* dimensions assess the basic directions along which personal growth and self-enhancement tend to occur in an environment. The exact nature of these dimensions varies somewhat among the different environments studied, depending on their underlying pur-

Table 1.1 Common Social Climate Dimensions Across Environments

Type of Environment	Relationship	Personal Development	System Maintenance and System Change
(1, 2) Hospital and community programs	Involvement Support Spontaneity	Autonomy Practical Orientation Personal Problem Orientation	Order and Organization Clarity Control
(3) Correctional institutions	Involvement Support Expressiveness	Autonomy Practical Orientation Personal Problem Orientation	Order and Organization Clarity Control
(4) Military companies	Involvement Peer Cohesion Officer Support	Personal Status	Order and Organization Clarity Officer Control
(5) University student living groups	Involvement Emotional Support	Independence Traditional Social Orientation Competition Academic Achievement Intellectuality	Order and Organization Student Influence Innovation

	Relationship dimensions	Personal growth dimensions	System maintenance and system change dimensions
(6) Junior high and high school classrooms	Involvement Affiliation Teacher Support	Task Orientation Competition	Order and Organization Rule Clarity Teacher Control Innovation
(7) Social, task-oriented, and therapeutic groups	Cohesiveness Leader Support Expressiveness	Independence Task Orientation Self-Discovery Anger and Aggression	Order and Organization Leader Control Innovation
(8) Work milieus	Involvement Peer Cohesion Staff Support	Task Orientation Competition	Work Pressure Clarity Control Innovation Physical Comfort
(9) Families	Cohesiveness Emotional Support Conflict	Independence Achievement Orientation Intellectual–Cultural Orientation Recreational Orientation Moral–Religious Emphasis	Organization Control

poses and goals. For example, in families these dimensions indicate the directions along which families may wish to develop—for example, Independence (the extent to which family members are encouraged to be self-sufficient and to make their own decisions); Active Recreational Orientation (the emphasis on such pursuits as individual or team sports, camping, fishing, bowling, etc.); and Moral–Religious Emphasis (the extent to which the family emphasizes and discusses ethical and religious issues and values).

The personal growth goals of university student living groups differ somewhat from those of families. Therefore, a different set of Personal Development dimensions is identified for them (e.g., Independence, Competition). Psychiatric and correctional programs emphasize still other, but related, areas of personal growth. In these environments the Personal Development dimensions assess the program's overall treatment goals—for example, Autonomy (the extent to which people are encouraged to be self-sufficient and independent); Practical Orientation (the extent to which the program orients an individual toward training for new jobs, looking to the future, setting and working toward concrete goals); and Personal Problem Orientation (the extent to which individuals are encouraged to be concerned with their feelings and problems and to seek to understand them). Thus Personal Development dimensions differ among the nine environments depending on their basic purposes and goals.

3. *System Maintenance and System Change* dimensions, which are relatively similar across all nine environments, deal with the extent to which an environment is orderly, is clear in its expectations, maintains control, and is responsive to change. The basic dimensions are Order and Organization, Clarity, Control, and Innovation. For example, Clarity in a work milieu indicates how accurately workers know what to expect in their daily routines and how explicitly rules and policies are communicated. Clarity in a classroom assesses the emphasis on following a clear set of rules and on students knowing the consequences of disobedience.

Only three variations occur in these dimensions. First, Order and Organization and Clarity may merge into one dimension (e.g., in university living groups and work milieus). Second, a separate dimension of Innovation (System Change) is identified in only some environments, either because there is relatively little innovation in the environment (e.g., military companies) or because innovation is linked to expressiveness and spontaneity in certain environments (e.g., families). Third, a unique System Maintenance dimension of Work Pressure is identified in work environments. This dimension assesses the emphasis on pressure, deadlines, and time urgency in the work milieu. It is a dimension that is not particularly relevant to the other environments.

Thus the evidence indicates that social environments may be conveniently categorized along three common sets of dimensions. This overall concept holds as well for scales developed by other investigators as for the nine Social Climate Scales (see Moos, 1974b; Chapter 14). For example, Stern (1970) identified several major types of dimension based on extensive research with an Organizational Climate Index. The first two dimensions—Closeness and Group Life—appear to be Relationship dimensions. Three of Stern's dimensions seem to reflect Personal Development: these are called Intellectual Climate, Personal Dignity, and Achievement Standards. Stern's last two factors—Orderliness and Impulse Control or constraint—are System Maintenance factors. Other investigators have found conceptually similar dimensions in high schools (Halpin and Croft, 1963), in classrooms (Walberg, 1969), in insurance agencies and other work environments (Litwin and Stringer, 1968; Schneider and Bartlett, 1970), and in treatment environments (Fairweather et al., 1969). Having three broad categories of dimensions provides us a convenient framework for reviewing relevant research.

The Impact of Treatment Environments.   *Evaluating Treatment Environments* (Moos, 1974b) described in detail our work in hospital-based and community-based psychiatric treatment programs. Techniques to measure the social climates of these treatment programs were developed by asking patients and staff individually about the usual patterns of behavior in their program. These techniques were the Ward Atmosphere Scale (WAS), which assesses the treatment milieus of hospital-based treatment programs, and the Community-Oriented Programs Environment Scale (COPES), for the evaluation of treatment milieus of community-based programs. Data were collected from more than 200 hospital programs in the United States, Canada, and the United Kingdom, and from more than 75 community programs in the United States and the United Kingdom. The work on treatment programs involved characterizing the psychometric characteristics of the scales, describing the range and diversity of different program types, comparing patient and staff views of programs, making cross-cultural comparisons between British and American programs, and using the scales in several program evaluation and program change studies.

These scales were successfully used in implementing social change in treatment programs. There were important relationships between the social climate of a treatment program and its size and staffing; for example, programs of smaller size and/or higher staffing tend to have more emphasis on Relationship and Personal Development dimensions and less emphasis on Staff Control. Certain characteristics of the treatment environment were related to both attitudinal and behavioral outcome criteria; thus programs with high dropout rates were found to have few social activities, little emphasis on involving patients in the program, and poor planning of patient activities. Finally, deviant perceptions and expectations generally have negative effects in relation to patient adaptation but may have positive effects in particular program milieus. Some of these findings are discussed in this book in relation to the current findings in correctional and community settings.

The work presented here represents an attempt to replicate our work in psychiatric programs in correctional settings. We wanted to relate both perceptual and objective measures of correctional programs to different indices of adaptation in correctional programs. As the work progressed it became apparent that the conclusions would be of greater utility if data from other settings were obtained. This consideration led to the work in family, classroom, and military settings.

Chapter 2 presents the development of the Correctional Institutions Environment Scale (CIES). The descriptive work with this scale is discussed in Chapters 3 and 4. Chapter 5 introduces a taxonomy of six similar types of programs in both correctional and psychiatric settings. Chapters 6 through 9 discuss the use of the CIES in various program comparison and evaluation studies. Chapters 10 through 12 deal with applications of the work in community-based correctional settings, in families, and in military training companies. Chapter 13 summarizes the work and presents some overall implications for assessing and evaluating social institutions.

REFERENCES

Alker, H. Is personality situationally specific or intrapsychically consistent? *Journal of Personality*, **40:** 1–16, 1972.

Allinsmith, W. The learning of moral standards. In D. R. Miller & G. E. Swanson (Eds.), *Inner conflict and defense.* Holt, Rinehart & Winston, New York, 1960, pp. 141–176.

Arthur, R. J. Success is predictable. *Military Medicine*, **136:**539–545, 1971.

Bandura, A. *Principles of behavior modification.* Holt, Rinehart & Winston, New York, 1969.

Bandura, A. & Walters, R. H. *Adolescent aggression.* Ronald Press, New York, 1959.

Bem, D. J. Constructing cross-situational consistencies in behavior: Some thoughts on Alker's critique of Mischel. *Journal of Personality*, **40:**17–26, 1972.

Burton, R. V. Generality of honesty reconsidered. *Psychological Review,* **70**:481–499, 1963.

Bushnell, J. Student culture at Vassar. In N. Sanford (Ed.), *The American college: A psychological and social interpretation of higher learning.* Wiley, New York, 1962, pp. 489–514.

Couch, A. The psychological determinants of interpersonal behavior. In K. Gergen & D. Marlowe (Eds.), *Personality and social behavior.* Addison-Wesley, Reading, Mass., 1970.

Cressey, D. Prison organizations. In J. March, *Handbook of organizations,* Rand McNally, Skokie, Ill., 1965.

Endler, N.S. The person versus the situation—A pseudo issue: A response to Alker. *Journal of Personality,* **41**:287–303, 1973.

Endler, N. S. & Hunt, J. McV. Sources of behavioral variance as measured by the S–R Inventory of Anxiousness. *Psychological Bulletin,* **65**:336–346, 1966.

Endler, N. S. & Hunt, J. McV. S–R Inventories of hostility and comparisons of the proportions of variance from persons, responses, and situations, for hostility and anxiousness. *Journal of Personality and Social Psychology,* **9**:309–315, 1968.

Fairweather, G., Sanders, D., Cressler, D., & Maynard, H. *Community life for the mentally ill: An alternative to institutional care.* Aldine, Chicago, 1969.

Findikyan, N. & Sells, S. Organizational structure and similarity of campus student organizations. *Organizational Behavior and Human Performance,* **1**:169–190, 1966.

Fischer, L. *The life of Mahatma Gandhi.* Collier Books, Macmillan, New York, 1962.

Glass, A., Ryan, F., Lubin, A. Ramana, C., & Tucker, A. Psychiatric prediction and military effectiveness, Part I. *U.S. Armed Forces Medical Journal,* **7**:1427–1443, 1956a.

Glass, A., Ryan, F., Lubin, A., Ramana, C., & Tucker, A. Psychiatric prediction and military effectiveness, Part II. *U.S. Armed Forces Medical Journal,* **7**:1575–1588, 1956b.

Goffman, E. On the characteristics of total institutions: The inmate world. In D. Cressey (Ed.), *The prison: Studies in institutional organization and change.* Holt, Rinehart & Winston, New York, 1966a.

Greenberg, J. *I never promised you a rose garden.* Holt, Rinehart & Winston, New York, 1964.

Gump, P., Schoggen, P., & Redl, F. The camp milieu and its immediate effects. *Journal of Social Issues,* **13**:40–46, 1957.

Halpin A. & Croft, D. The organizational climate of schools. Mid-West Administration Center, University of Chicago, Chicago, 1963.

Hartshorne, H. & May, M. *Studies in the nature of character, studies in deceit,* vol. 1. Macmillan, New York, 1928.

Hughes, E., Becker, H., & Geer, B. Student culture and academic effort. In N. Sanford (Ed.), *The American college: A psychological and social interpretation of higher learning.* Wiley, New York, 1962, pp. 515–530.

Hunt, J. McV. Traditional personality theory in the light of recent evidence. *American Scientist,* **53**:80–96, 1965.

Kesey, K. *One flew over the cuckoo's nest.* Viking, New York, 1962.

Ketchum, J. D. *Ruhleben: A prison camp society.* University of Toronto Press, Toronto, 1965.

Kozol, J. *Death at an early age.* Houghton-Mifflin, Boston, 1967.

Leary, T. *Interpersonal diagnosis of personality.* Ronald Press, New York, 1957.

Leopold, N. F. *Life plus 99 years.* Victor Gollancz, London, 1958.

Lewin, K., Lippitt, R., & White, R. Patterns of aggressive behavior in experimentally created "social climates." *Journal of Social Psychology,* **10**:271–299, 1939.

Litwin, G. & Stringer, R. Motivation and organizational climate. Division of Research, Harvard Business School, Cambridge, Mass., 1968.

Megargee, E. The prediction of violence with psychological tests. In C. Spielberger (Ed.), *Current topics in clinical and community psychology.* Academic Press, New York, 1970, pp. 98–156.

Milgram, S. Group pressure and action against a person. *Journal of Abnormal and Social Psychology,* **69**:137–143, 1964.

Mischel, W. *Personality and assessment.* Wiley, New York, 1968.

Monahan, J. The prediction and prevention of violence. In *Proceedings of the Pacific Northwest Conference on Violence and Criminal Justice.* Issaquah, Wash., December 6–8, 1973.

Moos, R. Differential effects of ward settings on psychiatric patients: A replication and extension. *Journal of Nervous and Mental Disease,* **147**:386–393, 1968.

Moos, R. Sources of variance in response to questionnaires and in behavior. *Journal of Abnormal Psychology,* **74**:405–412, 1969.

Moos, R. Conceptualizations of human environments. *American Psychologist,* **28**:652–665, 1973.

Moos, R. *The Social Climate Scales: An overview.* Consulting Psychologists Press, Palo Alto, Calif., 1974a.

Moos, R. *Evaluating treatment environments: A social ecological approach.* Wiley, New York, 1974b.

Moos, R. & Clemes, S. Multivariate study of the patient–therapist system. *Journal of Consulting Psychology,* **31**:119–130, 1967.

Moos, R. & MacIntosh, S. Multivariate study of the patient–therapist system: A replication and extension. *Journal of Consulting and Clinical Psychology,* **35**:298–307, 1970.

Murray, H. *Explorations in personality.* Oxford University Press, New York, 1938.

Nelson, P. D. Personnel performance prediction. In R. W. Little (Ed.), *Handbook of military institutions,* Sage Publications, Beverly Hills, Calif., 1971.

Pace, R. Implications of differences in campus atmosphere for evaluation and planning of college programs. In R. Sutherland, W. Holtzman, E. Koile, & B. Smith (Eds.), *Personality factors on the college campus,* University of Texas Press, Austin, 1962.

Pace, C. & Stern, G. An approach to the measurement of psychological characteristics of college environments. *Journal of Educational Psychology,* **49**:269–277, 1958.

Purcell, K. & Brady, D. *Assessment of interpersonal behavior in natural settings.* Final Progress Report, Childrens' Asthma Research Institute and Hospital, Denver, Colo., 1964.

Rausch, H., Dittman, A., & Taylor, T. Person, setting, and change in social interaction. *Human Relations,* **12**:361–378, 1959.

Riesman, D. & Jencks, C. The viability of the American college. In N. Sanford (Ed.), *The American college: A psychological and social interpretation of higher learning,* Wiley, New York, 1962, pp. 74–192.

Russell, B. *The autobiography of Bertrand Russell 1872–1914.* Little, Brown, Boston, 1967.

Schneider, B. & Bartlett, C. Individual differences and organizational climate. II: Measurement of organizational climate by the multi-trait multi-rater matrix. *Personnel Psychology,* **23**:493–512, 1970.

Simpson, J. A method of measuring the social weather of children. In R. Barker (ed.), *The stream of behavior.* Appleton-Century-Crofts, New York, 1963.

Solzhenitsyn, A. *One day in the life of Ivan Denisovich.* Dutton, New York, 1963 (original Russian edition in *Novy Mir,* November 1962).

Stern, G. *People in context: Measuring person–environment congruence in education and industry.* Wiley, New York, 1970.

Van der Veen, F. Effects of the therapist and the patient on each other's therapeutic behavior. *Journal of Consulting Psychology,* **29**:19–26, 1965.

Walberg, H. Social environment as a mediator of classroom learning. *Journal of Educational Psychology,* **60**:443–448, 1969.

Ward, M. *The snake pit.* Random House, New York, 1946.

White, R. W. *The enterprise of living: Growth and organization in personality.* Holt, Rinehart & Winston, New York, 1972.

Wichlacz, C, Del Jones, F., & Stayer, S. Psychiatric predictions and recommendations: A longitudinal study of character and behavior disorder patients. *Military Medicine,* **137**:54–58, 1972.

Withall, J. The development of a technique for the measurement of social emotional climate in classrooms. *Journal of Experimental Education,* **17**:347–361, 1949.

PART TWO

Assessing Correctional Milieus

CHAPTER TWO

The Social Climates
of Correctional Programs

Assessing Correctional Programs. The literature briefly reviewed in Chapter 1 illustrates the popularity and productiveness of research on the concepts of social and organizational climates. The concepts have often been discussed in relation to correctional institutions; and many investigators and administrators feel that the "social climate" of correctional programs is of critical importance.

The consensus of opinions about specific programs has been systematically assessed, and some investigators have developed methods for measuring resident and staff perceptions of unit climates. Eynon et al. (1971) evaluated the effect of a juvenile correctional program on residents, using resident and staff perceptions of institutional impact. A 60-item, 6-subscale Perception of Impact Scale was developed for residents. The subscales were constructed using a factor analysis on an initial item pool of 320 items. Inmate Code and Inmate Pressure, which assess opinions about the inmate subculture, might be considered to be Relationship dimensions. Interpersonal Approach and Self-Labeling are measures of self-concept, thus are really person variables rather than measures of the milieu. Rejection of Institution and Rejection of Positive Impact are general satisfaction scales rather than measures of either person or environmental variables. This mixture of variables indicates that Eynon was attempting to measure the general impact of the program on inmates rather than to directly assess the milieu or climate.

Wood et al. (1966) related troublemaking behavior to inmate perceptions of institutional life. A 36-item scale measured inmate perceptions of the institution as an opportunity structure and as an authority structure. Opportunity questions covered areas of potential personal development and asked about the opportunity to learn interpersonal skills, to develop a positive self-image, and to make a fresh start in life. The Authority items dealt with system or program maintenance areas and asked about rules and regulations and about custodial officers. A group of high-consensus troublemakers saw less opportunity, less reasonable and sympathetic authority, and greater arbitrariness in the institution than did either low-consensus troublemaker or control groups.

Street et al. (1966) assessed perceptions of institutional milieus at six juvenile correctional institutions using separate scales for inmates and staff. The staff and inmate scales had four and six sets of items, respectively. The six institutions were divided into three categories varying along a custody-treatment continuum (i.e., obedience/conformity, re-education/development, and treatment-oriented). The staff items focused mainly on perceptions of institutional goals, attitudes toward delinquents, and job satisfaction. Staff responses generally paralleled the official goals of the institution. Treatment-oriented institutions had staff who espoused treatment goals, whereas the staffs of custodial institutions espoused custodial goals.

The inmate items focused on attitudes toward staff and toward the program, the strictness of discipline, modes of adaptation to the institution, self-perceptions, and so on. Inmate responses were somewhat more positive in the treatment-oriented than in the custodial institutions; however, there was substantial inmate negativism in all settings. Overt behavioral conformity was favored in custodial institutions, whereas inmates were more likely to recommend giving evidence of personality changes in treatment institutions. Thus although some aspects of treatment program and system maintenance areas were covered, most of the staff and inmate subscales assessed attitudes and opinions, satisfaction variables, self-concepts, and other person-related dimensions, rather than dimensions of the institutional milieu.

Jesness (1968) developed several experimental treatment programs in a CYA training school. Experimental subjects were assigned to housing in lodges by maturity level subtype. Experimental treatment programs were then developed for each lodge in an attempt to design programs to best match the needs of the boys residing in the different lodges. Jesness recognized the importance of measuring the total social environment of each lodge. He felt that the lodge milieus were an integral aspect of the treatment programs. He developed two methods for assessing program environments.

The first method used three types of observers: lodge treatment teams, lodge ward panels, consisting of selected residents of the lodges, and research team members. Meetings were held with each group and opinions were compared, to arrive at a detailed consensus description of the social environment of each lodge.

The second method was an 81-item questionnaire called the Post Opinion Poll, designed to assess the residents' perceptions of the operations of their living units and to measure their attitudes about the behavior of staff, the behavior of their peers, and so on. Five dimensions, identified from one factor analysis of 29 items, were categorized as Subject-Perceived Treatment dimensions. The factors assessed were residents' perceptions of staff involvement and trust, permissiveness, equalitarianism, acceptance, and fairness.

The remainder of the Post Opinion Poll items were subjected to an independent factor analysis. The nine factors emerging were categorized as Subject-Perceived Group Living factors and were labeled as follows: (1) good evaluation of staff, (2) high clique delinquency, (3) hostile group climate, (4) lodge cohesiveness, (5) perception of change in self, (6) satisfactory school experience, (7) pessimism, (8) clique orientation, and (9) poor peer adjustment to the institution.

These 14 factor dimensions seem to be divided between Relationship dimensions (e.g., the Subject-Perceived Treatment dimensions of involvement, acceptance, and fairness, and the Subject-Perceived Group Living factors of lodge cohesiveness and clique orientation), and general satisfaction, opinion, and behavioral items that do not directly assess the treatment environment (e.g., all the remaining Subject-Perceived Group Living factors except for hostile group climate). Only one Treatment Program dimension (equalitarianism) and one System Maintenance dimension (Permissiveness) are assessed. All the treatment program dimensions differentiated between the experimental programs, the control programs, and a special psychiatric control unit, but Jesness found it very difficult to relate them to the detailed consensus descriptions of each lodge's social environment.

Thus four groups of investigators have attempted to assess the social environments of correctional institutions in different ways. However, Eynon et al. (1971) measured only perceptions of certain relationship dimensions, Wood et al. (1966) measured only perceptions of certain aspects of treatment program and system maintenance dimensions, and Street et al. (1966) measured only perceptions of practical orientation and of certain aspects of staff control. Jesness has done the most relevant work in this area. His opinion scales assess mainly relationship dimensions, although they cover some aspects of treatment program and system maintenance functions. In addition, these scales are only applicable to residents. Street derived a scale to assess values and goal orientations, but this was applied only to staff. Our goal was to develop an assessment technique that would elicit information on a broad range of dimensions characteristic of the social environments of correctional programs; the data would be helpful in assessing people's value orientations about correctional programs and would be similarly applicable to both residents and staff.

The Correctional Institutions Environment Scale (CIES). Our purpose was to develop a way of assessing the social climates of correctional programs by asking residents and staff individually about the usual patterns of behavior in their program. From a practical point of view we wanted to provide institutional administrators and their staff with a relatively simple means of assessing a program's social climate. The hope was that the information resulting from this type of assessment could be used for both short- and long-range staff and program development and for ongoing efforts to change and improve the program's living and working environment. We also felt that the technique might be useful in periodic assessments of the social milieu of an institution, and that it might thus be capable of detecting or bringing to light institutional tensions before violent crises occurred. To accomplish these goals it seemed important that each individual resident and each individual staff member have an opportunity to present his or her perceptions of the institution.

Thus the Correctional Institutions Environment Scale (CIES)* was developed to measure the social climates of correctional institutions as perceived by residents and staff. An overview of the various forms of the CIES (see Table 2.1) will be helpful to the reader. There are four different forms of the CIES: (1) a 90-item Form R to assess the actual (Real) program, (2) a 36-item Form S (Short Form) for rapid assessments of the actual (Real) program, (3) a 90-item Form I (Ideal Form) to assess perceptions of an ideal program, and (4) a 90-item Form E (Expectations Form) to assess expectations about a program. Both residents and staff answer exactly the same items.

The items in the CIES were adapted from the initial form of the Ward Atmosphere Scale (WAS) and from other perceived climate scales, by residents and staff who were intimately familiar with correctional

*The initial version of the CIES was called the Social Climate Scale (SCS). The name of the scale was later changed to more accurately indicate the type of institutional climate being assessed.

Table 2.1 Summary of Different Forms of the Correctional Institutions Environment Scale (CIES)

Actual program (long form)	90 items, 9 subscales, CIES Form R
Actual program (short form)	36 items, 9 subscales, CIES Short Form S (First 36 items of Form R)
Ideal program	90 items, 9 subscales, CIES Form I (parallel to Form R)
Program expectations	90 items, 9 subscales, CIES Form E (parallel to Form R)

institutions. The choice of items was guided by a set of environmental press categories derived from Murray's (1938) and Stern's (1970) lists (See Chapter 1). Twelve press categories that appeared to be particularly relevant to correctional institutions were initially chosen: Involvement, Affiliation, Support, Spontaneity, Autonomy, Practicality, Insight, Aggression, Order, Clarity, Submission, and Variety.

The choice of items was guided by the concept of environmental press. For example, the following question was asked: What items identify the characteristics of an environment that exerts a press toward Involvement, or toward Autonomy, or toward Order? What might there be in an environment which would be satisfying to or would tend to reinforce or reward an individual who has a high need for Involvement, or for Autonomy, or for Order? Environmental press are the characteristic demands or features of the environment as seen by those who live in that environment.

For example, a press toward involvement is inferred from items of the following kinds: "Residents put a lot of energy into what they do around here," and "Residents here really try to improve and get better." A press toward Autonomy is inferred from these items: "Residents are expected to take leadership on the unit," "Staff encourage residents to start their own activities," and "Residents have a say about what goes on here." A press toward Order and Organization is inferred from still other items: "The staff make sure that the unit is always neat," "Residents' activities are carefully planned," and "This is a very well organized unit."

Additional items were added to identify individuals with strong positive or negative halo in their perceptions of an environment. Some residents or staff might agree with extremely positive items, (e.g., "This is the most interesting place I could possibly imagine," "Residents on this unit never fight," and "Residents can leave the unit whenever they want to."). Whereas some residents or staff might wish to describe their correctional units in an overly positive light, others might wish to describe them in an extremely negative light by agreeing with items like: "The staff here are just terribly stupid," "Staff want to make residents feel inferior," "None of the staff here care about any of the residents." In addition to measuring positive or negative halo, it was thought that these items would also help to identify "crazy" or inconsistent answering by noting the degree to which subjects accepted both extremely positive and extremely negative items.

The resulting 194-item initial version of the CIES was administered to residents and staff on 16 correctional programs. These programs included seven units from a training school for boys ranging in age from 16 to 20 years; four units from a training school for boys and young men between the ages of 18 and 30 years with an extensive program of academic and vocational education; two units from a juvenile hall, one for males and one for females with average ages of approximately 15 years; and three boys' camps with extensive vocational programs for boys whose average age was approximately 16 years. Further background characteristics of these programs are given elsewhere (Moos, 1968, pp. 178–179).

A total of 384 residents and 92 staff were tested. All residents and staff also completed the Marlowe-Crowne Social Desirability Scale (Crowne and Marlowe, 1964) in addition to the CIES; this permitted us to identify and eliminate items that were particularly sensitive to social desirability. The first question investigated was whether each item discriminated significantly (one-way analysis of variance) among the programs for the residents. The analyses indicated that 163 of the 194 items (84%) discriminated significantly among programs at the .05 level and that 145 of these items (75% of the 194) discriminated significantly among programs at the .01 level.

Items were then selected for the second version of the CIES on the basis of three criteria: (1) the item should discriminate significantly among units (more than 95% of the items chosen did significantly differentiate among units for residents' responses); (2) the overall item split should be as close to 50–50 as possible, to avoid items characteristic only of extreme units; and (3) the items should not correlate highly with the Marlowe-Crowne Social Desirability Scale (only five of the items selected correlated above .20 with the Marlowe-Crowne). The use of these criteria resulted in a 120-item second version of the CIES—that is, there were 12 press dimension subscales, and each was measured by 10 items.

Two halo scales were constructed from the group of extreme positive and negative items using the following criteria:

1. The items should not discriminate significantly among units.

2. The items should be answered in the scored direction by fewer than 15% of the residents in the total sample. This criterion was met for the positive halo scale, on which an average of about 10% of residents answered the items in the scored direction, but it was not quite met for the negative halo scale, on which an average of almost 20% of residents answered the items in the scored direction.

3. The two scales should each have 10 items, 5 scored true and 5 scored false. This was to allow for the differentiation between acquiescence response set and a positive or negative halo response set.

The two scales were constructed according to these criteria. Thus the second version of the CIES had 140 items. There were 120 content items (10 on each of 12 press subscales) and 20 halo items (10 on each halo scale).

The CIES Final Real Program Form (Form R).   The second version of the CIES was administered to residents and staff in extensive normative samples gathered from more than 100 juvenile and 90 adult correctional programs in the United States and the United Kingdom. These standardization samples are described more fully in the next chapter. The final 90-item CIES was derived from these data in the following manner. Two samples, one of residents and one of staff, were chosen randomly from residents and staff from each of 95 juvenile correctional units in proportion to their size. There were 713 cases in the resident sample and 651 cases in the staff sample. Two additional samples, one of residents and one of staff, were identified from the adult male correctional units tested. A total of 1341 male residents in 41 correctional units and 526 staff in 15 correctional units were used in the adult samples. Both juvenile and adult samples were used in the derivation of the CIES to assure the utility of the scale for the widest variety of correctional programs.

Item intercorrelations, item-to-subscale correlations, and subscale intercorrelations were calculated on each of the four samples. The results, which were highly similar across the four samples, showed that the 12 a priori subscales generally had excellent psychometric properties, except for the Variety subscale, which showed very low item intercorrelations and item-to-subscale correlations. Thus Variety was dropped from subsequent analyses. Since Affiliation and Involvement were highly intercorrelated (.70, .69, .60, and .59 in the four samples), these two subscales were collapsed into one 10-item subscale labeled Involvement. The 10 items that showed the highest item-to-subscale correlations and/or the least extreme item splits were included in the new Involvement subscale.

The Aggression subscale also had several items with relatively extreme item splits and some others that showed low item-to-subscale intercorrelations. In addition, some of the items correlated much more highly with subscales other than Aggression. Upon reflection it did not seem logical to have an Aggression subscale in correctional programs. The CIES is designed to measure the press or emphasis given to certain dimensions in a program or institution. Whereas staff in treatment environments may strongly emphasize the open expression of anger and aggression (making this is a relevant dimension of the social climate of psychiatric programs), this is clearly not true of most correctional programs. Thus the Aggression subscale was dropped from the CIES for both empirical and theoretical reasons. Since correctional staff do not usually emphasize the open expression of aggression, aggression is not a basic dimension of environmental press in correctional programs. Aggression in correctional programs might be more appropriately viewed as a "dependent" variable; that is, rule breaking, deviant behavior, and violence show a differential incidence in different programs, presumably partly dependent on the social climate.

Aside from dropping the Variety and Aggression subscales, and combining the Affiliation and Involvement subscales into a revised Involvement subscale, only relatively slight changes were made in deriving the 90-item final Real Program Form (Form R). Items with low item-to-subscale correlations or extreme item splits were eliminated. The scale was shortened as much as was consistent with psychometric adequacy and subscale meaningfulness. Table 2.2 lists the nine CIES subscales* and gives brief definitions of each. The full 90-item scale and scoring key are given in Appendix A.

*Since some investigators have used the original 12 CIES subscales in research projects, it should be noted that the correlations between the Form R subscales and the equivalent subscales in the original form were calculated for the two juvenile and two adult samples. The average correlations are above .90 for all nine subscales and above .95 for four of the subscales. Thus statistical analyses (e.g., correlations) on the Form R subscales and on the equivalent nine subscales in the original form are essentially interchangeable and are treated as such in subsequent analyses.

Table 2.2 Correctional Institutions Environment Scale (CIES)

Subscale Descriptions

1.	*Involvement:*	measures how active and energetic residents are in the day-to-day functioning of the program (i.e., interacting socially with other residents, doing things on their own initiative, and developing pride and group spirit in the program)
2.	*Support:*	measures the extent to which residents are encouraged to be helpful and supportive toward other residents, and how supportive the staff is toward residents
3.	*Expressiveness:*	measures the extent to which the program encourages the open expression of feelings (including angry feelings) by residents and staff
4.	*Autonomy:*	assesses the extent to which residents are encouraged to take initiative in planning activities and take leadership in the unit
5.	*Practical Orientation:*	assesses the extent to which the resident's environment orients him toward preparing himself for release from the program: training for new kinds of jobs, looking to the future, and setting and working toward goals are among the factors considered
6.	*Personal Problem Orientation:*	measures the extent to which residents are encouraged to be concerned with their personal problems and feelings and to seek to understand them
7.	*Order and Organization:*	measures how important order and organization are in the program, in terms of residents (how they look), staff (what they do to encourage order), and the facility itself (how well it is kept)
8.	*Clarity:*	measures the extent to which the resident knows what to expect in the day-to-day routine of his program and how explicit the program rules and procedures are
9.	*Staff Control:*	assesses the extent to which the staff use regulations to keep residents under necessary controls (i.e., in the formulation of rules, the scheduling of activities, and in the relationships between residents and staff)

The Involvement, Support, and Expressiveness subscales measure *Relationship* dimensions. These dimensions assess the involvement of residents in the program, the amount of support residents receive from staff, the amount of support residents receive from each other, and the degree of spontaneity and free, open expression within all these relationships. The variables measure the type and intensity of personal relationships among residents, and between residents and staff.

The next three subscales (Autonomy, Practical Orientation, and Personal Problem Orientation) are personal development or *Treatment Program* dimensions. Each of these subscales assesses a dimension that is particularly relevant to the type of treatment orientation the program has developed. Autonomy assesses the extent to which residents are encouraged to be self-sufficient, independent, and responsible for their own decisions. This important treatment program variable indicates a major value orientation by staff. The subscales of Practical Orientation and Personal Problem Orientation reflect two of the major types of treatment orientation currently in use in correctional programs. For example, some programs emphasize practical preparation for the resident's release through academic and vocational training. Other programs place great emphasis on a personal problem orientation and seek to increase the resident's self-understanding and insight. Some correctional units emphasize both these dimensions just as some emphasize neither one.

The last three subscales, Order and Organization, Clarity, and Staff Control, assess *System Maintenance* dimensions, which are system-oriented in that they are all related to keeping the correctional unit or institution functioning in an orderly, clear, organized, and coherent manner. The CIES thus assesses correctional programs along nine salient dimensions rather than simply categorizing them along one custodial–treatment dimension.

The positive and negative halo subscales were dropped from the final revision of the CIES for the following reasons:

1.   The items in the nine content subscales were only minimally correlated with the halo scores, indicating that positive and negative halo response tendencies are essentially independent of the content subscales.

2.   Individuals who answer the CIES inconsistently and/or do not understand the items either do not finish the scale or omit a substantial number of items. Since stringent criteria are applied before a test is included in the sample from a unit (fewer than 10 missing items, no obvious "runs" of trues and/or falses or alternations between the two), these response set scores proved to be unnecessary. With the use of these criteria, random or inconsistent answering can be detected without help of the halo subscales.

3. One of our research interests is to investigate the correlates of deviant perceptions of the environment (see Chapter 9). The largely unsuccessful attempt to weed out those residents and staff who have deviant subscale scores is incompatible with the goal of characterizing individuals who perceive their correctional environments in a discrepant manner.

CIES Form R (Real Program Form) Test Statistics

Subscale Internal Consistencies and Intercorrelations. Table 2.3 shows the internal consistencies (Kuder-Richardson formula 20) and the average item-to-subscale correlations for each of the 10 subscales for a sample of residents and staff. Internal consistencies were calculated using average within-unit variances for the items, as suggested by Stern (1970). The average item-to-subscale correlations are quite high, ranging from a low of .38 for Clarity in the resident sample to a high of .56 for Order and Organization in the staff sample. Table 2.3 indicates that the overall average item-to-subscale correlation in the juvenile male sample was .46 for residents and .49 for staff. The results for the adult male sample were very similar to those for the juvenile sample (e.g., the overall average item-to-subscale correlations were .51 and .53, respectively, for residents and staff in adult male units). Table 2.3 also reveals that the subscale internal consistencies are all in an acceptable range, varying from moderate (e.g., Expressiveness, Personal Problem Orientation, Clarity) to substantial (e.g., Involvement, Order, and Organization). The internal consistencies of the subscales were very similar for the adult resident and staff samples.

The nine subscale scores were intercorrelated for each of the two resident and the two staff samples. The actual correlations were given in the CIES Manual (Moos, 1974a). Only a few of the correlations were as high as between .40 and .50 (except for the correlations between Involvement and Support), accounting for only between 16 and 25% of the variance. The subscale intercorrelations for the adult male sample were generally somewhat higher than for the juvenile sample, indicating a relative lack of differentiation within adult prison environments. Most juvenile correctional institutions have broken away from the "total institution" model provided by the typical adult prison and have developed more differentiated program environments and social climates. That this change has not occurred to the same extent in adult prisons is in part indicated by the higher intercorrelations of the CIES subscales in the adult sample.

Table 2.3   Average Internal Consistencies and Item–Subscale Correlations for CIES Form R on Juvenile Male Samples

	Internal Consistencies		Item–Subscale Correlations	
Subscales	Residents (N=22 Units)	Staff (N=22 Units)	Residents (N=713)	Staff (N=651)
1. Involvement	.72	.81	.50	.54
2. Support	.62	.69	.46	.47
3. Expressiveness	.56	.73	.43	.49
4. Autonomy	.68	.80	.48	.53
5. Practical Orientation	.70	.61	.48	.45
6. Personal Problem Orientation	.54	.66	.41	.47
7. Order and Organization	.72	.83	.49	.56
8. Clarity	.62	.54	.38	.42
9. Staff Control	.75	.68	.49	.44
Mean	.66	.71	.46	.49

Test–Retest Reliability and Profile Stability.   The test–retest reliabilities of individual scores on the nine CIES sub-scales were calculated on 31 residents in one correctional unit who took the scale twice, with a one-week interval between testings. All the test–retest reliabilities were in an acceptable range varying from a low of .65 for Support and Order and Organization to a high of .80 for Autonomy (see Moos, 1974a, Table 5, for the actual figures).

The question of the stability of the CIES profile for a correctional program over various periods was investigated by utilizing the intraclass correlation (Haggard, 1958). First, one correctional program was re-tested with a one-week interval between the testings. The intraclass profile correlation between these two testings was .94, indicating very high stability over this short time interval. We also tested two programs with a one-month interval and one program with a two-year interval between testings. These programs were chosen because their basic orientation had remained relatively stable over the test-retest time interval. We were concerned about the stability of the CIES profile, given a basic stability in the correctional program and in the types of residents in that program. The CIES profile correlations were .96 and .95 for the two programs tested one month apart and .91 for the program with a two-year interval between testings. These results indicate that given a stable program, the CIES will remain stable over relatively long periods, even though all residents and most of the staff members have changed, owing to discharge and turnover.

A related issue is whether the CIES profile reflects change when change has occurred. In one juvenile correctional unit a new treatment-oriented program was instituted and the CIES was utilized before and after the change. The CIES profile reflected the program change as indicated by the intraclass profile correlation which was only .52. Twelve other juvenile correctional units, on which extensive new program developments occurred over a two-year interval, were tested with the CIES both before and after the program change. The degree of change shown varied considerably from unit to unit; however, the average intraclass profile correlation for the 12 units was only .35, indicating substantial change. Thus the CIES profile is stable when the program is stable; the profile is sensitive to program change when change occurs.

These results are consistent with the findings of Street et al. (1966) and with our earlier findings in psychiatric treatment environments. Street administered inmate and staff questionnaires twice at each of four institutions. Two of the institutions had stable programs during the one-year interval between testings and showed little change on either questionnaire. The other two institutions attempted to change their programs. Both displayed considerably more change than the first two institutions, even though one was retested only one month after the program changes were initiated.

Our results on treatment environments indicated that the Ward Atmosphere Scale (WAS) profile stability of programs with a consistent treatment philosophy was very high over relatively long periods. This was true for both patients and staff, although the stabilities for staff were somewhat higher than those for patients, particularly over the longer intervals. Profile stabilities for eight different programs with test–

retest intervals between 24 and 40 months averaged about .75 for patients and .85 for staff. Since very few if any of the same patients were
tested on both occasions, this indicated that the social climate of a program may remain highly stable despite a complete turnover in patient
population. The results on the stability of the CIES corroborate these
findings (see Moos, 1974b, Chapter 3, and Moos, 1974d).

Differences Among Correctional Programs. We were concerned
about the actual proportion of subscale variance accounted for by differences among programs. This is similar to the problem of the relative
proportion of variance accounted for by persons, settings, and person
by setting interactions in responses to questionnaires and in behavior.
The proportions accounted for by different sources vary greatly depending on the particular sample of residents, programs, and specific
subscales under study. Thus there is no single answer to this question.
The analysis of variance of CIES subscales among programs is almost
always statistically significant for both residents and staff, particularly
when the programs are sampled from different institutions.

Estimated omega squared (Hays, 1963) was used to calculate the average proportion of the total subscale variance accounted for by differences among programs. Three different samples comprising 16 and 22
juvenile programs and 20 adult programs were used. The proportion
of variance accounted for by differences among programs varied from
a low of under 5% to a high of over 40%. Differences among programs
accounted for about 25% of the variance for resident responses and
about 20% of the variance for staff responses. Thus the proportion of
variance accounted for by differences among programs may be quite
substantial. This proportion is similar to the proportion of variance that
is usually attributable to individual difference measures of personality
traits (Mischel, 1968). On the other hand, an important proportion of
subscale variance can be ascribed to individual differences of perception
among residents and among staff within programs. Correlates of these
individual differences are discussed in Chapters 8 and 9.

These results are similar to those obtained in psychiatric programs.
Differences among hospital-based programs accounted for 20 to 25%
of the variance of patient perceptions and 25 to 30% of the variance
of staff perceptions. Differences among community-based programs accounted for an average of 20% of the variance of members' perceptions
and 27% of the variance of staff perceptions (Moss, 1974a, 1974d). Ellsworth and Maroney (1972) have dealt with this issue in relation to
the Perception of Ward scales, and Centra (1970) has discussed it with
respect to the student perception section of the Questionnaire on Stu-

dent and College Characteristics. Ellsworth and Maroney found that only between 2 and 11% of the total variance of Perception of Ward subscales was between-ward variance. This rather low proportion may have been found because the wards were sampled from a restricted range of hospitals. Centra derived 8 student perception factors from a broadly representative sample of 116 colleges and universities. He discovered that the proportion of total factor variance attributable to differences among institutions ranged from 21 to 68% with a mean of 35% for the 8 factor scales, and from 3 to 75% with a mean of 21% for the 77 items. Thus the proportion of variance due to differences among colleges can be quite substantial, although it is usually still less than that due to differences among students within colleges.

Relationships Between Subscales and Background Variables. The effects of individual background characteristics on resident and staff responses to the CIES were investigated by calculating separately for 384 residents and 92 staff members the correlations between the nine CIES subscales and the background characteristics of age and length of stay (or time worked) on the unit. In the resident sample only 2 of the 20 correlations were above .20, and in the staff sample only one of the 20 correlations was above .20. There was a slight tendency for older residents to perceive their units more negatively, but there was essentially no relationship (all correlations were less than .10) between length of stay on the unit and any of the nine subscales. There were no particular trends in the results for the staff sample. Wenk and Halatyn (1973) calculated correlations between the CIES subscales and the inmate background variables of age, length of sentence, time incarcerated, and number of times sentenced. Only 2 of the resulting 36 correlations were above .20, indicating that the CIES subscales are relatively independent of these background variables.

These results are consistent with findings on other perceived environment scales—for example, low correlations between the Ward Atmosphere Scale subscales and age, sex, and length of stay of patients in psychiatric treatment programs (Moos, 1974b, Chapter 3), and close similarity between male and female residents' perceptions of three coed dormitories (Gerst and Moos, 1972). More work is needed in this area because there may be significant relationships between perceptions of institutional atmosphere and personality factors or background variables other than age and length of stay.

The current status of this line of research suggests that some relations exist between individual personality and/or background characteristics of subjects and their perceptions of the environment, but such connections seldom appear to be very substantial. It is also unclear how well they reflect differences in the subenvironments actually experienced by individual perceivers. On the other hand, it seems reasonable to suppose that an individual who is under high environmental uncertainty and high need will answer an environmental item in a way that conforms to or is congruent with his particular need structure. The role position of an individual in an environment (e.g., resident or staff, inmate leader or follower) may also have a substantial effect on his perceptions of that environment. Thus personality and background variables might be correlated with environmental perceptions through the mediating effects of role position (see Moos, 1974b, Chapter 3).

Assessing Ideal Correctional Programs. The CIES Real Program (Form R) items and instructions have been reworded to permit residents and staff to answer them in terms of the type of correctional unit they would ideally like. This ideal program form (Form I) was developed to measure the goals and value orientations of residents and staff. For example, we wanted to determine the areas in which resident and staff goals are basically similar and in which they are basically different. To what extent do staff goals vary within an institution from one living hall or cell block to another? To what extent do staff goals differ among institutions? To what extent do the value orientations about ideal correctional units of judges and parole officers differ from those of institutional administrators and staff? To what extent do staff of different role orientations (e.g., guards, counselors) have different views of ideal correctional programs?

Another rationale for the development of the ideal form involved giving residents and staff an opportunity to compare real and ideal program profiles, thus to identify areas in which they wished to institute change. This rationale is particularly relevant for juvenile and community programs experimenting with different treatment modalities for the rehabilitation of juvenile offenders. A final purpose was to relate the degree of similarity or dissimilarity of real and ideal program perceptions to various other variables, such as general level of satisfaction with the institution and the incidence of antisocial behaviors in the institution.

Street, Vinter, and Perrow (1966) have used a conceptually similar approach. These investigators related staff goals, as formulated by the chief administrators of six correctional institutions, to staff beliefs about the proper modes of interaction with residents and to resident perspectives on the institution and staff. Executive goals were assessed by interviews with the chief administrative officer of each institution. Goal orientations fell into three categories, as previously described. Staff beliefs about the possibility of understanding delinquents, as assessed by a staff attitude questionnaire, were much more optimistic in programs with treatment-oriented goals than in programs that stressed reeducation/ development or obedience/conformity. The degree of permissiveness recommended in disciplining delinquents was much greater at the two treatment-oriented institutions than at the other four. Thus administrators' goal orientations may have important effects both on staff opinions and on the manner in which staff actually handle residents. Unfortunately Street did not measure resident, staff, and administrators' goals and perceptions on parallel subscales. This is what the CIES real and ideal program forms are intended to do.

The CIES ideal program form (Form I) may be used in conjunction with the real program form (Form R) to identify specific areas in which residents and staff feel that change should occur. The ideal program form may also be used by itself if an investigator simply wishes to assess the general value orientations or possible value changes in a program or institution. The final version of the ideal program form has 90 items directly parallel to the real program form items. That is, each of the ideal form items has the same content as the equivalent real form item, but it is worded somewhat differently to indicate that perceptions of an ideal environment are being sought. When filling out the ideal form, residents and staff are given the following instructions:

> Please think about an *ideal unit*. There are 90 statements in this booklet; they are statements about correctional units. Answer each statement to describe an *ideal unit*. Remember, do not describe the unit you are on but rather describe an *ideal unit*.

The ideal program form has been given to residents on 81 units (44 juvenile and 37 adult) and to staff on 62 units (45 juvenile and 17 adult). Item-to-subscale correlations and internal consistencies were calculated for the nine ideal form subscales for a subsample of 22 male juvenile units (838 residents and 229 staff). The average item-to-subscale correlations varied from a low of .32 for the Practical Orientation subscale for residents to a high of .53 for the Involvement subscale for staff. The subscale internal consistencies were all in an acceptable range, varying from a low of .61 for Practical Orientation for residents to a high of .89 for the Support subscale for staff. Thus the ideal form has adequate psychometric characteristics, although more normative data would be desirable. The overall ideal form means and standard deviations are given in the CIES Manual (Moos, 1974a), as are the ideal form items.

Assessing Expectations of Correctional Programs. The CIES real program (Form R) items and instructions have also been reworded to let residents and staff answer them in terms of their expectations about the correctional program or unit they are about to enter (Form E). How accurate are these expectations? To what extent does providing systematic information about correctional programs result in more accurate expectations? Evidence from individual and group psychotherapy and from our studies of community-based treatment programs (Moos, 1974b; Chapter 12) and of military basic training companies (see Chapter 12) indicates that certain types of inaccurate expectation may result in poor functioning, absenteeism, and premature dropout. The expectations form (Form E) is also directly parallel to the real program form (i.e., it has 90 items, and each one parallels an item in the real program form). Separate psychometric data have not yet been obtained on the expectations form. The Form E items and instructions are given in the CIES Manual (Moos, 1974a).

Details of Test Administration. The various forms of the CIES may be given as paper-and-pencil questionnaires or by utilizing tape-recorded instructions and special answer sheets. Various considerations involving different aspects of test administration, including the issues of obtaining cooperation from residents and staff, confidentiality, and anonymity of results, are discussed in an overview of all the Social Climate Scales (Moos, 1974c).

The 36–Item CIES Short Form (Form S). A 36-item Short Form of the CIES was developed for use by investigators or correctional staff who wish to make a relatively rapid assessment of a program's social climate. Four items were chosen from each of the nine CIES subscales in the following manner: items with the highest item-to-subscale correlations were chosen, provided there was an equal or 3:1 item split between items scored in the true direction and items scored in the false direction. When two chosen items had similar wording, one was dropped in favor of another less similar item, to cover the subscale content more adequately.

Means and standard deviations were then calculated separately for residents and staff for these nine 4-item subscales for a sample of 95 juvenile units for residents and 87 juvenile units for staff. Standard scores were obtained for each. Intraclass profile correlations (Haggard, 1958) between the nine Form R and the nine Form S standard scores were calculated for each unit, separately for residents and staff. These correlations assess the similarity between the CIES profile based on only four representative items from each subscale and the profile based on all the items in each subscale. The intraclass correlations between Form R and Form S were above .80 for 72, and above .70 for 85 of the 95 units in the resident sample. For the staff sample the intraclass correlations were above .80 for 70 and above .70 for 83 of the 87 units. Utilizing Form S, therefore, generally results in profiles highly similar to those obtained with the regular Form R.

The Short Form should be especially useful in following changes in a program over time. However, there are too few items on each subscale to warrant making comparisions among individuals. The 36 items included in the Short Form are marked with an asterisk on the scoring key given in Appendix A. The Short Form means and standard deviations for residents and staff for the juvenile, the male adult, and the female adult reference group samples are given in the CIES Manual (Moos, 1974a).

Random Samples on Units of Varying Sizes.   We studied psychiatric treatment programs to determine the proportion of subjects in a milieu who must answer a Social Climate Scale if an adequate characterization of that milieu is to be obtained. We took 50% random samples of patients and staff who completed the Ward Atmosphere Scale, derived separate profiles for these samples, and assessed the similarity of the resulting two profiles with the intraclass correlation (Haggard, 1958). For example, on hospital-based programs the average intraclass correlation for 67 wards with 30 or more patients was above .80. There was not a single correlation below .80 on any ward on which there were 20 or more staff members. Thus a tentative guideline for sampling was established—namely, that a 50% random sample in units with 30 or more patients (or residents) and/or 20 or more staff members would provide adequate profiles. Similar analyses were carried out for a sample of community-oriented psychiatric programs. The mean intraclass correlation was .88 for seven programs with 21 or more members and .92 for three programs with 11 or more staff.

In the present sample of juvenile correctional units many relatively large units were encountered. It was therefore decided to investigate the adequacy of 25% random samples taken from units with 40 or more residents and 20 or more staff. Two 25% random samples were taken from each of the 22 units that met these size criteria. Intraclass correlations were computed for each unit between each of the 25% sample subscale means and the subscale means of the complete sample. All of the resultant intraclass correlations were above .90, indicating that 25%

random samples are highly adequate means of characterizing the social milieu of an environment under the specified size conditions.

Thus, the most reasonable guidelines are that 50% samples are adequate when sampling correctional programs with 30 or more residents and/or 15 or more staff members, and 25% samples are adequate when sampling correctional programs with 40 or more residents and/or 20 or more staff members. This sampling must be done randomly; that is, 25% samples of volunteers will most likely provide a biased estimate of the unit social climate. The advantages of using 25 or 50% samples are twofold. First, the total quantity of data analysis is greatly reduced. Second, if both Real and Ideal forms are to be administered, or if replication is desired, different subsamples of residents and staff can take a different form or can provide desired replication. (This procedure is relevant only if the investigator wishes simply to assess the general social environment or the general value orientations of residents and staff. More complete samples are necessary if one wishes to relate individual resident or staff characteristics to either real or ideal program perceptions.)

The Effects of Subject Anonymity. Previous work on the effects of anonymity of subject responses has indicated that anonymity is an important issue under conditions of high threat to the respondent (Moos, 1974b; Chapter 2). Three of the Ward Atmosphere Scale (WAS) subscales significantly differentiated between random samples of patients on one ward who were given name and no-name instructions in a high-threat condition. Patients who put their names on the WAS perceived significantly more Involvement and Order and Organization and significantly less Staff Control. Thus patients in the name condition viewed their wards somewhat more positively than did patients in the no-name condition. Differences on other subscales were generally in the same direction, although not statistically significant. The magnitude of the subscale differences between the two conditions was about 0.5 standard deviation. However, there were no differences between two random samples of patients on another ward who took the WAS under low-threat conditions.

Work by other investigators in various milieus shows a similar pattern of results. Ash and Abramson (1952), Corey (1937), Gerberich and Mason (1948), Hamel and Reif (1952), and Olsen (1936) all report no significant response distortion by subjects who put their names on questionnaires. Pelz (1959) compared anonymity to confidentiality (subjects identified only to survey staff) and found almost no difference between the two conditions. However, Klein, Maher, and Dunnington (1967) investigated the responses of employees under high-threat conditions (employees randomly assigned to test groups). They reported significantly more response distortion under the high-threat condition. These authors also suggest that items of different content may be differentially susceptible to change under conditions of identification. They found that items dealing with salary and with ratings of top management produced consistent positive distortions, whereas items dealing with the subjects' situation (i.e., work pressure and subject's manager) produced little or no distortion even under conditions of high threat. Since the items in the CIES ask about the environment rather than about either personality or attitudes, they should produce relatively little distortion.

Moderate distortion may be produced by lack of anonymity or confidentiality under high-threat conditions. Answering questions about the environment of correctional institutions is likely to be perceived as a high-threat situation by both residents and staff. This is particularly true in the institution resembling a total institution model of Goffman (1961). The rigid hierarchial social structure of such an institution produces anxiety in low-status staff members and even lower-status residents when an unfamiliar and uncertain procedure, such as a potentially evaluative survey, is introduced. The difficulties of getting reliable and undistorted responses from residents and staff in this type of situation or, indeed, of getting any response at all are described by McCleery (1961). McCleery's study of incorrigible residents in certain units of maximum security prisons nearly failed because the interviewer did not make clear his purposes in conducting the study. It is thus best for investigators to grant anonymity to respondents to the CIES and other instruments, unless they wish to relate individual responses to other measures (see Moos, 1974b, Chapter 2; and 1974c).

REFERENCES

Ash, P. & Abramson, E. The effect of anonymity on attitude-questionnaire research. *Journal of Abnormal & Social Psychology,* **46:** 722–723, 1952.

Centra, J. A. The college environment revisited: Current descriptions and a comparison of three methods of assessment. College Entrance Examination Board Research and Development Reports, Number 1, August 1970.

Corey, S. Professed attitudes and actual behavior. *Journal of Educational Psychology,* **28:**271–280, 1937.

Crowne, D. and Marlowe, D. *The Approval Motive.* Wiley, New York, 1964.

Ellsworth, R. B. & Maroney, R. Characteristics of psychiatric programs and their effects on patients' adjustment. *Journal of Consulting and Clinical Psychology,* **39:**436–447, 1972.

Eynon, T., Allen, H., & Reckless, W. Measuring the impact of a juvenile correctional institution by perceptions of inmates and staff. *Journal of Research in Crime and Delinquency,* **8:**93–107, 1971.

Gerberich, J. & Mason, J. Signed versus unsigned questionnaires. *Journal of Educational Research,* **42:**122–126, 1948.

Gerst, M. & Moos, R. Social ecology of university student residences. *Journal of Educational Psychology,* **63:**513–525, 1972.

Goffman, E. On the characteristics of total institutions: The inmate world. In D. R. Cressey (Ed.), *The prison: Studies in organization and change.* Holt, Rinehart & Winston, New York, 1961.

Haggard, E. *Intraclass correlation and the analysis of variance.* Dryden Press, New York, 1958.

Hamel, L. & Reif, H. Should attitude questionnaires be signed? *Personnel Psychology,* **5:**87–91, 1952.

Hays, W. *Statistics for psychologists.* Holt, Rinehart & Winston, New York, 1963.

Jesness, C. *The Preston typology study.* Institute for the Study of Crime and Delinquency, Sacramento, Calif., 1968.

Klein, S., Maher, J., & Dunnington, R. Differences between identified and anonymous subjects in responding to an industrial opinion survey. *Journal of Applied Psychology,* **51:**152–160, 1967.

McCleery, R. H. Authoritarianism and the belief system of incorrigibles. In D. R. Cressey (Ed.), *The prison: Studies in organization and change.* Holt, Rinehart & Winston, New York, 1961.

Mischel, W. *Personality and assessment.* Wiley, New York, 1968.

Moos, R. The assessment of the social climates of correctional institutions. *Journal of Research in Crime and Delinquency,* **5:**174–188, 1968.

Moos, R. *Correctional Institutions Environment Scale Manual.* Consulting Psychologists Press, Palo Alto, Calif., 1974a.

Moos, R. *Evaluating treatment environments: A social ecological approach.* Wiley, New York, 1974b.

Moos, R. *The social climate scales: An overview.* Consulting Psychologists Press, Palo Alto, Calif., 1974c.

Moos, R. *Ward Atmosphere Scale Manual.* Consulting Psychologists Press, Palo Alto, Calif., 1974d.

Murray, H. *Explorations in personality.* Oxford University Press, New York, 1938.

Olson, W. The waiver of signature in personal reports. *Journal of Applied Psychology,* **20:**442–449, 1936.

Pelz, D. The influence of anonymity on express attitudes. *Human Organization,* **18:**88–91, 1959.

Stern, G. *People in context.* Wiley, New York, 1970.

Street, D., Vinter, R., & Perrow, C. *Organization for treatment: A comparative study of institutions for delinquents.* Free Press, New York, 1966.

Wenk, E. & Halatyn, T. The assessment of correctional climates. National Council on Crime and Delinquency Research Center, Davis, Calif., 1973.

Wood, B., Wilson, G., Jessor, R., & Bogan, J. Troublemaking behavior in a correctional institution: Relationship to inmates' definition of their situation. *American Journal of Orthopsychiatry,* **36:**795–802, 1966.

CHAPTER THREE

Real and Ideal
Correctional Programs

Juvenile Correctional Programs. A large and varied sample of juvenile correctional units was tested with the CIES in an attempt to obtain a normative sample, representative of the wide range of currently existing juvenile correctional programs. The goal was to provide a new measurement technique that would be standardized well enough to be generally applicable to all correctional programs. Units with innovative treatment programs for their residents were included, as were more traditional custodial and vocationally oriented units. To secure a varied regional representation of programs, the juvenile normative sample included programs located in seven states: California, Hawaii, New York, Oregon, Washington, West Virginia, and Wisconsin. The summary characteristics of this sample are given in Table 3.1. We assessed 112 programs located in 28 correctional facilities, 14 of them in California. Since it is generally felt that the California juvenile correctional system is one of the best in the country, the results probably present a positively biased picture of conditions in juvenile correctional facilities.

The juvenile normative sample includes 68 male units from seven training schools. Two of these schools were involved in a major research project at the time the CIES was administered (see Chapter 6). The other five training schools were more traditional juvenile correctional institutions, although all were basically treatment oriented. The first school was for relatively unsophisticated, immature boys in the 13- to

Table 3.1   Summary Characteristics of Normative Samples

CIES Form	Number of Correctional Facilities	Number of Facilities in California	Number of States Represented	Number of Units	Number of Residents Tested	Number of Staff Tested
CIES Form R (Real Program Form)						
Juvenile sample (male and female)	28	14	7	112	3651	858
Adult male sample	26	1	14	51	3151	895
Adult female sample	9	2	9	32	552	143
Totals	63	17	18	195	7354	1896
CIES Form I (Ideal Program Form)						
Juvenile male sample	11	11	1	45	1429	393
Adult male sample	14	0	6	37	1289	467
Totals	25	11	7	82	2718	860

18-year-old range. A program of shop training, horticulture, academic work through the high school level, and extensive training furloughs was offered. Psychotherapy was provided by a staff of three psychologists, six social workers, and a part-time psychiatrist for the school's population of about 600 boys. Each boy received small group and large group counseling led by a youth worker under the guidance of a psychologist or social worker, plus individual counseling by the youth worker.

The second training school was composed of 350 boys ranging in age from 14 to 17 years. It provided a program of shop training and academic education through the high school level. Small and large group counseling followed a pattern similar to that of the first training school. Psychiatric treatment was available for severely disturbed boys.

A third school took about 600 boys, 16 to 20 years of age, and offered academic instruction through the high school level, extensive vocational training, particularly in agricultural fields and general shop trades (metal, wood, electrical, print, and garment) as well as the usual large and small group counseling. Three innovative research-oriented projects were in process when the CIES was administered. The first was a vocational rehabilitation program that included training and counseling at the institution, job placement, on-the-job training, and assistance in living arrangements after release from the school. The second project was a drug treatment program exploring various approaches to the rehabilitation of drug users. The third project explored the utility of differential housing and treatment approaches for delinquents of different maturity levels.

A fourth training school had about 450 boys, 16 to 20 years of age; it featured preemployment training in 25 vocational fields, among them office machine repair, food service, upholstery, painting, masonry, refrigeration, and architectural drawing. The training was augmented by a half-day work experience within the institution and by academic instruction leading to a high school diploma. Small and large group counseling was offered, but no psychiatric care was available. Two special programs were in operation—a drug treatment program and a community orientation program designed to facilitate the transition from institutional to community life, primarily through the obtaining of a prerelease job guarantee for participants.

The fifth training school, which also had about 450 boys, catered to older juvenile or young adult offenders. It provided education to the college level; remedial and high school courses were offered at the school, and college courses were available by correspondence. Various vocational shops were accompanied by on-the-job training in bedding and mattress making, upholstering, manufacture of metal and wood furniture, and dairy and hog farming. Psychiatric services were available only at the school's adjustment center. The boys at this school were described as fairly mature but requiring a good deal of external control.

Other units in the reference group sample include four units from a reception and guidance center. Boys referred by the courts were given a battery of tests at the center, including intelligence, psychological, and vocational evaluations. Reports on boys were obtained from family, friends, and other agencies. A case summary was written for each boy and was used to develop a plan of custodial care, which was then put into effect at the state training school deemed most appropriate for the boy. Severely disturbed boys were usually sent to a state medical facility rather than to a training school.

There were broad similarities in the background characteristics of the delinquents committed to these different institutions. About 50% were Caucasian—this varied from a low of about 35% to a high of about 60%. About 15 to 20% were Mexican-American and the other 30 to 35% were black. Almost all the boys were between 14 and 20 years of age. Their commitment offenses varied widely (e.g., truancy and incorrigibility, narcotics use, rape, auto and other thefts, burglary, assault, robbery, and homicide). Staffing patterns in these training schools ranged from fewer than 3 to more than 12 residents per staff member.

Additional units included a vocational school and a work release program for boys, nine units in a variety of additional state-administered juvenile correctional facilities, and four units from an academic and vocational training school for boys and young men ranging in age from 18 to 30 years. The remaining units, which are described in more detail later, came from county juvenile halls (4 female and 10 male units) and ranches and camps (3 female and 14 male units).

A total of 3651 residents and 858 staff completed the CIES in these 112 juvenile programs. The overall means and standard deviations for residents and staff for this normative sample are given in the CIES Manual (Moos, 1974a). Figure 3.1 graphically compares the resident and staff means on the nine CIES subscales. Staff means are significantly higher on all subscales except Staff Control, which is significantly higher in the resident sample ($p < .001$ for all subscales). Thus staff members perceive the conditions in their units considerably more positively than do the residents in the same units. This strongly corroborates the existence of distinctly different resident and staff subcultures (see also Lohn, 1974). These results are consistent with findings in psychiatric treatment programs (Moos, 1974b, Chapter 3), although the average differences observed between residents and staff in correctional programs are considerably larger than those observed between patients and staff in psychiatric programs.

As Figure 3.1 indicates, the overall differences between the opinions of residents and staff on juvenile correctional units are very large. The average differences are 2 mean raw score points or greater on the Relationship dimensions of Involvement and Support and on the Treatment Program dimension of Autonomy. There is a difference of more than 1 mean raw score point on each of the other six CIES subscales. These statistically significant differences occur on individual subscales, which themselves have a total of only nine or ten items. To identify items on which residents and staff showed particularly large

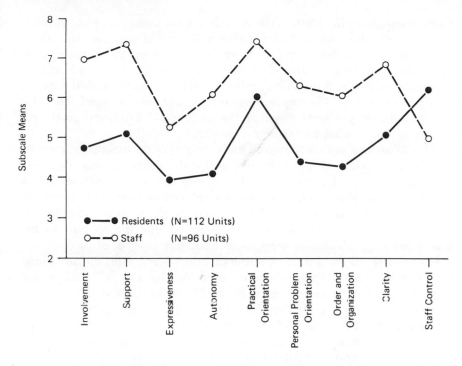

Figure 3.1 Comparison of resident and staff perceptions of juvenile correctional programs.

differences, we calculated the average proportion of true responses for each of the items separately for all the residents and staff in the normative sample.

Residents and staff showed differences of 30% or greater on 11 items. Some items on which staff answered true at least 30% more often than residents were: "Discussions are pretty interesting on this unit," "This is a friendly unit," "Staff go out of their way to help residents," "Staff act on resident's suggestions," and "Staff set an example for neatness and orderliness." Some items on which residents answered true 30% more often than staff were: "There is very little group spirit on this unit," "It is hard to tell how residents are feeling on this unit," "There is very little emphasis on making residents more practical," "Residents are rarely asked personal questions by the staff," "Staff are always changing their minds here," and "Residents will be transferred from this unit if they don't obey the rules." These item examples concretely illustrate that staff perceive correctional units considerably more positively than do residents.

Comparing Juvenile Halls with Ranches and Camps.   The perceptions of residents and staff in juvenile halls and in ranches and camps
were compared to determine whether differences existed in their social
environments. The 10 juvenile hall units housed between 14 and 78
residents (mean = 35). The number of staff per unit varied from 2
to 7 (mean = 3.8). The resulting resident/staff ratio ranged from 3.8
to 16 residents per staff member (mean = 8.5). The average length
of stay of the residents was about 5 weeks.

The programs in these juvenile halls were very custodially or system-
maintenance oriented. For example, although bedrooms and lavatories
were seldom locked during the day, shower times were almost always
prescribed, and showers were supervised by staff in most units. Supervision levels varied from minimal to extremely close, as indicated by a
comment from a staff respondent who stated that the 35 boys in his
unit went through the showers once each day in groups of five, the
entire process taking a total of one-half hour! Many halls did not allow
residents to smoke. Those that did allow residents over 16 to smoke
required a signed parental consent form. The units usually had a moderate amount of recreational equipment, such as a television set, radio,
books and magazines, and game tables. The use of these items was regulated by residents in some units and by staff in others. The telephone
was without exception regulated by staff. When a resident entered one
of these units, some or all of his personal belongings were taken from
him and placed in temporary storage. Mail was censored in six of the
units, and in five units silverware was counted after meals.

Some of the units had psychotherapy programs. Few had a large
professional staff, but some group and/or individual counseling was
offered in most units. Staff in some units were officially encouraged
to develop warm, personal, and trusting relationships with residents.
Behavior modification and positive reinforcement techniques were often
used as a basic management technique. The sample included a special
treatment unit for boys with mental–emotional or organic problems of
great severity, as well as a "halfway house" unit whose function was
to prepare residents for placement in a foster home or open institution.

The 14 ranches and camps ranged in size from 14 to 80 residents
(mean = 49). The number of staff per unit ranged from 3 to 19 (mean
= 9.3). The resident/staff ratio varied from 2 to 16, with a mean of
6 residents per staff member. The average length of stay for residents
was about 6 months, with a range among units from 3 to 8 months.

The other structural characteristics relating to custody functions and
system maintenance were similar to the juvenile halls just described.
Great variation existed in the relative emphasis on regimentation and

staff control, as in the case of the juvenile halls. The biggest difference between the camps and the juvenile halls was in the area of therapy and rehabilitation programs. Rehabilitation in the camps was supposed to result primarily from work and school experiences in the active outdoor environment provided by these institutions.

A more detailed program description was available from one of the typical ranches in our sample, located in the foothills about 30 miles from a large city. Residents were 13- to 17-year-old boys. Psychotic and drug-dependent individuals were not accepted, nor were there any boys with long institutional histories. Boys progressed through a three-step classification system during their stay at the ranch, which averaged 6 to 7 months. Each class carried greater responsibilities and was accompanied by more favorable work assignments. Promotion was discussed on a monthly basis by staff, using school and work progress reports. Individualized instruction was used in the academic program, which allowed boys with deficiencies in specific areas to learn necessary skills. Work experience consisted of caring for a herd of livestock which provided much of the ranch's food supply, and of janitorial, gardening and kitchen jobs. Athletic, church, and social activities furnished a measure of community contact for the residents. Staff made an effort to acquaint new residents with the purpose of the ranch and the rules by which the program operated.

The CIES results for staff correspond closely with what would be expected on the basis of the foregoing descriptions. Ranches and camps place much more emphasis on the Relationship dimensions of Involvement and Support and on all three of the Treatment Program dimensions. The differences on Autonomy and Practical Orientation are particularly large. However, there are no significant differences in staff perceptions of the three System Maintenance dimensions. Although ranches and camps probably emphasize Order and Organization and Clarity as much as juvenile halls, the results on Staff Control seem to be contrary to the impression that juvenile halls are more restrictive than ranches and camps. Our finding makes more sense when one looks at the actual items on Staff Control (e.g., "Once a schedule is arranged for a resident he must follow it," "All decisions about the unit are made by the staff and not the residents," and "The unit staff regularly check up on the residents.") These elements of staff control are as frequent in ranches and camps as they are in juvenile halls (see Figure 3.2).

The differences between the perceptions of residents in juvenile halls and those in ranches and camps generally parallel those for staff. Residents in ranches and camps felt that there was significantly more emphasis on the Relationship dimensions of Involvement and Support and on

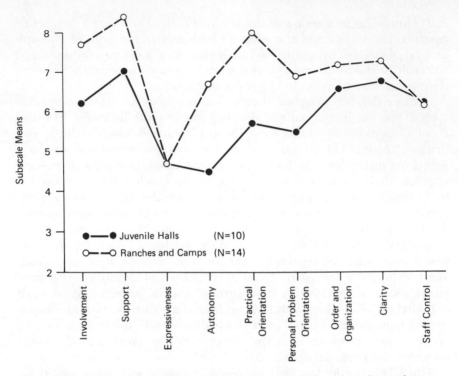

Figure 3.2   Comparison of staff perceptions of juvenile halls and ranches and camps.

the Treatment Program dimensions of Autonomy and Practical Orientation than did residents in juvenile halls. There were no differences between residents' perceptions on the three System Maintenance dimensions. Consistent with the earlier results, residents in both juvenile halls
and ranches and camps perceived their social environments much more
negatively than did staff.

Adult Correctional Programs.   The adult male normative sample consists of 51 units located in 14 states (see Table 3.1). Data were obtained
from 26 correctional facilities. The 14 states were Alaska, Arkansas, California, Connecticut, Georgia, Hawaii, Kentucky, Maryland, Mississippi,
New Mexico, Oklahoma, Texas, and Vermont. Most of the data were
collected in collaboration with Ernst Wenk of the National Council on
Crime and Delinquency and William Megathlin of Georgia State College.
The types of correctional units included dormitories and barracks, cell

houses, adult training centers, honor units, vocational farms, units from medical facilities for inmates requiring intensive psychiatric care, and a drug and alcohol abuse center.

The institutions, programs, and types of inmates varied widely. For example, the following types of institution were included: (1) an institution for first offenders 25 years of age or younger, (2) an institution mainly for young second offenders, (3) a medium security institution for younger recidivists, (4) various maximum security institutions for older multirecidivists, (5) a maximum security institution for older recidivists who were specifically high "escape risks and malcontents," (6) a minimum security institution for older first offenders who were able to work on minimally supervised farm units, and (7) a minimum security institution for inmates who had 6 months or less to serve and were participating in a work furlough program. Since a broad range of adult programs was included, the results are probably generally representative of the social climate conditions in adult correctional facilities.

The institutions involved also ranged widely in size and staffing patterns. The smallest programs had fewer than 50 residents, whereas the largest had more than 2000 residents. Staffing patterns varied from fewer than 5 to more than 10 residents for each staff member. The entire range of staff members working on these units were included (e.g., yard security personnel, tower guards, administrative staff, service staff, and medical facility staff). Minimum, medium, and maximum security facilities and units with treatment and rehabilitative programs, as well as units with more traditional and custodial programs, were included (see Wenk and Moos, 1972, for further details on this sample).

A sample of adult female correctional units was collected from prisons in nine states: Alaska, Arkansas, California, Connecticut, Hawaii, Kentucky, Mississippi, New Mexico, and Washington (see Table 3.1). Included in this sample were a women's unit in a prison with five male units, units from community-oriented correctional and treatment centers, cell block units in custodially oriented prisons, and cottage and hospital units. The relatively small size of the sample (32 units for residents but only 6 units for staff) means that it must be viewed as only a preliminary normative reference group.

Figure 3.3 compares the adult male resident and staff means on the nine CIES subscales. The actual means and standard deviations for both residents and staff for this adult male sample (as well as those for the adult female sample) are given in the CIES Manual (Moos, 1974a). Consistent with previous results in juvenile institutions, the staff in adult male units also perceive their programs much more positively than do the residents. The staff means are significantly ($p < .01$) higher on all

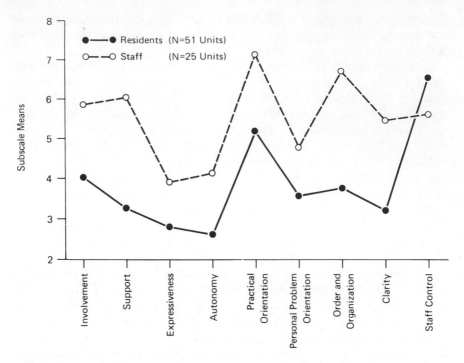

Figure 3.3   Comparison of resident and staff perceptions of adult male correctional programs.

subscales except Staff Control, on which they are significantly lower. The resident–staff differences were exactly the same in the adult female sample, except that the staff in female units perceived much more emphasis on Practical Orientation than did the residents. Staff in both male and female units rate their programs lower on Staff Control than do the residents.

As with the juvenile units, some of the resident–staff differences are quite substantial. The differences on Support, Order and Organization, and Clarity are greater than 2 mean raw score points. The differences on the Involvement, Expressiveness, Autonomy, Practical Orientation, and Personal Problem Orientation subscales are all between 1 and 2 mean raw score points.

For example, staff on adult male units agreed with the following items at least 25% more often than did residents: "Discussions are pretty interesting on this unit," "Staff go out of their way to help residents," "Staff try to help residents understand themselves," and "Staff tell residents when they are doing well." On the other hand, residents agreed with the following items at least 25% more often than did staff: "This unit has very few social activities," "Staff have very little time to encourage residents," "The staff give residents very little responsibility," "There is very little emphasis on making residents more practical." Each of these items discriminated between residents and staff in exactly the same way in the adult female sample. Thus the finding that correctional staff see their programs substantially more positively than do residents holds for both the juvenile and the adult samples.

Comparing Juvenile and Adult Programs.   Comparison of Figures 3.1 and 3.3 indicates that residents and staff on juvenile units generally see their social environment in a more positive light than do residents and staff on adult units. The differences are not extremely large, but they are in the same direction for both residents and staff on all but one subscale (Order and Organization). The differences are greatest for the Relationship dimensions of Support and Expressiveness, the Treatment Program dimension of Autonomy, and the System Maintenance dimension of Clarity (between 1 and 2 mean raw score points).

For example, items on which juvenile residents responded true at least 25% more often than adult residents include: "The residents are proud of this unit," "Staff encourage group activities among the residents," "Staff and residents say how they feel about each other," "Residents are encouraged to plan for the future," "Residents are expected to take leadership on the unit," "Staff try to help residents understand themselves," "Staff tell residents when they are doing well," and "The residents know when counselors will be on the unit." These items indicate that the overall emphasis on Support, Expressiveness, Autonomy, and Clarity is somewhat higher in juvenile than in adult correctional programs.

Ideal Correctional Environments.   Chapter 2 mentioned the development of an additional form of the CIES (Form I) to obtain information about residents' and staff members' views of ideal correctional programs. A brief description of the juvenile and adult reference group samples for this ideal program form is given here (see Table 3.1). The juvenile reference group sample consists of residents from 44 units and staff members from 45 units, all in California. These juvenile units were in correctional institutions of the following types: two county juvenile halls, two state training schools, and seven ranches and camps. The adult Form I reference group sample consists of residents from 37 correctional units and staff members from 17 units. The adult sample, collected in collaboration with Ernst Wenk, consisted of units from male prisons in Arkansas, Kentucky, Hawaii, New Mexico, Oklahoma, and Vermont. The Form I data were collected in the juvenile and adult facilities already described. The fairly broad samples probably give a good indication of the views of residents and staff regarding ideal correctional programs.

Figure 3.4 compares resident and staff views of ideal correctional environments. The results from the juvenile and adult samples were very similar and have been combined. The actual Form I means and standard deviations are given in the CIES Manual (Moos, 1974a). Staff in adult and juvenile correctional institutions ideally want much more emphasis on all three Relationship dimensions, on all three Treatment Program dimensions, and on two of the three System Maintenance dimensions than do residents ($p < .01$ for all subscales). The two groups want about the same emphasis on Staff Control. These findings provide additional support for the concept of separate subcultures for residents and staff. Staff perceive actual correctional programs considerably more positively than do residents. Staff are considerably more positive about ideal correctional programs than are residents. The differences between residents and staff are again of substantial magnitude. For example, the resident–

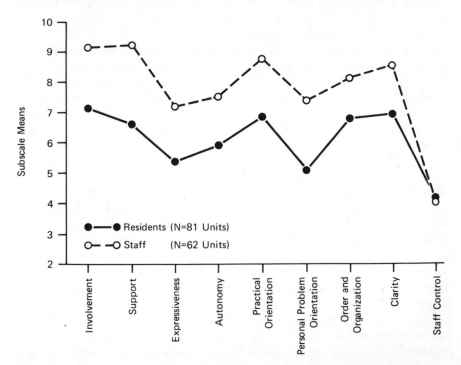

Figure 3.4 Comparison of resident and staff perceptions of ideal correctional programs.

staff discrepancies are about 2 mean raw score points (on subscales having only 9 or 10 items) for all three Relationship dimensions and for the Treatment Program dimensions of Practical Orientation and Personal Problem Orientation. Thus there are fundamental differences in the way in which residents and staff view both real and ideal correctional milieus.

The vast differences between real and ideal correctional environments may be seen by comparing Figure 3.3 (resident and staff perceptions of adult male correctional programs) with Figure 3.4 (resident and staff perceptions of ideal correctional programs). The differences between real and ideal are greater than 3 mean raw score points for both residents and staff on four of the nine CIES subscales: Involvement, Support, Autonomy, and Clarity. The differences are greater than 2 mean raw score points on Expressiveness (both residents and staff), Personal Problem Orientation (staff), Order and Organization (residents), and Staff Control (residents). These differences are all statistically significant $(p < .01)$. The real–ideal differences are somewhat less for juvenile units, but they are still of substantial (and statistically significant) magnitude on most subscales.

The standard deviations of the nine Form I subscales are quite substantial for residents and staff alike, indicating that there are important differences of opinion about the ideal correctional milieu. This suggests what many correctional practitioners feel—that is, different residents want and presumably would do better in different types of social environments. This is presumably also true for staff. Systematic attempts to place residents and/or staff in programs that have social environments consistent with their orientation and preferences might prove valuable.

A somewhat different way of organizing the data highlights the pervasive negative social conditions currently found in correctional institutions. For example, Table 3.2 shows some of the items with which more than 75% of all the residents in adult male correctional programs agree. Table 3.3 gives some of the items with which more than 75% of these residents disagree. These items indicate that there are few social activities, that group spirit or cohesion is lacking, that residents are fearful of and tend not to express themselves with the staff, and that there is a strong feeling of unclear expectations about what will happen to residents within an environment that is rigidly controlled by staff. Staff do not usually help and support residents and do not encourage resident autonomy, independence, or leadership.

The situation is better in juvenile correctional units, although juvenile residents tend to respond like adult residents to the items listed in Table 3.2 and 3.3. Better social conditions are possible, as indicated by some of the specific examples of programs discussed in Chapters 5 and 6.

Thus present conditions in the majority of adult and juvenile correctional institutions are in no sense necessary. The variability of current conditions, and existing examples of cohesive, active, and involved treatment-oriented correctional programs, illustrate the potential for beneficial change in the system.

Table 3.2   CIES Items on Which at least 75% of All Adult Residents Respond "True"

The unit has very few social activities.
There is very little group spirit on this unit.
Counselors have very little time to encourage residents.
Residents are careful about what they say when staff is around.
It is hard to tell how residents are feeling on this unit.
Residents tend to hide their feelings from the staff.

Staff rarely give in to resident pressure.
There is no resident government on this unit.

Residents never know when a counselor will ask to see them.
Residents never know when they will be transferred from this unit.
Staff are always changing their minds here.
Once a schedule is arranged for a resident, he must follow it.
Residents will be transferred from this unit if they don't obey the rules.
All decisions about the unit are made by the staff and not by the residents.

Table 3.3   CIES Items on Which at Least 75% of All Adult Residents Respond "False"

The residents are proud of this unit.
Staff go out of their way to help residents.
Staff are interested in following up residents once they leave.
The staff help new residents get acquainted on the unit.
The more mature residents on this unit help take care of the less mature ones.
Staff and residents say how they feel about each other.

The staff act on residents' suggestions.
Residents are expected to take leadership on the unit.
Staff encourage residents to start their own activities.
Residents have a say about what goes on here.
Staff are mainly interested in learning about residents' feelings.
Personal problems are openly talked about.

Residents may criticize staff members to their faces.
Residents can call staff by their first names.

Multiple Methods of Assessing Correctional Programs. This section is concerned with the extent to which resident and staff perceptions of their social environments are related to other more usual ways of describing and differentiating among correctional programs. For example, to what extent do perceptions of environments provide information congruent with that extracted from more objective structural variables. The detailed program comparisons presented in Chapter 6 clearly show that correctional units of essentially identical size, staffing, resident background, and architectural characteristics may have quite different social environments. On the other hand, there is an overall relationship between the structural characteristics of programs, such as size and staffing, and their social environments.

Two major dimensions by which environments have been characterized are of special relevance here. First are the dimensions of organizational structure and functioning, such as size and staffing ratios. Correctional programs, like psychiatric treatment programs, are usually compared in terms of readily observable indices of this sort (e.g., number of residents, number of staff, degree of control or security, type of occupational or vocational rehabilitation programs). Much of the classical work on organizational characteristics in different institutions has utilized such dimensions (March, 1965). Typical examples include work on the properties of organizational structure in industrial institutions in relation to job attitudes and job behavior (Porter and Lawler, 1965) and work on the relationship between such objective institutional factors as number of students and faculty, amount of tuition, size of library, amount of money spent on scholarships, and the vocational and educational development of students (Astin, 1968; Astin and Panos, 1969).

The second category of relevant dimensions takes in the personal and behavioral characteristics of the inhabitants of the milieu (i.e., the residents in correctional institutions). Various individual characteristics—average age, socioeconomic background, length of incarceration, and so on—may be considered to be situational variables in that they partially define important characteristics of the environment. Relevant research studies utilizing this basic approach include the Environmental Assessment Technique (EAT) used by Astin and Holland (1961), the Inventory of College Activities (ICA) developed by Astin (1968), and certain portions of the Questionnaire on Student and College Characteristics (QSCC) developed by Centra (1968). These studies, together with earlier work on treatment environments, indicate that different methods of assessing institutional environments must be used in conjunction (Moos, 1974b; Chapter 6).

The Unit Information Form (UIF).   The Unit Information Form (UIF) for correctional units was adapted from the Ward Information Form developed by Kellam et al. (1966). The UIF obtained data on five dimensions differentiating among correctional units. There are two structural dimensions (unit census and staff–resident ratio), two resident characteristics (length of commitment and total amount of aggressive behavior), and one program policy dimension (adult status).

"Unit census," the number of residents on the unit at the time of testing, was essentially identical to total unit size, since almost every unit was filled to capacity. All full-time day staff were counted in computing the staff–resident ratio. This complement included counselors and social workers when these individuals were basically assigned to the unit. The average length of time the residents had been on the unit was estimated to the nearest week.

The aggressive behavior dimension was assessed by asking staff about the number of residents who (1) damaged or destroyed unit property, their own personal property, or someone else's property; (2) were assaultive to other residents; (3) refused to follow an order given by a staff member; (4) broke one or more of the unit rules; (5) played practical jokes on other residents or staff; and (6) brought "contraband" into the unit (e.g., liquor, drugs, knives). Since relatively complete disciplinary records are kept on most correctional units, it was possible to obtain a reasonably accurate count of the number of residents who engaged in each of these activities during the 30 days prior to the CIES testing.

The adult status dimension of the UIF assesses the degree to which residents on the unit are allowed to "maintain basic symbols of adulthood." Kellam et al. initially constructed this dimension on the hypothesis that "a patient on a ward which allowed possession of more symbols of adulthood would not tend to regress as severely as a patient who was treated on a ward which allowed possession of fewer" (1966, p. 563). We felt that a similar hypothesis was reasonable for correctional units and that the degree of adult status might be related both to unit social climate and to parole outcome. Data were obtained on such basic policies of correctional units as: (1) whether the residents' bedrooms are locked for any period during the day, (2) whether the lavatories are locked for any period during the day, (3) whether the toilet stalls have doors, (4) the proportion of residents that can take showers with and without supervision, (5) whether residents may smoke without supervision, (6) whether there is a silver count at mealtime, and (7) whether the unit censors the residents' incoming and/or outgoing mail. Information about the extent to which residents regulate the use of television, radio, telephone, books, magazines, game tables, and other items on the unit was also included.

Complete information on these UIF variables was obtained for 78 of the 112 units in the juvenile normative sample. Since we were primarily interested in the relationships between size and staffing and social climate, and since 27 of the 78 units were almost identical in size and staffing (they had between 47 and 53 residents), these 27 units were not used in the subsequent analysis. The relationships among the five UIF variables over the remaining 51 juvenile correctional units were calculated first. The correlations among these five variables were generally moderate to low, with none as high as .50. The highest correlation was one of −.47 between the number of residents on a unit and the staff–resident ratio, indicating that larger correctional units are more poorly staffed. Larger units also show a tendency to have residents whose average stay in the unit is longer (.41). Finally, the staff–resident ratio was positively related to the extent of aggressive behavior (.35), indicating that residents show more aggressive behavior on better staffed units (or that units on which there are more aggressive residents, are better staffed).

Structural Dimensions: Size and Staffing.   Correlations were computed between the nine CIES subscale means and the five UIF dimensions over the 51 juvenile units, separately for residents and staff. The results were highly similar for residents and staff, thus only the results for residents are presented in Table 3.4. The results indicate that as the size of a correctional unit increases, the emphasis on the Relationship dimensions of Support and Expressiveness decreases, as does the emphasis on the Treatment Program dimensions of Autonomy and Personal Problem Orientation and the System Maintenance dimension of Clarity. These relationships are of moderate to substantial magnitude. The results for staff–resident ratio are almost exactly identical, although of course they are in the opposite direction. Some of the social climate dimensions (e.g., Involvement, Practical Orientation, Order and Organization, and Staff Control) show only minimal relationships with size and staffing, suggesting that certain dimensions of the social environment may be more closely related to size and staffing than others.

The results are basically consistent with those obtained on a sample of American and British psychiatric treatment programs (Moos, 1974b; Chapter 6). However, the magnitude of the relationships between size and staffing and social environment was somewhat higher in the correctional than in the psychiatric sample. This confirmed our clinical impres-

Table 3.4   Relationship Between Residents' CIES Means and Unit Information Form (UIF) Scores *(N = 51 Juvenile Units)*

Subscales	Structural Dimensions		Resident Characteristics		Program Policy
	Number of Residents	Staff–Resident Ratio	Average Length of Resident's Stay	Total Aggressive Behavior	Adult Status
Involvement	−.24	.17	−.14	.02	−.21
Support	−.49**	.39**	−.15	.12	−.28*
Expressiveness	−.57**	.45**	−.26	.57**	−.07
Autonomy	−.42**	.33*	.03	.22	.00
Practical orientation	−.21	.28*	.09	−.02	.09
Personal problem orientation	−.33*	.29*	−.15	.15	−.09
Order and organization	−.02	−.07	−.27*	−.38**	−.34*
Clarity	−.49**	.38**	−.30*	.07	−.13
Staff control	.21	−.12	−.08	−.25	−.32*

$*p < .05.$
$**p < .01.$

sion that the variability in social environmental characteristics among different correctional institutions is greater than the variability among psychiatric treatment programs. In addition, the CIES subscale standard deviations over units are generally higher than the WAS subscale standard deviations over wards. The actual magnitude of the differences between large and small programs varied between 1.5 and 3 mean raw score points, indicating that there are quite important differences related to unit size and staffing.

Is there greater disagreement among residents and/or among staff in larger and/or more poorly staffed programs? Larger and more poorly staffed programs may have less well developed and integrated social climates; thus we might expect residents and staff to show less agreement among themselves in describing these environments. To check this hypothesis, the standard deviations of each of the nine CIES subscales were correlated with size and staffing over the 51 units, separately for residents and staff. Program size was positively related to five of the nine resident and six of the nine staff subscale standard deviations, and three of each set of these correlations were statistically significant (p < .05). Thus there is less agreement both within the resident group and within the staff group as program size increases. Similar correlations were calculated for staffing ratios with similar results; the actual correlations were of quite similar magnitude. Thus smaller and more highly staffed correctional programs have somewhat more coherent and integrated social environments.

The Effects of Size and Staffing. The results are in agreement with previous findings on size and staffing in other environments ranging from treatment-oriented institutions such as hospital-based and community-based psychiatric programs, to educational institutions such as colleges and universities, and to business and industrial organizations. A substantial amount of work has been done on the effects of institutional size, which has been related to a variety of important outcomes— absenteeism (Indik, 1963), turnover rates (Porter and Lawler, 1965), productivity (Revans, 1958), and satisfaction and morale (e.g., Katz, 1949). A review of this literature and a conceptualization of the effects of size and staffing in psychiatric treatment programs are given elsewhere (Moos, 1974b, Chapter 6).

Researchers studying the effects of treatment and rehabilitation programs for offenders have long been aware of the importance of the size and staffing of correctional units. Several previous studies have been primarily concerned with comparing treatment-oriented programs and more custodial programs. These studies have concluded that small size of the living unit is an indispensable prerequisite to the success of the therapeutic strategies being tested. Other studies reviewed below have focused more directly on size and staffing as well-defined and distinct variables affecting the social milieu and the treatment strategy.

Weeks (1958) compared a group of subjects from a large custodial reformatory to a second group, matched in terms of background characteristics and assigned to a small residential treatment program called Highfields. Highfields attempted to rehabilitate offenders by using guided group interaction sessions and by housing boys in an informal, homelike atmosphere in which the boys' normal living patterns would not be greatly disrupted. Rabow and Elias (1969) state that boys at Highfields engaged in community-relevant behavior patterns, whereas reformatory inmates had to conform to standards of behavior that were irrelevant to life outside the institution. Weeks noted that the small size of Highfields was essential to the therapeutic strategy. Guided group interaction requires small and cohesive therapy groups, which are more difficult to create and maintain in a reformatory. A family or homelike atmosphere is impossible to maintain with a very large group of inmates.

McCord and McCord (1959) compared two correctional programs that housed delinquent boys who were relatively similar in background and personal characteristics. One institution (Wiltwyck) heavily emphasized the potential therapeutic benefits of the social milieu and organized the boys into living groups of 12, with two counselors for each group. The other institution (New England) was also organized into living units, but there were 35 boys in each unit. Study of closely matched samples of boys from the two institutions revealed that those who were organized into smaller living units showed superior progress on several levels (e.g., they showed greater affection toward and identification with counselors; there was a greater decrease in insecurity and prejudice). Adjustment to society, defined as a lack of criminal convictions during a 3-year period after release, was 71% at Wiltwyck and only 53% at New England. Knight (1971) points out that these effects cannot necessarily be attributed to living unit size alone. However, he indicates that both rapport with counselors and the fact that group living was guided by counselors instead of delinquents may well have been facilitated by small size.

Jones (1964) compared a private institution housing about 300 residents in cottages of 16 to 20 boys with a public institution having a total population of about 500 residents, housed in cottages of 16 to 32 boys. The private institution emphasized individual therapy as its rehabilitation strategy, whereas the larger public institution emphasized overt behavioral conformity and the importance of a routinized milieu. Again, size and treatment effects are confounded, but Jones explicitly recognizes that the smaller cottage size at the private institution was essential to the use of individual therapy. Close personal relationships between residents and staff were felt to be necessary for the success of the therapeutic strategy, and such relationships would have been difficult to achieve in larger cottages.

Jesness (1965) has done one of the most carefully designed studies of the effects of size on institutional climate and outcome. The Jesness study was conducted at a correctional ranch (Fricot) operated by the California Youth Authority. Fricot residents were housed in 50-bed cottages staffed by a cottage supervisor and a small number of assistants, including one social worker. A junior high school level academic program was supplemented by an extensive outdoor recreational program, including camping trips. A single 20-bed unit was constructed at Fricot for especially disturbed boys. Jesness used this special 20-bed unit and one of the ranch's 50-bed units in his study.

Boys were randomly assigned to the 20- and 50-bed units from a pool of subjects eligible for assignment to the 20-bed unit. Every effort was made to keep the therapeutic program of the two units comparable, although the smaller size of the 20-bed unit was expected to result in a somewhat more intensive program. More staff time was available per resident in the small cottage, since the number of staff was the same in both units.

Milieu differences between the small and large units were readily apparent to all observers. The decreased number of management problems posed by the smaller unit was felt to be the primary reason for the differences. Staff in the 20-bed unit had an opportunity to develop supportive individual relationships with residents, whereas in the 50-bed unit staff were almost entirely concerned with orderly management of the immature and often hostile boys. This management consisted largely of military-style regimentation, frequent use of group and individual punishment, and reliance on peer-group leaders among the residents for help in controlling other residents. In contrast, the 20-bed unit was described as a friendlier and much less regimented place in which to live. Strict group discipline was almost nonexistent, and reason and rewards were used to positively motivate residents wherever possible. Staff showed greater willingness to become involved with the residents' personal problems and to interact informally with them. On the basis of sociometric tests, Jesness concluded that boys in the small unit made friends more easily and were more aware of the boys they disliked than were boys in the large unit.

These differences in milieu and size were accompanied by a more favorable parole outcome for the residents in the smaller unit. Jesness (1972) found that 42% of the experimental subjects in a matched random group violated parole during the first 15 months of exposure to parole, as compared with 68% of the controls. In an intriguing additional finding, Jesness noted that boys classified as "neurotic" in the experimental program showed a parole violation rate of only 30% as compared with 61% for those "neurotic" boys assigned to the larger living unit. "Nonneurotic" boys appeared to gain as much if not more from the control program, as assessed by similar parole violation rates. The results may have been due either to the milieu created in the smaller unit with a higher staff–resident ratio, or to the difference in the actual treatment received by each boy as a direct result of the social milieus of the two units. For example, boys in the small unit received almost five times as much staff time in one-to-one contact or in small group activity counseling meetings than did boys in the large unit.

Knight (1971) discusses the mechanisms by which size and/or decreased staffing create pressures toward a more rigid organizational structure, increase staff need to control and manage, decrease the degree of resident independence and responsibility and the amount of support and involvement that staff are able to give residents, and so forth. He points out that:

1.   Large living units reduce the proportion of intimate or close relationships. Group cohesion tends to decrease as group size increases.
2.   Large living units limit the time available per event and per group member. These time limitations provide impetus to the need for control and reduce the opportunity for personal intimacy.
3.   The social distance between residents and staff, which is wider in larger living units, facilitates the development of separate resident and staff subcultures.
4.   Shared misunderstandings may occur among residents as a result of reduced intimacy, decreased group cohesion, and distance between residents and staff. People in large groups are especially likely to lack adequate information about, thus to misinterpret, one another's real feelings and intentions.
5.   Increasing regimentation leads to a restriction of the personal satisfactions and social rewards of residents.

Knight concludes that these conditions result in "high interference with treatment involvement" and that "big group delinquent contagion" is the inevitable resulting problem. Inmates are "freed" from positive staff influence precisely when situational pressures toward deviance are the greatest. Under such conditions a staff member not only has scant influence to guide or support but in fact may come to be seen as "the man"—an aloof representative of a controlling but relatively uninterested authority.

The generally negative effects of large size and poor staffing may sometimes be ameliorated by changing certain aspects of the social environment. There are examples of large relatively well staffed and small relatively poorly staffed psychiatric programs which have quite positive treatment programs. We studied one Veterans Administration Hospital ward that was both large (156 patients) and relatively poorly staffed (staff–patient ratio of 1:11) but still had a positively perceived treatment environment (i.e., both patients and staff agreed that there was above-average emphasis on all the Relationship and all the Treatment Program dimensions). Clinical case studies of large and/or relatively poorly staffed correctional programs that maintain cohesive social environments might be useful.

Ullmann (1967) has indicated that the negative effects of large hospitals may be partially alleviated by a unit system in which the hospital is functionally divided into smaller sections. In an analogous way some large programs may benefit from organizing residents and staff into smaller teams or groups. Porter and Lawler (1965) have hypothesized that the effects of large size in industrial organizations may be partially or wholly counteracted by small subunits. Indik (1965) has suggested that the negative effects of large size can be avoided by having the manager of a large organization take steps to ensure high rates of internal communication, thereby facilitating interpersonal attraction and maintaining motivation to participate.

Resident Characteristics: Length of Stay and Aggressive Behavior. Correlations were also calculated between resident and staff CIES subscale means and average length of resident stay and total aggressive behavior. The results were similar for resident and staff perceptions, and only the results for residents appear in Table 3.4. Average length of resident stay is essentially unrelated to social climate, although there is a slight tendency for programs in which residents stay longer to show less emphasis on Order and Organization and Clarity. There was a significant positive relationship between Expressiveness and aggressive behavior and a significant negative relationship between Order and Organization and aggressive behavior. Apparently, then, resident aggressive behavior is higher in correctional programs that emphasize and encourage the open expression of feelings (including angry feelings) and which de-emphasize the importance of order and organization.

A Program Policy Dimension: Adult Status. Adult status seemed to constitute a basic dimension of program policy in correctional institutions, especially since it is linked to Goffman's (1961) concept of the "total institution." Many investigators have discussed a dimension of this sort, which is usually believed to discriminate between "good" and "bad" institutions. King and Raynes (1964) have operationally devised a measure of inmate management in residential institutions. They argue that the characteristics of total institutions may be regarded as having a common orientation "in that individual differences among inmates and unique circumstances are disregarded in favor of an emphasis on the routine running of the institution" (p. 43). They define such practices as institutionally oriented, whereas practices in which individual differences and unique circumstances are given recognition are called inmate oriented.

The relationships between the nine CIES resident subscale means and the program policy dimension of adult status are shown in Table 3.4.

As adult status in a program increases, the amount of emphasis on Support, Order and Organization, and Staff Control decreases; however, the magnitude of these relationships is quite small. This may be partly because there was a somewhat skewed distribution of adult status scores among the 51 units, with very few units having scores greater than 60 (theoretical score range is from 0 to 100). Most correctional programs simply have very little emphasis on adult status.

The Need for Different Measures. The results indicate that a variety of methods are needed to assess correctional programs. More important, each method provides some reliable information that is not supplied by any of the other methods. Objective organizational dimensions, such as size and staffing, clearly give some important information about a program, but they do not necessarily tell the whole story. The same conclusions hold for the other types of dimensions (i.e., average length of resident stay, resident aggressive behavior, and adult status). For example, contrary to some previous literature, it may not be possible to predict much about the social climate of a program from knowing the average length of time the residents have been incarcerated.

These conclusions are quite similar to those obtained in treatment environments and in educational environments (Moos, 1974b; Chapter 6). For example, Centra (1970) administered the Questionnaire on Student and College Characteristics to upper class students at over 200 institutions. The items in the instrument elicit student perception and student self-report information about each institution. Centra compared three methods of assessing the college environment—student perceptions, student self-reports, and objective institutional data—by use of multimethod factor analysis. He concluded that

> while in a majority of instances a predicted relationship was found, there were enough exceptions to question the indiscriminate use of the three methods as sources of the same information about colleges. . . . Each method seems to tap *some* information not predictably obtained by other methods. Quite likely then there are certain kinds of information that can be obtained by only one method even when it appears that two or more methods assess the same domain." (Centra, 1970, p. 39).

These studies indicate that different methods of assessing institutional environments must be used together. A related point involves the utility of different sources of information about the environment. Information about the social climate may be most relevant for facilitating short-term environmental change. Information about the characteristics of the milieu inhabitants may be best used to give prospective residents and staff an idea of what they are likely to encounter in the environment. For example, it may be important for a prospective staff member to learn that staff in a particular correctional program spend approximately 12 hours a week in meetings, since that will indicate the kinds of interpersonal behavior he will probably need to engage in. Finally, information about more objective institutional characteristics may be most valuable for making relatively quick comparisons among institutions and for the overall planning of long-term changes.

REFERENCES

Astin, A. W. *The college environment.* American Council on Education, Washington, D.C., 1968.

Astin, A. W. & Holland, J. L. The environmental assessment technique: A way to measure college environments. *Journal of Educational Psychology,* **52**:308–315, 1961.

Astin, A. W. & Panos, R. *The educational and vocational development of college students.* American Council on Education, Washington, D.C., 1969.

Centra, J. Development of the Questionnaire on Student and College Characteristics. Research Memorandum 68-11, Educational Testing Service, Princeton, N.J., 1968.

Centra, J. The college environment revisited: Current descriptions and a comparison of three methods of assessment. College Entrance Examination Board Research and Development Reports, No. 1, August 1970.

Goffman, E. The moral career of the mental patient. In *Asylums,* Doubleday, Garden City, N.Y., 1961.

Indik, B. P. Some effects of organization size on member attitudes and behavior. *Human Relations,* **16**:369–384, 1963.

Jesness, C. The Fricot Ranch study. Research Report No. 47, California Youth Authority, Sacramento, 1965.

Jesness, C. Comparative effectiveness of two institutional treatment programs for delinquents. *Child Care Quarterly,* **1**:119–130, 1972.

Jones, J. The nature of compliance in correctional institutions for juvenile offenders. *Journal of Research in Crime and Delinquency,* **1**:83–95, 1964.

Katz, D. Morale and motivation in industry. In W. Dennis (Ed.), *Current trends in industrial psychology.* University of Pittsburgh Press, Pittsburg, 1949, pp. 145–171.

Kellam, S. G., Shmelzer, J., and Berman, A. Variation in the atmospheres of psychiatric wards. *Archives of General Psychiatry,* **14**:561–570, 1966.

King, R. D. & Raynes, N. V. An operational measure of inmate management in residential institutions. *Social Science & Medicine,* **2**:41–53, 1968.

Knight, D. The impact of living-unit size in youth training schools. Unpublished manuscript, California Youth Authority, Division of Research and Development, Sacramento, 1971.

Lohn, H. Occupational status and its relationship to perceptions of the organizational climate. M.S.W. thesis, University of Maryland, College Park, 1974.

March, J. (Ed.) *Handbook of organizations.* Rand-McNally, Skokie, Ill., 1965.

McCord, W. & McCord, J. Two approaches to the cure of delinquents. In S. Glueck (Ed.), *The problem of delinquency.* Houghton Mifflin, Boston, 1959.

Moos, R. *Correctional Institutions Environment Scale Manual.* Consulting Psychologists Press, Palo Alto, Calif., 1974a.

Moos, R. *Evaluating treatment environments: A social ecological approach.* Wiley, New York, 1974b.

Porter, L. W. & Lawler, E. E. Properties of organization structure in relation to job attitudes and job behavior. *Psychological Bulletin,* **64**:25–51, 1965.

Rabow, J. & Elias, A. Organizational boundaries, inmate roles, and rehabilitation. *Journal of Research in Crime and Delinquency,* **6**:8–16, 1969.

Revans, R. W. Human relations, management and size. In E. M. Hugh-Jones (Ed.) *Human relations and modern management,* North Holland Publishing Co., Amsterdam, 1958, pp. 177–220.

Ullmann, L. *Institution and outcome: A comparative study of psychiatric hospitals.* Pergamon Press, Oxford, 1967.

Weeks, H. *Youthful offenders at Highfields: An evaluation of the effects of the short-term treatment of delinquent boys.* University of Michigan Press, Ann Arbor, 1958.

Wenk, E. & Moos, R. Social climates in prison: An attempt to conceptualize and measure environmental factors in total institutions. *Journal of Research in Crime and Delinquency,* **9**:134–148, 1972.

CHAPTER FOUR

Case Studies of
Correctional Programs

RUDOLF H. MOOS, JEAN OTTO,
AND DAVID A. PRITCHARD

The Diversity of Correctional Milieus. The CIES provides detailed information about how residents and staff perceive the social milieu of their program. Resident and staff perceptions can be compared and their similarities and differences noted. Individual programs may be compared with each other or with one of the normative groups. The Ideal Form (Form I) of the CIES may be used to identify resident and staff values and to determine how closely the current program matches the stated values. This information can be fed back to staff, allowing them to reevaluate their program and to focus on specific factors of interest and concern.

CIES results can be summarized in profile form to make them clear and easy for staff to interpret. Respondents indicate whether the items are true or false of their program. The number of items on each subscale which are answered in the scored direction is the scale score for each individual. These scale scores are averaged separately for residents and staff. For the CIES real program (Form R) profile, these average scores are converted to standard scores based on the separate normative groups of juvenile and adult programs. This profile allows staff to determine the extent to which their program is above or below average in emphasis in each of the nine program areas. These profiles identify the most salient aspects of an individual program and serve to illustrate the diversity of current correctional milieus.

The Form R profiles of five programs are presented here to demonstrate the kind of information that can be obtained from the CIES and to illustrate the variations found in individual treatment-oriented correctional programs. Each unit serves juvenile offenders, and the profiles compare the programs against our juvenile normative sample of 112 units. The Form I profiles (Ideal Form) are shown for the last program to demonstrate the utility of this information.

A Boys' Unit in a Correctional School.   Figure 4.1 shows the CIES Form R (Real program) results for residents and staff in Unit 167, which had a total of 48 boys who stayed in the program an average of 9 months. There were 10 full-time staff members. The institution was a state training school for adjudicated delinquents ranging in age from 12 to 18. About 60% of the boys were either black or Mexican-American; the rest were Caucasian. Most came from lower socioeconomic status homes. Their offenses ranged from drug use to homicide. The boys were involved in a behavior modification program. Each boy attended a weekly small group counseling session with his caseworker and a daily unit meeting with the youth counselors, casework supervisor, and teachers. The institution offers regular high school classes and has three industrial and two arts and crafts shops. Reading and math specialists and a school psychologist assist program staff with individual residents.

There is wide variation in the amount of emphasis placed on the nine different areas, but residents and staff agree closely in their perceptions of their program. Very high emphasis is placed on the open expression of feelings. More than 80% of the residents and staff felt that residents say anything they want to counselors and that residents are encouraged to show their feelings. In addition, staff felt that residents receive a good deal of support in the program. More than 80% of staff reported that they went out of their way to help residents and that they were involved in resident activities. In contrast, residents indicated that there was about average emphasis on Support (e.g., only 19% felt that staff went out of their way to help them).

The next three subscales measure the treatment approaches of the program. Residents and staff felt that the primary orientation of the unit was toward encouraging autonomy and teaching residents to learn to understand their personal problems. More than 80% of the residents and staff felt that residents are expected to take leadership on the unit and are encouraged to be independent. In addition, both groups felt that staff try to help residents understand themselves and that residents

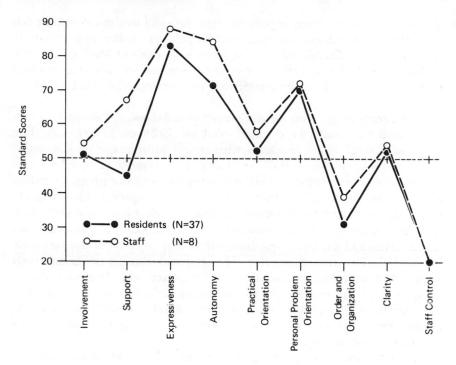

Figure 4.1 CIES Form R profiles for residents and staff on Unit 167.

are expected to share their personal problems. The emphasis on residents learning to plan and prepare for the future (Practical Orientation) was rated as average.

The last three subscales assess the structure and organization of the unit. The clarity of rules and expectations is about average as compared with other juvenile units. However, both the orderliness of the unit and the degree to which staff have the primary responsibility for making rules and planning activities (Staff Control) are clearly below average. More than 80% of the residents and staff agreed that the unit usually looks a little messy, that the unit is not very well organized, that not all decisions about the unit are made by the staff, and that residents may criticize staff members to their faces. This unusually low level of Staff Control is consistent with the above-average emphasis placed on Autonomy in this program.

In summary, this program places primary emphasis on the personal development of its wards by encouraging the open expression of feelings (Expressiveness), the development of independent modes of behavior (Autonomy), and the understanding of personal problems and feelings

(Personal Problem Orientation). Neither the staff nor the residents felt that there was much emphasis on staff keeping the unit neat and orderly or under tightly disciplined control. The close resident–staff agreement, in the context of a treatment-oriented program, implies clear mutual communication and shared understanding between the two groups.

A Contrasting Boys' Unit in a Correctional School. Twenty-two residents and four staff were tested on Unit 102 (see Figure 4.2). The unit had a total of 54 residents who stayed an average of 7 months. There were six full-time staff members. This sample of residents and staff is adequate to provide a reliable assessment of the program milieu according to the sampling criteria discussed in Chapter 2. The program was designed to handle first-time offenders, to develop social skills, and to train residents in at least one marketable job skill. The background characteristics of the boys were basically similar to those of the residents in Unit 167. The institution offers 11 vocational training programs, such as electrical maintenance, printing, and culinary arts. Academic classes ranging from the elementary to the junior college level are available. The unit placed particular stress on individual counseling of the residents, most of whom were characterized as having internal conflicts and feelings of inadequacy.

Unit 102 shows greater disagreement between resident and staff responses than Unit 167. Residents and staff in Unit 102 see more emphasis on Involvement and Support than the respondents in Unit 167. For example, more than 80% of the residents and staff agreed that 102 was a friendly unit (Involvement), that staff went out of their way to help residents, and that staff were involved in resident activities (Support). They also stated that the residents openly disagreed with each other and that staff and residents openly expressed their feelings about each other (Expressiveness). Although the resident–staff differences were larger for this unit, residents and staff agreed that there was above-average emphasis on the Relationship dimensions.

Residents and staff also agreed that all three of the Treatment Program dimensions were above average. Both groups agreed that stress was placed on residents' developing autonomy and independence, on residents' understanding their personal problems and feelings, and on residents' preparing themselves for the future. More than 80% of residents and staff felt that residents were encouraged to be independent (Autonomy), to plan for the future and to work toward their goals (Practical Orientation), and to more fully understand themselves and their motivations (Personal Problem Orientation).

On the System Maintenance dimensions, residents evaluated the em-

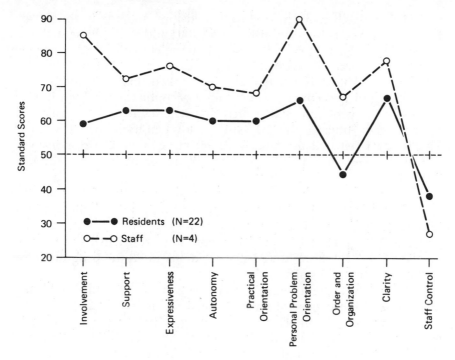

Figure 4.2 CIES Form R profiles for residents and staff on Unit 102.

phasis on Order and Organization as below average. For example, most of them agreed that things were sometimes very disorganized and that the day room and the entire unit usually looked messy. Staff, on the other hand, felt that the unit was fairly well organized and that they kept it relatively neat. Residents and staff agreed that Clarity was above average and that there was relatively little emphasis on Staff Control. More than 80% of the residents and staff agreed that staff tell residents when they are doing well and that new residents are shown around and told how the unit operates (Clarity). Most of the staff felt that residents could criticize staff members to their faces (Staff Control).

In summary, this program emphasizes friendly, supportive, open relationships between residents and among residents and staff. Residents are encouraged to be independent, to prepare for the future, and to solve their personal problems. Program expectations and rules are clear to both residents and staff.

An independent evaluation was made of this unit. Both subjective and objective information was gathered from the unit's staff, from residents, and from independent observers (Jesness, 1968). The staff observed that the boys formed close friendships and rarely fought and that they desired close relationships with staff and were willing to discuss personal problems. These comments are parallel to the CIES assessment that Unit 102 emphasized Involvement, Support, and Personal Problem Orientation. The staff felt that the boys asked many questions about unit rules and procedures, which might account for the high level of Clarity in the program. Staff stated that strict conformity to rules was not enforced. Similarly, the CIES showed low emphasis on Staff Control. Finally, staff felt that the boys were encouraged to take responsibility for making rules and following them; this is corroborated by the high level of Autonomy shown by the CIES.

Seminars with some of the boys from the unit indicated that they saw the unit as friendly and felt that mutual support was high. However, unlike the staff, they felt that they did not receive sufficient attention and counseling. They felt that some staff were restrictive and nonsupportive. The CIES also showed that residents rated the program lower in Support than did staff.

Observers who spent several 6-hour sessions on the unit agreed that there was a high degree of trust between residents and staff and that there was emphasis on self-understanding rather than on conformity to rules. They also noted the discrepancy between resident and staff perceptions of the amount of counseling time available.

A more objective assessment of the unit was made using the 81-item Post-Opinion Poll of resident perceptions. The items measure five treatment dimensions (e.g., involvement, permissiveness, and equalitarianism) and nine group living factors (e.g., good evaluation of staff, cohesiveness and optimism—see Chapter 2). The residents had a favorable attitude toward staff and felt that staff wanted to help them and were accepting and complimentary (similar to Support). Residents reported spending a lot of time openly talking with staff. They indicated that they were allowed to make plans and rules for the unit and that there was a significant level of equalitarianism in the unit program (high Autonomy, low Staff Control).

Senior group supervisors were asked 71 open-ended questions about their unit. Three experts then rated the responses on the dimensions of involvement, permissiveness, and equalitarianism. The rank-order of this unit (as compared with other units in the same institution) was similar for both experts' and residents' ratings on these three dimensions. These independent sources of information on Unit 102 quite closely paralleled the information obtained with the CIES.

A Boys' Ranch. Unit 193 is a small cottage living group in a county-operated boys ranch. The profile in Figure 4.3 is based on the CIES

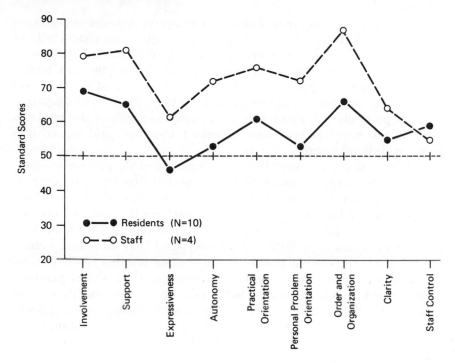

Figure 4.3 CIES Form R profiles for residents and staff on Unit 193.

results for all 10 residents and 4 staff in the group. The average length of stay of these boys is 8 months. The ranch accepts boys from 12 to 15 years of age who can be maintained in a minimum security setting. About 60% of the boys were Caucasian. Most were from lower socioeconomic status homes. Their offenses included truancy, auto theft, burglary, and narcotics use. Besides the typical academic program offered by most institutions for boys this age, the ranch had a variety of farm animals for which the boys learned to care. Each boy was placed in a small living group that met several times a week and was designed to focus on the needs of the individual boys. Figure 4.3 shows that there are significant differences between resident and staff perceptions of the program in almost every area.

The residents saw the program as encouraging them to be involved in activities and as providing them with above-average help and support. All residents thought discussions were quite interesting, and 70% of them felt that staff helped new residents get acquainted. The emphasis on the open expression of feelings, however, was slightly below average. The residents felt that they had to be careful about what they said to the counselors and that staff thought it was not healthy to argue. Practical Orientation was the only Treatment Program dimension perceived by residents as clearly above average. For example, more than 90% of the residents felt that they were expected to work toward their goals and that they had to make concrete plans before leaving the unit. Unlike the other two programs discussed, the residents saw all three System Maintenance dimensions as being above average. Order and Organization was particularly high on this unit; more than 90% of the residents felt that the unit was very well organized and that resident activities were carefully planned.

Staff agreed with residents that Involvement and Support were important elements in the program, but they also felt that residents were allowed to express themselves freely. Most of the staff felt that residents were encouraged to show their feelings. Staff felt that the unit encouraged boys to prepare for leaving the program (Practical Orientation), that the boys had considerable autonomy, and that they were helped to work out their personal problems. All staff agreed that residents were expected to take leadership and were encouraged to be independent. Staff also felt that they tried to help residents understand themselves and that discussions on the unit stressed understanding personal problems. Finally, staff agreed with residents that the System Maintenance dimensions, particularly Order and Organization and Clarity, were emphasized.

In summary, residents and staff agreed that involvement and supportive help of staff were of primary importance. Staff felt that residents were allowed to express their feelings openly. Both groups felt that emphasis was placed on preparing the boys for leaving the program within an organized, well-disciplined unit structure.

A Juvenile Hall Unit for Boys.   Figure 4.4 is the CIES profile of an urban county juvenile hall unit for boys, on which 25 residents and 5 staff were tested. The unit has about 35 boys, aged 15 to 16 years, who stay for an average of 1 to 2 weeks. There are only two staff on the unit at any one time. Like most juvenile halls, this unit is primarily a holding center for boys awaiting court dates or referral to other county or state facilities following a court decision.

Residents and staff agree closely on the characteristics of this unit. The three Relationship dimensions of Involvement, Support, and Expressiveness are each seen as average or below average by both residents and staff. More than 80% of the residents and staff thought that residents did not put a lot of energy into what they did on the unit and that there was very little group spirit. Residents felt that there was slightly more emphasis on the open expression of feelings than did staff;

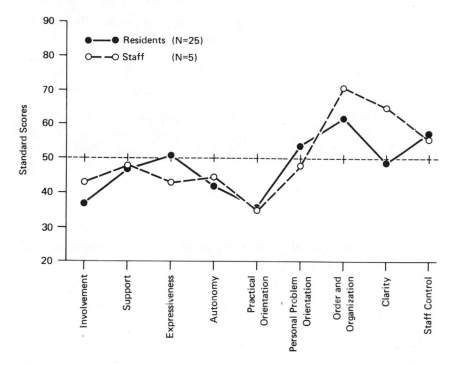

Figure 4.4   CIES Form R profiles for residents and staff on Unit 185.

88% of the residents, but only 20% of the staff, agreed that people say what they really think on the unit. However, more than 60% of both groups agreed that residents tend to hide their feelings from the staff.

There was no particular emphasis on the Treatment Program dimensions. Practical Orientation was especially low in this program. Only 20% of the residents and staff felt that the unit stressed training for new jobs, and a similarly low percentage of both groups felt that residents must make plans before leaving the unit. Residents and staff did feel, however, that Personal Problem Orientation was about average.

The System Maintenance dimensions on this unit were similar in degree of emphasis to those on the ranch unit. Here, too, Order and Organization was most important. More than 75% of the residents and staff agreed that the staff make sure that the unit is always neat and that the unit is very well organized. The staff also felt there was above-average emphasis on Clarity; all agreed that staff tell residents when they are doing well and that residents know when the counselors will be on the unit. Staff Control was slightly above average (e.g., more than

80% of the residents and staff agreed that staff order the residents around). In summary, this unit primarily provides an organized, structured setting in which boys may be held until an appropriate placement is determined for them. There is no significant amount of emphasis on developing resident–staff relationships or on initiating treatment.

A Juvenile Hall Unit for Girls.   The final example is particularly interesting because it involves the first female correctional unit discussed, and because of the distinctive variation between resident and staff opinions of the program. We tested 27 girls and 7 staff on this unit, which has a total of 38 residents, aged 15 to 16 (see Figure 4-5). About half the girls were Caucasian; the other half were black or Mexican-American. Again, most came from lower socioeconomic status homes. Their offenses included truancy, prostitution, forgery, and theft. Girls stayed for an average of about one month. The unit was in the same juvenile hall as the boys unit.

Because of the considerable variation of the resident and staff scores, their perceptions are discussed separately. The girls on Unit 183 saw Involvement and Expressiveness as above average. More than 85% agreed that staff and residents express what they feel about each other and that people really say what they think on the unit. This is quite a different picture from that on the boys' unit. Like the other unit, however, none of the treatment variables was strongly emphasized. For example, only 67% of the girls felt that residents talked about their personal problems with other residents. The girls felt that Order and Organization and Clarity were not strongly emphasized, but they reported Staff Control as above average; the vast majority felt that all decisions were made by the staff rather than by the girls.

The staff have a somewhat different picture of the unit. They agree with the girls that Involvement is slightly above average, and they rate Support in the same way. Most of the staff (71%) felt that staff go out of their way to help residents and that staff are involved in resident activities. Interestingly, they thought that there was much less emphasis on Expressiveness than did the residents (e.g., only 28% agreed that staff and residents say how they feel about each other). In terms of treatment, staff felt that the unit provides the residents with at least some opportunity to exercise autonomy (e.g., 85% agreed that staff encourage residents to start their own activities). They also felt that neither Practical Orientation nor Personal Problem Orientation was particularly important. The greatest differences between residents and staff are seen in the System Maintenance areas. Staff saw both Order and Organization and Clarity as significantly above average. Almost all (86%) agreed that

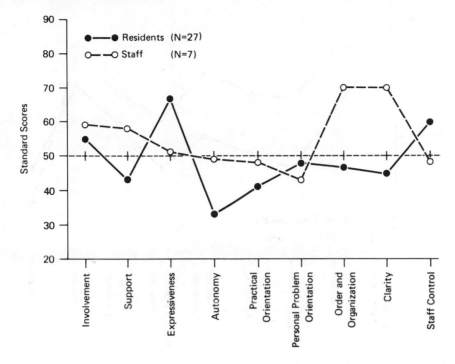

Figure 4.5 CIES Form R profiles for residents and staff on Unit 183.

staff make sure that the unit is always neat, that residents' activities are carefully planned, and that residents know what will happen to them if they break the rules.

In summary, the girls in Unit 183 are moderately involved in program activities and express their feelings openly, even though considerable control is exerted over them by staff. The staff see the program as providing an involving, supportive environment that is well organized and has clear rules and expectations.

Real and Ideal Program Profiles. The residents and staff on Unit 183 also completed Form I (Ideal Form) of the CIES. In this form residents and staff are asked to describe an ideal correctional program on the same nine dimensions on which they have described their current program. The number of items answered in the scored direction is the *scale score*. The averages of these scores for residents and staff are displayed on the profile in Figure 4.6. The Ideal Form profiles plot the *raw score* averages of residents and staff rather than the standard scores.

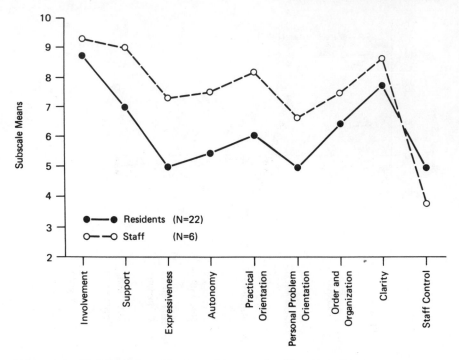

Figure 4.6   CIES Form I profiles for residents and staff on Unit 183.

This is done because staff usually want to compare *their* perceptions of an ideal milieu with *their* current program (see Figure 4.7). When Real–Ideal comparisons are made, staff are more interested in how their own results compare than in how their program compares with a large sample of other programs.

The residents and staff basically agreed on the type of correctional program that would be ideal, except that the girls would place less emphasis on Support, Expressiveness, Autonomy, and Practical Orientation. This profile indicates the extent to which the residents and staff have similar value orientations with respect to the social milieu of their program. In the present profile it is clear that residents and staff shared generally similar value orientations, although there were some differences.

The next profile is designed to indicate what changes residents and/ or staff would make in their current program to have a more ideal program. It also indicates which program areas are satisfactory in relation to the two groups' ideals. The average raw score from the *real*

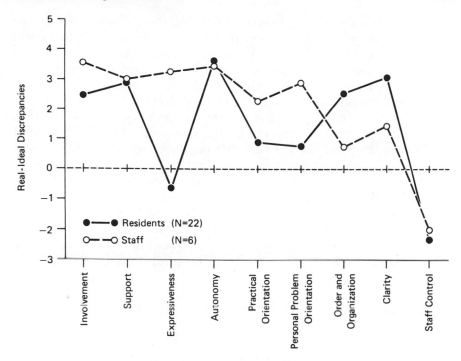

Figure 4.7 Real–ideal program discrepancies as perceived by residents and staff on Unit 183.

form (Form R) testing is subtracted from the average raw score from the *ideal* form (Form I) testing for each subscale. When the ideal score is higher than the real score, a positive number is obtained, indicating that respondents would like to see an *increase* in that area. When a negative number is obtained, respondents would like to see a *decrease* in emphasis in that area. If the ideal score is the same as the real score the difference is 0, indicating *no* change is desired in the program. This "0" score is marked by a straight line across the center of the profile, as in Figure 4.7.

Residents and staff would like to see substantial increases in the emphasis on the involvement of girls in program activities (Involvement) and on the amount of support residents receive from staff and other residents (Support). Residents are satisfied with the freedom of expression they feel the unit allows (real–ideal differences were very close to zero), but staff would like to see a significant increase in this area. Both groups would like much more emphasis on Autonomy and Independence. Residents are fairly satisfied with the Treatment Program areas of Practical Orientation and Personal Problem Orientation, whereas staff would like an increase in these areas. The opposite is true for the System Maintenance areas of Order and Organization and Clarity, in which staff feel the emphasis is relatively satisfactory while residents would prefer fairly large increases. Staff Control is the only program area in which both residents and staff would like to see a decrease.

Using this profile, it is easy for staff to identify areas either they themselves or the residents would like to change. For example, staff evaluating the profile might note that both they and the residents wish significant increases in Involvement, Support, and Autonomy. Program changes consonant with these mutual desires could be planned. Whereas the staff indicated some desire to also increase Expressiveness, the residents are currently satisfied with it. Staff, then, might choose not to make any specific plans for working in this area. Thus the profile serves as an evaluative technique that allows staff to assess *their* program using *their* own stated values as measured by the Ideal Form of the CIES.

Milieu Variation in Adult Units.   Adult correctional units using the CIES show variations in social climate similar to those reported in juvenile units. For example, a small correctional community center, where inmates work in the daytime and have group counseling in the evenings, showed strong agreement between inmates and staff, indicating that the program was above average. Involved supportive relationships were very highly emphasized. There was very strong encouragement of inmates to be independent and to gain an understanding of their problems. In addition, the program was rated as being fairly well organized and as having clear expectations. In contrast, a more traditional camp facility showed fairly large discrepancies between inmate and staff perceptions. Inmates perceived most areas of the program as about average, whereas staff rated all areas but Staff Control as above average. Both groups agreed that there was only slightly above-average emphasis on Autonomy. Two units in another closed correctional facility placed very low emphasis on Involvement, Support, and Order and Organization. Inmates rated all other areas as slightly below average. Thus there are substantial variations in the social environments of adult correctional units. (See Wenk and Moos, 1972a, 1972b, for several examples of adult program profiles.)

Staff Reactions to CIES Profile Feedback.   Feedback sessions were held for all the units in which staff completed both the CIES Forms R and I. The information given was much like that in the profile examples just presented. A member of the research team explained the rationale of the nine subscales and the method of scoring and then interpreted the profiles. Feedback questionnaires were distributed in 17 of the units to evaluate the accuracy and completeness of the profiles as the staff perceived them.

The majority of staff (about 75%) felt that the CIES profiles portrayed their treatment milieus relatively accurately and completely. The majority also felt that definite changes in their program were suggested by the evaluation. There were many positive comments, although some staff indicated areas they felt were not covered or that might be misinterpreted. Two staff members of a juvenile hall commented that the Practical Orientation subscale did not apply to their institution because the residents were only there for a short time. One staff member felt that Autonomy was rated inaccurately because staff and residents had unclear personal definitions of this area. Another claimed that staff encouragement of girls to be independent could be construed as lack of support. On one of the ranches tested a staff member said that a boy's view of his situation (punitive or rehabilitative) would affect his rating of the unit. One person was concerned that race relations were not covered in the scale.

Thus the CIES allows staff to define more accurately the type of program they have, not only in terms of their own perceptions but also as it is seen by the residents. A self-initiated type of analysis results, as discussion of the real profile leads to interest in the differences and similarities of resident and staff perceptions. This nonevaluative analysis opens staff to discussing key areas of concern rationally rather than emotionally. Furthermore, as a natural consequence of this discussion, staff begin exploring their own and resident ideals and relating these ideals to actual program performance. The CIES serves as a concrete guideline for discussion. As a result of feedback, staff have been able to identify specific changes by which to improve their program as suggested by the definition of their own goals and values.

Facilitating Social Change. Research results have been successfully used to stimulate social change in organizations of many types. Standardized surveys are generally useful because they help individuals focus on specific elements of their environment, and they provide some guidelines for evaluation. When staff can concentrate their attempts to change their program on a few commonly defined areas, change can take place in an orderly, structured manner. This reduces the possibility of confusion or conflicting behavior.

For example, a psychiatric unit in a teaching hospital used the Ward

Atmosphere Scale (WAS) to help change the program. Two issues of concern were lack of clarity and lack of involvement of patients in ward activities. Staff discussions were held following an initial administration of the WAS and feedback of results. A second administration of the WAS showed essentially no change in staff perceptions of the ward milieu. Specific plans for changes that would improve the milieu were then formulated. Decisions were made to make the ward activities more relevant to the age distribution of the patients. In addition, it was decided that the ward treatment teams would handle all disciplinary matters and would see to it that the rationale for their actions was understood by the patients. Staff expectations of patients, including ward norms and values, would be more frequently discussed at the community meeting, to ensure consistency of behavior by staff and clarity of understanding by patients.

The WAS was readministered after these and other changes were initiated. Staff saw increases in Involvement and Clarity. Patients saw increases in Support and Autonomy. For example, more patients and staff answered "true" to the following items at the second testing than at the first: "Patients often do things together on the weekends," "Patients set up their own activities without being prodded by the staff," and "The healthier patients on this ward help take care of the less healthy ones."

In an adolescent program discussions were held with residents and staff following the initial administration and feedback of results of the Community-Oriented Programs Environment Scale (COPES). Clarity and Order and Organization were two of the areas this group felt needed improvement. Positions of crew job chairman (to supervise the work duties of other residents) and food manager (to help plan the meal preparation) were instituted. New residents were asked to keep a journal of their relationships and problems during their first few weeks in the program, so that they could more readily set concrete behavior goals for themselves. A second administration of COPES was given two months after the initiation of these changes. Staff felt that emphasis on Involvement, Spontaneity, and Clarity had increased, whereas residents felt that there was greater stress on Order and Organization and Clarity. In each of these three examples the program changed and became closer to an ideal program after assessment, feedback, and change attempts were instituted. Thus feedback of social climate scale results can help to successfully facilitate and evaluate social change. A discussion of the methodology underlying attempts to change programs, as well as some of the sources of resistance to change and some methods for coping with this resistance, has been presented elsewhere (Moos, 1974; Chapters 4 and 11).

The Process of Institutional Consultation. This section describes the use of the CIES in gathering information about an institution. Just as the therapist builds a mental model of his patient to guide him in therapy, so the consultant creates an image of his institution to assist him in his task. The consultant's image consists of observations and speculations about the structure, the function, and the dynamics of an institution.

The consultant relies on numerous sources of information about the institution. The CIES may provide a valuable input to his working image. The discrepancy between the CIES and other information can be the source of new information for the consultant. Furthermore, the measurement–feedback–planning sequence constitutes an assessment of variables relevant to the consultant's task (e.g., amount of resistance to change, resources for generating and maintaining innovations, values and priorities of institution staff). The reactions of the staff are valuable clues to the functioning of the institution.

Use of the CIES in an assessment process is illustrated in a 4-month project conducted by one of the authors (David A. Pritchard) at a male juvenile institution within the Wisconsin Division of Corrections. The CIES (Form R) was administered to boys and staff of three cottages at the school. The resulting profiles were discussed with staff and suggestions for program change were debated.

New School (a pseudonym) was a 10-year-old facility that received adjudicated delinquents from the state's Reception Center, located in another institution. It consisted of three "complexes" of four ranch-style cottages each, a central academic and vocational school, an interdenominational chapel, an administration building, and a food service center where meals were prepared for delivery to each cottage. The school was headed by a superintendent who was assisted by three treatment directors with primary responsibility for the three complexes; each cottage was managed by a team of one social worker, two teachers, and three youth counselors. The decentralized organization and multidisciplinary teams were intended to encourage differentiation of programs within the institution and improved communication among staff.

New School was a relatively new juvenile institution populated by boys between the ages of 12 and 18 years. Boys were committed for an indefinite term up to the age of 18 (the age of mandatory release from juvenile status). The average age of the boys was a little over 15 years and their average length of stay a little more than 5 months. Residents were of low socioeconomic status and only moderate intelligence (average verbal IQ was only a little over 80) and reading ability (average reading level was a bit better than fifth grade). The boys were committed for a wide range of offenses.

The school offered programs in academic and technical training as well as sports and recreations activities. Staff consisted of a clinical services staff (psychologists and psychiatrists) and cottage teams (social worker, counselor, and school teachers). The resident–staff ratio was approximately 3:1.

When the CIES project was introduced, one of the cottages was already operating an experimental program reputed to differ radically from the programs of other cottages. Several innovations had been introduced in an attempt to change the way in which boys were disciplined, the way privileges and rewards were allocated, the way decisions regarding cottage activities were made and, in general, the way staff related to boys. Discipline was handled solely by the youth counselors (instead of by supervisors, who were called into the cottage to judge the problem and assign a punishment). Counselors were permitted to talk privately with boys who appeared upset or who requested advice, rather than being restricted to mere supervision of the boys as a group. Cottage meetings were scheduled weekly rather than irregularly and were discussion- rather than lecture-oriented. Boys could pursue private projects rather than being restricted to group activities. The broad intent was to structure cottage activities and relationships in ways that would encourage the boys to adjust to reasonable authority, to be active and assertive, to develop self-control, and to build a sense of self-respect and personal competence.

But the cottage's reputation within the school was based as much on rumor and speculation as on any of the innovations. Most institutional staff never had firsthand experience with the experimental cottage. Their impressions of the program were based on brief contacts with the boys and staff from the cottage and on stories that circulated throughout the school. Their view of the cottage as "special" was enhanced by the intense involvement in the cottage of the school's chief psychologist and by the publicity the administration gave the cottage in annual reports and on visitors' tours. Did the experimental cottage deserve this special reputation? It is possible, for example, that the reputation developed even though the actual differences between this cottage and other cottages at New School were no longer as great as when the experimental program began. In testing this possibility, the CIES was administered in the experimental cottage and in two comparison cottages selected from the same complex.

The project was first proposed to the school superintendent, to one of the treatment directors, and to the chief psychologist. Their response was immediate and favorable. After this administrative approval, the social workers of the three cottages were asked for their cooperation.

Like the administrators and psychologists, each social worker expressed interest and agreed to assist in implementing the project in their cottage. However, the teachers and youth counselors were less than unanimous in their response. Some of them agreed to participate; others were openly hostile and resistant, claiming that valid answers on the CIES would jeopardize their jobs. They suggested that current events in the state made their positions insecure and that it would be risky to criticize the school in filling out the CIES. The anxiety-producing events included recent layoffs of staff at several state institutions (including New School) due to reduced populations and the publication of a controversial report from the Governor's Task Force on Corrections, which recommended permanently closing several correctional institutions.

The different reactions to the project of administrators, psychologists, and social workers, on the one hand, and teachers and youth counselors, on the other, was important information. Was the resistance understandable in terms of the job insecurity of counselors and teachers, or did it reflect a conflict among staff members about the worth of evaluation and program change? Since all staff participated in the project once anonymous answer sheets were promised, it may be that the initial resistance of the counselors and teachers was due to fear of reprisals. There was no evidence that the resisters genuinely disliked accountability and program development.

The CIES results from the three cottages (Figure 4.8) generated many questions about the school. The highest scales for the two comparison cottages were Order and Organization and Clarity, indicating that the traditional programs placed greatest emphasis on orderliness of the cottages and neatness of the residents, on regimented routine and on clear expectations. Since the traditional cottages also had somewhat elevated scores on the three Relationship dimensions, it was clear that the emphasis on Order and Organization and Clarity was not oppressive. Rather, it seemed that the first priority of these cottages was to maintain a smoothly functioning program; it appeared that other priorities (e.g., developing group spirit or discussing personal problems) were pursued only in that context.

Analysis of the staff logs of the three cottages revealed that the experimental cottage punished boys less frequently for late rising, for "horseplay" in the cottage, for leaving the doors to their rooms open at night, for doing a poor job on their assigned cottage chores, for having a messy room, and so on. Thus the experimental cottage did indeed place less emphasis on Order and Organization than did the traditional cottages. A number of observed differences between the experimental and the traditional cottages also confirmed the relative lack of emphasis on

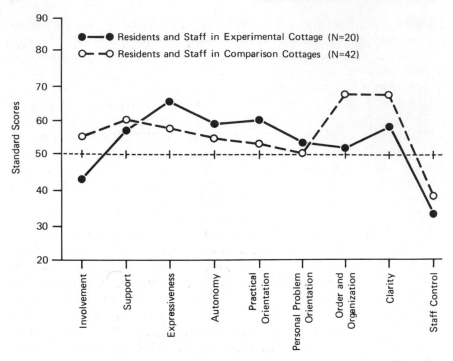

Figure 4.8   CIES Form R profiles for residents and staff in experimental and comparison cottages.

Clarity in the former; for example, the experimental cottage sometimes punished boys for offenses against order and organization, whereas they ignored such offenses most of the time. Such inconsistent enforcement of rules contributed to the relatively low Clarity score in this cottage.

There were no consistent differences between the experimental and the traditional cottages on the Relationship and Treatment Program dimensions. In fact, the profiles of the three cottages overlapped considerably on these dimensions. Analysis of the three cottages indicated that the experimental and traditional cottages did not differ in program elements like regular cottage meetings, home furloughs, assigned cottage chores, and family therapy. Furthermore, they all shared such institution-wide programs as school, church, psychological services, movies, and school events. In addition, they were all constrained by the same institutional regulations regarding visits, mail, off-campus activities, and population flow.

But if the three cottages overlapped considerably in program elements, where was the experiment in the experimental cottage? In view of the similarity among the cottages, how did the experimental cottage currently differ from the traditional cottages? The CIES detected the relatively lower emphases on Order and Organization and Clarity. Were there additional differences not reflected in the CIES profiles? Careful observations of the three cottages indicated that there were some procedural differences among them, but no additional substantive differences were discovered.

The discrepancy between the CIES description and observations of the experimental cottage, and the reputation of that cottage throughout the school, needed explanation. In studying this reputation, we learned that it involved more than detached perception and judgment of the experimental cottage. Some staff were highly critical of the cottage and its innovations, implying that it was too permissive and too heavily dominated by the boys. There was little support for the experimental cottage and, on occasion, outright "persecution." Obviously the experimental cottage was situated in a hostile environment.

The Feedback and Planning Sessions.   The CIES profiles for each cottage, and interpretations of the profiles, were distributed in a written report to cottage team members. After they had had an opportunity to read the report and discuss it among themselves, separate team meetings were scheduled to go over the results in detail. There was general agreement that the cottage descriptions were accurate. No one felt that his cottage program had been completely misrepresented, although there were some questions of minor consequence. Some team members expressed dismay at their cottage's score on some aspects of the profile, but they accepted those scores as accurate indices of their program.

All three cottage teams said that the feedback was useful in generating discussion about program change, but they differed in how the feedback was used in such discussion. The experimental cottage used the profile as a conceptual framework within which to discuss their program. The team focused on the meaning of the CIES subscales and their relation to the program. Consequently, they generated few concrete suggestions for program change; the outcome of their discussion was a commitment to use the scale-concepts in discussing their program, in future planning of changes, and in elevation of future developments. The feedback meeting in the experimental cottage involved the "trying out" of new concepts and a new vocabulary, rather than the selection of strategies for changing the cottage program.

In contrast, the traditional cottages used the CIES more as a barometer to detect the high and low pressure centers of their cottage atmospheres. They congratulated one another on the generally favorable state of the cottage and made specific suggestions for improving scores they wished to see changed. Generally the suggestions were for importing activities or procedures from other cottages in New School or increasing the frequency or intensity of current program elements. Suggestions for program changes were limited by a rejection of any that seemed too "permissive" and by a fear of anything that would encourage "manipulation" by the boys.

The reaction of the traditional cottages implied a general satisfaction with their programs and a perceived need to introduce only slight modifications. Such modifications were not to be innovative, nor were they to overstep the limits of "permissiveness." This underlying attitude was consistent with the desire of the traditional cottages to develop programs only in the context of high Order and Organization and Clarity. According to this conception, the traditional cottages would support program changes only so long as they did not undermine the priority of System Maintenance functions.

The reaction of the experimental cottage was consistent with previous inputs indicating that maintenance functions were of low priority; staff discussion of the feedback was not colored by fears of "permissiveness" and "manipulation." The team's discussion of the feedback indicated that they saw the need for an integrated systematic program guided by a clear conception of rehabilitation. In contrast, the traditional cottages were uninterested in a program whose elements were justified by a systematic model of rehabilitation. The justification of program elements derived from their face validity and, more important, from their congruence with practices in the other cottages.

The working image of New School was fairly well developed at the end of the feedback discussion sessions. Initial reaction to the project sensitized the consultant to the current mood of the school and, as indicated, political events in the state had decreased staff morale and job security at New School. Within this context of uncertainty, most cottages operated by emphasizing Order and Organization and by supporting only program innovations that were compatible with this priority. In this context the experimental cottage developed the reputation of being radically different—a reputation based primarily on reordered priorities. The experimental cottage differed from other cottages mainly in its emphasis on Order and Organization and Clarity, in procedural matters, and in the orientation of its staff toward the development of an integrated rehabilitation program. These differences were sufficient to signal other staff that the experimental cottage had reordered its priorities and, consequently, to elicit negative reactions from those staff.

This information is clear enough to permit a consultant to choose

alternative strategies for dealing with the experimental and the traditional cottages. For example, it appears that the future existence of New
School as a juvenile institution is in doubt. The consultant might decide,
therefore, to await clarification of the school's future before proposing
any program innovations or, at least, to propose only minimal changes.
To do otherwise would be to ask a demoralized and unmotivated staff
to exert effort on a task they saw as senseless.

If minimal changes are proposed, the information suggests what kind
of changes they ought to be—namely, changes that do not interfere
with the smooth functioning of the cottages. To propose that boys be
free to roam the grounds would be completely unacceptable. But to
propose that boys be allowed to use the dayroom while they successively
showered, instead of waiting in their rooms until everyone had completed showering, might be acceptable. Assuming that the school continues as a juvenile institution, the information also suggests appropriate
strategies for introducing radical change. For example, it would seem
unprofitable to test out a radical innovation in the experimental cottage,
because its reputation would interfere with the adoption of the innovation by other cottages. It might be more advisable to have the school
superintendent impose the change on all cottages simultaneously, or at
least on an entire complex, giving traditional staff a more diffuse target
for their criticisms. Such a procedure would also assure that the innovation had support from some portion of the school, if unanimous acceptance seemed unlikely. Additional strategies or suggestions for change
can be formulated in a similar way.

Planning for Program Change.   We have discussed the value of the
CIES and the assessment–feedback–planning sequence as an aid to developing a working image of an institution. By a judicious interpretation
of the CIES, of staff reactions to each phase of the sequence, and of
information that conflicts with the CIES, an image of each residential
unit and of the institution as a whole can be generated. This image
can then serve the consultant in the same way a good personality assessment serves the therapist.

In addition to illustrating this clinical use of the CIES, the project
suggests several advantages of employing the CIES in consultation with
correctional institutions. One striking benefit is the helpful effect of the
CIES on the establishment of the consultative relationship. In many correctional settings the entry phase of consultation is the most critical
period in the implementation of the consultant's role. Even functioning
programs sometimes bear the marks of an inadequately negotiated

relationship between the consultants and the institution staff (e.g., Kotkin, 1972). In the present example the entry phase was completed without problem, primarily because the administration was ready to endorse
program development and because the CIES project offered an acceptable vehicle for such development. The project spoke to the needs of
the administration (not necessarily to the needs of the line staff) and
suggested a procedure that was originally unknown to the school but
on examination seemed to be relevant and efficient. Consequently, the
project was approved and supported by the administration within a
month of its being proposed. Such unanimous and speedy endorsement
would be unlikely with a less systematic or less structured consultative
procedure.

It appears in retrospect that even more structure would probably have
enhanced the productiveness of the project. The discussion of feedback
with multidisciplinary teams led to overcontribution by higher-status
team members and undercontribution by lower-status team members.
Psychologists, social workers, and administrators in each cottage commented and made suggestions more often than teachers and youth counselors. This imbalance could be avoided by utilizing a structured group
discussion technique, such as a modification of the nominal group technique (Delbecq and Van de Ven, 1971), which regulates the contributions of each discussant. This procedure would also have assured participation of staff who criticized the project as well as those who supported
it.

An incidental benefit derived from the use of the CIES was the exposure of staff to a differentiated framework for thinking about their programs and problems. Regardless of the program changes that might
or might not have followed discussion of feedback, the project gave
staff a new vocabulary for construing and discussing their cottages. Instead of locating their programs in a two-dimensional space defined by
"security" and "rehabilitation," staff were encouraged to use at least nine
dimensions (the CIES scales). This cognitive change alone will facilitate
future change, since it precludes resistance to change in the name of
"security" and eliminates the division of staff into punitive (security)
and permissive (rehabilitation) factions. As staff becomes more consistent
in using the new vocabulary, discussion of program change should gen-
erate less conflict.

A final benefit inherent in the CIES project was the opportunity it
gave team members to redefine their roles. After one year's experience
as members of cottage teams, most staff had settled into the role of
"case manager"; during team meetings they dispensed rewards and punishments to individual boys, and they assigned these boys to special pro-

grams such as family therapy or work-study. The discussion of feedback, however, shifted their concern from individual boys to the cottage as a whole and its impact on all residents. Suddenly team members were regarded as responsible for the programs and policies of their cottage. Their role expanded to include program designing and planning. At least part of the difficulty experienced by the traditional cottages during discussions was due to the novelty of these new responsibilities. The experimental cottage was more familiar with the role of design and planning after one year's experience of running an experimental program. It is likely that further discussion with the traditional cottages would have facilitated their familiarity with the new role.

The project at New School illustrates the value of the CIES as an assessment instrument for the clinician or consultant who wishes to better understand his institution or to maximize his effectiveness in the system. Besides furnishing input to the professional's image of an institution, the CIES contributes directly and indirectly to the institution itself. New programs or modification of old programs often derive from staff discussion and feedback. The use of the CIES may prepare an institution for later change by clarifying the conceptual framework of the staff and by encouraging staff to adopt the role of program designer and planner. Such indirect contributions help to ease an institution toward more flexible and responsive correctional programs.

REFERENCES

Delbecq, A. & Van de Ven, A. A group process model for problem identification and program planning. *Journal of Applied Behavioral Science,* **7**:466–492, 1971.

Jesness, C. The Preston typology study. Institute for the Study of Crime and Delinquency, Sacramento, Calif., 1968.

Kotkin, E. Psychological consultation in a maximum security prison: A case history and some comments. In S. Golann & C. Eisdorfer (Eds.), *Handbook of community mental health.* Appleton-Century-Crofts, New York, 1972.

Moos, R. *Evaluating treatment environments: A social ecological approach.* Wiley, New York, 1974.

Wenk, E. & Moos, R. Social climates in prisons: An attempt to conceptualize and measure environmental factors in total institutions. *Journal of Research in Crime and Delinquency,* **9**:134–148, 1972a.

Wenk, E. & Moos, R. Prison environments: A study of the social ecology of correctional institutions. *Crime and Delinquency Literature,* **4**:591–621, 1972b.

CHAPTER FIVE

Toward a Typology
of Correctional Programs

The Importance of Typologies. In this chapter we attempt to develop a typology of correctional programs. The literature contains many hypotheses about the differential treatment of offenders of various types; however very little work has been directed toward the construction of an empirical typology of treatment programs. This is a necessary step if we wish to systematically test hypotheses regarding the amenability of different types of offender to different types of treatment program.

Gibbons (1965) has made one of the few attempts to logically categorize different forms of treatment. He distinguishes between psychotherapy, which generally assumes that delinquency is psychogenic, and environmental therapy, which generally assumes it to be sociogenic. He divides psychotherapy into three major types—individual or depth psychotherapy, group psychotherapy, and client-centered therapy. He also distinguishes among three types of environmental therapy—group therapy, milieu management, and environmental change. His distinction between group psychotherapy (essentially individual therapy in a group setting) and group therapy (the entire group rather than only the individuals in it is the focus of treatment and change attempts) is not widely accepted. However, the general categorization of types of treatment is a step in the right direction.

Gibbons also proposes two offender typologies, one for delinquents and one for criminals. The typology of delinquents includes categories such as predatory gang delinquent, casual gang delinquent, automobile thief or "joyrider," overly aggressive delinquent, and "behavior problem" delinquent. The typology of criminals includes categories such as professional thief, property offender or "one-time loser," naïve check forger, white collar criminal, embezzler, and violent sex offender. Gibbons advances specific treatment recommendations for the 9 delinquent and the 15 criminal types. For example, the automobile thief or "joyriders" are "promising candidates for group therapy rather than for some kind of intensive individual treatment. The problems to which these boys are responding can best be tackled through a group situation in which the offender's peers can be led to attribute high status to him for acts other than stealing cars and related aggressive activity" (Gibbons, 1965, p. 243).

The increasingly compelling evidence that environmental variables powerfully influence individual and group behavior has led to systematic efforts to characterize social situations or settings. Our approach has suggested the potential utility of describing a broad range of social settings by three major types of dimension: (1) Relationship dimensions, (2) Personal Development or Personal Growth dimensions, and (3) System Maintenance and System Change dimensions. An important next step is an attempt to develop taxonomies of these settings. For example, Craik (1973) has recently reviewed the literature on environmental psychology and has pointed out that "a taxonomic interest in the descriptive properties of places is a prerequisite to substantive research on man–environment relations" (p. 404). Cowen (1973) has identified a similar need in his recent review of social and community interventions: "to understand the effects of settings on growth requires that we first develop systematic frameworks for describing settings—something we currently lack" (p. 434).

Price and Blashfield (1973) have noted that at least three issues must be confronted in developing a workable taxonomy of social situations. First, the entity to be classified must be identified. In our case the setting or situation is a correctional or psychiatric treatment program. The second issue concerns the selection and summary of variables used to describe the situation (i.e., correctional programs). In our case the characteristics of programs are described by their results on the relevant Social Climate Scale (e.g., the nine subscale dimensions of the CIES).

The third issue is "How will settings be sampled and classified once they have been defined and described according to a set of variables or dimensions?" (Frederickson, 1972). This problem involves the sampling of settings from some larger population and their classification into a number of relatively homogeneous and distinct groups or classes. Examples of attempts of this kind include Hemphill's (1959) classification of executive positions and Findikyan and Sells' (1966) empirical classification of 60 student organizations into relatively homogeneous clusters. The six categories were: athletic teams, departmental scholastic clubs, fraternities, religious organizations, ROTC squads, and student congress committees.

Findikyan and Sells used a similarity index (based on the differences in group means on the 13 dimensions of the Group Dimensions Description Questionnaire) and a hierarchical grouping procedure that selected subcategories or subtypes from the overall sample of 60 groups, thus keeping the average distances within the subcategories at a minimum. The empirical grouping of student organizations was relatively similar to the a priori classification. The fraternities, the ROTC squads, the student congress committee, and the athletic teams were more similar to one another than they were to any other group or cluster. However, the clustering of religious organizations and departmental scholastic clubs did not converge into classifications resembling the a priori grouping. These groups, especially the religious organizations, fell into several different heterogeneous composites. Thus the empirical results seriously called into question the validity of classifying all religious organizations into one subgroup. An empirical typological analysis may identify clusters of settings which are not obvious from a purely rational approach.

Thus the classification of settings requires that (1) some definition of the population of settings be provided, (2) a procedure for sampling the population be developed, and (3) a basis for classification be decided on. Classification may then proceed on either a rational or an empirical basis (Bailey, 1973). Empirical classifications usually employ multivariate procedures that aim to form homogeneous groups of entities based on similarities and differences of the measured characteristics of the entities. Although a relatively large number of cluster analysis procedures have been designed to serve this purpose (e.g., McQuitty, 1956; Rubin, 1967; Tryon and Bailey, 1970), the goal is the formation of groups that maximize intragroup similarity and intergroup differences.

Six Types of Correctional Program

Juvenile Treatment-Oriented Programs. There were 84 juvenile correctional programs on which both residents and staff responded to the CIES and on which there were also complete Unit Information Form (UIF) scores. The 9 resident CIES standard scores for each of the 84 programs were used in the cluster analysis. Intraclass correlations (Haggard, 1958) were computed between each set of two programs to measure their similarity. The intraclass correlation is a conservative index of program similarity, since it is affected by both relative position differences (i.e., one program is high on Expressiveness and low on Staff Control, whereas the other is low on Expressiveness and high on Staff Control) and level differences (i.e., both programs obtain their highest scores on Staff Control, but one program has a standard score of 80 on Staff Control, whereas the other has a standard score of 60). This analysis produced an 84 × 84 correlation matrix. This correlation matrix furnished a measure of the similarity of every program with every other program in terms of their residents' average perceptions of the social environment.

The similarity matrix was then subjected to a cluster analysis algorithm developed by Carlson (1972). In Carlson's method for identifying homogeneous classes within a heterogeneous sample, the objects within a class must be different from the objects not in the class, and similar to each other. Thus the objects in each cluster formed from Carlson's algorithm have higher similarity indices with all other members in their cluster than any of their similarity indices with an object not in their cluster. Since this procedure often identifies only very small and numerous clusters (usually no more than two or three objects would cluster together by the foregoing criteria), Carlson introduced an optional modification that allowed 5% of the comparisons for an object to be deviant. More specifically, an object was no longer required to have all the similarity indices for members of its cluster higher than its similarity indices for nonmembers: 5% of these indices could now be exceptional. Thus the method identifies clusters that are homogeneous and distinct, and it leaves room for some margin of error, which presumably is an inherent aspect of psychological data and should be considered in any formal classification method. The choice of this procedure resulted in the identification of six major clusters or types of correctional programs.

The Therapeutic Community Program. The first cluster, which consisted of six units, was identified as a "Therapeutic Community" cluster. The average resident CIES profile for these six programs (Figure 5.1) indicates considerably above-average emphasis on all three Relationship dimensions and on all three Treatment Program dimensions (i.e., they foster resident autonomy and independence, they have a practical "down-to-earth" task orientation, and they emphasize the open expression of personal problems and feelings). This occurs in a context that is relatively highly structured but not strictly controlled. These programs are orderly and well organized, and the program rules and regulations are reasonably clear. However, Staff Control is de-emphasized. Thus this cluster identifies a very active, highly treatment-oriented therapeutic community milieu. This is almost the "ideal" type of program, so often described in the literature (e.g., Jones, 1953). There were only six such programs in the juvenile sample, indicating that therapeutic community type of program is relatively rare in institutional correctional settings.

The Relationship-Oriented Program.   The second cluster consisted of ten of the 84 programs. The average resident CIES profile for this cluster also appears in Figure 5.1. The 10 programs are substantially above average on Involvement and Support and on Order and Organization and Clarity, and average on Staff Control. The programs strongly emphasize relationships among their members and between members and staff within the context of a relatively high degree of structure (i.e., both Order and Organization and Clarity are well above average). Although all the Treatment Program dimensions are somewhat above average, there is no special emphasis on any of them. Thus this cluster identifies correctional programs that might be characterized as "warm

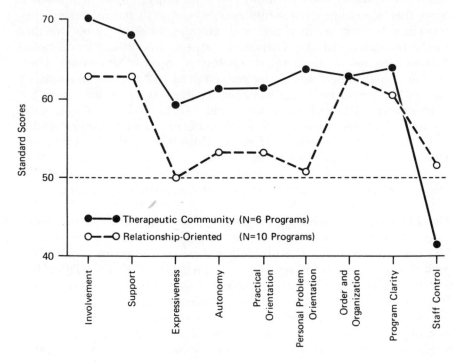

Figure 5.1   CIES Form R profiles for residents in Therapeutic Community and Relationship-Oriented correctional programs.

and clear." We label them Relationship-oriented because of our feeling that the basic therapeutic ingredients in these programs are the strongly supportive interpersonal relationships.

The Action-Oriented Program. Figure 5.2 shows the average resident standard score profile for the 17 "Action-oriented" juvenile programs that fell into a third cluster. These programs are clearly differentiated from those included in the first two clusters. The emphasis on Relationship dimensions and cohesiveness is only about average, and the emphasis on the System Maintenance dimensions of Order and Organization and Clarity is average or below average. These characteristics are in sharp contrast to the first two Treatment-oriented program clusters. The programs in the Action-oriented cluster are primarily characterized by above-average emphasis on Expressiveness and Autonomy and moderately above-average emphasis on both a practical and a feeling orientation.

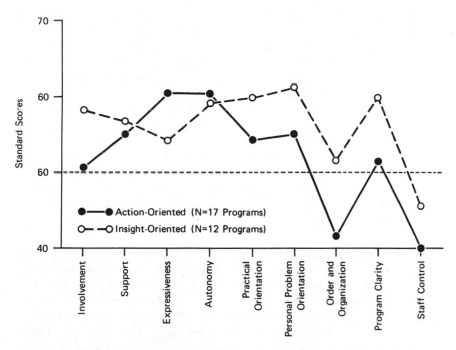

Figure 5.2 CIES Form R profiles for residents in Action-Oriented and Insight-Oriented correctional programs.

There is much stress on activity and on getting things done in these programs, as evidenced by the following items with which the residents strongly agree: "Staff encourage residents to start their own activities," "Residents are expected to take leadership on the unit," "Residents have a say about what goes on here." This is in the context of an expressive milieu, as evidenced by the following items with which residents also agree: "Residents say anything they want to the counselors," "People say what they really think around here," "Staff and residents say how they feel about each other," "On this unit staff think it is a healthy thing to argue," and "Personal problems are openly talked about."

The high degree of independence and expressiveness, in conjunction with the relatively low degrees of cohesion and of System Maintenance, is linked to an elevated amount of assaultive and violent behavior as shown by information from the UIF. The Action-oriented programs had a moderately high proportion of residents who damaged property, were assaultive, refused orders, broke one or more program rules, and so forth.

The Insight-Oriented Program.   Figure 5.2 also shows the average resident CIES profile for a fourth cluster, which consists of 12 programs with a somewhat different social milieu. The Relationship dimensions are moderately emphasized, but in a context in which both Practical Orientation and Personal Problem Orientation are also stressed. This occurs within the overall context of a high emphasis on Clarity but only a moderate emphasis on Order and Organization. Staff in Insight-oriented programs often feel that attaching too much importance to Order and Organization constrains the treatment process by reducing the openness and spontaneity of self-expression. This cluster is somewhat similar to the second cluster. However, the second cluster identifies programs oriented more strongly to the Relationship dimensions, whereas this cluster identifies programs oriented more strongly to the Treatment Program dimensions.

Adult Treatment-Oriented Programs.   Are there similar clusters of treatment-oriented programs in the adult sample? We inspected all the resident CIES adult program profiles and identified 44 programs that appeared to have "treatment-oriented" milieus. These programs fell into the same four categories described earlier, although there was somewhat less differentiation among the clusters. Four programs were in the Therapeutic Community category, 10 were Relationship-oriented, 10 were Insight-oriented, and 20 were Action-oriented. The average resident profiles for these four adult program categories were similar to those shown in the juvenile sample. Only 7 of the 51 male normative sample programs fell into the Therapeutic Community, the Relationship-oriented, or the Insight-oriented categories; whereas 17 of 32 of the female programs fell into these three categories. On the other hand, 11 of the 20 Action-oriented programs were for males, whereas only 9 were for females. These results illustrate further the differences between male and female adult programs briefly discussed in Chapter 3.

Thus a substantial proportion of adult correctional programs are treatment-oriented, at least in the sense that they fall into the four basic treatment-oriented program clusters. The Therapeutic Community and the Relationship- and Insight-oriented treatment programs are considerably more prevalent in female institutions. The Action-oriented programs are more prevalent in male institutions. The results indicate the existence of four quite similar clusters of treatment-oriented correctional programs in both the juvenile and adult program samples.

The results suggest that it would be advisable to rethink the basic characteristics of program environments. For example, Sinclair (1971) has described successful British hostel programs as being "warm and strict." The Relationship-oriented category identifies a set of correctional programs that are warm (high involvement and Support), are characterized by a high degree of Order and Organization with regard to program activities, and have clearly defined rules and procedures. However, they are not necessarily strict, at least in the sense that residents perceive Staff Control to be low. High Staff Control or strictness is not a necessary component of programs otherwise high on System Maintenance. It is likely that most of Sinclair's successful hostels would fall into the Relationship-oriented program cluster (see Chapter 7 for further discussion of Sinclair's project).

The four clusters named constitute four broad categories into which individual treatment-oriented programs can be placed. There are of course a great variety of individual programs, some of which are illustrated in the profile examples presented in Chapter 4. There are programs that strongly emphasize Personal Problem Orientation to the virtual exclusion of the other treatment program dimensions. A few programs are high on Order and Clarity and Control. Together, however, the four clusters illustrate the basic categories of treatment-oriented correctional programs; considerable variability of course exists within each category.

The results also illustrate the importance of doing an entire profile analysis of a program, rather than attempting to interpret each subscale individually. High Staff Control in a program that strongly emphasizes Involvement and Support may mean something quite different from high Staff Control in a program low on Involvement and Support. Configurational analyses of the CIES profiles are necessary.

The 48 juvenile treatment-oriented programs were drawn from 14 correctional institutions, of which 11 also had programs that were classified into one of the other two clusters, discussed below. Thus one cannot classify correctional programs simply by identifying the institution in which they are located. A custodial institution may have one or more treatment-oriented programs, and a treatment-oriented institution may have one or more custodial programs. The variability of the social environments of correctional programs within institutions is almost as great as the variability among institutions.

The Control-Oriented Program.   The fifth cluster, which has been labeled Control-oriented, characterizes a very familiar type of program. Figure 5.3 shows the average resident CIES profile for the 26 juvenile programs which fell into this cluster. Such programs strongly emphasize Staff Control to the virtual exclusion of all other areas except Order and Organization. All three Relationship dimensions receive substantially below-average emphasis, as do all three Treatment Program dimensions. The clarity of program rules and regulations is well below average. This cluster clearly represents a custodial Control-oriented program which is characterized mainly by close adherence to rules and procedures and a regimented bureaucratic approach to residents.

The 26 programs were typically relatively large (average size was 94 residents) and had a very low staff–resident ratio (the average was 1 staff member to each 23 residents). This contrasts sharply with the first four clusters in which the average size was less than 50 residents and the average staffing pattern was approximately one staff member for each dozen residents. The Control-oriented programs are almost twice as large as those in the first four clusters, and they are also considerably less well-staffed. This cluster represents the classic, large, regimented "two-subculture" programs that have been discussed in detail by Goffman (1961) and others. Eight of the 26 custodial programs were located in county juvenile halls and 11 in maximum security juvenile institutions. The remaining seven were in several different institutions, most of which were reputed to be oriented toward treatment or at least toward rehabilitation.

The average resident CIES profile for the 26 adult programs that were Control-oriented or custodial was almost identical to that for the juvenile units in Figure 5.3, except that Order and Organization was also de-emphasized in the adult custodial cluster. These programs typify the human warehouses and snake pits of which so many authors speak.

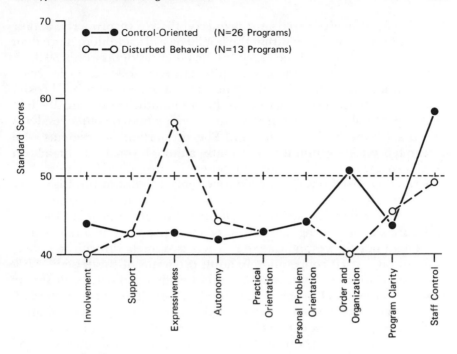

Figure 5.3 CIES Form R profiles for residents in Control-Oriented and Disturbed Behavior correctional programs.

Twenty-four of the adult programs were male and only two were female, indicating that Control-oriented programs are considerably more prevalent in male than in female prisons. This is exactly what would be expected on the basis of our earlier results.

The Disturbed Behavior Program.   Our sixth and last cluster comprises programs that deal mainly with particularly hard-to-manage "disturbed" juveniles and adults. Figure 5.3, which shows the average resident CIES profile for the 13 juvenile programs in this cluster, indicates a moderately high emphasis on Expressiveness and Staff Control. Since these programs stress neither Involvement and Support nor Personal Problem Orientation, the emphasis on Expressiveness appears to refer to the open expression of anger more than the constructive expression of personal feelings. This conclusion is strongly supported by the data obtained on these 13 programs on the Unit Information Form (UIF).

This cluster of programs was characterized by more disturbed and aggressive behavior than any of the other clusters, including the Action-oriented cluster, displayed. For example, about 20% of the residents had damaged or destroyed unit property, their own property, and/or somebody else's property within the last 30 days. In addition, more than 20% of the residents had been assaultive to other residents within 30 days. Almost 40% of the residents had recently refused to follow an order given by a staff member. More than three-quarters of the residents had broken one or more of the program rules in the last month. More than 40% had played practical jokes (with an aggressive connotation) on other residents or on staff within the last month. The proportion of residents who attempted suicide within the last month, although small, was higher on these programs than on any of the other five program clusters.

Five adult programs (four male, one female) fell into the Disturbed Behavior category. The average resident profile for these programs was very similar to that for the juvenile Disturbed Behavior programs shown in Figure 5.3. Such programs are much more prevalent in adult institutions than our figures indicate, but it was extremely difficult to obtain resident (and staff) cooperation in adult programs of this type.

To sum up, the cluster analysis indicates that at least six different types of correctional program can be identified. The exact clusters of programs derived from an analysis of this sort are to some extent arbitrary. However, the six clusters just described make excellent conceptual and empirical sense. There are four groups of treatment-oriented programs. The Therapeutic Community programs emphasize all the Relationship and Treatment Program dimensions. The Relationship-oriented programs emphasize mainly cohesion and organization (i.e., both Relationship and System Maintenance dimensions). The Insight-oriented programs put the most stress on insight and clarity of program expectations. The Action-oriented programs emphasize Independence and Expressiveness and de-emphasize Organization and Control. The Control-oriented programs, on the other hand, emphasize Organization and Control, to the virtual exclusion of all the Relationship and Treatment Program dimensions. Finally, the Disturbed Behavior programs attempt to emphasize Control, but Expressiveness is also elevated primarily because the residents involved are particularly aggressive and difficult to control.

Resident–Staff Agreement.   Do the staff agree with the resident descriptions of the six program clusters? The staff view each type of program considerably more positively than do the residents. However, the differences among the staff in their perceptions of the six types are basically consistent with the differences among the residents. For example, staff on the Therapeutic Community, Relationship- and Insight-oriented programs have the highest scores (as compared with staff on the other programs) on six of the nine CIES dimensions—namely, the Relationship dimensions of Involvement and Support, the Treatment Program dimensions of Practical Orientation and Personal Problem Orientation, and the System Maintenance dimensions of Order and Organization and Clarity. This exactly matches the subscales that are highest in the resident sample from these programs. Staff on the Action-oriented programs have the highest scores on Autonomy and Expressiveness and the lowest score on Staff Control. These are the same dimensions on which the residents in these programs show their highest and lowest scores.

Staff in the Control-oriented programs did not agree as closely with the residents in these programs, as might be expected. Whereas the average resident–staff discrepancy on the four groups of treatment-oriented programs was between 1 and 1.5 standard deviations, the average discrepancy in the Control-oriented programs was greater than 2 standard deviations. In addition, resident–staff difference on Staff Control was less than 1 standard deviation in the treatment-oriented clusters, but it was more than 3 standard deviations in the Control-oriented cluster. Thus residents and staff in custodial programs have totally different perceptions of these programs, clearly corroborating the "two-subculture" notion of resident and staff groups who function side by side but have little or no common communication. On the other hand, none of the four treatment-oriented programs can be described in this manner.

Residents and staff of the Disturbed Behavior programs also show relatively large disagreements; that is, the discrepancies are greater than 2 standard deviations on six of the nine CIES subscales. But residents and staff have almost identical perceptions on Expressiveness and Control, the two subscales that characterize these programs as perceived by the residents. Thus there is at least some agreement, even though the staff feel that there is considerably more emphasis in all the other areas than do the residents.

It is instructive to compare the Therapeutic Community, Relationship-, and Insight-oriented programs with the Control-oriented programs in terms of the amount of disturbed and aggressive behavior shown by their residents. We see that the amount of this behavior is almost identical in these three types of programs. In the three clusters of programs, the proportions of residents who damaged property, were assaultive, attempted suicide, refused an order, broke program rules, played practical jokes, and brought "contraband" into the unit were essentially identical! Thus there is no evidence whatever that a program that emphasizes resident and staff cohesion and a treatment orientation is necessarily associated with more aggressive or rule-breaking resident behavior. To put it another way, the data provide no evidence that programs emphasizing Staff Control necessarily reduce the amount of aggressive and rule-breaking resident behavior. The Therapeutic Community, Relationship-, and Insight-oriented programs were about half the size of the Control-oriented programs, and had about twice the staffing. Given these size and staffing constraints, it is highly unlikely that the custodial programs could have successfully decreased their emphasis on Staff Control and/or increased their emphasis on Relationship and Treatment Program dimensions without at least a temporary rise in violent and aggressive behavior. The data indicate that high Staff Control may have considerably less impact on certain indices of resident behavior than has commonly been thought.

Six Types of Psychiatric Program.   Do psychiatric programs fall into similar clusters? We collected data on 160 American hospital-based psychiatric programs (Moos, 1974, Chapter 3). There were 143 programs on which Ward Atmosphere Scale (WAS) data were obtained from patients and staff and on which pertinent size and staffing data had also been collected. Cluster analyses on the patient WAS data led to the identification of six clusters of programs. There was remarkable similarity (although there are some differences) to the six clusters identified in correctional programs.

The Therapeutic Community Program.   A group of 19 psychiatric programs was identified as belonging to a Therapeutic Community cluster. The average patient profile for these programs appears in Figure 5.4. The programs show considerably above-average emphasis on all three Relationship and all four Treatment Program dimensions. In these characteristics they are almost identical to the correctional Therapeutic Community cluster. Unlike the correctional Therapeutic Community cluster, however, the psychiatric programs are low on all three System Maintenance dimensions.

Patients in these programs are seen as active and involved, as spending time constructively, and as having group spirit and pride in the program. They express their feelings relatively freely and emphasize the discussion of personal problems and the open expression of anger and aggression. Encouraged to be self-sufficient and independent, they are oriented toward preparing themselves for release from the hospital. The programs are somewhat disorganized and lack clarity, probably because of

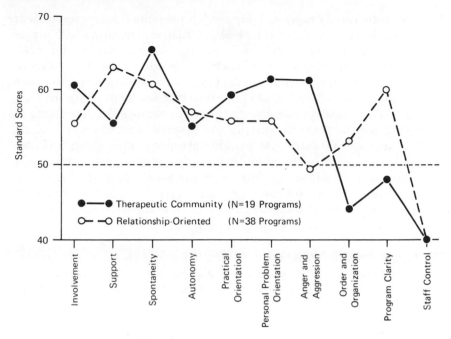

Figure 5.4 WAS Form R profiles for patients in Therapeutic Community and Relationship-Oriented psychiatric programs.

their highly individualized treatment orientation. These programs tend to be located in university teaching hospitals, to be small, and to be very highly staffed.

The Relationship-Oriented Program.   A group of 37 programs was identified as belonging to a Relationship-oriented cluster. The average patient profile for this cluster also appears in Figure 5.4. These programs have moderately high emphasis on the three Relationship dimensions, slightly above-average emphasis on three of the Treatment Program dimensions, and moderately to substantially above-average emphasis on Clarity and Order and Organization. Staff Control is strongly de-emphasized. The programs' primary stress is on the Relationship dimensions of Involvement and Support and on the System Maintenance dimensions of Order and Organization and Clarity. Staff Control is played down. Programs of both types show only moderate emphasis on the Treatment Program dimensions. The actual similarity between the correctional and psychiatric Relationship-oriented cluster profiles is striking, as can be noted by comparing Figures 5.1 and 5.4

The Action-Oriented Program. Figure 5.5 presents the average patient profile for the Action-oriented type of psychiatric program, which places very high emphasis on patient autonomy and independence, and moderate emphasis on Staff Control. Each of the other eight WAS dimensions is below average. This cluster represents a high-turnover prerelease program in which patients are expected to take leadership, are strongly encouraged to be independent and to assume responsibility, are engaged in making specific plans for leaving the hospital, and so on. The Staff Control element indicates that patients are not simply given a choice about whether to be independent; rather, they are strongly encouraged in the direction of autonomy. However, the highly individualized program, in conjunction with the high turnover rate, is linked with very low involvement and cohesiveness and with substantial patient confusion regarding program policies and procedures.

The Insight-Oriented Program. Figure 5.5 also shows the average patient profile for the 19 programs in the Insight-oriented cluster. These programs are also characterized by a lack of emphasis on the Relation-

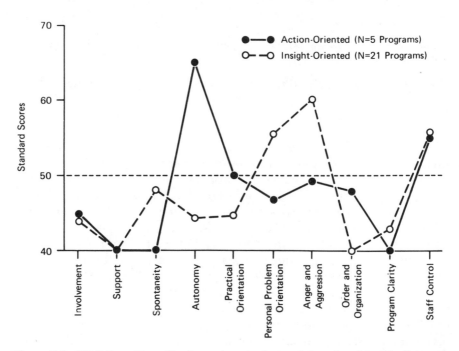

Figure 5.5 WAS Form R profiles for patients in Action-Oriented and Insight-Oriented psychiatric programs.

ship dimensions. They strongly de-emphasize Staff Control. Since they also play down Order and Organization and Clarity, all three System Maintenance dimensions receive below-average emphasis. However, the Treatment Program dimensions, particularly Personal Problem Orientation and Anger and Aggression, are emphasized much more highly than in the Relationship-oriented programs.

This cluster is relatively similar to the Insight-oriented cluster identified in the correctional sample, but there are two major differences. In the psychiatric cluster the emphasis on the open expression of feelings (as shown by Spontaneity and Anger and Aggression) is higher, whereas the emphasis on Clarity is lower. This is because psychiatric staff are more likely than correctional staff to foster expressiveness and spontaneity. This situation often engenders a good deal of confusion on the part of the patients. The program rules and procedures tend to be unclear, precisely because the orientation of the program is to individualize as many decisions as possible. Although this "democratization" is instituted to achieve laudable aims, it often has the effect of raising uncertainty and confusion among the patients.

The Control-Oriented Program.   A surprising total of 50 of the 143 psychiatric programs fell into a custodial cluster. The average patient WAS profile for these 50 programs is given in Figure 5.6. Again, there is a striking similarity between this average patient WAS profile derived from psychiatric programs, and the average resident CIES profile derived from correctional programs (see Figure 5.3). The psychiatric Control-oriented programs show below-average emphasis on all three Relationship and all four Treatment Program dimensions. In addition, they reveal below-average emphasis on Program Clarity. The only two dimensions receiving average or above-average ratings are Order and Organization and Staff Control, exactly as in the correctional Control-oriented cluster. Psychiatric programs are usually described as treatment-oriented, whereas correctional programs are often described as custodial. These results indicate that a substantial proportion of the programs in both correctional and psychiatric institutions are custodial, at least in the sense that Relationship and Treatment Program areas receive little if any emphasis.

The Disturbed Behavior Program.   Eleven of the 143 programs were placed in a Disturbed Behavior cluster; Figure 5.6 gives the average patient WAS profile for these programs. There is above-average emphasis only in the areas of Anger and Aggression and Program Clarity.

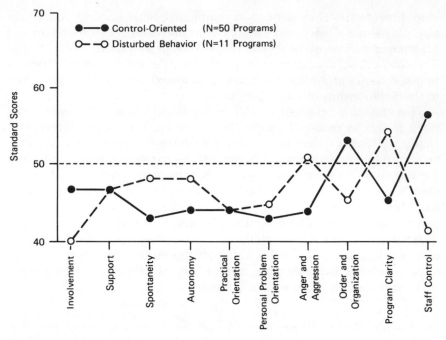

Figure 5.6 WAS Form R profiles for patients in Control-Oriented and Disturbed Behavior psychiatric programs.

All the other dimensions are well below average. This profile is quite similar to the profile for correctional Disturbed Behavior programs (Figure 5.3). The main difference is that the correctional programs showed their elevation on Expressiveness, but this is because the CIES has no Anger and Aggression dimension. Most of the psychiatric programs in the cluster are state hospital admission programs with relatively acutely disturbed and/or acting-out impulsive patients.

Size and staffing indices differentiated among the major psychiatric program clusters and among the correctional program clusters in the same manner. More specifically, the psychiatric Control-oriented programs were almost twice as large (averaging about 55 patients) and half as well staffed (averaging about 1 staff member for each 7.6 patients) as were the four treatment-oriented clusters (which averaged about 30 patients, and 1 staff member for each 4 patients). The Disturbed Behavior programs were slightly larger than the Therapeutic Community programs but were almost as well staffed (see Price and Moos, 1975, for more details).

Toward Differential Programs and Differential Treatment. The findings indicate that the clusters of correctional programs fall into six major types, which are almost identically replicated in psychiatric programs. The custodial type of program has already been extensively described in the literature. Disturbed Behavior programs exist in many correctional institutions, but there is very little research on these programs. In this respect the results simply call attention to a type of program that needs to be studied further. The results may be most interesting in relation to the Treatment-oriented clusters, since there seem to be at least four distinctly different types of treatment-oriented program. It is not adequate to call a correctional program "treatment-oriented," since "treatment orientation" may be defined quite differently across programs.

The findings are important from several perspectives. One of the major points is that empirical relationships identified in one cluster of programs may or may not generalize to another cluster. This may help explain some of the discrepant findings that appear in the literature. For example, there is evidence that individuals who perceive environments deviantly are generally less satisfied and do worse in those environments. However, deviant perceptions may be related to greater individual satisfaction and to better performance when the environment itself is particularly negative and/or undifferentiated. Thus although deviancy per se has negative consequences in most situations, the relationship between deviancy, satisfaction, and performance in an environment varies as a function of the characteristics of the environment itself.

Residents who perceive Therapeutic Community or Relationship-oriented programs deviantly may adapt more poorly in such programs. Residents who perceive Control-oriented programs deviantly may adapt better in programs of this type. Discrepant perceptions in Control-oriented programs might constitute an adaptive reaction. These considerations suggest that research findings may not generalize across social settings precisely because the settings have important differential characteristics. The CIES may thus have utility both in selecting correctional environments in which replication studies should be carried out and in suggesting explanations for the failure of certain relationships to be replicated in different programs. In addition, they may help specify the exact generality of certain relationships (e.g., do they hold equally well for both Therapeutic Community and Control-oriented programs?).

Perhaps the major reason for characterizing types of correctional programs is the possibility of identifying certain offender types who might be more likely to benefit from one program than another. This is, of course, most likely in relation to the four treatment-oriented clusters. To make progress in this area, it is necessary to have a typology of both delinquents and correctional programs.

Sheldon and Eleanor Glueck (1970) have recently presented an extensive review of this area and have proposed an empirically derived typology of three clinical types of juvenile offender. Type 1 lacks certain personal characteristics usually associated with antisocial behavior (e.g., defiance, adventuresomeness, and acquisitiveness). This type comes from generally positive family backgrounds in which the homes are orderly, clean, and stable, as well as cohesive and supportive. The relationship between the delinquent and his parents is generally positive. The Gluecks point out that type 1 boys are exceptional in that they become delinquent despite the relatively low probability of this behavioral outcome. Thus the boys are thought to present "promising human behavior to which therapists might devote special effort" (p. 62).

The Gluecks' second type identifies boys who are more likely to be defiant, adventurous, and unconventional, and less likely to be masochistic and self-punishing. Many of the type 2 boys were also raised in relatively cohesive families; however a certain proportion came from homes with either delinquent mothers and/or incompatible parents, and were not adequately supervised by their mothers. Interestingly, the Gluecks suggest that type 2 might be broken into two subtypes, one made up of boys with relatively favorable individual traits and family backgrounds, and the other of boys in whom relatively unfavorable individual traits are paired with relatively unfavorable social factors.

The Gluecks' third type represents what they consider to be the "core" group of serious juvenile delinquents. The boys tend to be defiant, adventurous, unconventional, and irresponsible; they come from parents and households that "run almost the entire gamut of family pathology" (p. 63).

Although the Gluecks are extremely modest in the claims they make for their typology, they believe that it is relevant for intervention and treatment, particularly in that the risk of continued delinquency significantly differentiates among the three types (rising from type 1 to type 3). It is of course pure speculation, but it is reasonable to suppose that these three delinquent types might react differently to the four treatment-oriented types of programs. The Gluecks' type 1 delinquent would probably do best in either a Therapeutic Community or an Insight-oriented program. Since these boys have certain internal controls, they may not need a high degree of external control. In addition, they may be more likely to benefit from the substantial emphasis on the Treatment Program dimensions, particularly Personal Problem Orientation, which is present in such programs. In this respect they may be similar to the neurotic delinquents identified by Rubenfeld (1967).

The Gluecks' type 2 delinquent may be most likely to do well in a Relationship-oriented program. These delinquents would probably benefit from the support and cohesiveness shown in these programs; however, most of them probably need relatively clear and consistent guidelines within which their conduct will be judged. Relationship-oriented programs might also be particularly beneficial for the power-oriented delinquents described earlier.

Finally, the Gluecks' third type of delinquent might find the Action-oriented type of program most beneficial. These boys need more opportunity to engage in constructive and active behavior, and they may not be able to develop the type of cohesiveness required in the two foregoing programs. In addition, if they did develop this cohesiveness it might be antithetical to normative staff values. These suggestions are purely hypothetical; however, they illustrate the possibility of attempting to match clinical juvenile offender types with currently existing types of correctional treatment program. Other examples of suggested strategies for the differential treatment of juvenile offenders can be found in Glueck and Glueck (1970). They are also discussed further in Chapters 6 and 10.

Some studies have shown that there are differential patterns of response to different treatment modalities among various groups. For example, Price and Curlee (1973) assessed 51 consecutive admissions to an alcoholism treatment program. The patients evaluated each of eight treatment modalities on each of eight response dimensions. The treatment modalities included lectures, group therapy, individual counseling, family counseling, and free time. The treatment response dimensions included perceived worth ("it was important to me"), pleasantness ("I was pleased"), vigor ("I felt lively"), therapeutic benefit ("it helped me get well"), and participation ("I talked freely and openly"). Price and Curlee carried out a cluster analysis of patients in terms of their response patterns to the different treatment modalities. This analysis yielded three patient clusters representing distinctly different response patterns to the treatments. One cluster of patients saw coming into the hospital and individual counseling as being of high therapeutic benefit. A second cluster saw coming into the hospital as highly beneficial but felt that individual counseling had little therapeutic value. For a third cluster, coming into the hospital had little if any therapeutic benefit.

Price and Curlee then showed that the three patient clusters differed on several subscales of the Minnesota Multiphasic Personality Inventory

(MMPI). The patients in cluster A showed elevated scores on the Psychopathic Deviate (Pd) and Hypomania (Ma) scales. They also had significantly lower Social Introversion (Si) scores, which is consistent with their positive ratings of individual counseling and group therapy.

Patients in cluster B had an MMPI profile characteristic of individuals displaying neurotic depressive diagnoses and passive aggressive personality disorders. This group also had relatively high scores on the Psychasthenia (Pt) and Schizophrenia (Sc) subscales. Price and Curlee conclude that the apparent threat-proneness of this group of patients is quite consistent with the relatively low ranking they give to individual counseling.

Finally, cluster C obtained an MMPI profile frequently characterized by a depressive psychophysiological diagnosis. Individuals with these profiles are usually described as "manifesting hypochondriacal tendencies" and "presenting self as physically, organically sick." This is the group that rated coming into the hospital as being of little or no therapeutic benefit to them, indicating that they feel that environmental change is not particularly helpful in dealing with their problems. Consistent with their preoccupation with physical symptoms, this group rated the lectures, which contain information about the physiology of alcoholism, as therapeutically important. Thus the three patient clusters identified by Price and Curlee displayed personality differences on the MMPI which were consistent with their differential response to various aspects of their treatment program.

Palmer (1965) took this approach one step further by identifying types of treators (probation officers) from clinical assessments and analyses of interviews with delinquent youngsters. He identified three groups of officers whose characteristics overlap remarkably the characteristics of three of our treatment program types. The first group—the "relationship–self-expression" oriented officers, often became personally and emotionally involved with the youngsters they were seeing. They were concerned with establishing an open direct relationship with the youths. They were concerned about issues relating to personal accomplishment, lack of self-confidence, and independence–dependence conflicts. The boys were likely to see the officers as counselors or friends.

Another group of officers, labeled as "surveillance–self-control" oriented, were described as "sharp-eyed police officer" and/or "hard-nosed parole officer." The boys saw them as focusing primarily on their peer relationships, on employment opportunities, and on control of the boys' behavior. The officers were said to be relatively tough-minded and exacting, and wishing to maintain considerable social distance and formality in their relationship with their youngsters. The middle or "group two" officers were described as a blend of the first two groups; that is, they were both Relationship- and Control-oriented. They were typically described as energetic, candid, and open in their manner of expression.

Analyses of satisfaction and effectiveness ratings showed that the relationship–self-expression officers had their best results with delinquents of the (a) communicative–alert, (b) impulsive–anxious, and (c) verbally hostile and defensive types. These delinquents tended to come from intact rather than broken family settings. They were moderately independent and were actively planning to achieve important educational and vocational goals. Officers of the surveillance–self-control orientation achieved their best results with the dependent–anxious type of delinquent—the most compliant, nonsuspicious, and malleable members of the sample. These delinquents were least likely to show resistance to control, and most likely to place positive value on the main objective of the Control-oriented officers (i.e., the control of behavior). The youths displayed little hostility or defiance, thus were unlikely to arouse counterresistance and impatience in the Control-oriented officers. They were prepared to accept direction from the authority figure. The Control-oriented officers were prepared to "keep them out of more serious trouble" and "tell them what to do and what not to do."

Palmer points out that the dependent–anxious delinquents did not do as well with the Relationship-oriented probation officers as they did with the Control-oriented group. These delinquents did not have the necessary future-oriented or adult-oriented goals; they preferred to remain with the status quo and were not very interested in bringing about fundamental changes in their life situation. The Relationship-oriented officers wanted the youngsters to overcome and work on rather than avoid their problems. These officers also preferred a more equalitarian interaction between themselves and the delinquents and were not comfortable with the "son or daughter role" with which the dependent–anxious delinquents seemed to be at ease.

One of the most successful combinations of youngsters and officers constituted the group two officers, who emphasized both relationship and control, and the delinquent who "wanted to be helped and liked." This type of delinquent wanted not only the direction and guidance of authority figures, but also an open expression of support and reassurance from them. These youngsters felt that they would be able to manage their own lives effectively if they were given approval and direction from adult and/or parent figures. The group two officers were generally able to fulfill these needs. Palmer concludes as follows:

> No single group of officers seemed able to work in a highly effective manner with all kinds of groups—or for that matter even equally well

with all groups. . . . In at least this particular probation setting none
of the three groups of officers seemed in terms of satisfaction–
effectiveness to work in a highly effective manner with some groups of
youths. . . . It was therefore quite plain that no 'all around heroes' and
no 'all around villains' appeared among our three empirically derived
group of officers." (p. 22)

Warren (1969) has cogently presented the case for the differential
treatment of delinquents with special reference to the Community Treatment Program (CTP), and Palmer (1968) followed up some of his earlier
results in CTP. One set of data includes 88 delinquents drawn from
the caseloads of 34 CTP parole agents. The 88 cases were broken down
into two categories—those with whom the agents were closely matched
and those with whom they were not closely matched. The two groups
of delinquents were not significantly different on variables such as age,
intelligence, nature of committing offense, socioeconomic level, and race.
However, they were strikingly different in their "failure rate": the 15-
month parole revocation rate was 19% for the well-matched group,
whereas it was 43% for the poorly matched group. This is a striking
difference by any criteria. Palmer (1973) has recently updated these analyses and has confirmed the importance of matching. Jesness (1970) also
found that the development of treatment programs uniquely suited to
delinquents of specific maturity levels decreased management problems,
serious rule infractions, difficulties with peers, and the incidence of reported behavioral problems. However, this matching had no differential
impact on parole performance (see Chapters 6 and 7).

To sum up, the most important aspect of the results presented here
is the notable similarity between the six major types of correctional and
psychiatric programs. It is not accurate to characterize correctional programs as wholly custodial or control-oriented; neither is it accurate to
call psychiatric programs wholly therapeutic or treatment-oriented.
There is considerable range and diversity of program characteristics
within both the correctional and the psychiatric systems. Perhaps the
most surprising aspect of these results is that the proportion of control-
oriented programs in the psychiatric system is remarkably high. A relatively large proportion of psychiatric programs simply do not have any
treatment component whatever, at least as assessed by the Relationship
and Treatment Program dimensions. The results also indicate that the
phrase "treatment-oriented" is not sufficient to describe the major characteristics of either correctional or psychiatric programs. The relevant
question is, What aspects of a treatment orientation are particularly
strongly emphasized?

The foregoing typology of programs may be most useful in ruling out rather than in making program assignments. It may be easier to identify programs that probably *will not* work for a particular youngster than to choose programs that probably *will* benefit him. For example, it might be unwise to place an impulse-oriented youngster in a Therapeutic Community or an Insight-oriented program, or to place a controlling, power-oriented youngster in a Relationship- or Action-oriented program. This notion achieves additional importance in the light of the evidence that both individual therapy (Bergin, 1971) and group therapy (Lieberman, Yalom and Miles, 1973) may produce detrimental results with considerably greater frequency than anyone has previously supposed. Finally, there is no reason for not converting the large proportion of control-oriented programs in correctional and psychiatric settings into treatment-oriented programs of appropriate types. This would, at the very least, enhance the satisfaction and morale of the residents and staff who live and function in these programs.

REFERENCES

Bailey, K. D. Monothetic and polythetic typologies and their relation to conceptualization, measurement and scaling. *American Sociological Review*, **38**:18–33, 1973.

Bergin, A. The evaluation of therapeutic outcomes. In A. Bergin & S. Garfield (Eds.), *Handbook of psychotherapy and behavior change: An empirical analysis*. Wiley, New York, 1971.

Carlson, K. A method for identifying homogeneous classes. *Multivariate behavioral research*, **7**:483–488, 1972.

Cowen, E. Social and community interventions. *Annual Review of Psychology*, **24**:423–472, 1973.

Craik, K. H. Environmental psychology. *Annual Review of Psychology*, **24**:403–422, 1973.

Findikyan, N. & Sells, S. Organizational structure and similarity of campus student organizations. *Organizational Behavior and Human Performance*, **1**:169–189, 1966.

Frederiksen, N. Toward a taxonomy of situations. *American Psychologist*, **27**:114–123, 1972.

Gibbons, D. C. *Changing the lawbreaker*. Prentice-Hall, Englewood Cliffs, N.J., 1965.

Glueck, S. & Glueck, E. *Toward a typology of juvenile offenders. Implications for therapy and prevention*. Grune & Stratton, New York, 1970.

Goffman, E. *Asylum: Essays on the social situation of mental patients and other inmates*. Anchor Books, Doubleday, Garden City, N.Y., 1961.

Haggard, E. *Intraclass correlation and the analysis of variance*. Dryden Press, New York, 1958.

Hemphill, J. K. Job descriptions for executives. *Harvard Business Review*, **37**:55–67, 1959.

Jesness, C. The Preston typology study. *Youth Authority Quarterly*, **23**:26–38, 1970.

Jones, M. *The therapeutic community: A new treatment method in psychiatry*. Basic Books, New York, 1953.

Lieberman, M., Yalom, I., & Miles, M. *Encounter groups: First facts.* Basic Books, New York, 1973.

McQuitty, I. Agreement analysis: Classifying persons by predominant patterns of responses. *British Journal of Statistical Psychology,* 9:5–16, 1956.

Moos, R. *Evaluating treatment environments: A social ecological approach.* Wiley, New York, 1974.

Palmer, T. Types of treators and types of juvenile offenders. *Youth Authority Quarterly,* 18:14–23, 1965.

Palmer, T. Recent research findings and long-range developments at the Community Treatment Project. Community Treatment Project Research Report No. 9, Part 2, California Youth Authority, Sacramento, 1968.

Palmer, T. Reply to Lerman critique. Community Treatment Project, Sacramento, 1973.

Price, R. & Blashfield, R. Explorations in the taxonomy of behavior settings: Analysis of dimensions and classification of settings. *American Journal of Community Psychology,* in press, 1975.

Price, R. & Curlee-Salisbury, J. Person-treatment interaction among alcohol patients. *Quarterly Journal of Studies on Alcohol,* in press, 1975.

Price, R. & Moos, R. Toward a typology of inpatient treatment environments. *Journal of Abnormal Psychology,* in press, 1975.

Rubenfield, S. *Typological approaches and delinquency control: A status report.* National Institute of Mental Health, Chevy Chase, Md., 1967.

Rubin, J. Optimal classification into groups: An approach for solving the taxonomy problem. *Journal of Theoretical Biology,* 15:103–144, 1967.

Sinclair, I. *Hostels for probationers.* Home Office Research Studies, Her Majesty's Stationery Office, London, 1971.

Tyron, R. C. & Bailey, D. *Cluster analysis.* McGraw-Hill, New York, 1970.

Warren, M. Q. The case for differential treatment of delinquents. *Annals of the American Academy of Political and Social Science,* 381:47–59, 1969.

PART THREE

Program Comparisons and Evaluations

CHAPTER SIX

Divergent Treatment
Programs:
Behavior Modification
and Transactional
Analysis

CHAPTER SEVEN
The Impact of
Correctional Programs:
Morale, Personality,
and Parole Performance

CHAPTER EIGHT

The Impact of
Correctional Programs:
Absconding

CHAPTER NINE

Congruence and
Incongruence in
Correctional
Environments

Divergent Treatment Programs: Behavior Modification and Transactional Analysis

RUDOLF H. MOOS AND PAUL SOMMERS

The Background and Setting of the Youth Center Research Project. The Youth Center Research Project was a direct outgrowth of earlier studies conducted by Jesness. Jesness (1965) compared the effects of two treatment programs at a California Youth Authority (CYA) ranch. One program was an intensive, internally oriented program in a small living unit; the other was externally oriented, less intensive, and functioned in a large living unit. Subjects in the more intensive program appeared to do better; that is, they had lower 12-month parole revocation rates than subjects in the less intensive program. The more neurotic subjects in the intensive program did particularly well. However, as Jesness notes, the effects of differential treatment were confounded with the effects of size (see Chapter 3). Thus the better outcome shown by the intensive treatment program may have been largely a result of its size.

In the Preston typology study Jesness (1968) explored the feasibility of classifying juvenile inmates by personality development types and defining a treatment strategy for each type. Subjects were classified by Interpersonal Maturity (I) Levels and subtypes within each I-level, using a methodology based on Sullivan et al. (1957). There are seven maturity levels in this typology, and three were used in the study. The higher levels correspond to greater maturity, each level being defined by crucial interpersonal problems that must be resolved before a higher level can be achieved.

Level 2 or I_2 subjects tend to be egocentric, impulsive, and unrealistic. They relate to another person only in terms of whether the person gives or takes something away. I_2 subjects do not understand the effects of their behavior on others and do not understand what others expect of them. An I_2's delinquency may stem from poor impulse control or inability to cope with external pressures, including pressures from peers. Two subtypes are distinguished at this level:

> *Unsocialized Aggressive* subjects react with anger or hostility to frustrations or adult demands.
>
> *Unsocialized Passive* subjects tend to complain or withdraw in similar situations.

Level 3 or I_3 subjects attempt to manipulate their environment to get what they desire. The external social environment is seen in terms of stereotyped roles (strict father, nice teacher, big policeman) rather individual personalities. The I_3 subject tries to manipulate the holders of these roles through "conning" or conforming to the perceived power structure. Three subtypes are distinguished by the typical mode of manipulation:

> *Immature Conformist* subjects conform to the demands of persons immediately around them.
>
> *Cultural Conformist* subjects demonstrate surface conformity to the external power structure.
>
> *Manipulator* subjects overtly manage persons and objects to gain or maintain power over others.

Level 4 or I_4 subjects have an internalized set of standards by which to judge behavior. These standards may or may not be socially acceptable; thus the delinquency of I_4 subjects may result from internal conflict or from a clash between the values of society and those of the delinquent.

> *Neurotic Acting-out* subjects are characterized by guilt and anxiety resulting from internalization of a negative and inadequate self-image. These subjects are usually reluctant to reveal this negative self-image and thus strive for autonomy. Delinquent acts are frequently the acting-out of a family problem or internal conflict.

Neurotic Anxious subjects share the negative self-image of the Acting-out subtype but place greater value on introspection. Thus they are more likely to seek relationships with adults and peers who approve and accept their good traits while forgiving the "bad me."

Situational Emotional subjects have a more positive self-image but experience distress and conflict in relation to a particular family or personal problem, which precipitates their involvement in delinquent activities.

Cultural Identifier subjects tend to internalize the values of a deviant subculture. These values typically include antipathy toward middle-class mores and the perception of racial and socioeconomic injustices. This subtype's delinquency is a means of expressing loyalty to the subculture and of attacking middle-class white society.

A more detailed discussion of I-level theory can be found in Appendix A of Jesness et al. (1972) and in Warren (1966).

Boys were randomly assigned to experimental and control groups. The experimental group was classified by I-level and subtype, then assigned to lodges by subtype, in an attempt to segregate maturity levels and, if possible, to segregate some of the most common subtypes. Each experimental lodge developed its own treatment program, using techniques staff felt would be most helpful to the particular personality types assigned to the lodge. The control group participated in the traditional CYA program of academic and vocational training accompanied by group counseling sessions.

The development of treatment strategies was most successful in the experimental lodges housing Cultural Conformist, Manipulator, and Neurotic Acting-Out subtypes. Psychological data (the Jesness Inventory) showed that Manipulator subjects had become less autistic, less alienated, and more aware of interpersonal relationships during their stay than had their control counterparts. Cultural Conformist and Neurotic Acting-out subjects had become less aggressive, less alienated, and more responsible than the comparable controls (Jesness, 1968, pp. 313; 1971a, pp. 45–46).

The experimental program also had an impact on management problems. Reports of serious behavior incidents and the use of detention facilities declined in the experimental units. In the Neurotic Anxious and Immature Conformist lodges the reduction of reports of rule infractions was especially dramatic (Jesness, 1971a, pp. 45). Thus the introduction of new treatment strategies apparently gave staff more flexibility and additional options in dealing with behavior problems.

On parole outcome, the standard measure of program effectiveness, there was no difference between experimental and control groups, either as a whole or broken down by I-level subtype. At 15-months parole exposure 54% of both groups had in some way violated the conditions of their parole, and at 24-months exposure 62% of all subjects had been returned to an institution. Jesness (1971a) concludes that any behavior change achieved within an institution must be maintained and supported by community programs.

The Preston study pointed to the need to develop explicit and integrated treatment strategies for juvenile delinquents of various types. Two innovative unit programs at Preston were successful enough that a more rigorous testing of these strategies was suggested. One unit used a token economy and the other a transactional analysis program. These two strategies were selected for further testing in the Youth Center study.

The Youth Center study took place at the Karl Holton and O. H. Close California Youth Authority (CYA) training schools in Stockton. The two institutions were similar in physical design, organizational structure, and staffing patterns. Both were meant to house 400 youths in eight 50-bed living halls.

Prior to the start of the Jesness study both Holton and Close were treatment-oriented institutions in terms of the treatment–custody classification system of Street et al. (1966). Staff attempted to rehabilitate delinquents by improving the boys' interpersonal behavior and self-concepts, and by increasing their ability to think and act realistically. Large and small group counseling was used. The large group sessions were community meetings mainly devoted to management problems, whereas the small group sessions tended to be loosely structured rap sessions. The boys participated in a wide range of educational and recreational activities. Some interaction with the outside community was arranged via trial furloughs, day passes, and group trips (see Campos, 1967; Jesness et al., 1972).

Random assignment procedures were started at the CYA Northern Reception and Guidance Center one year prior to the start of the treatment project, so that comparable populations would be in residence at the two schools when the project began. Boys in the 15- to 17-year-old range who were assigned to Stockton by the CYA during a 2½–year period from August 1968 to March 1971 were considered as experimental subjects and randomly assigned to either Holton or Close. A pool of 1130 eligible subjects was assigned to the two schools by the CYA. Of the subjects randomly assigned to Close, 460 were available for pre- and posttesting, and of the subjects assigned to Holton, 444 were available for pre- and posttesting.

The effects of the two treatment programs were measured by parole outcome and several "in-house" measures (i.e., personality and behavioral changes). Academic progress was measured by general reading and arithmetic tests. Two personality tests, the Jesness Inventory and the Loevinger Sentence Completion Test, were administered to each subject shortly after entering and shortly before leaving the institution. The Jesness Inventory is a personality and attitude test designed to discriminate between delinquent or disturbed, and nondelinquent children; its 155 true–false questions yield scores on 11 scales, including one scale called Asocial Index, which is related to delinquency proneness (Jesness, 1966). The Loevinger Sentence Completion Test consists of 36 open-ended sentences which subjects complete as they see fit. A revised 15-item Short Form of the test developed by the Jesness project was used at the Youth Center (see Jesness et al., 1972, p. 45; Loevinger, 1970).

Behavior within the institution was measured by the frequency of written reports of serious incidents of misbehavior and the use of detention, and by the Behavior Check List (BCL). The BCL consists of 80 statements describing nonintellectual social behaviors in very precise language. An observer rates a person on each item on a scale from 1 to 5, depending on the frequency with which the behavior is observed. The 80 items are scored on 14 scales developed through a factor analysis as described by Jesness (1971b). The BCL was filled out by three staff members for the observer form of the scale and by each resident describing himself for the self-appraisal form. Both forms were filled out on two occasions, shortly after the boy arrived and shortly before he left.

Residents' attitudes toward the schools and staff were tapped just before they left by competence and likeability ratings of staff members, and by the Post-Opinion Poll (POP). The POP consists of 42 items asking about prior delinquency, attitudes toward school and home environments, and self-concepts. Finally, the CIES was used as a measure of the actual social environment developed within the two schools.

The Holton Behavior Modification Program.   Behavior modification refers to the utilization of environmental contingencies in a planned way to alter a person's responses to given stimuli. Modification strategies used at Holton included systematic desensitization, extinction of undesirable responses, training in assertiveness, counterconditioning, and conditioning of avoidance responses. The most basic technique was positive reinforcement of desired responses to increase the frequency of those responses.

The fundamental mechanisms of positive reinforcement at Holton were a token economy and a parallel parole-contingent point system. Boys earned Behavior Change Units (BCUs) for exhibiting three types of desired behavior:

1. Convenience behaviors (i.e., neatness, courtesy, following rules). These were behaviors required for efficient and orderly operation of the school and were related to successful parole adjustment in that they are necessary to success in any school or work situation.

2. Academic behaviors (i.e., educational achievements as measured by successful completion of courses).

3. Correction of critical behavior deficiencies, defined as behavior deficiencies most likely to increase the probability of success or failure on parole.

To be recommended for parole, boys had to earn a total number of BCUs set at the time of admission. Of this total, 45% had to be earned by convenience behaviors, 28% by academic behaviors, and 27% by correction of critical behavior deficiencies. The great emphasis on convenience behaviors ensured efficient and orderly operation of the living halls. The three-part BCU goal also required residents to demonstrate satisfactory progress in three distinct aspects of the institutional program. For each BCU earned, a boy received a Holton dollar, which could be used to purchase immediate reinforcements (e.g., use of a lounge, a private sleeping room, snacks, entrance to movies, the opportunity to go on a field trip outside the institution).

The formal reinforcements were supplemented by social reinforcements, such as verbal approval from staff, and bonus money in Holton dollars dispensed by staff to reinforce behaviors deemed especially critical. Two punishments were used: fines on the boy's Holton dollar balance (but not applied to BCUs accumulated toward release) and deprivation schedules prohibiting participation in certain events or access to certain positive reinforcers such as snacks or use of lounges. Staff also tried to develop something in between positive reinforcement and punishment, a period of no reinforcement of any kind. This was done by setting up "time-out" areas, which were bland, well-lighted rooms containing no furniture except perhaps a chair, and no reading material or recreational equipment. The rooms were used to stop all positive reinforcement for short periods without resorting to punishment. No formal detention facilities were available at Holton; the time-out areas were staff's only way of removing a boy from the living hall other than transferring him permanently to another institution.

Critical behavior deficiencies were identified by the Jesness Behavior

Check List, in which 80 clearly defined behaviors are grouped into 14 categories. Some of the categories had been found to be predictive of parole success or failure in an earlier study (Jesness, 1968). Modification of these deficiencies was attempted through contingency management. Contingency management is a motivational technique for increasing the probability that a person will exhibit a desired behavior by making his high-priority, high-probability behaviors contingent on satisfying staff objectives. That is, a boy did something staff wanted him to do in return for something he wanted and staff had control over.

Contingency management operated through the institution of formal contracts between subjects and staff. Contracts described target behaviors, a method for identifying the achievement of the target and the reinforcement to be given on completion of the contract. A staff member had to secure the written agreement of a boy for each contract. A sample packet of 100 contracts was written up to aid staff in the contracting process. The contracts covered the same ground as the Behavior Check List, plus such additional areas as obesity and drug use. Contracts in the package were arranged hierarchically in incremental steps, which gradually led to complete correction of a deficiency.

The following case study (adapted from Jesness et al., 1972, pp. 222–227) demonstrates the techniques of contracting with a boy and gradually shaping his responses in the desired directions. George, a black 17 year old in the eleventh grade of an inner-city high school, was committed to the Youth Authority following conviction for assault with a deadly weapon. George had been involved in a racial incident at his high school which turned into a riot after he shot another youth in the arm with a pistol. He had had six previous encounters with the judicial system, having been charged with five burglaries and one assault.

Psychological and psychiatric reports showed no marked disorders. Intelligence tests placed George on the borderline between dull and normal, and academic achievement tests revealed very poor reading and arithmetic abilities. Staff observers at Holton rated George's behavior at the school as deficient on three factors of the Behavior Check List: Depression, Alienation, and Anxiety. Specific items needing improvement included:

Seldom talks to counselor about himself.
Doesn't seek conversations with adults.
Withdraws or isolates himself from others.
Appears nervous, anxious, or tense.
Does not contribute in meetings or discussions.
Speech is difficult to understand.

George also rated himself very low on these items.

Thus his behavior within the institution was nonobtrusive and retiring. He simply wanted to be left alone to "do his time." His counselor set five goals for George's program at Holton. The goals included increasing George's rate and quality of verbal behavior with staff, increasing his rate of approaching adults, decreasing his anxiety responses to persons in authority, increasing his assertiveness with adults and peers, and increasing his approach behaviors toward peers of other ethnic backgrounds.

Several contracts were written to shape behaviors related to the first three goals. The first contracts dealt with speaking to staff members when he first saw them each day and writing down each situation in which he had difficulty dealing with adults. Later contracts required him to make a specified number of contributions in group meetings; first, contributions agreeing with the majority opinion, then contracts requiring him to take an opposing stand.

To reduce George's anxiety in dealing with adults, he was asked to describe situations in which he became anxious. After instruction in deep muscle relaxation, he was asked to practice relaxation in the situations he described as anxiety provoking. When he subsequently reported experiencing less anxiety in contacts with both adults and peers, George was given the job of hall manager, which required him to have many daily contacts with staff and residents.

George was paroled after a 9-month stay at Holton. His early release was a result of excellent performance in the Holton program, both in the living hall and in the academic program, where he earned 27 high school credits and made substantial gains in reading and arithmetic. Just before release, George was rated as having improved more than 1 standard deviation on 11 of the 14 BCL factors. He was rated as more independent, having greater rapport with peers and adults, and being less anxious. After 158 days on parole, there had been no reports of delinquent behavior.

The O.H. Close Transactional Analysis Program.   The theory of transactional analysis assumes that people are capable of experiencing alternative ego states representing various life stages. Three ego states are emphasized in therapy: the Child, the Parent, and the Adult. The Child ego state is characterized by reactions typical of a little girl or boy. The Parent ego state resembles an actual or imagined parent's responses to a situation. The Adult ego state is inferred from an objective and autonomous appraisal of a situation. The concept of autonomy states that individuals are capable of choosing among the three ego states, which implies that individuals have a variety of possible responses to a given life situation. The goal of transactional analysis is to make individuals aware of these alternatives and to help them realize a nondestructive and nondelinquent alternative to their present life style.

The interaction of persons in a social situation can be analyzed in terms of transactions between ego states. One person may choose a childish response to the parental-sounding comment of another person. Such an interaction would be called a Parent–Child transaction. A fixed set of transactions is called a "game" if it meets the following criteria: the set frequently occurs in common social situations, it involves two or more ego states, and it has repetitious, superficially plausible moves with a concealed motivation or snare that results in a payoff of some kind to one of the players. The payoff may seem to be positive or negative, and the game need not be fun or enjoyable. In fact, most games are destructive to the persons involved (e.g., see Berne, 1964, pp. 48–49).

Soon after a boy entered O. H. Close he was interviewed by a social worker or youth counselor, to secure information about the boy's life script and his general expectations on entering the institution. The life script concept is that of a broad pattern of behavior or repetitious life plan, which in the case of a delinquent frequently appears to doom him to continued failure and delinquency. The interviewer also sought information about the boy's desire to change his behavior. At the conclusion of the interview, a summary of the boy's life script was written up, and staff on the living hall used this report in devising an individualized treatment program for the boy.

Life scripts were analyzed at Close in small group counseling meetings in which the therapist tried to make each subject aware of the chain of transactions, the ego states involved in each transaction, the games being played, and the possible effects of calling on alternative ego states at each stage of the script. Role playing was one of the primary therapeutic techniques. Members of the therapy group assumed the roles of family members or friends involved in a boy's life script, and the boy thus revealed his games to the group and had a chance to experiment with new ego states and game-free sets of transactions.

When an alternative life script became apparent to a boy, he made a contract with the therapist to try to implement it. The contract included a statement of the new script, which the boy himself had to compose, and a specification of the ways in which progress toward it could be observed within the institution. The choice of appropriate new goals was up to the boy; however, progress toward them had to be observable within the institution. Also, the goals had to be socially accept-able, nondelinquent goals—not, for example, learning to be a better pickpocket!

The following case study (adapted from Jesness et al., 1972, pp. 216–220) demonstrates the analysis of games and the formulation of new life scripts in life script interviews and counseling sessions at Close. Art, who was white and nearly 18, was classified as an I₄. Situational Emo-tional subtype. His extensive police record included petty theft, malicious mischief, possession of marijuana, incorrigibility, intoxication, and drug abuse.

During his life script interview, Art said that he had been taught by his parents that life is mostly hard work and that the best way to live is to keep a tight rein on the Child's bad drives by stern, moralistic Parent controls. Art thought that he was essentially bad, and he only occasionally felt happy. Thus he began to use drugs to quiet the preach-ing Parent in his head, but this behavior promoted guilt, leading to more drug use. The vicious circle had ended in hospitalization and a resolution to stop using drugs and hurting his parents. Art broke this promise, however, and ended up at Close, more guilty and moralistic than before. He stated intentions of controlling his weak will by setting and working toward firm educational and vocational goals.

In the first few group sessions, Art used transactional analysis princi-ples to reinforce his Parent moralizing. The therapist attempted to show Art other possible options, by asking, for example, what the youth really liked to do when he reported feeling depressed. In session 14 Art said he had decided to give up drugs but that it would be hard work. The therapist suggested that he was giving the same old Parent message of "Work hard but don't enjoy yourself." Art learned that he could bypass his Parent and decide to get "high on life" rather than drugs.

After 16 sessions Art went home on emergency furlough because his mother was seriously ill with cancer. He returned to Close for a few days, but his mother died, and he went home again for the funeral. Art returned to Close very guilt-stricken and withdrawn. His therapist tried to make him aware of the possibility of saying goodby to his mother and of dropping his guilt feelings, since there was nothing he could do to change the fact of his mother's death. In a subsequent counseling session, Art felt bad because he could never prove to his mother that he could succeed. The therapist asked him about his chances to prove to himself that he could succeed. In session 20 Art described his proce-dures for getting and holding a job to the group. It was a very Adult presentation, not embellished with Art's usual "shoulds" and "you have tos." In the next session Art continued his use of the Adult ego state by asking the therapist for advice about the possibility of living with his older sister after release.

Staff on Art's hall agreed that his decision to stop using drugs may have been made before coming to Close but that he was headed for a Parent-dominated and not very enjoyable life. At Close Art learned that he had options other than living as a constantly moralizing Parent, and he decided to create his own happiness without drugs. Staff speculated that his original life script called for a fall, a conversion, then a zealot's life, saving others on the way down. They felt that his new life script offered better chances of success than the zealot role. Art apparently made a successful adjustment to life outside. After 350 days on parole, there were no reports of drug use or other delinquent activity.

The Social Climates at Holton and Close

Contrasting Treatment Milieus. The CIES was first administered at Holton and Close when the schools were quite new. The Jesness project had not yet reached the operational phase in which staff were using the two treatment strategies in treating residents. The CIES profiles of the two schools were essentially identical at this time, both for the residents and the staff. Both schools placed moderately high emphasis on the Relationship dimensions of Involvement and Expressiveness, on the Treatment Program dimensions of Autonomy and Personal Problem Orientation, and on the System Maintenance dimension of Clarity. The remaining dimensions (Support, Practical Orientation, Order and Organization, and Staff Control) received average or below-average emphasis. Staff at both schools were more positive than residents, as is usually the case.

Two years later, during the middle of the active operational phase of the Jesness project the CIES was again administered on all living halls at both schools. Although virtually no change in social climate had taken place at Close, residents reported that the emphasis on almost all dimensions had dropped at Holton. Staff at Holton thought that the climate at Holton was nearly unchanged. Thus two schools, identical in physical plant and identical in the demographic characteristics of residents, developed distinctly different treatment strategies over a 2-year period. Essentially no changes in social climate were found at Close over this period, whereas Holton became less positively perceived by its residents.

Figure 6.1 compares residents' perceptions of the social climates at Holton and Close, for the second administration of the CIES. The Close residents are clearly more positive about their school's climate than the Holton residents are about theirs. Close residents are at least 1 raw score point higher on five of the nine subscales. They report higher emphasis on all three Relationship dimensions (especially Involvement), on all Treatment Program dimensions, and on two of the System Maintenance dimensions. On the remaining dimension of Staff Control, Holton residents report a slightly higher score. There are three similarities in the two profiles. Practical Orientation is the most strongly emphasized dimension at both schools. Order and Organization receives the least emphasis at both schools, and Staff Control is quite strongly emphasized at both.

Figure 6.2 shows the perceptions of staff at Holton and Close at the second testing. Staff are in general quite positive about the social milieus they work in. However, staff agree with residents that the Holton milieu places less emphasis on the CIES dimensions. The differences between schools are smaller on some subscales than in the resident sample, but staff at Holton report a lower emphasis on every subscale. Whereas residents at the two schools felt that Practical Orientation was clearly less

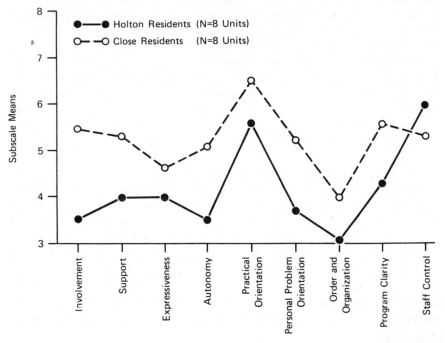

Figure 6.1   CIES Form R profiles for residents at Karl Holton and O. H. Close (second testing).

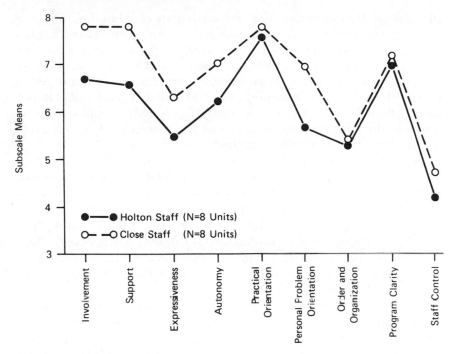

Figure 6.2   CIES Form R profiles for staff at Karl Holton and O. H. Close (second testing).

emphasized at Holton, staff reported that the difference was very small. Residents saw fairly large differences between schools on all three System Maintenance dimensions, but staff saw much less difference between schools on these dimensions.

   In summary, the Close milieu featured moderate emphasis on the Relationship dimensions. Involvement of residents in the day-to-day operation of the program, giving of support to residents by staff and other residents, and (to a lesser extent) allowing residents to freely express their emotions and feelings, were emphasized at Close. The independence and freedom of residents within the program were moderately emphasized, as was a concern with understanding the personal problems of residents. Planning ahead and preparing residents vocationally and academically for the postrelease period were heavily stressed. The orderliness and neatness of the living hall was not a strong concern. The clarity of rules and routines was moderately emphasized, and staff control of resident activities was emphasized.
   Holton, on the other hand, placed little emphasis on the Relationship

dimensions. Residents were not very actively involved in their program, residents and staff gave little support and encouragement to each other, and residents were not encouraged to freely express their emotions and feelings. Independence of resident activities and insight into residents' personal problems were not emphasized. Planning ahead and getting prepared for the postrelease period were accorded a good deal of importance. Orderliness and neatness received very little emphasis, but the clarity of the daily routine and the rules was emphasized, as was strong staff control over residents' activities.

The differences between Holton and Close are illustrated by items to which Close residents answered "true" at least 15% more often than Holton residents: "Residents here really try to improve and get better" (Involvement), "Staff go out of their way to help residents" (Support), "Residents are encouraged to show their feelings" (Expressiveness), "Residents are expected to take leadership on the unit" (Autonomy), "Residents are encouraged to learn new ways of doing things" (Practical Orientation), and "Staff try to help residents understand themselves" (Personal Problem Orientation).

These clear-cut differences between the schools existed even though the background characteristics of the two resident populations were essentially identical. Jesness et al. (1972) found no significant differences between the two schools' residents on I-level, I-level subtype, age and racial distributions, first offenders versus readmissions, history and seriousness of drug involvement, and academic abilities as measured by reading comprehension, reading vocabulary, and arithmetic computation tests. The random assignment procedures were very effective in providing closely matched samples of residents at the two schools; therefore the milieu differences observed could not have been a function of the personal characteristics of the residents.

The more negatively perceived climate at Holton makes good sense in relation to the type of treatment program introduced. The pre-Jesness program, which emphasized small and large group counseling sessions, was changed to feature indirect controls and systematic manipulation of rewards to achieve desired resident behavior. Given the rather large size of the living halls, such a policy is likely to de-emphasize the Relationship dimensions and concentrate on overt behavior rather than understanding residents' personal problems. The Close CIES results are also reasonable consequences of the transactional analysis program. An existing therapeutic milieu orientation was only slightly modified by the introduction of a uniform, school-wide, and systematic treatment philosophy. Small and large group counseling sessions continued as before, but a new vocabulary was introduced.

The similarities between Holton and Close found on the Practical Orientation, Order and Organization, and Staff Control subscales point to very real similarities between the actual programs. Holton staff did not totally ignore internal feelings and personal problems of residents. Social reinforcers (compliments, extra snacks) were offered as rewards for exemplary resident behavior. Systematic desensitization techniques were taught to residents to give them a way to cope with feelings of tenseness and anger. Close staff made explicit behavior change contracts with their residents just as Holton staff did with their residents. The only difference between schools was the specific type of behavior included in the contracts. A resident's rate of smiling might be a change relevant to Holton staff, whereas at Close the same resident would be contracted with to increase the number of Adult interactions he held with his peers. These program similarities would lead one to expect only small differences between schools in some of the Relationship and Treatment Program dimensions. Both schools controlled and organized resident activities within the constraints of their respective treatment philosophies. Thus it is reasonable to find an emphasis on Order and Organization and Staff Control at both schools.

Contrasting Responses to Treatment. The social milieu differences were related to differential resident ratings of staff competence and likeability between schools. Residents were asked to rate their youth counselor, their living hall staff, and each of their teachers on a 7-point competence scale and a 6-point likeability scale. The ratings were positive overall, indicating that residents at both schools liked their counselors and teachers, and thought that the staff were performing their jobs well. However, Close residents were significantly more positive than Holton residents on both questions. Close residents were also more likely to describe their counselors as knowing a lot about their work, as feeling confident, as being positive and considerate, and as treating everyone fairly.

Sections of the POP substantiate the more positive milieu at O. H. Close. For example, 15% more of the Close residents described themselves as spending a considerable amount of time talking to staff, and 20% more felt that counselors knew and understood their feelings. Holton residents felt that their counselors were stricter, more demanding, and less likely to let them take part in making rules and plans in the living hall (differences significant at $p < .001$). These responses support the CIES findings that the Relationship dimensions were more heavily stressed at Close, whereas Staff Control received more emphasis at Holton. More of the Holton subjects reported having to work hard to get good grades or points. Jesness concludes that these responses supported the research staff's subjective impression that the more negative reaction of Holton residents was partly due to the greater pressure to perform, both in class and in the living hall.

Close residents were more likely to report that they liked their classes and their teachers, that their teachers were doing a good job, and that their teachers found something good to say about them. They were also less aware of an inmate subculture antithetical to staff goals. On questions about roughing up an unliked boy, finding friends similar to those chosen at home, playing it safe within the school, and not telling staff about everything that was going on, fewer Close residents responded affirmatively than did Holton residents.

On the posttest battery, residents at both schools were asked to select the 5 most helpful program components at their school from a list of 11. Jesness then rank-ordered the percentage of residents choosing each item, separately for each school. Close residents chose the following five items most frequently: small group counseling (90%), schoolwork (87%), individual counseling (79%), community meetings (42%), and the experience of living with other boys (38%). The five most frequently chosen components at Holton were schoolwork (92%), individual counseling (72%), the experience of living with other boys (41%), gym classes (39%), and small group meetings (37%). Clearly small group meetings and perhaps other group experiences played a much larger role in the Close than in the Holton program.

The Jesness Behavior Check List (BCL) was used as a measure of observable behavior change of the residents at the two schools. The BCL was completed by three staff members on two occasions for each resident at the two schools, as described previously. T-tests on the average BCL changes over time (posttest minus pretest) showed two significant differences between schools: Holton residents demonstrated greater decreases on Unobtrusiveness and on Anger Control. Since decreases on these scales are considered undesirable, Holton residents' behavior deteriorated more than that of Close residents on these two scales. On most of the remaining scales boys at both schools received slightly better posttest scores, but there was little differential effect between schools. The self-appraisal form of the BCL, filled out by each subject to describe himself, did not replicate the observer form findings. Only one scale significantly differentiated between schools. On Enthusiasm, Close residents rated themselves as having improved more than Holton residents.

The Jesness Inventory provided evidence that some I-level subtypes did better at Close, whereas others benefited more from the Holton program. Pre- and posttest changes on the Inventory showed more positive personality changes for Immature Conformist, Manipulator, Neurotic Acting-out, and Neurotic Anxious residents at Close, whereas Unsocialized Passive and Cultural Conformist residents displayed more positive changes at Holton. Overall significant differential changes were found on seven scales, and all these differences favored Close. The mean change scores decreased more at Close on Social Maladjustment, Value Orientation, Alienation, Withdrawal, and Social Anxiety, and greater increases were found at Close on Repression and Denial. The scoring of the Inventory is such that all seven changes are interpreted as positive personality changes for most subtypes.

The Loevinger Sentence Completion test provided no evidence of differential maturity level change between the two schools. The small difference between schools in the number of subjects advancing to a higher maturity level was not significant, nor was the slightly larger difference in the number of subjects shifting to a lower maturity level. Changes in reading and arithmetic test scores were similar in the two schools, although there was some evidence that middle maturity (I_3) boys did better at Close, whereas higher maturity (I_4) boys did better at Holton.

There were somewhat more rule violations, behavior incidents, fights, and residents sent to detention at Close. The latter finding may have been partly attributable to the "time-out" rooms on each living hall at Holton, whereas Close had a physically separate detention unit. Jesness et al. (1972) also suggest that different methods of limit-setting, differential reporting, and/or different procedures for handling behavioral problems may have influenced these results.

Parole failure rates (revocations of parole) were the only available data on the Youth Center subjects' adjustment after release. The two treatment programs were successful in reducing parole failure rates 10 to 15% below the rates of other comparable CYA training schools (see Jesness et al., 1972, p. 310). This substantial reduction may be at least partially due to parole agent and court discretion. In 1969 before the treatment programs were initiated at Holton and Close, the parole failure rate for 12-months parole exposure was 44.0% for Close and 42.3% for Holton. Residents released in 1970 comprised about half the sample of experimental subjects in the new treatment programs. At 12-months parole exposure these subjects showed failure rates of 31.4% at Close and 31.9% at Holton. These rates were prorated to account for the slight difference in age distributions between schools, since younger releasees are more likely to be returned to custody. Breakdown of releases by I-level subtype indicated no significant difference in rates between schools, although the I_2 Unsocialized Passive subtype may show a significant difference favoring Holton when the total cohort data are obtained. Thus no overall difference was found between the two schools on parole outcome.

Variations Within Schools: Amador and Humboldt Halls.   Differences among individual units within each school were fairly large. Not all units at Holton became more negatively perceived after behavior modification was introduced as the official treatment strategy. Some Close units were more positively perceived after the transactional analysis program was started, but some were not. One unit became more negatively perceiced and similar to the Holton profile at the second testing. This was Glenn Hall, which maintained a token economy program throughout the Jesness project, even though it was also involved in transactional analysis. Two O. H. Close units, Amador and Humboldt, are used as examples of the climate variations and the differential impact of living hall climates found within the Youth Center schools. It is important to note that even when staff are using a well-defined treatment strategy at an entire school, very large social climate variations exist among the individual living units in the institution.

Before the transactional analysis program started in Amador Hall, the social milieu was quite negatively perceived. Residents reported about average emphasis on Expressiveness, Autonomy, and Staff Control, and below-average emphasis on the remaining six dimensions. Figure 6.3 shows the CIES profiles of residents and staff at the second testing with the CIES in Amador, when the transactional analysis program was in full operation. Resident perceptions are dramatically higher than at the first testing, and staff perceptions are still higher than residents'. Residents reported well-above-average emphasis on every dimension except Staff Control. At the first testing, they had reported below-average emphasis on six dimensions. Staff reported an emphasis 1 to 2 standard deviations above residents on every dimension except Staff Control, on which they were about 1 standard deviation below residents.

The transactional analysis program had succeeded in getting residents actively and energetically involved in the day-to-day functioning of the program and in encouraging residents to be concerned with and to seek to understand their personal problems and feelings. This occurred in a context of above-average emphasis on giving support to other residents, openly expressing emotions and feelings, preparing and planning for the future, and orderly, neat, and clear organization and operation of the living hall. Staff control over resident activities was at an average level on this hall.

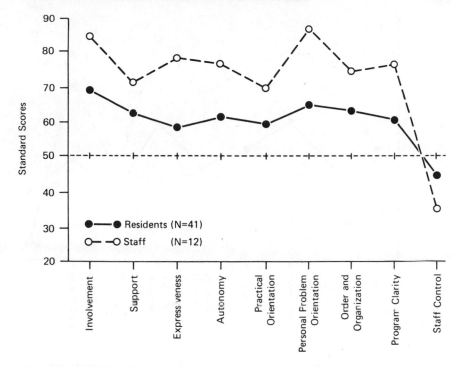

Figure 6.3   CIES Form R profiles for residents and staff in Amador Hall (second testing).

Not all the Close living halls were as successful as Amador in implementing the transactional analysis program. Humboldt started with a social climate within 1 standard deviation of the average on all the CIES subscales. Involvement, Autonomy, and Practical Orientation were slightly above average; the remaining subscales were at or slightly below average. Figure 6.4 is the second CIES profile for residents and staff on Humboldt Hall. Staff present quite a positive picture of their hall, nearly as positive as Amador staff. They report above-average emphasis on every subscale except Order and Organization and Staff Control.

Residents disagree markedly with staff perceptions of the social climate on Humboldt Hall. The extent of resident–staff disagreement exceeds 2 standard deviations on all the Relationship and Treatment Program dimensions, and it is fairly large on two of the three System Maintenance dimensions, as well. Humboldt residents see their hall as emphasizing the free and open expression of feelings and emotions, and as oriented toward understanding personal problems. Staff Control over resident activities is not strongly emphasized. On these three subscales Humboldt residents report emphases quite close to Amador residents.

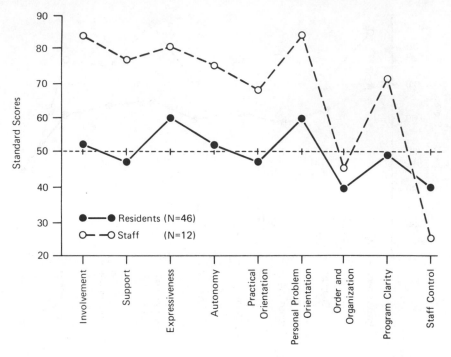

Figure 6.4 CIES Form R profiles for residents and staff in Humboldt Hall (second testing).

However, Humboldt residents report average or below-average emphasis (and they are 1 to 2 standard deviations below Amador residents) on the remaining subscales. Residents feel that they are only minimally involved in the program, that they are not particularly encouraged to take initiatives and leadership roles, that the hall is somewhat disorderly and not well kept up physically, and that there is little clarity and explicitness about program rules and routines.

The Utility of the CIES in Program Comparisons.   Several conclusions may be drawn regarding the utility of the CIES from the results of the Youth Center Research Project. First, the initiation of an innovative experimental program may or may not result in changes in the perceived climate of the program as rated by the residents and the line staff. Both Karl Holton and O. H. Close were treatment-oriented institutions prior to the initiation of the project. It is thus not surprising that the initiation of a compatible treatment strategy (transactional analysis) simply served to maintain the already existing social climate, whereas the initiation of a less compatible treatment strategy (behavior modification) resulted in more negative evaluations of the social climate by both residents and staff. This illustrates the well-known fact that unintended negative consequences may occur subsequent to the initiation of a new program.

Second, there may be large variations in the social climates of presumably similar treatment programs, even when they are using the "same" overall treatment strategy. Our previous work in this area has indicated that the individual program, not the overall institution, is the appropriate unit of analysis. Variations among programs within one institution are often as large as variations among programs in different institutions. This conclusion holds for both correctional and psychiatric programs (see Moos, 1974, Chapters 4 and 5).

Third, the social climate or milieu differences among different programs may develop even though the background characteristics of the residents in those programs are essentially identical: Holton and Close developed quite different social milieus, although they had essentially identical resident populations. Thus the social climate of the program is not necessarily a function of the types of resident in it. The type of resident in a program does not necessarily determine the social climate of that program. This conclusion is identical to that derived from studies of psychiatric programs; that is, psychiatric programs with essentially identical patient populations may develop very different treatment environments.

Fourth, the differences between the social milieus of the two schools were directly related to certain resident morale and satisfaction differences and, somewhat less, to certain differences in personality changes as measured by the Jesness Inventory. These differences generally indicate that the residents at O. H. Close were more satisfied with their program and showed more beneficial personality change than did the residents at Karl Holton. However, there were few if any behavioral differences between the residents at the two schools either in the program (as assessed by the BCL and by reading and arithmetic tests) or after the youths left the program (as assessed by parole revocation rates).

These results coincide exactly with those of earlier studies. For example, Jesness (1968) discovered that attitudes and behavior within an institution were not necessarily correlated. Daniels (1970) found a lack of relationship between symptom checklist and job performance criteria of psychiatric treatment outcome, and Smith (1968) noted a similar lack of relationship between self-assessed mood and supervisor-assessed performance criteria in Peace Corps volunteers. Furthermore, Ellsworth et al. (1968) have pointed out the surprising absence of relationship between measures of patient symptoms obtained in and out of hospital. These issues are discussed more fully in Chapter 7. The main conclusion is that the social climate correlates of morale, satisfaction, and attitudes may be more consistent than, and quite different from, the social climate correlates of more objective indices of such institutional outcomes as task performance and parole revocation.

Fifth, regular administration of a social climate scale and feedback of the results to staff may aid staff to control and develop their unit's climate in the desired directions. Holton might have maintained its more positive initial climate if staff had been given this type of information. More units at Close might thus have developed more positive treatment environments. The work reported in Chapter 4 suggests that feedback of CIES results can be an effective and practical aid in the development of a program.

Sixth, perceived climate scales provide a means of systematically describing institutional milieus, as well as a methdology for use in longitudinal and cross-sectional comparisons of milieus. The work done with the Ward Atmosphere Scale in these areas has been reviewed elsewhere (Moos, 1974; Chapters 4 and 5). In brief, the WAS has been used in a longitudinal comparison of an experimental intentional social systems treatment program, including a hospital-based, patient-operated employment service, with a more traditionally organized control program (Daniels, 1970). It has also been used to describe the treatment milieu of an innovative peer confrontation program dealing with alcoholic and drug addict patients (Van Stone and Gilbert, 1972), to investigate the effects of group therapy training on the social milieu of state hospital wards (Leviege, 1969), and to document the impact of instituting a token economy program with relatively chronic female patients (Gripp and Magaro, 1971).

Carte and Rohrbaugh (1971) used the CIES to describe the social climate at the Hillcrest institution for female delinquents in Oregon. Background information from residents and staff was correlated with the CIES subscales. In general, there were very few significant relationships; however, staff with a longer period of employment at Hillcrest perceived less emphasis on Order and Organization ($p < .05$), and residents who had been admitted to Hillcrest more than once rated the social environment lower on Autonomy ($p < .001$) and on Support ($p < .05$).

Carte and Rohrbaugh discussed the resident and staff CIES profiles. Practical Orientation and Order and Organization were emphasized more than the other dimensions, according to residents. Expressiveness, Autonomy, and Personal Problem Orientation received much less stress, and the remaining subscales of Involvement, Support, Clarity, and Control were accorded intermediate emphasis. Staff responses followed this general pattern closely, except that they were much more positive. The overall impression is that of an orderly program with a strong practical orientation, emphasizing planning for the future, learning new skills, and residents' involvement in program activities.

Katrin (1972) used the CIES as one measure of the effects of a staff training program. Fourteen female correctional officers, about one-third of the staff at a state correctional facility for women in Georgia, received 40 hours of training over a 4-month period. The training was designed to increase the ability of the officers to be supportive and helpful in their relationships with inmates. Training of just one-third of the staff resulted in two significant changes on the resident CIES responses— decreased emphasis on Order and Organization and on Clarity. Thus the new initiatives of staff resulted in some confusion and disorderliness in the eyes of residents. This can be expected in the short run from any program change that has not had an opportunity to "settle in."

Frank and Michel (1972) also used the CIES as a measure of the effects of program change. A new payroll system introduced at a federal reformatory involved giving inmates higher pay for more difficult and responsible jobs, and giving supervisors discretionary authority to vary payment according to the quality and/or quantity of output. Among the results of this change were reduced sick call rates, reduced number of requests for job changes, and reduced number of disciplinary reports for the inmates involved in the new system. The CIES was administered to all inmates at the institution before the change was made, and again 4 months later. Specific subscale scores are not reported, but Frank and Michel state that positive changes were found for most of the inmates who participated in the pay change. These changes might have been due to "halo effects." On the other hand, the actual implementation of a specific innovation is often associated with more general changes in the social milieu.

Wilkinson and Reppucci (1973) administered the CIES to residents and staff at a state training school for male delinquents. Residents were housed in small cottages holding 15 to 20 boys and staffed by 9 to 12 cottage parents, teachers, caseworkers, and parole officers. Two cottages in which token economy programs had been in operation for more than a year were compared with two cottages in which no systematic treatment philosophy was followed. Wilkinson and Reppucci administered a shortened 7-subscale version of the CIES. The token economy cottages were perceived more positively than the other two cottages by both residents and staff. In particular, residents of the token economy cottages reported higher emphasis on Spontaneity, Autonomy, Personal Problem Orientation, Order and Organization, and Clarity, which in the authors' words "tend(s) to dispel the notion that a token economy system eliminates individual freedom and makes 'automatons' of its participants" (p. 40).

Program comparisons and evaluations have also been carried out with the CIES in adult correctional institutions in Alaska (Hill, 1973) and Kentucky (Scully, 1973). Daniels (1973) used the CIES to plan and evaluate in-service training in the development and operation of correctional treatment programs. Jones (1974) and his associates have successfully used the CIES to compare open and closed prisons in the United Kingdom. Heal, Sinclair, and Troop (1973) have used the CIES as a basis from which to develop a social climate questionnaire for British correctional schools and community homes.

Finally, published information about the characteristics of correctional programs may or may not be congruent with the characteristics of these programs as they are perceived by their own residents and staff. The accuracy, thus the utility, of correctional program descriptions might be enhanced if information about the psychosocial characteristics and social climate of the program were systematically included. Some guidelines for the development of more accurate and complete program descriptions are presented in Chapter 10.

REFERENCES

Berne, E. *Games people play: The psychology of human relationships.* Grove Press, New York, 1964.

Campos, L. Developing eight "therapeutic communities" at a school for boys. *Youth Authority Quarterly,* **20:**20–31, 1967.

Carte, J. & Rohrbaugh, P. The social climate at Hillcrest: A study. Hillcrest School of Oregon, Oregon Division of Corrections, 1971.

Daniels, D. The in-vivo therapeutic community through task groups: The Dann Services program. Department of Psychiatry, Stanford University, Palo Alto, Calif., 1970.

Daniels, D. *The treatment team effectiveness development project,* Vol. I. Electromagnetic Systems Laboratories, Sunnyvale, Calif., 1973.

Ellsworth, R., Foster, L., Childers, B., Arthur, G., & Kroeker, D. Hospital and community adjustment as perceived by psychiatric patients, their families, and staff. *Journal of Consulting Clinical Psychological Monographs,* **32:**1–41, 1968.

Frank, C. & Michel, R. Inmate performance pay demonstration project. Federal Reformatory, El Reno, Okla. Task Force Report to U.S. Bureau of Prisons, 1972.

Gripp, R. & Magaro, P. A token economy program evaluation with untreated control ward comparisons. *Behavioral Research and Therapy,* **9:**137–139, 1971.

Heal, K., Sinclair, I., & Troop, J. Development of a social climate questionnaire for use in approved schools and community homes. *British Journal of Sociology,* **24:**222–235, 1973.

Hill, M. Inmate and staff perceptions of Alaskan correctional institutions. Systems and Research Unit, Alaska Division of Corrections, Anchorage, 1973.

Jesness, C. *The Fricot Ranch study.* Research Report No. 47, California Youth Authority, Sacramento, 1965.

Jesness, C. *The Jesness Inventory.* Consulting Psychologists Press, Palo Alto, Calif., 1966.

Jesness, C. *The Preston typology study.* Institute for the Study of Crime and Delinquency, Sacramento, 1968.

Jesness, C. The Preston typology study: An experiment with differential treatment in an institution. *Journal of Research in Crime and Delinquency,* **8**(1):38–52, 1971a.

Jesness, C. *The Jesness Behavior Checklist.* Consulting Psychologists Press, Palo Alto, Calif., 1971b.

Jesness, C., DeRisi, W., McCormick, P., & Wedge, R. *The Youth Center Research Project.* American Justice Institute and California Youth Authority, Sacramento, 1972.

Jones, H. A study of open and closed prisons. *Social Science Research Council Newsletter,* No. 23, 2–4, May 1974.

Katrin, S. The effects on women inmates of facilitation training provided correctional officers. Ph.D. dissertation, University of Georgia, Athens, 1972.

Leviege, V. Group relations: Group therapy with mentally ill offenders. M.A. thesis, Fresno State College, Fresno, Calif., 1969.

Loevinger, J. *Measuring ego development I & II.* Jossey-Bass, San Francisco, 1970.

Moos, R. *Evaluating treatment environments: A social ecological approach.* Wiley, New York, 1974.

Scully, C. Resident and staff perceptions of the prison environment: A psychosocial evaluation. Division of Research Statistics, Kentucky Department of Corrections, Frankfort, 1973.

Smith, M. B. Competence and socialization. In J. A. Clausen (Ed.), *Socialization and society.* Little, Brown, Boston, 1968.

Street, D., Vinter, R., & Perrow, C. *Organization for treatment: A comparative study of institutions to delinquency. Psychiatry,* **20:**373–385, 1957.

Sullivan, C., Grant, M., & Grant, J. The development of interpersonal maturity: Applications to delinquency. *Psychiatry,* **20:** 373–385, 1957.

Van Stone, W. & Gilbert, R. Peer confrontation groups: What, why and whether. *American Journal of Psychiatry,* **129:**583–589, 1972.

Warren, M. Interpersonal maturity level classification: Juvenile: Diagnosis and treatment of low, middle and high maturity delinquents. California Youth Authority, Sacramento, 1966.

Wilkinson, L. & Reppucci, N. Perceptions of social climate among participants in token economy and non-token economy cottages in a juvenile correctional institution. *American Journal of Community Psychology,* **1:**36–43, 1973.

CHAPTER SEVEN

The Impact of Correctional Programs: Morale, Personality, and Parole Performance

Introduction and Theoretical Rationale.   We treat social environments as active entities, directed with respect to their inhabitants. People have plans or personal agendas that impel their behavior in specific directions. Environments have programs that organize and shape the behavior of their inhabitants. Dimensions characterizing physical and social environments have important consequences for individual and group behavior (e.g., Barker, 1968; Maslow and Mintz, 1956; Porter and Lawler, 1965). The work reported here involves the assessment of the differential impact of the social climates of correctional programs. The underlying logic is similar to that used in studying psychiatric programs. In brief, the particular pattern of press in an environment creates a group atmosphere or social climate that must be considered as a real entity having demonstrable effects (Lewin, 1951). The individual members of a group tend to fall in line with the norms of that group. Thus an individual in a group that inhibits the expression of aggression will tend to express little aggression, whereas the same individual in a group that characteristically facilitates the expression of aggression will tend to express a high amount of aggression. The same logic holds for involvement, support, autonomy, and so on.

These notions were supported in three studies of psychiatric treatment milieus. Emphasis on the Relationship and Treatment Program dimensions (except for Anger and Aggression) was positively related to patient satisfaction, liking for staff, perceived opportunities for personal development, and initiatives in the areas of self-revealing and the expression of anger. The emphasis on Staff Control was negatively related to each of these variables. Patients' satisfaction with the program and their liking for other patients and for staff was a general reaction that could be tied to a variety of program elements. There are a number of alternative ways in which staff can change the social climate, and any of them can have the effect of increasing patients' liking for each other and for staff, thus the extent of patient–patient and patient–staff contact and mutual therapeutic influence.

In another study the emphasis on Anger and Aggression was shown to be negatively related to helping behavior. This supported the notion that some programs with active treatment milieus oriented toward emphasizing the open expression of anger might make patients more uncomfortable, thus resulting in a decrease in the amount of helping behavior. We viewed the findings as indicating the variables mediating between treatment environment and treatment outcome. For example, patient-perceived Practical Orientation was related to release rate in two independent studies of treatment outcome. Practical Orientation was also positively related to patient helping behavior in the areas of friendship and enhancement of self-esteem, and to staff helping behavior in the areas of friendship and directive teaching. We felt that these helping activities were related, in turn, to the rapid turnover rate in treatment programs with a high emphasis on Practical Orientation.

A study on community-based programs was performed in an attempt to replicate some of the above-mentioned relationships. The three Relationship dimensions were again highly related to general satisfaction, liking for staff, and personal development. When the Relationship dimensions are strongly emphasized, morale is high, and members feel more satisfied, like each other and the staff more, and are more hopeful about treatment. Emphasis on the Treatment Program dimensions of Autonomy, Practical Orientation, and Personal Problem Orientation is usually also positively related to these patient reactions. There was not a single example of significant negative correlation between the emphasis on these three Treatment Program dimensions and any of the foregoing reactions to treatment programs. The relationships between treatment environment and reactions to programs are least clear and consistent for the System Maintenance dimensions, although Order and Organization and Program Clarity are generally positively related, whereas Staff Control is generally negatively related, to satisfaction, liking for staff, and hopefulness about treatment.

Two studies linking treatment environment, as perceived by patients and staff, to objective indices of treatment outcome were also completed. Psychiatric programs with high dropout rates tend to have few social activities, little emphasis on involving patients in the program, and somewhat poor planning of patients' activities. Patients in these programs do not interact much with one another. They have a good deal of free time with little or no guidance. Staff discourage criticism from patients and are unwilling to act on patients' suggestions. Patients tend to gripe and criticize the staff, perhaps because the program is seen as poorly organized. Programs with high dropout rates are rather unfriendly; patients do not feel comfortable or at ease, and staff seem to be somewhat unhappy with the environment and with one another.

Programs with high release rates typically emphasize making plans for getting out of the hospital, for training patients for new kinds of jobs, and for making concrete plans before leaving. There is a fair amount of staff control, but staff are personally interested in the patients and tell them when they are making progress. There is relatively little emphasis on expressiveness; for example, patients rarely argue with one another, and they keep their disagreements to themselves. Neither patients nor staff see much support in these programs. However, even though the programs are practical and "unexpressive," they engender a certain pride in involvement in their members.

Programs that keep patients out in the community the longest emphasize the free and open expression of feelings, particularly angry feelings. Staff think it is healthy to argue, are seen arguing among themselves, and sometimes start arguments in group meetings. Patients are expected to share their personal problems and feelings with one another and with staff. This emphasis on personal problems and the open expression of anger occurs within a context that also emphasizes autonomy and independence, a practical orientation, order and organization, and a reasonable degree of staff control. For example, patients are transferred from the program if they do not obey the rules, but they are treated with respect by the staff and are encouraged to be independent. (See Moos, 1974, Chapters, 7, 8, and 12 for more details on these studies.)

Our studies in correctional environments represent an attempt to replicate and extend the finding just outlined. We investigated whether correctional programs that differed in social climate were also demonstrably different on four sets of dependent variables: (1) general resident morale, satisfaction, and reaction to the program; (2) initiatives that residents perceived themselves as taking to cope with and change the program environment; (3) personality and both self-reported and observer-related behavioral changes; and, (4) parole performance. It was hypothesized that programs emphasizing individual resident responsibility (e.g., Autonomy), general freedom of emotional expression (Expressiveness and Personal Problem Orientation), and high staff–resident and resident–resident interaction (Involvement and Support) would tend to have residents who were generally more satisfied, liked each other and the staff more, felt that the program was having a greater impact on them, and would tend to show more personality and behavioral changes.

Morale and Personal Growth.   Three independent samples of correctional programs were studied to investigate the relationship between social climate, morale, and personal development. The first sample of 16 units was picked to obtain a variety of diverse units in different types of correctional institutions. There were seven units from a training school for boys ranging in age from 16 to 20 years; four units from a training school for boys and young men ranging in age from 18 to 30 years, in which there was an extensive program of academic and vocational education; two units from a juvenile hall, one for males and one for females; and three boys' camps with extensive vocational programs for boys whose average age was 16 years.

The second sample included 14 generally similar types of correctional units. Five male units were sampled from two different juvenile hall programs for boys of approximately 15 years of age; one boys' ranch with an extensive educational program for youths about 15 years old was included; and there were eight units from a training school for boys approximately 13 to 15 years old. Since these samples both included programs located in different correctional institutions, there was the possibility of confounding interprogram and interinstitutional differences. Thus we selected a third sample of 15 correctional units, all located within two training schools for boys between the approximate ages of 14 and 17 years. These units were all physically similar and were also of similar size and staffing. Since most extraneous variables were controlled, we felt that this sample would provide a particularly stringent test of our hypotheses.

Residents and staff on all the units took the CIES and another short questionnaire designed to assess general reactions to the program. The latter questionnaire included six items asking residents and staff to rate their general satisfaction with the program (6-point scales), how much they liked the residents and the staff in the program, how nervous or tense they generally felt while in the program, and the extent to which they felt the program gave them a chance to test their abilities and develop their self-confidence (5-point scales).

Table 7.1 presents the correlations between the CIES subscales and the residents' reactions to the unit, averaged over the three samples. The general satisfaction and liking for residents items were combined because they were highly correlated. The abilities and self-confidence items were combined into one item labeled "personal development" for the same reason.

The overall results are quite clear-cut. As the emphasis on the three Relationship and the three Treatment Program dimensions increases, residents report that they like the staff more and that they have greater opportunities for personal development within the program. The same relationships hold for Clarity, but the reverse relationships hold for Staff Control. Thus as Staff Control increases, residents like the staff less and feel that they have less to gain from the program. There were no relationships between any of the CIES subscales and the variable of anxiety. General satisfaction increases as emphasis on the Relationship and Treatment Program dimensions increases, but the correlations are only of moderate magnitude.

The results for liking of staff, anxiety, and personal development were very similar across the three samples studied. The results for general

Table 7.1   Average Correlations over Programs Between CIES Subscales and Resident Reactions

Subscales	General Satisfaction	Like Staff	Anxiety	Personal Development
Involvement	.42	.56**	.06	.61**
Support	.41	.57**	−.14	.58**
Expressiveness	.27	.58**	−.05	.34
Autonomy	.38	.63***	−.01	.65***
Practical orientation	.28	.49*	.28	.63***
Personal Problem orientation	.43*	.67***	−.35	.48*
Order and organization	.32	.19	.01	.17
Clarity	.33	.50**	−.33	.57**
Staff control	−.38	−.67***	.10	−.53**

Note: with $N = 15$
  *$R.10 = .43$
 **$R.05 = .50$
***$R.01 = .62$

satisfaction, however, differed sharply in the three samples. There were only limited relationships between the CIES subscales and general satisfaction in the first two samples. The third sample of 15 programs, which presented the most stringent test of our hypotheses, showed highly significant relationships between several of the CIES subscales and satisfaction. These programs were the most treatment-oriented group of correctional units studied. Thus social climate may have only a moderate impact on residents' satisfaction and morale, except when the program is strongly relationship- and treatment-oriented. As would be expected, correctional residents generally show much lower levels of program satisfaction than do psychiatric patients.

The same relationships were computed for staff. All three Relationship dimensions, all three Treatment Program dimensions, and the System Maintenance dimensions of Order and Organization and Clarity were positively related to staff general satisfaction and staff feelings about the extent of personal growth they could attain in the program. The relationships were of moderate magnitude, and only those for Involvement and Support were statistically significant ($p < .05$). There were no significant or even generally consistent relationships between the CIES dimensions and either staff liking for other staff or staff anxiety. Thus the social climates of correctional programs may have somewhat different correlates for residents and staff. Residents' liking for staff is related to the social climate, but residents' general satisfaction is not. Staff members' general satisfaction is related to the social climate, whereas their liking for other staff is not. The social climate does relate to both residents' and staffs' feelings about the amount of personal growth they can attain in the program.

Coping and Adaptive Behavior.   Residents in the 16 correctional programs tested in the first sample were also administered the Resident Initiative Scale (RIS). Items in the RIS indicate initiatives residents can take in correctional programs. For each item residents are asked how often (i.e., always, often, sometimes, never) they act in a given way while in the program. Items in the scale are sensitive to differences among programs and relatively free of social desirability response set. The RIS was patterned after the Ward Initiative Scale (Form A) originally developed by Houts and Moos (1969) to measure the initiatives taken by patients on psychiatric programs.

Items from several sources were selected for inclusion in the RIS. Items from the CIES often suggested parallel items about resident initiatives. Interviews with residents and staff on a heterogeneous sample of correctional programs formed a major source of items. An initial 122-item questionnaire was constructed. All items referred to potential resident behaviors, and for each item residents were asked how often they acted that way while in the program. All items confusing to less educated residents were discarded, as were all items that were significantly correlated with the Crowne-Marlowe Social Desirability Scale. The remaining items were subjected to one-way analyses of variance to determine the degree to which they differentiated among the 16 programs. There were 57 items that discriminated at the $p < .20$ level; these were initially sorted into seven categories based on similar content and similarity to the CIES subscales. However, two of the subscales were dropped in subsequent analyses because of low internal consistency.

The remaining five subscales were labeled as follows: Affiliation (10 items), Self-Revealing (6 items), Aggression (7 items), Autonomy (15 items), and Submission (7 items). The item scores were summed into five subscale scores. One-way analyses of variance were calculated for each of the subscale scores, all of which discriminated significantly ($p < .05$) among the programs. An additional subscale intended to measure social desirability responses was constructed from items that correlated significantly with the Crowne-Marlowe Social Desirability Scale. Nine items were selected on the basis of high correlations with and similar content to the Crowne-Marlowe.

The items in the RIS are indicative of concrete initiatives residents can take in correctional programs. For example, Affiliation initiatives are inferred from items such as: "I try to become friends with other people on the unit," "If I am interested in a conversation I will join in and give my opinions," "I hang around with groups of residents on the unit." Self-Revealing initiatives are inferred from these items: "I try to share my personal problems with other residents," "I ask other people on the unit if they think I'm in bad shape," "I tell people on the unit what I'm thinking about." Aggressive initiatives are inferred from these items: "I gripe about the unit," "I try to get the staff to argue with each other," "I let off steam on the unit." Autonomy initiatives are inferred from items like: "I ask my counselor if he thinks I am improving," "I make suggestions to the staff," "I tell the staff what I want," "I say anything I want to my counselor." Finally, Submission initiatives are inferred from items like: "I try to talk about things that the staff think are important," and "I do things that the staff ask me to do, even if I don't like to."

Mean scores were obtained for residents on each of the 16 programs for each of the RIS subscales. Correlations were calculated between the 9 CIES subscales and the 5 RIS subscales over the 16 units. There were statistically significant ($p <$ .05) positive relationships between program social climate and resident initiatives. More specifically, the greater the emphasis on the Relationship and Treatment Program dimensions, the more Affiliation, Self-Revealing, Autonomy, and Submission initiatives were taken by the residents. The results were similar for Clarity, but they were in the reverse direction for Staff Control. There were no significant relationships between social climate and initiatives in the area of Aggression. (See Moos, 1970, for further details.)

Personality and Behavioral Change.   Residents in the Youth Center Research Project (see Chapter 6) were given the Jesness Inventory and a self-appraisal form of the Jesness Behavior Check List (BCL) shortly after the boy arrived (pretest) and shortly before he left (posttest). The observer form of the BCL was also filled out twice by three staff members for each boy. Does the social climate of the unit relate to the extent of change shown by the units' residents on the Jesness Inventory and the BCL subscales?

Jesness Inventory and BCL subscales on which mean pre–post changes were at least 5 standard score points (i.e., 0.5 standard deviation) were chosen for analysis. Only three of the Jesness Inventory subscales met this criterion at O. H. Close (Withdrawal, Social Anxiety, and Denial), and only one subscale (Social Anxiety) met it at Karl Holton (Jesness et al, 1972, p. 251). Three of the self-appraisal BCL subscales (Independence, Enthusiasm, and Calmness) met this criterion at Close, whereas none qualified at Holton (Jesness et al., 1972, p. 260). However, the following eight observer BCL subscales met this change criterion at both schools (Jesness et al., 1972, p. 268): Responsibility, Considerateness, Independence, Rapport, Enthusiasm, Sociability, Communication, and Insight.

Individual change scores were calculated for each of the residents at the two schools for these variables. Mean change scores for all the residents on each unit at the two schools were then calculated. Spearman rank-order correlation coefficients were computed between the unit mean CIES subscale scores and the resulting mean change scores, separately for the two schools. Table 7.2 shows the correlations for the three Jesness Inventory subscales for the seven O. H. Close units. The results indicate that boys on units high on the Relationship and Treatment Program dimensions (as perceived by staff) tended to improve more (i.e., their scores showed greater decreases from pre- to posttesting) on the dimensions of Withdrawal and Social Anxiety. The results were in the same direction for the CIES Clarity subscale, but were reversed for

Staff Control. There were no significant correlations between changes on the Denial subscale and the social climate of the unit. The significant correlations for Social Anxiety were not replicated for the eight Holton units.

Table 7.3 shows the Spearman rank-order correlations between the CIES subscales and the three relevant self-appraisal BCL mean change scores for the seven Close units. The results generally indicate that boys in units high on the three Relationship dimensions, the three Treatment Program dimensions, and the dimension of Clarity changed in more beneficial directions on the self-appraisal BCL dimensions of Independence and Calmness. The results were in the opposite direction for the System Maintenance dimension of Staff Control. On the other hand, there were no consistent relationships between the CIES subscales and changes on the BCL self-appraisal Enthusiasm subscale.

Spearman rank-order correlations were also computed between the CIES subscales and observer BCL mean change scores for the Responsibility, Considerateness, Independence, Rapport, Enthusiasm, Sociability, Communication, and Insight subscales. At O. H. Close there were significant $(p < .10)$ correlations between the Autonomy and Personal Problem Orientation subscales and the degree of positive change on Responsibility and Insight. In addition, there were significant relationships be-

Table 7.2   Rank-Order Correlations Between CIES Subscales and Jesness Inventory Mean Change Scores for O. H. Close Units $(N = 7)$

Subscales	Withdrawal	Social Anxiety	Denial
Involvement	.81**	.95**	−.01
Support	.52	.61*	.54
Expressiveness	.47	.64*	−.07
Autonomy	.63*	.89***	.00
Practical orientation	.32	.64*	.02
Personal problem orientation	.56*	.77**	−.41
Order and organization	.00	.25	.52
Clarity	.72**	.71**	.40
Staff control	−.67*	−.68**	−.31

*$p < .10$
**$p < .05$
***$p < .01$

Table 7.3   Rank-Order Correlations Between CIES Subscales and Self-Appraisal Behavior Check List Mean Change Scores for O. H. Close Units (N = 7)

Subscales	Independence	Enthusiasm	Calmness
Involvement	.96***	.36	.77**
Support	.75**	.04	.46
Expressiveness	.54	.14	.50
Autonomy	.68**	.25	.61*
Practical orientation	.43	.04	.36
Personal problem orientation	.47	.34	.59*
Order and organization	.32	−.36	−.11
Clarity	.86***	.32	.64*
Staff Control	−.79**	−.21	−.61*

$*p < .10$
$**p < .05$
$***p < .01$

tween the Personal Problem Orientation subscale and the degree of positive change on Rapport ($p < .10$), Enthusiasm ($p < .05$), Sociability ($p < .05$), and Communication ($p < .10$). There were no other significant correlations between any of the CIES subscales and any of the observer BCL mean change scores. The statistically significant correlations were not replicated at Karl Holton.

Thus the results support the conclusion that boys on units with more "positive" social climates showed more beneficial changes on certain Jesness Inventory and self-appraisal BCL dimensions. When the social climate emphasizes the three Relationship dimensions, the three Treatment Program dimensions, and Program Clarity, and de-emphasizes Staff Control, boys in the transactional analysis program showed greater decreases on two Jesness Inventory subscales: (1) Withdrawal–Depression, which measures dissatisfaction with self and others and the tendency toward isolation from others, and (2) Social Anxiety, which refers to perceived emotional discomfort associated with interpersonal relationships.

Boys on these units also showed greater increases on two self-appraisal BCL dimensions: (1) Independence, which characterizes people who attempt to cope with tasks and make decisions without undue reliance on others, and (2) Calmness, which is defined by the presence of self-confidence, composure, personal security, and high self-esteem.

These data present some additional evidence of the beneficial impact of certain social climates, at least within a dynamically and motivationally oriented therapeutic model (i.e., transactional analysis). On the other hand, both the Jesness Inventory and the self-appraisal BCL constitute self-report measures. The relationships between social climate and the observer BCL changes were less consistent, except for the CIES dimensions of Autonomy and Personal Problem Orientation. The emphasis on these two Treatment Program dimensions at O. H. Close was clearly related to positive change on several of the observer BCL dimensions. Thus there is some additional weak but supportive evidence to suggest that the Relationship and Treatment Program dimensions relate to beneficial personality and behavioral changes. The "in-house" personality and behavioral changes in the Youth Center Research Project were generally quite small. It is possible (though of course not necessary) that the relationships between unit social climate and personality and behavioral changes would have been more substantial if the overall changes had themselves been somewhat greater.

Parole Performance.   The evidence presented thus far supports the conclusion that the social environments of correctional programs have differential "in-house" correlates. Does program environment affect other indices of program outcome, such as postinstitutional recidivism? Carl Jesness kindly shared his Youth Center Research Project parole data with us to make it possible to carry out relevant analyses. Parole performance data were provided on 663 boys who had been paroled from the two schools.

The total number of months a boy was not in custody during the first 24 months after release was used in this analysis. This variable was chosen partly because it was a continuously distributed variable (in comparison with custody status, which is dichotomous) and because it seemed to be a differentiated criterion of program success. It also allows residual scores to be reported as the number of months a boy stays out of custody (i.e., remains in the community) more or less than predicted from his Base Expectancy score.

A parole Base Expectancy score—derived from a boy's race, age at release, and number of prior commitments—was also available for use in obtaining the number of months a boy was expected to remain in the community. The actual number of months he remained in the community was subtracted from the expected number of months to give a residual score. This score reflected the degree to which a boy performed better or worse than predicted from his initial background characteristics.

The residual scores were averaged for all residents in each of the seven units at O. H. Close and each of the eight units at Karl Holton. These mean residuals made it possible to rank-order the units in each school in terms of their relative standing on the "community tenure" criterion. There were differences on this criterion among the units at both Close and Holton, although these differences were not very substantial. The average number of months in the community for all boys was 17.96 (SD = 5.98). The best unit at Close kept boys in the community an average of 1.44 months longer than expected; whereas the worst unit had boys who were in the community about 1 month less than expected. The differences at Karl Holton were 1.8 months better than expected for the best unit and 1.6 months less than expected for the worst unit. These differences are not very large, although they do indicate that the differences between the best and worst units at each of the two schools are about 2 to 2.5 months per individual.

Are these differences on the "community tenure" criterion related to the social environment of the unit? The basic question is whether there are consistent characteristics of correctional milieus that correlate with the community tenure criterion. Each of the CIES items is answered either true or false. First, the percentage true was calculated for residents for each item for each of the units at Close and Holton. Next, each item was correlated with the community tenure outcome criterion. These were Spearman rank-order correlations in which the units in each school were rank-ordered on the outcome criterion and on the percentage of residents who answered the items in the true direction.

The Community Tenure Scale.   A substantial number of items displayed moderate to high correlations with the outcome criterion. There were 12 items that correlated .30 or above with community tenure at both schools. These 12 items constitute a Community Tenure Scale, which is highly related to unit mean residual "community tenure" scores. The rank-order correlation between the Community Tenure Scale mean and the mean residual was .96 for the seven Close units and .71 for the eight Holton units. Thus the Community Tenure Scale identifies characteristics of correctional programs which are highly related to the average success of their residents even after relevant initial background characteristics (as measured by parole Base Expectancy scores) have been taken into account.

Table 7.4   CIES Community Tenure Scale Items and Scoring Key

| | | Percentage of Residents Answering in Scored Direction | | | |
| | | Close | | Holton | |
Scored Direction		High Tenure Unit	Low Tenure Unit	High Tenure Unit	Low Tenure Unit
F	The staff very rarely punish residents by restricting them.	.95	.68	.88	.54
T	If one resident argues with another, he will get into trouble with the staff.	.71	.58	.69	.44
F	Residents can call staff by their first names.	.32	.30	.86	.63
T	Residents are expected to share their personal problems with each other.	.32	.14	.17	.16
T	Things are sometimes very disorganized around here.	.95	.73	.88	.86
T	Staff sometimes argue with each other.	.35	.19	.51	.27
F	The staff discourage talking about sex.	.78	.49	.79	.64
F	Staff have very little time to encourage residents.	.76	.59	.48	.35
F	Counselors have very little time to encourage residents.	.61	.61	.43	.32
F	Very few things around here ever get people excited.	.51	.38	.57	.35
F	Residents here really try to improve and get better.	.37	.31	.64	.38
F	Staff encourage group activities among residents.	.44	.30	.43	.36
	Mean	7.1	5.3	7.3	5.3

Table 7.4 gives the items on the Community Tenure Scale grouped by similar content areas. The scoring direction for each item is also given, as is the percentage of residents in the highest and lowest community tenure units at both Close and Holton who answered the item in the scored direction. As Table 7.4 shows, the mean Community Tenure Scale scores for residents for the highest community tenure units were 7.1 and 7.3 at Close and Holton, respectively; whereas it was 5.3 for the lowest community tenure units at both schools.

From Table 7.4 we can infer that programs with higher community tenure rates are seen by their residents as having somewhat stricter controls than programs with lower community tenure rates. Residents are more likely to feel that staff punish residents by restricting them. Residents also feel that if they argue with one another they are more likely to get into trouble with the staff. In addition, they feel less free to call staff by their first names. However, this emphasis on control is not so rigid and strict that openness and expressiveness are discouraged. For example, residents in programs with higher community tenure rates are more likely to feel that they are expected to share their personal problems with one another. They are more likely to agree that things are sometimes very disorganized in the program and that staff sometimes argue openly with one another. In addition, they feel that staff are less likely to discourage talking about sexual matters.

These residents also feel that there is somewhat more support and involvement in their program. They are more likely to feel that counselors and other staff have at least some time to encourage residents, and that certain things that happen in the program are involving. On the other hand, residents in the high community tenure programs are less likely to feel that they are really trying to improve and get better. They are also less likely to feel that staff encourage group activities among them. Thus high community tenure programs are characterized by moderate degree staff control, interpersonal communication, resident-staff openness, and staff support, and moderate emphasis on involvement.

In general, staff showed similar perceptions of the social climates of the units on the 12 Community Tenure Scale items, although the differences between the highest and lowest community tenure units were not quite as large. The mean Community Tenure Scale scores for staff for the highest community tenure units were 6.3 and 7.2, at Close and Holton, respectively; whereas it was 5.5 for the lowest community tenure units at both schools. The rank-order correlations between staff Community Tenure Scale means and the community tenure criterion were .43 and .36 at Close and Holton, respectively.

These results provide some evidence that the social environment of a correctional program may relate to parole performance over and above the expected relationship as predicted by Base Expectancy scores. This influence appears to be relatively small, even in the heavily treatment-oriented programs which existed at O. H. Close and Karl Holton.

In addition, Base Expectancy scores may not have adequately controlled for other personality, behavioral, or community factors differentiating among the boys in different units. It is possible that the boys in the best community tenure units should have been expected to do as well as they did on the basis of information not included in their Base Expectancy scores. On the other hand, the results did hold for both O. H. Close and Karl Holton, even though the two schools had undertaken quite different treatment regimes. The items in the Community Tenure Scale may have some generality across different types of treatment.

The results are clearly preliminary and in need of replication. But the findings, and the methodology used, are of some interest, especially since this represents the first attempt to systematically relate correctional environments to objective indices of correctional outcome.

Other Correctional Outcome Studies

Within-Program Effects. A host of previous studies have shown that "positive" or treatment-oriented correctional milieus are associated with more positive perceptions and attitudes of residents and staff, at least while they are in the program. The question of whether this makes any difference for residents once they leave the program is considerably more difficult and ambiguous.

For example, Street, Vinter, and Perrow (1966) examined six institutions for male delinquents which differed widely in goals—from primarily disciplinary to educational to treatment-centered (see Chapter 2). They found that residents in the treatment-oriented institutions had more positive perspectives toward the institution and staff than did residents in the obedience–conformity institutions. In general, the results observed in the educationally oriented institutions were closer to those of the treatment-oriented than those of the obedience–conformity organizations. Some of the specific differences were very close to those we found between correctional units high and low on the Relationship and Treatment Program dimensions. For example, the residents in the treatment-oriented institutions were more likely to respond positively to items such as: "Hang around with two or more boys," "Have two or more close friends here," "Want to see all or most inmates again after release," and "Would talk to other inmates about a personal problem."

Grusky (1959) has shown that inmate leaders in an experimental treatment-oriented prison camp were likely to receive higher adjustment ratings and to manifest more favorable attitudes toward the camp officials, the camp itself, and its program of treatment than were nonleaders. Grusky also found that inmate leaders were less likely to request transfers, to be transferred for disciplinary reasons, or to escape from the camp. He assumes that staff emphasis on custody promotes resident hostility, whereas their emphasis on treatment encourages resident cooperation. Grusky concluded

> that the social organization of a prison may be extensively influenced by a program of quasi-milieu treatment and thereby help establish the conditions determining the program's therapeutic effectiveness. . . . The goal of treatment in small custodial prisons may help to promote the informal co-optation of the inmates leaders in such a manner as to further the acceptance of the treatment goal. . . . When treatment is a dominant goal in a small prison a pattern of cooperation between the informal leaders and the authorities may be established which promotes rather than hinders treatment. (p. 67)

Wilson (1968) obtained generally similar results in a study of prison inmates' adaptations and relations with staff and fellow inmates. He related three types of inmate adaptation to two patterns of management. The patterns of management were classified in terms of how staff involved the inmates in decisions. Cooperative inmate adaptations occurred much more frequently under participative management practices, whereas opportunistic adaptations occurred more frequently under bureaucratic management practices. Even more important, the proportion of inmates showing an alienated type of adaptation was considerably lower in the participative than in the bureaucratic units. In addition, opportunistic and alienated types of adaptation increased with time spent in the bureaucratic units, whereas cooperative adaptations grew steadily with exposure to participative management. Inmates living under participative management were more likely to communicate with staff than were inmates in bureaucratic units.

Seckel (1965) conducted two studies to assess the institutional and postrelease impact of three counseling programs involving group treatment. He found clear indications that the treatments, especially large and small group counseling together, were accompanied by favorable changes in the attitudes of the boys and their adjustment within the institution. The counseled boys moved toward less delinquent attitudes on the Jesness Inventory subscales and received fewer disciplinary reports and more staff commendations. Subjective evaluations from staff indicated that the boys who experienced group treatment developed more benign social climates in which informal delinquent groupings became less frequent, tensions were diminished, and staff became more actively involved with specific problems of individual boys.

Jones (1964) collected data on resident compliance in two correctional programs for young delinquents. The public institution emphasized behavioral conformity, concern with neatness and routine, scheduling of resident activity, and an explicit system of rules and regulations. The private institution had an individualized approach to rehabilitation. A permissive environment was created, the expression of inner feelings was encouraged, and the behavior of residents was evaluated in terms of the meaning of the act for the therapeutic progress of the individual. Jones found that the boys at the private institution were more likely to feel that staff wanted them to change and that the changes pertained to more than mere conformity to institutional rules and routines.

The proportion of moral compliance (feeling that the staff member had a right to request the change) was greater in the private institution, whereas the percentage of calculative compliance (feeling that more was to be gained by simply overtly agreeing to change) was greater in the public institution. This is consistent with our finding that submission to the staff (as well as autonomy from the staff) increased with program emphasis on the CIES Relationship and Treatment Program dimensions. Jones' results also indicate that residents may be as much or more compliant with staff in treatment-oriented as in custodially oriented correctional programs.

It would have been extremely interesting to have actual CIES results from some of the studies just mentioned. However, from the data reported, it is likely that Street's treatment-oriented institutions, Grusky's treatment-oriented prison camp, Seckel's group counseling programs, and Jones' private institution were relatively high on the Relationship and Treatment Program dimensions and low on the Staff Control dimension. It is also likely that Wilson's participative management unit would have been similarly differentiated from his bureaucratic units. The results reported in Chapter 6 also strongly corroborate these findings. Residents and staff perceived the O. H. Close environment as emphasizing the Relationships and Treatment Program dimensions more than the Karl Holton environment. The Close residents were generally more satisfied, had better relationships with and liked the staff more, and had more positive attitudes toward the institution than did the Holton residents. Thus the results of these studies show a high degree of consistency.

Importantly, there is specific evidence in each study that resident background factors cannot account for the observed differences. The background characteristics of the residents in the Close and Holton schools were very closely matched. Wilson (1968) introduced background characteristics as control variables and found that "the relation between pattern of management and type of adaptation is unaffected" (p. 152). Street et al. performed similar analyses and concluded:

> To the extent that background variables have any relationship with perspectives beyond random associations, they seem to do so mostly in interaction with the institutional environment. Background attributes apparently take on their primary significance through the emphasis and interpretations staff personnel give to them and the staff behavior toward the inmate that follows from these perceptions. (p. 220)

The evidence that the organization or social climate of a correctional institution affects the residents in predictable ways over and above what would be expected from knowledge about their background characteristics is highly persuasive and consistent across studies.

Postinstitutional Outcome.   Unfortunately, there is very little evidence that institutional climate factors (or for that matter any other institutional characteristic) differentially affect more "objective" postinstitutional outcome indices such as parole performance and recidivism. The evidence for this conclusion is also highly consistent and persuasive. Sheldon and Eleanor Glueck (1930) made this point many years ago in their study of 500 criminal careers. They concluded that reformatories did not reform, nor did any of the current methods for dealing with criminals lead to demonstrable reduction in their antisocial conduct. Bailey (1966) reviewed 100 studies evaluating correctional outcomes and concluded that "on the basis of this sample of outcome reports with all of its limitations, evidence supporting the efficacy of correctional treatment is slight, inconsistent, and of questionable reliability" (p. 157).

More recently, Lerman (1968) has reviewed several evaluative studies of institutions for delinquents and has formulated very similar conclusions. He argues that residential programs for young delinquents are characterized by high rates of potential failure, regardless of the type of program. His conclusion is that treatment-oriented institutions do not increase the probability of parole success; however, they also do not decrease it. In any case, there is no demonstrable differential impact on community adjustment of different types of institutional program.

This conclusion is supported by follow-up data from many recent projects. Seckel (1965) found no difference in 30-month postrelease recidivism rates between his counseling and control programs. He also found no difference in 24-month recidivism rates between an experimental 5-month work-therapy program and a control program (Seckel, 1967). Knight (1970) found no difference in parole violation rates between a short-term therapeutic community treatment program and a control program. Jesness (1971) found no difference in 24-month parole violation rates between a set of I-level experimental programs and control programs. Indeed, 62% of the boys violated parole and were returned to an institution within 2 years of release. Jesness et al. (1972) report no difference in early parole violation rates for the residents in the O. H. Close versus those in the Karl Holton school (see Chapter 6). Kassebaum, Ward, and Wilner (1971) found no evidence that group counseling in a prison setting beneficially affected parole behavior.

These results are consistent with the results of controlled psychotherapy and counseling studies of young delinquents. Perhaps the classic study in this area is the Cambridge–Somerville, Massachusetts, youth study (Powers and Witmer, 1951) in which 650 boys were individually matched in pairs on variables such as age, IQ, school grade, and delinquency rating, and were randomly assigned to a treatment group or to an untreated control group. The two groups had almost identical rates of offenses and court appearances on follow-up. The differences that appeared were actually slightly in favor of the control group. There have been several other community-based delinquency prevention studies, and all have obtained similarly disappointing results (e.g., Craig and Furst, 1965; Hackler, 1966; Meyer, Borgatta, and Jones, 1965; Miller, 1962).

The most recent and best-designed study to obtain similar negative results is the Seattle–Atlantic Street Center Delinquency Prevention experiment conducted in Washington (Berleman, Seaberg, and Steinburn, 1972). Carefully matched experimental and control groups composed of central area junior high school boys were assessed on the frequency and severity of school disciplinary and police contacts. Intensive social services, which lasted for 1 to 2 years, were given to the experimental boys and their families. The boys and their families showed positive perceptions of the service and indicated that they would participate in a similar service again if offered.

However, the results failed to support the contention that the counseling and social services had any impact whatever in moderating the boys' acting-out behavior. As a matter of fact, some of the differences that were shown were in favor of the control group, prompting the authors to suggest that:

the inference can be drawn that the social service given the experimental
boys not only did not help but actually had a negative influence, or
enhanced the likelihood, that these boys would achieve acting-out levels
that they might not have attained had they remained untouched by the
service. (p. 342)

This experiment was conducted in a relatively high-delinquency, predom-
inantly black, ghetto area. No attempt was made to weaken friendship
group ties that might have reinforced acting-out behavior, since such
moves could have compromised the research design by "treating" some
of the boys in the control group who were, of course, friends of some
of the boys in the experimental group. This may have contributed to
the negative results. In any case, controlled correctional treatment outcome studies almost uniformly show little or no posttreatment differences between treated and control groups.

Program Outcome and the Social Milieu.   The findings regarding outcome in correctional programs are very similar to those derived from
controlled outcome studies of psychiatric treatment (e.g., Bergin, 1971).
It is reasonable to expect a program to affect the behavior of the
individuals who function within it. Why does it not seem to demonstrably affect the behavior of the same individuals once they leave it? As
has been pointed out elsewhere, people vary their behavior considerably
from setting to setting (Moos, 1969). For example, psychiatric patients
vary their behavior substantially from one psychiatric ward subsetting
to another. More important, Ellsworth et al. (1968) have shown that
there is very little relationship between staff-rated adjustment at the time
of hospital release and family-rated adjustment only three weeks later!
They argue that the belief that improvement or change is primarily
person-related (and therefore stable across situations), incorrectly
leads staff to assume that the residents who improve most in the institution will function better in the community. Since the community environment to which a delinquent must adapt is quite different from the
institutional or program setting, it may be unreasonable to expect a
significant relationship between institutional treatment and community
outcome.

Two recent studies of absconding or runaway behavior in correctional
institutions provide some within-institutional examples of the kinds of
analysis needed in relation to postinstitutional outcome (see also Chapter
8, pp. 195–199). Clarke and Martin (1971), who examined the personality characteristics of absconders and nonabsconders from approved

schools in the United Kingdom, found the personality characteristics of the two groups to be remarkably similar. They thus sought an explanation for their subjects' behavior in the environments of the schools. Measures of the environment were then related to absconding rates. The results indicated that absconding rates were high given one or more of the following conditions: for a short time after admissions and after holidays, on dark winter evenings, on particularly sunny or dull days within a given season, when absconding had not recently been punished by caning, among boys being admitted during busy periods and among boys exposed to other absconders early in their school careers. These environmental variables appear to affect absconding behavior in one of three ways: (1) a boy may be placed under stress, thus stimulated to abscond; (2) obvious opportunities for absconding may present themselves; (3) an instance of absconding may be positively rewarded both within the institution and outside it. Clarke and Martin's analysis supports the importance of various types of environmental factors.

Sinclair (1971) studied the characteristics of British probation hostels. He defined the failure rate of a hostel as the proportion of boys who left as the result of an absconding or an offense. The failure rates of 46 regimes (a regime was defined as the tenure of one warden in one hostel) varied enormously—from a low of 13.5% to a high of 78.1%. Sinclair found that these failure rates correlated highly with 1-year and 3-year reconviction rates and that the differences in failure rates among the regimes could not be explained either by the personal background characteristics or by the previous criminal histories of the boys. In fact Sinclair noted

> that 17 years' previous experience counted as little in comparison with the immediate impact of the hostel environment while the boys were in it. But the gratifying evidence of a hostel's ability to influence its present residents for good carries with it a less welcome corollary. If the effects of 17 years of family training can be modified almost overnight, how long can we expect the impact of one year's hostel training to last? It is not surprising that when boys have left the hostel it is not usually the differences in their past hostel environments that count, but the differences in the environments to which they go. (p. 78)

The basic conclusions to be derived from this and other similar work are: (1) that the social milieu is an important determinant of individual behavior, and (2) that individual background characteristics are relatively poor predictors of within-institutional behavior, such as running away or absconding. We also know that individual background characteristics and behavior or improvement within an institution do not adequately predict to postinstitutional behavior. For example, the correlation between Base Expectancy scores and the community tenure criterion for the 663 boys from Close and Holton used in the parole performance analysis above was a remarkably low .08! The inevitable conclusion is that the community settings in which released residents must function critically affect their postinstitutional behavior and outcome. The high recidivism rates of certain delinquents may simply occur because these residents are released to function in the same community and peer group settings in which they initially engaged in delinquent or criminal behavior. Recidivism may not mean that institutional correctional programs have failed: it may reflect the failure of the relevant social environments in the community.

The classical ecological studies of delinquency indicated that there were marked variations in the rate of juvenile delinquents and adult criminals among different areas in Chicago (Shaw et al., 1929). The rate of recidivism varied inversely with the distance from the center of the city. The delinquents living in areas of high delinquent rates were more likely to become recidivists. Furthermore, the recidivists from the high delinquent areas were more likely to appear in court three or more times than were recidivists from areas with low rates of delinquency (Shaw et al., 1929, pp. 198–204). These and other similar data indicate that indices of program outcome may be more dependent on the specific characteristics of the community settings in which a delinquent functions than on his background characteristics per se.

Toward a National Cooperative Outcome Study.   Our work relating treatment environment to treatment outcome in psychiatric programs led us to propose a national cooperative outcome study, the design of which is relevant for correctional program evaluations. In the first phase of the work, the program characteristics of a relatively large sample of correctional programs should be systematically assessed, to develop a typology of correctional programs; thus a representative sample of programs could be selected for more intensive outcome study.

Four categories of variables, representing the major methods by which program characteristics have been compared in industrial, educational, and psychiatric settings, are required in assessing program characteristics.

1. Information should be collected on structural characteristics of different programs (e.g., objective organizational variables such as size and staffing, program policy variables such as adult status, the degree to

which different modalities of rehabilitation are actually utilized in the program).

2. Information should also be collected on both resident and staff background characteristics. The kinds of resident background characteristic assessed should include personal history variables such as sex, age, ethnic background, marital status, previous institutionalization, and legal status. Educational and employment variables, such as highest educational level completed, present trade or profession, number months worked during the last 2 years should also be included.

Resident input characteristics are systematically assessed in most program evaluation studies, but staff input characteristics are usually neglected. Program characteristics may be determined as much by staff as by patient background variables. Information should thus be obtained on simple, objective staff background variables such as sex, age, education, previous employment history, and time worked in the program. The second method will identify the program characteristics in terms of the average background characteristics of the residents and staff who are in the programs. The general logic underlying the use of such variables in characterizing environments is briefly present elsewhere (Moos, 1973).

3. There should be a systematic assessment of the social atmosphere or climate of each program.

4. Detailed information about the specific treatment procedures and interventions which residents actually experience is also necessary. Information should be collected on the basic orientation of the program, the particular "problem" behaviors targeted for change, the relevance of these behaviors to the kinds of problem that brought residents to the program, the quality of contact with counselors and other staff, and so on.

Thus the overall assessment of program characteristics should include information on structural and organizational dimensions, on resident and staff background characteristics, on the social climates of the programs, and on actual treatment experiences. A typology of correctional programs could then be developed on the basis of the results of these assessments. This might be done by way of a procedure of hierarchical grouping similar to that used by Findikyan and Sells (1966) in developing a typology of university campus organizations. The procedure discussed in Chapter 5 to develop a typology of correctional programs based on the CIES could also be used. An overall systematic description of a broad range of correctional programs would result from this phase of the project.

Phase two of the study would involve the selection of a representative subsample of programs for an intensive study linking program characteristics to indices of program outcome. A subsample of somewhere between 25 and 30 programs might be selected for this more intensive study. The subsample should be as representative of the entire range of correctional programs as possible. These programs would be assessed on two occasions on the three categories of program descriptive variables discussed previously. Our earlier studies have indicated that there is relatively high stability over time on these three types of dimension. However, the second assessment of the intensively studied programs would be necessary to obtain information on the temporal stability of their program characteristics.

A minimum of 200 residents in each program should be studied more intensively, particularly with regard to residents' perceptions of the correctional program, to different indices of program outcome, to the community environments, and to the community services provided for residents. The residents would provide information about their individual background characteristics (e.g., educational level, previous employment history, previous drug usage). However, additional information about background variables should also be included. The two most relevant issues are motivational factors related to criminal behavior and the systematic description of the past community environments in which the resident has functioned. Various investigators have discussed motivational issues that may be related to involvement in a deviant subculture, to the attraction of counternormative and deviant behavior, and to the self-esteem and identity gains from peer group approval. Some attempt must be made to categorize these types of motivation and to assess their importance for individual residents. Different aspects of motivation for rehabilitation and change should be similarly assessed.

The residents should be followed for 24 months after discharge. Follow-up information would be obtained on outcome indices such as postinstitutional employment (e.g., proportion of days worked, absenteeism), income, various physical and mental symptoms (particularly anxiety, depression, and irritability), self-esteem, and type of living situation. Previous outcome studies have indicated that this information may be obtained with considerable completeness and accuracy (e.g., Ludwig, Levine, and Stark, 1970). Correctional studies have often used only various "delinquency" indices such as police arrests, parole revocation, and temporary detention, as outcome criteria. More positive outcome indices, such as employment and academic achievement, should also be included. These sets of criteria may or may not be related to each other.

Methods for assessing community environments are needed to identify the characteristics of the community situation to which the discharged resident must adapt. General community characteristics can be taken from census tract data, which have been shown to be highly related to the rate of social disruption such as narcotics violations, out-of-wedlock childbirths, school dropouts, and so on (Chein, 1966; Chein et al., 1964). The more specific immediately relevant social settings would be assessed by techniques that characterize the resident's family or living situation, his work situation, and the social groups to which he belongs. These three sets of environment represent the critical aspects of the resident's immediate social situation. The relevant Social Climate Scales could be utilized here (see Chapter 11).

This programmatic study should accomplish several important aims:

1. Individual background characteristics of residents could themselves be related to indices of program outcomes.

2. Overall program characteristics, and the specific characteristics of the rehabilitation programs individual residents have experienced, could also be related to indices of program outcome.

3. The individual's perception of the program climate could be related to program outcome criteria.

4. Information on the feasibility and utility of assessing community settings would be obtained.

5. Person–environment congruence could be assessed in several different ways (e.g., how closely do the individual resident background characteristics "fit" the resident's ideas about an ideal social climate).

The project could be a model outcome study systematically building on the strengths and weaknesses of past outcome studies in both psychiatric and correctional programs. The methodology described for characterizing programs and for relating a variety of different program characteristics, and the background characteristics of residents and staff, to different indices of outcome has not to our knowledge been previously utilized. In addition, measures of resident–environment congruence, and the characterization of community environments such as those of work groups and family or living situations, have not been included in previous outcome studies. The project would also meet some of the recent objections raised in relation to controlled outcome studies, particularly the lack of systematic information on the actual "treatments" characterizing different programs (Clarke and Cornish, 1972).

Identifying the environmental conditions in the community that facilitate success on probation or parole could have very important practical implications. The current tendency is to think of human behavior as an interaction between ecological or setting influences and personality traits in the individual. An important corollary of this notion is that environmental variables are alterable. If program outcome can be influenced through such alterations, a new source of therapeutic leverage becomes available. At a time when there is increased emphasis on keeping delinquents out of institutions and returning them to their communities, the identification of the psychosocial factors that favor successful adaptation in the community would be a valuable practical contribution.

Polak (1971a) has stated that the degree of similarity between the behavior of patients in psychiatric hospitals and the behavior of the same patients in the community might be taken as an indicator of the relevance of psychiatric hospitals to community settings. He reviews some evidence on this point and concludes that

> Psychiatric hospitals are basically irrelevant to the real world settings from which the patients come and to which they must return. It might even be speculated that good adjustment to psychiatric hospitals could be regarded as a predictor of unhealthy adjustment in the outside world. (p. 256)

Polak elsewhere (1971b) details concepts and techniques that are relevant to social systems intervention—that is, the application of therapeutic community principles to real life settings.

National cooperative studies are feasible and either have been or are being carried out in several areas, for example, chemotherapy studies conducted by the Veterans Administration, the Psychiatric Evaluation Project conducted by the Veterans Administration (Gurel, 1964), a proposed national outcome study including 40 psychiatric treatment programs in eight to ten VA hospitals (Ellsworth, 1973), and both the clinical drug trials and the multiple risk factor intervention trials sponsored by the National Heart Institute. Furthermore, an ecological orientation in behavior change studies has been suggested by Monroe (1964) with relation to drug treatment outcome and by Mausner (1973) with regard to cigarette smoking. Thus the logic and conditions for an ecologically oriented national cooperative correctional outcome study are quite favorable. Information derived from such a study may deter correctional officials from continuing to labor under certain erroneous assumptions. As Sinclair (1971) has pointed out

> Penology may be accepting a fallacy similar to that of the educational psychologists who believe that exercising the mind on Latin inevitably fitted it for yet more arduous intellectual tasks. It is no more certain that producing good behavior in an institution will insure good behavior outside. (p. 140)

REFERENCES

Bailey, W. Correctional outcome: An evaluation of 100 reports. *Journal of Criminal Law, Criminology and Police Science*, **57**:153–160, 1966.

Barker, R. *Ecological psychology: Concepts and methods for studying the environment of human behavior.* Stanford University Press, Stanford, Calif., 1968.

Bergin, A. E. The evaluation of therapeutic outcomes. In A. E. Bergin and S. L. Garfield (Eds.), *Handbook of psychotherapy and behavior change.* Wiley, New York, 1971.

Berleman, W., Seaberg, J., & Steinburn, T. The delinquency prevention experiment of the Seattle–Atlantic Street Center: A final evaluation. *Social Service Review*, **46**:323–346, 1972.

Chein, I. Psychological, social and epidemiological factors in drug addiction. In *Rehabilitating the narcotic addict*, Vocational Rehabilitation Administration, Government Printing Office, Washington, D.C., 1966, pp. 53–72.

Chein, I., Gerald, D., Lee, R., & Rosenfeld, E. *The road to H: Narcotics, delinquency and social policy.* Basic Books, New York, 1964.

Clarke, R. V. G. & Cornish, D. *The controlled trial in institutional research: Paradigm or pitfall for penal evaluators?* Her Majesty's Stationery Office, London, 1972.

Clarke, R. & Martin, D. *Absconding from approved schools.* Her Majesty's Stationery Office, London, 1971.

Craig, M. & Furst, P. What happens after treatment? A study of potentially delinquent boys. *Social Service Review*, **39**:165–171, 1965.

Ellsworth, R. Characteristics of psychiatric programs and their relationship to treatment effectiveness. VA Cooperative Studies Proposal, Veterans Administration Hospital, Salem, Va., 1973.

Ellsworth, R., Foster, L., Childers, G., Arthur, G., & Kroeker, D. Hospital and community adjustment as perceived by psychiatric patients, their families, and staff. *Journal of Consulting and Clinical Psychology Monograph*, **32**:No. 5, Part 2, 1968.

Findikyan, N. & Sells, S. Organizational structure and similarity of campus student organizations. *Organizational Behavior and Human Performance*, **1**:169–190, 1966.

Glueck, S. & Glueck, E. *500 criminal careers.* Knopf, New York, 1930.

Grusky, O. Organizational goals and the behavior of informal leaders. *American Review of Sociology*, **65**:59–67, 1959.

Gurel, L. Correlates of psychiatric hospital effectiveness. In L. Gurel (Ed.), *An assessment of psychiatric hospital effectiveness.* V.A. Psychiatric Evaluation Project, Intramural Report, 64–5, Washington, D.C., 1964.

Hackler, J. Boys, blisters and behavior: The impact of a work program in an urban central area. *Journal of Research in Crime and Delinquency*, **3**:155–164, 1966.

Houts, P. & Moos, R. The development of a Ward Initiative Scale for patients. *Journal of Clinical Psychology*, **25**:319–322, 1969.

Jesness, C. The Preston typology study: An experiment with differential treatment in an institution. *Journal of Research in Crime and Delinquency*, **8**:38–52, 1971.

Jesness, C., DeRisi, W., McCormick, P. & Wedge, R. *The Youth Center Research Project.* American Justice Institute and California Youth Authority, Sacramento, 1972.

Jones, J. The nature of compliance in correctional institutions for juvenile offenders. *Journal of Research in Crime and Delinquency*, **1**:83–95, 1964.

Kassebaum, G., Ward, D., & Wilner, D. *Prison treatment and parole survival: An empirical assessment.* Wiley, New York, 1971.

Knight, D. The Marshall program: Assessment of a short-term institutional treatment program. Part II: Amenability to confrontive peer-group treatment. Research Report No. 59, Department of the Youth Authority, State of California, Sacramento, 1970.

Lerman, P. Evaluative studies of institutions for delinquents. *Social Work*, **13**:55–64, 1968.

Lewin, K. Frontiers in group dynamics. In D. Cartwright (Ed.), *Field theory and social science*, Harper & Row, New York, 1951.

Ludwig, A., Levine, J., & Stark, L. *LSD and alcoholism: A clinical study of treatment efficacy.* Charles C. Thomas, Springfield, Ill., 1970.

Maslow, A. & Mintz, N. Effects of esthetic surroundings: 1: Initial effects of three esthetic conditions upon perceiving "energy" and "well-being" in faces. *Journal of Psychology*, **41**:247–254, 1956.

Mausner, B. An ecological view of cigarette smoking. *Journal of Abnormal Psychology*, **81**:115–126, 1973.

Meyer, H., Borgatta, E., & Jones, W. *Girls at Vocational High: An experiment in social work intervention.* Russell Sage Foundation, New York, 1965.

Miller, W. The impact of a "total-community" delinquency control project. *Social Problems*, **10**:181–191, 1962.

Monroe, J. An approach to drug addiction through the assessment of natural environments. In *Rehabilitating the narcotic addict.* Vocational Rehabilitation Administration, Government Printing Office, Washington, D.C., 1966, pp. 343–357.

Moos, R. Sources of variance in responses to questionnaires and in behavior. *Journal of Abnormal Psychology*, **74**:405–412, 1969.

Moos, R. Differential effects of the social climates of correctional institutions. *Journal of Research in Crime and Delinquency*, **7**:153–170, 1970.

Moos, R. Conceptualizations of human environments. *American Psychologist*, **28**:652–665, 1973.

Moos, R. *Evaluating treatment environments: A social ecological approach.* Wiley, New York, 1974.

Polak, P. The irrelevance of hospital treatment to the patient's social system. *Hospital and Community Psychiatry*, **22**:255–256, 1971a.

Polak, P. Social systems intervention. *Archives of General Psychiatry*, **25**:110–117, 1971b.

Porter, L. & Lawler, E. Properties of organization structure in relation to job attitudes and job behavior. *Psychological Bulletin*, **64**:23–51, 1965.

Powers, E. & Witmer, H. *An experiment in the prevention of delinquency: The Cambridge—Somerville youth study.* Columbia University Press, New York, 1951.

Seckel, J. Experiments in group counseling at two youth authority institutions. Department of the Youth Authority, Sacramento, 1965.

Seckel, J. The Fremont experiment: Assessment of residential treatment at a Youth Authority Reception Center. Research Report No. 50, Department of the Youth Authority, Sacramento, 1956.

Shaw, C., Zorbaugh, F., McKay, H., & Cottrell, L. *Delinquency areas.* University of Chicago Press, Chicago, 1929.

Sinclair, I. *Hostels for probationers.* Her Majesty's Stationery Office, London, 1971.

Street, D., Vinter, R., & Perrow, C. *Organization for treatment: A comparative study of institutions for delinquents.* Free Press, New York, 1966.

Wilson, T. Patterns of management and adaptations to organizational roles: A study of prison inmates. *American Journal of Sociology*, **74**:146–157, 1968.

CHAPTER EIGHT

The Impact of Correctional Programs: Absconding

MARY M. CHASE

Since its inception in 1960, the New York State Division for Youth (DFY) has established and operated a number of open, community-based residential programs for the treatment of delinquent and predelinquent adolescents aged 15 through 17 years (Luger, 1969). Annual follow-up statistics for a 2-year period after release show that 60% of the youths discharged from these facilities are not arrested after leaving the program and 90% do not have to be reinstitutionalized. A major function of the division's Research Department is to undertake intensive analyses that will explain the program process by which different outcomes of success and failure are achieved. The research discussed in this chapter is one such analysis of 395 males who were referred to 9 DFY programs during 1971. In particular, it examines how each youth's personal characteristics and perception of the program environment related to his successful or unsuccessful completion of the treatment and, later, to his postrelease adjustment.

DFY Programs and Philosophy.   Three major assumptions or operating beliefs underlie the DFY programs. First is the belief that the state's delinquency programs must be diversified and must provide some alternatives between the two extremes of closed, total institutions and probation. To help fill this huge gap, the division decided to experiment with three different kinds of treatment program. One is the conservation or work *Camp* designed to accommodate 60 youths and located in rural although not geographically isolated areas of the state. The Camp program consists of a supervised work experience in a forestry setting combined with reality-oriented group counseling, academic and remedial instruction, and recreational programs. The basic treatment units are 5 work crews consisting of 12 youths, each is assigned its own counselor and work supervisor, and a crew leader is chosen from among and by the youths themselves.

The second type of program is the *Urban Home,* designed to maintain youths in their home community with adult guidance and support. Youths are selected for this program if they have sufficient stability, ties, and strength to utilize community resources. Youths are programmed on an individual schedule for school or community employment while they receive residential care, counseling, tutoring, and other services in relation to their needs. Initially, Urban Homes accommodated 20 youths; later three physically separate apartment complexes, each housing 7 youths, were added. Thus more individualized services were offered, and it was found that neighborhoods accepted 7 youths more readily than 20.

Third is the *START* (Short-Term Adolescent Residential Training) Center, which serves the older, more sophisticated and manipulative type of delinquent. Each center, located near a large town, accommodates 20 youths; the treatment approach is primarily that of intensive, guided group interaction. After a daily supervised work experience in the community, youths meet with the director in a probing, confronting session to examine their innermost feelings and attitudes.

A second operating assumption common to all three programs is that the facilities should be open and should run without physical restraints. This approach is possible because from the outset the DFY insisted on control over its own intake and freedom to reject youths who needed the security and structure of a closed setting. In practice, youths are not committed to the program by the judiciary but are *accepted* as a condition of probation (75% of the intake) or as a voluntary referral with parental consent as a delinquency prevention measure (25% of the intake).

A third operating assumption is that the youths' contact with the community should be maximized. This applies even to the relatively remote and self-contained Camps.

Approximately 1000 youths are admitted annually to the DFY male experimental facilities. There are in operation currently 5 Camps, 12

Urban Homes, and 2 START centers. Some characteristics of the youths are as follows: approximately 42% are white, 40% black, and 18% are of Puerto Rican or other ethnic background. 45% are referred from New York City, the remainder coming from upstate New York. At the time of referral, 57% have had no previous arrest, whereas 43% have been arrested one or more times. The single largest type of complaint that brings a youth into DFY care is that of behavior problems (43%); 37% have criminal complaints, 6% are drug violators, and 14% have no current complaint. Nearly one-quarter (24%) of the youths come from families on public welfare. The average length of stay in DFY programs is about 8 months; there are wide variations, however, since youths tend to stay until they are considered by staff and peers to have proved their readiness for release.

Predicting Program Outcome. A major assumption underlying the diversification of delinquency programs is of course that youths have differential treatment needs. Programs that might benefit one type of youth may have little impact on, or even be harmful to, other youths. These may seem to be relatively simple treatment assumptions, but evaluating the effectiveness of different treatment models is a very complex research problem, especially when assignment of youths to treatment is nonrandom. As a step toward such evaluation, the DFY Research Department has undertaken several studies to discover how the personal characteristics of youths who are treatment "successes" differ from those of youths who are treatment "failures." (Treatment "failures" are defined as youths who recidivate within 2 years of program release.) One purpose of these studies is to develop tools that will enable intake workers and program staff to identify which youths have a high risk and which a low risk of postrelease arrest.

Prior to 1971, the characteristics that were studied for their relationship to treatment outcome had been limited to social–demographic background variables (e.g., age, previous offense history, ethnicity). There were small but significant relationships between these variables and postrelease arrest (Goldman, 1970). But it was felt that the prediction and explanation of postrelease arrest would be enhanced if personality variables and variables descriptive of the treatment environment were included. It would be of little value to know, for example, that certain high-risk recidivism cases responded better to program X than to program Y if we could not also specify what it was about program X that was so unique or helpful. This in turn meant finding a measure to describe or categorize the program environments. The Correctional Institutions Environment Scale (CIES) was adopted because it seemed to be a promising tool. The Jesness Personality Inventory (Jesness, 1966) was used as the personality measure.

A study was initiated in 1971 using these and other tests for data collection. The research had purposes too numerous for detailed elaboration here, but there were specific questions regarding the youths' perceptions of the treatment environment. From the earlier studies it was known that youths who failed to complete their DFY training were significantly more vulnerable to postrelease arrest than program graduates. We expected to find first that youths who did not graduate would rate or perceive the programs less favorably than graduates. By implication we also expected to find that youths who were arrested after release would rate the program less favorably than other youths. If a program is to help a youth change his behavior and attitudes, we reasoned, he should at least find the program involving, supportive, clear about goals, permitting him to express himself, and so on. To the extent that he perceived the program as lacking these characteristics, the treatment could be expected to have a lessened impact.

There are three types of nongraduation from DFY programs. Youths may fail to graduate because (a) they abscond permanently from the program, (b) they are dismissed by the staff or removed by court action for new offenses committed during treatment, or (c) they withdraw from the program for miscellaneous reasons, such as removal by parental request, enlistment in the armed forces, or removal to a mental hospital. Of these nongraduation categories, the first two are regarded as unsatisfactory outcomes; the withdrawal category has a more neutral connotation. In recent years approximately 45% of the annual intake to DFY programs have failed to graduate. It would clearly be of considerable practical importance to identify these potential nongraduates while they are still in the early stages of treatment. A negative or unusual rating of the social climate may well provide a reliable indication that a youth is a potential dropout.

There were also theoretical reasons for expecting the three nongraduation categories to differ *among themselves* in their social climate ratings. In particular, the absconder group was expected to rate the programs differently from other types of nongraduates.

The study population consisted of 395 youths who were resident in 9 DFY experimental programs between January and October 1971. The facilities were 4 Camps, 4 Urban Homes, and one START center. Youths in each facility were tested in small groups in the spring of 1971. The research team returned 6 months later to retest any youths still in the program and to test other youths who had been admitted in the interim. Five major types of data were obtained for each youth:

1. *Social-demographic (Background) Information.* These data include information on the youth's age, family, school, and work experience; offense history; place of geographical residence; and ethnic background. The information is collected routinely as part of the initial intake procedure and was obtained through the DFY's Statistical and Survey Unit.

2. *The Correctional Institutions Environment Scale (CIES).* This information was collected only from youths, not from staff.

3. *Jesness Personality Inventory* (Jesness, 1966, 1971). This is a 155-item, true–false, personality–attitude test designed to provide a personality typology of delinquents as well as a general delinquency-proneness index. The 11 scales that make up the Inventory are: Social Maladjustment, Value Orientation, Immaturity, Autism, Alienation, Manifest Aggression, Withdrawal, Social Anxiety, Repression, Denial, and Asocial Index. The Inventory was completed by each youth.

4. *Program Outcome Data.* This refers to the four categories of graduation and nongraduation described earlier indicating whether the youth graduated (successfully completed) the program or left for some other reason.

5. *Arrest–Commitment Data.* These were obtained from the New York State Department of Criminal Justice Services.

Social Climate and Program Outcome.   Of the 395 youths, 315 (80%) were in Camps; 50 (12%) were in Urban Homes, and 30 (8%) were in a START center; 298 (75%) of the youths graduated; 45 (12%) absconded; 35 (9%) were dismissed or removed by court action, and 17 (4%) withdrew.

We examined first whether nongraduates as a group differed from graduates in their ratings of the social climate of the programs. The results, given in Table 8.1 show that in general nongraduates rated the programs less favorably than graduates did. The differences were significant on Staff Control, Autonomy, Practical Orientation, and Clarity. The differences between the two groups approached significance ($p < .10$) on Involvement, Support, and Expressiveness. Nongraduates tended to rate the programs as possessing less of these characteristics than graduates did.

The differences between the two groups became more pronounced when the nongraduates were subdivided according to the various reasons

Table 8.1   Means and Standard Deviations on CIES Subscales for Different Types of Program Outcome

	Graduates (N = 298)		Total Nongraduates (N = 97)		Nongraduate Subgroups			
					Absconders (N = 45)		Others (N = 52)	
Subscales	Mean	S.D.	Mean	S.D.	Mean	S.D.	Mean	S.D.
Involvement	6.62	2.24	6.24	2.31	6.38	2.37	6.11	2.29
Support	6.65	2.08	6.28	2.10	6.56*	2.19	6.03	2.03
Expressiveness	5.45	1.72	5.12	1.97	4.82	2.19	5.39*	1.72
Autonomy	5.76*	1.70	5.38	1.81	5.49*	1.95	5.27	1.70
Practical orientation	7.01*	1.70	6.66	1.84	6.82*	1.87	6.52	1.83
Personal problem orientation	6.17	1.78	6.16	1.69	6.38	1.68	5.96	1.73
Order and organization	5.96	2.13	6.17	2.09	6.40	2.26	5.95	1.92
Clarity	6.04*	1.68	5.71	1.58	5.93*	1.45	5.49	1.69
Staff control	4.79	1.85	5.23*	1.80	5.33*	1.87	5.18	1.79

$*p < .05.$

for not graduating (i.e., absconded, dismissed by staff, removed by court action, or withdrew from the program). Using these finer groupings, only Involvement, Personal Problem Orientation, and Order and Organization failed to differentiate between graduates and one subgroup or the other at the .05 confidence level (see right-hand half of Table 8.1). It is not possible to determine from these data whether nongraduates were actually treated less favorably than graduates and experienced the programs more negatively for this reason, or whether nongraduates possessed personal characteristics that made them rate differently the identical conditions experienced by graduates.

In general, there are only slight relationships between an individual's background and personality characteristics and his perception of social climate. Thus one suspects that nongraduates in DFY programs were actually treated differently from graduates. It seems quite reasonable to assume, for example, that the program staff may have felt that some youths were less able to handle responsibility (Autonomy) than others or that some youths needed more Staff Control than others. These youths and/or youths who for other reasons found the programs less supportive or clear about goals were less likely to graduate. Thus a relatively negative rating of the social climate would have given some indication that youths were potential program dropouts.

Social Climate and Postrelease Recidivism. It was expected that youths who rated the program unfavorably would be less likely to benefit from the program and correspondingly more vulnerable to postrelease recidivism. To examine this assumption, product moment correlation coefficients were computed between each of the nine CIES subscales and (*a*) arrested/not arrested and (*b*) committed/not committed to a correctional institution within 2 years of program release. The results did not support the hypothesis. Of the nine scales, only Staff Control was significantly related to arrest, but the correlation ($r = -.09$) was too low to be of any practical value. Similarly, the results showed no relationship between perception of social climate and postrelease commitment. Youths who perceived the social climate more negatively were *not* more likely to be committed than other youths.

As a third measure, we examined the relationship between deviant perceptions of the social climate and postrelease arrest and commitment. For these analyses, a directional deviance score was used which measured the extent to which an individual perceived the social climate more positively or negatively than his reference group (i.e., other youths who were in the same program at the same time). High scores on the first eight subscales and a low score on Staff Control were considered to be the more positive directions. The results revealed that deviant perceptions of the social climate, whether positive or negative, were unrelated to postrelease recidivism.

These results are generally disappointing, but perhaps not too surprising in view of all the subjective factors that combine to make arrest and commitment unsatisfactory measures of postrelease success and failure. For example, not all youths who commit crimes after release are apprehended, and the police decision to arrest or not is itself fraught with subjective judgments (see Piliavin and Briar, 1965), as are court verdicts and the sentencing process. Stronger relationships between the within-treatment perceptions of social climate and postrelease adjustment might emerge if more numerous and more diverse measures of successful community adjustment were used.

In addition, Mischel (1968) may well be right to stress that improvements in the prediction of posttreatment adjustment cannot be expected unless characteristics of the posttreatment environment are taken into account. As this author points out, measures of the individual's within-treatment environment permit fairly accurate predictions of treatment outcome. But when the individual's environment changes, as it must upon release from the program, the new environment seems to determine the individual's behavior most critically. The present results showing that the within-treatment measures relate well to the treatment outcomes of graduation and nongraduation but not to postrelease recidivism reinforce Mischel's conclusions.

Finally, predictions of postrelease recidivism might be enhanced if youths were subdivided according to some classification system for offenders. For example, negative or deviant perceptions of the social climate may be indicative of postrelease arrest for some offenders but not for others.

Social Climate and Absconding. One example of the benefits to be gained from concentrating on a specific subgroup of offenders rather than the larger, undifferentiated mass of youths is provided by a study of the youths in the present sample who absconded from DFY programs in 1971 (Chase, 1973). The work provides a useful illustration of how program environment variables can be integrated with other within-treatment measures to yield a more complete explanation of treatment outcomes than can be achieved from examining single sets of variables, one at a time. Such analyses are now possible through the ready availability of computerized multiple-regression procedures. But important as these methodological considerations may be, there were even more pressing practical reasons for singling out absconders for special attention. The following were the most pertinent:

1. Approximately 45, or 12% of the sample studied in 1971, absconded permanently from the program. This figure of 12% is an underestimate of the annual number of abscondings from DFY experimental programs. For example, between 1968 and 1970, the average was 16% a year, and recent statistics show that the percentage is increasing. In addition, these statistics record only youths who terminate treatment by reason of absconding. They give no indication of the number of youths who abscond temporarily and return (or are returned) to the program. The latter group is also cause for concern for the several reasons listed below.

2. Absconding is often threatening to the local community in which DFY facilities are located, leading in some cases to fear and hostility toward the programs and demands for greater restriction of residents. This problem is likely to be accentuated as a greater number of "open" community-based facilities are established.

3. Absconding represents a problem for the facility, since it disrupts

programs and may have an unsettling influence on other youths.

4. Recovering absconders can be time-consuming for the staff and police and a source of concern to parents.

5. Absconding rates provide one measure of the effectiveness of DFY programs in eliciting rule-abiding behaviors among youths. That is, absconding during treatment can in itself be regarded as a form of delinquency, since it violates the rules and regulations of the facility. Thus, just as arrest and commitment represent criteria of failure *after* program release, absconding may be regarded as one criterion of program failure *before* release.

6. Previous research has also found that although absconding is not legally defined as a delinquent act, it is often accompanied by further offenses (e.g., a youth may steal money, food, or an auto during the course of absconding).

7. Some researchers have found an association between absconding and further offending even after normal program release from delinquency programs. Thus absconding may be indicative not only of program failure but of subsequent delinquency. A number of factors have been suggested to account for this relationship, but they are only speculative. One is that absconding reveals something about a youth's personality which is correlated with a general delinquency-proneness. Another is that absconding affects the youth, rendering him more likely to become delinquent again. For example, this may be because he is deprived of the rehabilitative influence of the program, because of delinquencies committed while absconding, or because the act of absconding confirms his sense of delinquent identity. Whatever the reason(s), it is fairly well established that absconding may be associated with further delinquencies, even after normal program release.

For all these reasons, a special study was made of those youths in the present sample who absconded permanently from the programs. It is important to note that many definitions of absconding are possible, varying from "any unauthorized absence from the facility no matter how temporary" to "failure to return to the facility by midnight." As the term is used here, it has the more precise meaning of "termination of treatment by reason of permanently absconding." This definition limits the number of youths studied much more drastically than the definitions employed in most other studies. In the latter, the number of times a given youth absconds has most frequently been used as the outcome or criterion measure. Accordingly, youths studied have included the "occasional" absconder who returns to the facility and completes the training program. In DFY programs, such occasional abscondings are not recorded as research statistics. It is reasonable to assert, however, that the present sample is broadly comparable to the "persistent" or "habitual" absconder category of other studies.

A second point concerns the significance to be attached to absconding. It is this writer's opinion that absconding is a problem worth investigating partly because of the reasons already listed and partly because it is itself a deviant act whose study may shed light on the causes of delinquency. However, it is recognized that some practitioners attach only minor importance to the problem. It has been argued, for example, that absconding is merely symptomatic or may actually be healthy, since it permits a youth to act out aggressive or rejected feelings that might otherwise be expressed in more antisocial ways. But as Lubeck and Empey (1968) have noted, any community-based delinquency program that continually ignores absconders may be courting disaster.

> If (community-based) institutions are to be effective, perhaps even to survive, they must find non-physical means for preventing runaways. The reasons are compelling. Not only are the public, the police and courts, and legislators and paroling authorities often resentful and fearful over the loss of physical control; but a continuing failure to find effective substitution for physical controls might defeat the corrective and integrative functions of the (community-based) program, the most compelling functions for which it was created. (Lubeck and Empey, p. 244)

This point of view is not necessarily incompatible with the position of those professionals who feel that one of the essential elements of a training program should be showing a youth that he is trusted and allowing him the opportunity to exercise choice and responsibility— including the choice and responsibility of whether to abscond. According to this school of thought, if the price for reducing abscondings is more restrictions and greater surveillance, the price is too high, since the many youths who do not abscond and benefit from the openness of the program would suffer at the expense of the few who do abscond. However, it may be possible to reduce the incidence of absconding by psychological means rather than by more restrictions and surveillance. This possibility is explored more fully after discussion of the present research findings.

Previous Work on Absconding.   The best available review of past research into the causes and incidence of absconding from juvenile correctional institutions is provided by Clarke and Martin (1971). Few studies have in fact concerned themselves with the problem, and of these, the majority have dealt only with the individual's characteristics. That is, they have tried to find out whether absconders have different personalities from nonabsconders. Based on their own and others' research, Clarke and Martin conclude that absconders differ very little from other youths with respect to individual or personality characteristics. On the other hand, three individual background characteristics have been consistently related to absconding: (1) absconders are more delinquent in terms of previous experience and future prognosis, (2) absconders more often have a history of absconding, and (3) once a youth has absconded, the older he is, the more often he runs away; age itself, however, is not related to the onset of absconding.

It seems therefore that background characteristics relating to previous offenses are more related to (predictive of) absconding than personality characteristics. In addition, situational or environmental factors seem to be more related to absconding than personality characteristics. Unfortunately, these situational factors have been studied even less than personality characteristics. Prior to the studies of Clarke and Martin and with the exception of the work of Lubeck and Empey, only a few variables in the facility had been demonstrated to be related to absconding. The main one was time during training when abscondings occur, the two major findings being that absconding is highest (a) soon after admission and (b) after holiday periods. A high incidence of absconding at these periods has been interpreted as reflecting anxiety and insecurity among boys recently removed from the familiarity of their home environments.

In their own studies of boys in British approved schools, Clarke and Martin pursued the investigation of environmental variables further by examining, among other things, whether youths who were extroverted or introverted (as measured by the Junior Eysenck Personality Inventory) would have different absconding rates depending on the kind of program environment in which they were placed. It was expected that introverted boys might be more likely to abscond from a school that emphasized team games and house spirit than from one in which an individual casework approach was preferred. This and other expectations were not confirmed. However, examination of the manner in which the environment of the schools was measured suggests that the findings might be different if more refined measures of social climate were used. For example, the regime of each school was described very simply according to the broad categories: "permissive–therapeutic" (casework), "traditional structured," "training school," and "paternalistic traditional." These descriptions were not obtained by any systematic or objective means but merely arrived at in consultation with the Headmaster of the classifying center that referred youths to the various schools. These gross descriptions of the school environments left much to be desired and did not permit a very intensive examination of the interaction between environmental and personality variables as they related to absconding.

This conclusion leads to the rationale for the present study: namely, when studying abscondings or any other treatment outcome, the assessment of facility environments must be systematic, and it is worth studying interaction effects more intensively. Before examining the results to see whether this approach was fruitful, there remains for consideration one other important study already mentioned in passing—that by Lubeck and Empey (1968).

These authors studied absconding rates in two different types of delinquency programs, one an institutional program that was located in a relatively isolated geographical area but was open in the sense of operating with few physical restraints. This was designated a "total" institution (without walls) and seems comparable in many respects to the DFY Camp facility. The second type of program was a small experimental, community-based program located in a residential section of Los Angeles. This program was also open and was termed a mediatory institution (since it mediated between the youth and his community). It seems generally comparable to a DFY Urban Home.

Four major types of variables were studied for their relationship to absconding: personality characteristics (measured by the Jesness Inventory), social background characteristics (including family relationships, age, social class), peer relations, and offense history. There were three main findings of interest. First, the battery of measures explained or accounted for more of the abscondings from the total institution than from the mediatory institution, suggesting that absconding may be more predictable at one kind of institution than at another. Second, of the four measures, the offense history group was most consistently related to absconding in both types of program. Third, the size of the relationship between each of the four measures and absconding varied not only between the two programs but also *within* each program at different times—notably before and after some major organizational changes occurred.

Considering these findings together, no static relationship emerges between a youth's personal characteristics and absconding. Rather, the relationship between absconding and personal characteristics varies depending on the program and its organizational structure.

Unfortunately the findings were much less definitive regarding exactly how the relationships vary. Despite this, some interesting suggestions have been taken up or developed further in the present study. For example, a major variable that may determine whether personality variables will be associated with absconding is the nature of the sentence the youth is serving. Lubeck and Empey found that when the total institution changed its rules or norms regarding length of sentences and granting furloughs, absconding became more related to personality. Prior to the rule change, youths had served a determinate sentence; after the change, length of stay was made indeterminate. This suggests that prior to the change, a youth could have coped with the system merely by adopting the attitude of "doing time," since there was an absence of normative pressures toward basic attitudinal or behavioral change. After the change, however, release became based on the youth's demonstrated capacity for behavioral and attitudinal change, and it was no longer possible to opt out of the system by taking a "doing time" attitude. As a consequence, Lubeck and Empey suggest that youths with personality problems (who would therefore be most subject to pressures for change) may have chosen to escape the strains and stresses of the system by absconding. This variable of determinate/indeterminate sentence could also explain why Clarke and Martin and perhaps other researchers have found no personality differences between absconders and nonabsconders. As far as can be ascertained, the Clarke and Martin samples consisted entirely of youths who were admitted to the schools for a determinate length of time.

In their discussion, Lubeck and Empey also suggest another interesting relationship between personality and absconding. During the study of the mediatory institution, a spate of abscondings occurred and prompted the staff to impose a severe sanction for absconding, in an attempt to placate the local populace. Immediately afterward, the capacity of the personality variables to predict absconding sharply increased. Lubeck and Empey note that there seemed to be a diminishing *tolerance of deviance* in the program and that boys who entered the program at this point were increasingly confronted with a program culture characterized by strict staff and peer controls and close scrutinization of behavior.

Lubeck and Empey's observations seem to suggest a more general proposition—namely, that programs having a low tolerance for deviance for *whatever reason* will have higher absconding rates. In an impressionistic article on absconding, Hildebrand (1968) lends credence to this proposition by the following assertion:

Allowance for more breathing room within the institution would make it less necessary to breathe from without the institution. Lacking an "out" while "in" increases the need to get out regardless of the means or consequences of getting there. It could be said that those who would make expression by inmates impossible make escape and internal tumult inevitable. (p. 66)

If absconding increases as tolerance of deviance decreases, one would expect abscondings to be more numerous in programs that restrict Expressiveness and emphasize Staff Control. Furthermore this tolerance of deviance might be directed at (thereby experienced most acutely by) youths who have strong feelings of anger and aggression, together with a tendency to act out their hostile impulses (Jesness Manifest Aggression Scale). Finally, if the program places a strong emphasis on changed attitudes and behavior as a precondition for release, it is likely also to place a strong emphasis on Personal Problem Orientation, which in turn is likely to provoke escape behavior in the youths with the most severe personality problems. Thus most of the Jesness scales should be related to absconding, especially in facilities that allow little room for expression, but stress Staff Control and Personal Problem Orientation.

Personality and Environmental Correlates of Absconding. To test the preceding hypotheses, absconders' perceptions of the program's social climate were compared with those of graduates. As Table 8.1 indicates, the 45 youths who absconded rated their programs as permitting significantly less Expressiveness and as putting more stress on Staff Control than graduates did. The two groups did not differ in their scores on the other CIES subscales, with the exception of a tendency ($p < .10$) for absconders to rate the programs higher on Order and Organization than graduates did.

From the earlier discussion, it was also expected that absconders would have more abnormal Jesness personality profiles than graduates. This expectation was strongly supported with respect to all the Jesness scales except Social Anxiety. The largest difference ($p < .01$) for any single scale was on the Manifest Aggression scale, where the means for absconders and graduates respectively were 64.3 (S.D. 11.9) and 56.5 (S.D. 11.7).

Next, since these analyses showed a significant differentiation between absconders and graduates, it was of interest to know how much the two types of variables (CIES and personality) added to each other in explaining or predicting absconding and whether they interacted with each other in any significant fashion. The data were analyzed using a hierarchical multiple regression technique (Cohen, 1968), whereby variables are successively examined for their increment to the prediction or explanation of the dependent variable as determined by multiple regression equations. Independent variables may be introduced separately or in sets according to some prespecified order. As they are introduced, a multiple regression equation is computed, with independent variables consisting of the newly introduced variable(s) plus all variables in the preceding sets. After each new set is added, the multiple correlation coefficient is computed and the increment in R^2 due to the new set is calculated. The increment represents the addition in predictive or explanatory power due to the newly introduced set, compared with that of preceding sets of variables. Single variables within sets may also be examined for their individual contributions to the increment.

We first tested the specific hypothesis elaborated earlier that youths were likely to abscond if they rated the program low on Expressiveness and high on Staff Control and Personal Problem Orientation, and if they had high Manifest Aggression. In testing this hypothesis, age and age squared were partialled out (controlled for) first, since age has often been shown to be related to delinquency. In addition, it was possible that if the tests and measures had been obtained *shortly before* a youth absconded or graduated, they would be more related to program outcome than if they had been obtained a long time before the youths absconded or graduated. Accordingly, the sample was divided into two groups—those who were within the last 0 to 2 months of treatment when tested, and those who stayed in the program more than 2 months after testing. This dichotomy, which will be referred to as the "time after" variable, was entered into the equation after age. The remaining variables were then entered into the regression equation in the order shown in Table 8.2, which also gives the results for the cumulative contribution of all the variables in predicting absconding.

The results confirmed the hypothesis. The multiple correlation coefficient for absconding after the first six sets of variables was .30, which is highly significant $(p < .01)$. Corrected for shrinkage, the adjusted coefficient was .25.

Referring to individual variables, both Expressiveness and Personal Problem Orientation were significantly $(p < .01$ and $p < .05$, respectively) related to absconding and in the anticipated directions. That is, youths who rated the programs as low on Expressiveness and high on Personal Problem Orientation were more likely to abscond than other youths. With these and the preceding variables controlled, perception of Staff Control was entered, but this variable was found to be unrelated to absconding at this point.

Next, Jesness Manifest Aggression scores were entered, and this variable provided a dramatic increase in the power to predict absconding.

Table 8.2 Cumulative Contribution of CIES and Jesness Scores to the Prediction of Absconding

Variable Sets	Multiple R	Multiple R-Square	Increment on R-Square	F-Ratio of Increment
1. Age at Admission Age Squared "time-after"	.11	.01	.01	1.26
2. CIES Expressiveness Personal Problem	.19	.04	.03	4.27**
3. CIES Staff Control	.20	.04	.01	1.74
4. Jesness: Manifest Aggression (M.A.)	.28	.08	.04	14.25**
5. Interactions: M.A. × Expressiveness; M.A. × Staff Control	.29	.08	.00	.29
6. CIES Interaction: Expressiveness × Staff Control	.30	.09	.01	3.80*

*$p < .05$.
**$p < .01$.

Moreover, with the entry of this variable, the significance of Expressiveness dropped considerably, suggesting that Expressiveness may have achieved some of its power to predict absconding because it was related to Manifest Aggression. This raises the interesting possibility that youths who have high Manifest Aggression may be more prone to perceive their surroundings as not permitting Expressiveness. This may be either because such youths are *actually* prevented from expressing themselves, or because they *feel* they cannot express themselves within their program environment.

In either case it is worth noting that the term Manifest Aggression is somewhat misleading, and any simple interpretation of the results to mean that angry youths were not allowed to express themselves in DFY programs is unlikely. High scorers on Manifest Aggression may, but do not necessarily, act out their hostility. In defining the meaning of the scale, Jesness (1971) holds that the term refers to the perception of unpleasant feelings, especially anger, and concern about their control, but no close relationship between high scores and actual outbursts of aggressive behavior should be assumed. In fact, it is not uncommon for persons who are highly concerned about controlling their feelings to display unusually conforming and overcontrolled behavior. It would not therefore be surprising to find that overcontrolled youths feel they cannot express themselves.

Two interaction terms were next entered—Manifest Aggression in interaction with Expressiveness, and Manifest Aggression in interaction with Staff Control. Neither of these was significant, indicating that the ability of Manifest Aggression to predict absconding was not enhanced or diminished by variations in levels of Expressiveness or Staff Control. This is an important and somewhat unexpected finding. It had been thought that environmental variables would interact with personality variables to add to the explanation of absconding, but the results for sets 2 through 5 show that only main effects were operative. Thus whereas one might expect a very high aggression score accompanied by a very low expressiveness score to produce an unusually high risk of absconding, the results show that this is not the case.

Finally, an interaction term representing Staff Control in interaction with Expressiveness was introduced, and this variable was significantly related to absconding: youths who rated the programs high on Staff Control and low on Expressiveness were more likely to abscond than youths who rated the programs high on both scales or low on both scales. It is important to note that this combination of variables is associated with absconding even after Manifest Aggression scores have been taken into account (partialled out).

In summary, the results support the hypothesis that youths who rate their programs low on Expressiveness and high on Personal Problem Orientation and high on Staff Control, and who themselves have high Manifest Aggression scores, are more likely to abscond than other youths. Given the foregoing set of characteristics, then, does it matter which type of facility a youth is placed in? To answer this question, facility type was entered as set 7 in one computer pass. This set did not significantly add to the predictive or explanatory power of the preceding variables. The implication is that the social climate variables in conjunction with Manifest Aggression had already accounted for differences in absconding rates among major facility types. Thus when we had taken into account youths' scores on Manifest Aggression and their perception of the facility's social climate, their likelihood of absconding was the same, irrespective of the facility they were in.

However, other analyses undertaken to assess the relationships between absconding and (a) background variables, (b) personality variables, and (c) program adjustment behaviors, showed that these variables—whether separately or together—were *not* capable of accounting for different absconding rates among individual facilities. For example, with these three types of variable controlled or taken into account, camp A still had a significantly higher absconding rate than camp D. It was only with the inclusion of the CIES data that the difference in absconding rates between camp A and camp D disappeared.

Examination of mean CIES scores confirms that camp A did in fact have a social climate different from camp D. For example, camp A was rated by the youths as highest of all camps on the Relationship and Treatment Program dimensions and was particularly high on Personal Problem Orientation. Camp D was among the lowest of the camps on these two dimensions and was intermediate on Personal Problem Orientation. Both camps had a similar mean score on the System Maintenance dimensions, including Staff Control. However, reference to the individual scales suggests that camp A was a particularly "gung-ho" place to be. For example, of all camps it ranked highest on Personal Problem Orientation, Support, Practical Orientation, Order and Organization, and Clarity. It ranked second highest on Involvement, Expressiveness, and Autonomy. This in turn suggests that if a youth is a "misfit" in a particularly enthusiastic and go-ahead facility, he is more likely to abscond than if he is a "misfit" in a lower-keyed facility (such as camp D).

Further examination of the data also confirms that youths who absconded from camp A rated the social climate of the camp very differently from camp A graduates. Absconders rated the program significantly lower than graduates on the Relationship and Treatment Program dimensions and significantly higher on the System Maintenance dimensions. Consistent with the results in Table 8.2, the differences between the two groups were particularly marked on the Expressiveness scale.

Practical Implications. Through exhaustive analyses of many other kinds of data and by a careful piecing together of the evidence, it was possible to develop a composite profile of the DFY absconder. After replication of the results, this profile can be used for "flagging" the high-risk case when he enters the program and for directing special treatment efforts toward him designed to reduce his likelihood of absconding. It will also be possible to evaluate the effectiveness of different treatment strategies by examining whether the high-risk case responds better to one kind of treatment environment than to another.

As was shown earlier, in developing the composite absconder profile, the youths' perceptions of the social climate of their program were a key component. Without studying this aspect it would not have been known which program conditions were most conducive to absconding for certain youths. Moreover, collecting the CIES data clarified not only which conditions encouraged absconding but also what practical steps might be taken to avert it. Such practical steps will include efforts to exert any necessary staff controls in a manner that will be less threatening to the potential absconder's sense of autonomy and responsibility, and encouraging him to express himself more openly.

When considering the practical usefulness of the CIES data, two further points are worth noting. First, although the youths' CIES ratings were related to absconding, for these results to be of any practical value we must know at what time during treatment the typical absconder CIES ratings can be identified. For example, if the potential absconder rates the program low on Expressiveness and high on Staff Control for only a week or two before he runs, there would be little time to avert it—even assuming CIES ratings were collected every two weeks, which would be unlikely.

The results for the "time after" variable, which was included in every multivariate analysis to indicate whether a youth was within 1 to 2 months of absconding or graduating when he completed the tests, showed that this variable was not significant. The conclusion is that the social climate data that were found to relate to absconding were predictive, irrespective of when they were obtained from the youths. That this must have been so is verified by determining how many absconders actually absconded within 2 months of being tested and how many stayed in the program for longer than 2 months. The results show that 60% or 27 of the absconders stayed in the program for 2 or more months after being tested. Thus their absconding characteristics were discernible for at least 2 months, and in many cases much longer, before they actually ran. This result held true for the other types of within-program measure and led to a direct program implication, namely, that if systematic assessments could be made of each youth at intake or shortly after, efforts to forestall absconding could be started much earlier, with a corresponding increase in the likelihood of averting such behavior.

Second, throughout the analyses, only the *individual's* perception of the social climate was used, but we might have used the group perception—that is, the mean perception of the youths who were in the same program at the same time. There are certain advantages to using the group perception: if group perceptions of the social climate are reliably related to abscondings or other program outcomes, these ratings could be taken into account when placing individual youths in programs. For example, one might decide against placing a potential absconder in a facility where the existing group rates the program as low on Expressiveness and high on Staff Control.

To investigate the relationship between group perceptions and absconding, the data of Table 8.2 were reanalyzed using group perceptions of social climate instead of individual perceptions. A sharp decrease appeared in the relationship between social climate and absconding. Neither Expressiveness nor Staff Control, nor the interaction between the two, was related to absconding. Only the group perception of Personal Problem Orientation remained predictive. The relationship was such that more abscondings occurred where the group rated the programs as putting stress on solving personal problems. This is an interesting finding, since it suggests that the Personal Problem Orientation scale gives a valid measure of how much importance the individual facilities attach to solving personal problems within their overall treatment strategies. It also implies that if the group as a whole perceives a high stress on resolving personal problems, the individual *with* personal problems (as indicated by the abnormal personality profile) will indeed begin to feel pressures to start solving his own. However, the general pattern of results for this analysis clearly shows that an individual's perception of the program climate may be highly idiosyncratic, and that program staff need to be sensitive not only to the general group feeling but also to individual variations.

Thus the CIES, in common with other within-program measures, has considerable value in predicting treatment outcomes such as whether or not youths are likely to complete treatment. However, individuals' perceptions did not relate to postrelease recidivism. Several reasons for the latter failure are discussed, such as the "softness" of the recidivism criterion, the need to study postrelease environments, and the difficulties of studying youthful offenders as a homogenous group without the refinement of subgroup classifications.

Despite these limitations, it was found that the within-program data, including the program environment measures, made a significant contribution to the explanation of absconding. This problem is likely to be of increasing concern to the public and to correctional authorities as a greater number of open, community-based facilities are established. In general, the most useful results were obtained when the CIES data were used (*a*) in conjunction with other kinds of data, notably personality measures and information regarding facilities of different types; (*b*) to test specific hypotheses derived from a reasonably coherent theoretical base; (*c*) to study a subgroup rather than the juvenile offender group as a whole; and (*d*) to explain a specific effect—in this case, absconding.

The finding that only certain CIES subscales were related to the dependent variable suggests that social climates may have quite specific effects. The instrument may be useful for gross comparisons among different types of programs, for understanding the processes that mediate different treatment outcomes, and for permitting practical suggestions for treatment innovations.

REFERENCES

Chase, M. M. *A profile of absconders.* New York State Division for Youth; Research Dept., World Trade Center, New York, 1973.

Clarke, R. V. G. & Martin, D. N. *Absconding from approved schools.* Home Office Research Studies, No. 12. Her Majesty's Stationery Office, London, 1971.

Cohen, J. Multiple regression as a general data analytic system. *Psychological Bulletin,* **70**:426–443, 1968.

Goldman, I. J. *Characteristics associated with recidivism.* New York State Division for Youth; Research Dept., World Trade Center, New York, 1970.

Hildebrand, R. J. The anatomy of escape. *Federal Probation,* **33**:58–66, 1969.

Jesness, C. F. *Manual for the Jesness Inventory.* Consulting Psychologists Press, Palo Alto, Calif., 1966 (revised 1971).

Lubeck, S. G. & Empey, L. T. Mediatory vs. total institution: The case of the runaway. *Social Problems,* **16**:242–260, 1968.

Luger, M. Innovations in the treatment of juvenile offenders. *Annals of the American Academy of Political and Social Science,* **381**:60–70, January 1969.

Mischel, W. *Personality and assessment.* Wiley, New York, 1968.

Piliavin, I. & Briar, S. *Police encounters with juveniles.* Center for the Study of Law and Society, University of California, Berkeley, 1965.

CHAPTER NINE

Congruence and Incongruence
in Correctional Environments

Resident and Staff Congruence. This chapter addresses two related issues. First, residents and staff in some programs agree closely on the characteristics of the actual and/or of an ideal social milieu; in other programs they disagree sharply. What are the correlates of the extent of agreement between residents and staff? Second, some residents in a program agree closely with the other residents on the characteristics of their program's social environment. Some residents, however, sharply disagree; that is, there are often important differences of opinion among residents (and among staff) on what the program is really like. What are the correlates of deviant perceptions? For example, are residents who perceive the program in a deviant manner less satisfied? Are they more likely to break unit rules?

Patients and staff in psychiatric programs usually agree quite well in their perceptions of the treatment environment. Although patient–staff agreement varies from program to program, the average agreement is much greater than would be expected by chance. There is also a relatively high degree of patient–staff agreement about ideal treatment milieus. Again, programs differ considerably in the extent of agreement, but the average agreement is considerably greater than would be expected by chance (Moos, 1974, Chapter 13).

At least two processes contribute to this congruence. First, patients and staff learn about the characteristics of their treatment milieus, and congruence develops out of a mutually shared reality of events. Congruence also develops through discussions of shared value orientations and through mutual attraction and personal influences directed toward increasing congruence. Second, patients and staff who do not share either the perceptions of the treatment milieu and/or the dominant value orientations about an ideal milieu tend to leave the program. However, in psychiatric programs the effects of self-selection and program selection are confounded with changes in perceptions and values that occur subsequent to entering a treatment milieu. Thus although there is evidence for a relatively high degree of program congruence, the exact reasons for this congruence are unclear. These results led us to investigate the degree of congruence in correctional programs, in which there is little or no self-selection, at least for residents.

Indices of congruence were derived from CIES data from two samples of correctional programs. There were the second and third samples used in the analyses relating social climate to morale and personal growth (see Chapter 7). Four program congruence scores were calculated: (1) agreement between residents and staff with respect to the actual social climate (CIES Form R), (2) agreement between residents and staff with respect to an ideal social climate (CIES Form I), (3) real–ideal social climate similarity (Form R vs. Form I) for residents, and (4) real–ideal social climate similarity (Form R vs. Form I) for staff. The CIES profile similarity scores were calculated by utilizing the intraclass correlation (Haggard, 1958).

The results, which were quite surprising, highlight the important differences between psychiatric and correctional milieus. The average CIES Form R profile correlations between residents and staff were $-.21$ and $-.31$, respectively, in the two samples. Thus there was essentially no agreement between residents and staff on the characteristics of their program's social climate. The average resident–staff profile correlation for the larger sample of 78 units discussed in Chapter 3 was .06. Residents and staff show no overall agreement whatever on the characteristics of their programs! This is in sharp contrast to the results on samples of psychiatric treatment programs, on which the analogous average profile correlations were .35, .57, and .65.

The correlations between the residents' real and ideal CIES profiles were .09 and $-.11$ in the two samples, indicating no relationship between the residents' views of their actual program and their views of an ideal program. This again contrasts markedly with the results in psychiatric programs, in which similar correlations ranged from .33 to .70. There was a minimal degree of congruence between resident and staff views of ideal correctional programs. The average intraclass profile correlations between resident and staff CIES Form I results were .25 and

.40 in the two samples. There was also some congruence between real and ideal program perceptions for staff (i.e., the relevant correlations were .22 and .43 in the two samples). Even here, however, the results are considerably lower than the congruence found in psychiatric programs; for example, the average patient–staff value congruences were .56, .76, and .78, in three samples of treatment programs.

These results indicate that the processes hypothesized earlier as responsible for increasing congruence in psychiatric treatment programs do not necessarily occur in correctional programs. Residents and staff in correctional programs do not share a "mutual reality of events." Discussions of value orientations about the program and about changes in the program are unlikely to occur. Patients and staff who do not share the perceptions of the treatment milieu and/or the dominant value orientations tend to leave psychiatric programs. This is less likely to occur for residents in correctional programs, and it may also be less likely to occur for staff. Since correctional programs seldom demand much staff interaction, it may be easier for "deviant" staff to function in a reasonable way in these programs. In any case, resident and staff congruence is no greater than would be expected on the hypothesis of random selection. To the extent that this is so, correctional programs are culturally or socially disorganized. These results furnish further support for the thesis that residents and staff generally constitute two surprisingly distinct subcultures.

Eynon et al. (1971) measured the impact of a juvenile correctional institution and also found essentially no congruence between the perceptions of inmates and staff. Their questionnaire measured six factors: interpersonal approach, inmate code, rejection of institution, inmate pressure, rejection of positive impact, and self-concept. The staff member who knew the departing boy best was asked to make an assessment of him on a 15-item rating scale covering these six areas. The correlations between the staffs' and the boys' ratings of impact were extremely low, leading the authors to conclude that they were essentially independent. There was hardly any relationship between the boys' perceptions of institutional impact and the staffs' evaluations of the boys' eventual outcome after release. As might be expected from our data, the staff ratings of the boys were considerably more favorable than the boys' perceptions of the impact of their institutional stay. This is only one of many correctional studies pointing to the lack of congruence between residents and staff.

However, the degree of resident–staff and real–ideal congruence does vary considerably from one program to another. In some programs (particularly Relationship- and Insight-oriented ones) the relevant intraclass profile correlations are over .70, whereas in others (particularly Control-oriented ones) they are as low as −.50. What are the correlates of the degree of congruence in a program?

In psychiatric programs the four congruence indices were positively related to patient general satisfaction, liking for staff, and opportunities for personal growth. For example, when patients and staff showed greater value congruence (i.e., about their ideal treatment environment) patients felt more satisfied and liked the staff more. Similar results were obtained for patient–staff congruence about the actual treatment milieu. Furthermore, real–ideal congruence was positively related to patient satisfaction and perceived personal development.

The results in the two samples of correctional programs were somewhat different. Table 9.1 shows that the agreement between the residents and staff about their social milieu was not related to any of the resident reactions to the program. But both residents' real–ideal congruence and resident–staff value congruence (i.e., about their ideal correctional environment) were positively related to resident general satisfaction, liking for staff, and opportunities for personal growth. Also, when staff showed real–ideal congruence, residents felt that they enjoyed greater opportunity for personal growth. Overall, however, the correlates of congruence in correctional programs are relatively weak. This is probably because the average degree of congruence in these programs is so low.

Table 9.1   Correlations Between Congruence Scores and Resident Reactions to the Program

Congruence Scores	Satisfaction	Like Staff	Anxiety	Personal Development
Resident–Staff (Real)	.12	.33	.04	.07
Resident–Staff (Ideal)	.49*	.50**	−.15	.48*
Resident (Real vs. Ideal)	.67***	.48*	.18	.42
Staff (Real vs. Ideal)	.21	.06	−.17	.45*

Note: with $N = 15$

   *R.10 = .43
  **R.05 = .50
***R.01 = .62

The Impact of Congruence.   Many studies have focused on the importance of value congruence or similarity, especially between patients and therapists. For example, Cook (1966) found that patient–therapist value similarity had an impact on change in meaning during brief counseling. Rosenthal (1955) showed that patients who were rated as improved by their therapists tended to adopt the moral values of the therapist, at least on the tested dimensions of sex, aggression, and discipline. In an intriguing study Burdock, Cheek, and Zubin (1960) found a relationship between psychoanalytic candidates' success in training and similarity with their supervisors' interest patterns, as measured by the Strong Vocational Interest Blank. They suggested that trained analysts may be equating criteria for the well-adjusted personality with their own interests or value systems.

Welkowitz, Cohen, and Ortmeyer (1967) found that patients who were rated as most improved by their therapists were closer to the therapist in values than patients rated least improved. They also found that values tend to move toward similarity in ongoing patient–therapist dyads. These and other studies (see Moos, 1974, Chapter 13) support the notion that individual value systems move toward greater similarity with the dominant values in the environment. Other relevant studies are reviewed by Meltzoff and Kornreich (1970, pp. 311–327) and by Goldstein, Heller, and Sechrest (1966).

Rogers et al. (1967) reported a definite difference between therapist views of the therapy relationship and the views of both judges (who rated tape recordings of the interviews) and patients. Therapists tended to make considerably more favorable evaluations of their interactions with patients than their patients did. The data indicated that in successful therapy there was a significant positive correlation between patient and therapist evaluations of the relationship (i.e., greater congruence). In less successful cases patient and therapist assessments were more divergent, actually correlating negatively with one another (i.e., less congruence). These findings are exactly the same as our own. Staff view correctional programs more positively than residents, but there is a variation in this tendency from program to program. Residents are more satisfied in those programs in which resident–staff value congruence is high.

Stern (1970) has done some relevant work in educational environments. He argued that the relative dispersion or scatter of environmental press scores around a group mean can be a measure of cultural heterogeneity. Stern found that cultural variability in male academic programs was directly related to a number of problems (e.g, problems involving organizational decision making, faculty quality, academic quality, and social and political freedom). The correlations were not of very substantial magnitude (between .23 and .37), but they supported the notion that some organizational problems may be more prevalent when cultural dispersion or heterogeneity is high.

Stern also derived an index he called cultural dissonance, which was measured by the average discrepancy between needs and social environmental press for all the individuals in a particular group. This measure is analogous to our real–ideal milieu discrepancy measure. Schools differed greatly in the amount of dissonance experienced by their students; for example, public institutions were more dissonant than private ones, and independent schools were more dissonant than church-related schools. High dissonance in public colleges was related to two types of institutional problems—more problems concerned with faculty quality and fewer problems concerned with social and political freedom. Stern also found that overall cultural dissonance was not related to the individual deviancy of student perceptions per se.

Thus the evidence indicates that lack of congruence is usually associated with more problems, individual symptoms, and so forth. More important, many studies have found that social environments exert a press toward increased congruence or conformity; for example, the career choices of college students tend to conform more and more closely over time to the dominant career choice in the college. When resident–staff interaction and congruence of views is minimal, the press for greater conformity will be almost totally exerted by other residents. Increasing adherence to the "innate code" and decreasing impact of normative staff values is the expected result. Increased resident–staff interaction and congruence can be expected to have a beneficial impact on residents. Correctional staff must learn to take maximum advantage of the press toward progressive conformity exerted by most social environments.

Increasing Resident–Staff Communication.   The foregoing considerations indicate that efforts to increase resident–staff congruence are needed. Piliavin and Vadum (1968) suggest a relevant technique. They argue that the conflict between custodial and professional treatment personnel is an important problem in correctional programs.

> Workers responsible for these respective aims assign different priorities to organizational goals, hold contrasting views of inmates and finally develop conflicting expectations of each other's appropriate organizational

roles. These differences in perspective and expectation result not only in the failure of staff to cooperate with each other, but in their lack of desire to cooperate. (p. 35)

Grusky (1959) has pointed out that serious role problems among prison officials arose directly from conflicts between treatment and custodial goals that came about because of the introduction of a milieu treatment program. Staff uncertainty, property damage, and a high escape rate ensued.

One solution to this problem is to reduce the discrepant views of custodial and treatment professionals by providing overlap in their respective roles—that is, give custodians some treatment duties and treatment professionals some custodial functions. Piliavin and Vadum studied custodial workers who volunteered to counsel inmate groups. Two other groups were used as controls. The results indicated that the custodians who served as counselors perceived greater utility in treatment programs and treatment personnel than did the custodians who did not serve as counselors. In addition, the counselors placed greater trust in inmates. Appropriate role changes may alter the attitudes of custodial staff. Custodians' undue suspicion and mistrust of residents may result in restrictive practices and in unnecessarily alienating the residents. Some overlap in custodial and treatment roles may be a viable device for enhancing congruence in correctional programs.

The importance of increasing the degree of staff interaction with residents, thus their influence on residents, can hardly be overemphasized. In his pioneering study, Clemmer (1958) developed the concept of "prisonization" to describe the changes residents undergo during periods of confinement. He believed that there was an inmate code or system of norms that required loyalty to other inmates and opposition to correctional staff. Clemmer defined prisonization as "the taking on in greater or lesser degree of the folkways, mores, customs and general culture of the penitentiary" (p. 299). Prisonization is an illustration of the more general processes of assimilation that occur whenever persons are introduced to a new culture or subculture. It is a specific example of "progressive conformity" theory. The problem for correctional staff is how to induce progressive conformity to staff rather than to inmate values.

This may not be as difficult as many people believe, particularly with younger offenders. Glaser (1964) points out that residents who are opposed to staff values are inclined to be verbally or physically aggressive against those who disagree with them. He concludes that these residents will publicly express their values much more than will the residents who are supportive of staff values. He thus proposes that "prisoners perceive other prisoners as having less commitment to staff supported values than is in fact the case" (p. 116). Glaser presents evidence that most residents are very concerned with trying to "go straight" and that:

> both they and sociologists are pluralistically ignorant of the distribution of this interest in their group . . . one might say that both inmates and others commonly err in assuming that the inmates membership group in the prison represents his primary reference group, especially in his orientation to life after release. (p. 116)

Wheeler (1961) and Glaser (1964) present cogent evidence that Clemmer's prisonization hypothesis must be modified. Wheeler found that residents' conformity to staff expectations decreased with length of time served. Wheeler also measured the extent of residents' involvement with other residents in terms of the number of close friendships established and the degree to which residents spent their free time with other residents or by themselves. He found that the speed and degree of prisonization were a function of informal resident involvement. He points out the basic incompatibility between being closely involved with other residents and conforming to staff expectations. The resident who values friendship with other residents and who also desires to conform to staff expectations faces a vivid conflict. Presumably residents must cope with this problem either by becoming more isolated from other residents or by shifting their attitudes away from the staff's.

Wheeler indicates that the structure of correctional programs makes conformity with staff norms possible only at the cost of isolation from other residents. Residents perceive the opinions of others to be more opposed to staff than they actually are. Thus residents who accept staff values probably feel more deviant than they actually are. Wheeler points out that the conforming resident may thus be "restrained from establishing supportive ties with others by both the official and the inmate systems" (p. 705).

There appears to be a U-shaped curve relating phase of institutional career to conformity to staff role expectations. Wheeler divided residents into three institutional career phases: (1) early phase (those who had served less than 6 months), (2) middle phase (those who had served more than 6 months, but still had more than 6 months left to serve), and (3) late phase (those who had less than 6 months remaining to serve). He found that residents in the early and late phases were more frequently oriented to conventional value systems. Residents in the late phase of their institutional career (i.e., prerelease) were more likely to show conformity to staff role expectations than were residents in the middle phase. This indicates that the effects of the inmate culture are clearly reversible and that staff could have considerably more influence on inmates than they do.

In support of this logic Glaser (1964) found a U-shaped pattern showing maximum aloofness between residents at the beginning and at the end of their prison terms. He also notes that strong resident–staff contacts and communication exist even in the most authoritarian prison institutions. He hypothesizes that inmate leaders probably have the greatest influence in correctional programs in which informal inmate–staff communication and contact are minimized. Glaser argues that inmate–inmate relationships might be radically altered if staff–inmate communication were expanded. If any inmate can easily make contact with staff, then staff contact can no longer enhance the status of certain inmates only.

The evidence that increased resident–staff contact should lead to increased resident–staff agreement and greater staff influence on residents is substantial. Glaser summarizes these considerations very succinctly:

> Staff influence on inmates varies directly with staff manifestation to inmates of the same types of personal behavior that cause a man to be liked in non-prison relationships. (a) Inmates are most influenced by staff who act towards them in friendly and considerate—rather than hostile—tone and manner. (b) Inmates are most influenced by staff who treat them with fairness and predictability. (1964, p. 133)

The possibility of using residents in limited staff roles to increase resident–staff communication and congruence has been extensively explored, but the results have been mixed. There are many reports of residents taking over almost the entire responsibility of certain functions at correctional institutions (e.g., Sutherland and Cressey, 1960, pp. 490–491), but total resident control is unlikely to work out successfully (or for that matter to be attempted) in the majority of situations. The use of a resident government or resident council with limited authority over matters directly affecting residents is the most likely channel for increasing resident–staff communication. Patient governments have been extensively used in psychiatric treatment facilities. The use of residents to help govern or run certain aspects of correctional programs is increasing in both juvenile and adult institutions. Our data suggest that the proportion of correctional programs with some sort of resident government is still fairly low. We found that 30% of the staff in adult programs and 40% of the staff in juvenile programs indicated that there was some sort of resident government in their program. Indeed, more than 75% of juvenile and adult staff indicated that they would ideally like to have some kind of resident government in their program. This shows that further change along these lines is likely to occur.

Resident–Program Congruence and Satisfaction.   The notion of behavior as a function of person–environment congruence or fit has recently received increased attention (Pervin, 1968). These investigations move away from a personological or "trait" orientation to an interactional or transactional perspective, in which a person's environment and his perception of that environment are given explicit consideration.

Research emanating from this perspective is still relatively rare in the area of crime and delinquency. Some studies have focused on the personality characteristics of delinquents (Aichorn, 1935; Glueck and Glueck, 1950), whereas others have investigated certain aspects of the social structure of correctional institutions. Very few have assessed the interaction of person and environment. The importance of investigating the interaction of delinquent and institution is emphasized in the efforts of the Preston typology study (Jesness, 1968) and the Paso Robles Differential Treatment Project (Warren, 1969) to match "types" of delinquents with specific treatment programs.

In the following work, which was done in collaboration with Ed Trickett, we deal with the relationship between the delinquent–environment "fit" and a delinquent's satisfaction with his correctional program. On entering a correctional institution, a delinquent must define himself with respect to a variety of new reference groups, such as the other residents, the youth counselor, and the guards. Our hypothesis was that the delinquent's satisfaction with respect to these groups would be related to the degree to which he sees himself as similar to them. If, however, he sees himself as a "fish out of water," as vastly different from a particular group, he will report dissatisfaction with that group. The hypothesis derives from research indicating that perceived similarity is positively related to interpersonal attraction (Brown, 1962; Lott and Lott, 1965).

The work followed some related research conducted in college environments. Pervin (1967a) studied college characteristics and student-by-college interaction using the Transactional Analysis of Personality and Environment (TAPE), an instrument based on the semantic differential. Students from 21 colleges rated the following concepts on 52 different scales: my college, myself, students, faculty, administration, and ideal college. Ratings of satisfaction with different aspects of college life were also made. In general, discrepancies between students' perception of themselves and of their college were related to dissatisfaction with college. Discrepancies between perceptions of self and other students were most highly related to reports of feeling uncomfortable with students. Discrepancies between perceptions of self and perceptions of faculty were most highly related to reports of dissatisfaction with faculty. Discrepancies between perception of self and of the administration were most highly related to reports of disagreement with the administration. Pervin (1957b) replicated these results and reported that satisfaction with the environment was not simply a function of satisfaction with self.

The study took place in a correctional institution for male adolescent delinquents. Incoming groups of delinquents underwent a 10- to 14-day orientation and testing program and lived in two separate "housing units" with separate staffs. The two units allowed for a replication of the study within the original design. The subjects were 75 residents from one unit and 60 from the other. Ages in both groups ranged from 15 to 18 with a median of 17 years and both groups had comparable average reading scores (eighth grade) and I.Q. (100).

The semantic differential technique was used to assess the residents' perceptions of themselves and their environment. Each resident was asked to rate six concepts: (1) myself, (2) the way I'd like to be, (3) the other residents, (4) the counselor, (5) the housing unit officer, and (6) the disciplinary committee. Each concept was rated on a 9-point scale for each of 11 adjective word pairs, chosen because of its applicability to the sample and the setting. Examples of word pairs include: honest–dishonest, fair–unfair, friendly–unfriendly, tough–not tough, and helpful–not helpful.

The questionnaire also asked about satisfaction with various aspects of the institution in six different areas: (1) general satisfaction, (2) satisfaction with other residents, (3) satisfaction with the staff, (4) satisfaction about the opportunity for personal development in the institution, (5) satisfaction with the orientation program ("In general, do you feel that the orientation program gave you useful information about the program here?"), and (6) satisfaction with the group meeting ("How useful do you feel the group meeting is?").

The CIES was given to residents to assess the social climate of the two units and to provide evidence on the similarity of their social milieus. The residents were given these questionnaires near the end of the 10- to 14-day orientation and testing program. By this time all residents were familiar with the various groups mentioned in the semantic differential questionnaire.

The results of the CIES indicated that the two units had essentially identical control-oriented social environments. Both units were substantially above average on the System Maintenance dimensions of Order and Organization and Staff Control. Both units were somewhat below average (between 0.5 and 1 standard deviation) on all three Relationship dimensions, all three Treatment Program dimensions, and Clarity. The two units did not differ from each other by even as much as 0.5 standard deviation on any of the nine subscales. Since the social environments on the two units were essentially identical, it was felt that they could be used as replicates of one another (see Trickett and Moos, 1972).

Similarity scores were calculated for the following five pairs of concepts: self–ideal self, self–other residents, self–counselor, self–housing officer, and self–disciplinary committee. For each of the 11 adjective pairs for each concept, the absolute difference on the rating between the first concept and the rating on the second concept was calculated. A similarity score was obtained for each pair of concepts by summing the 11 difference scores.

Correlations were calculated between the resulting five similarity scores and the six satisfaction scores, separately for each. There were significant postive relationships between self–staff similarity (self–counselors, self–housing officer, self–disciplinary committee) and satisfaction with institutional staff. These correlations, which ranged from a low of .37 to a high of .62 were replicated in both units. There were also strong positive relationships between self–staff similarity and satisfaction with different aspects of the institutional program. For example, residents who saw themselves as more similar to staff were more likely to feel that the orientation program was clear and helpful (correlations ranged between .22 and .42), that the group meeting was useful and its purpose clear (correlations ranged between .22 and .58), and that the institutional program helped them to develop their abilities and self-confidence (correlations ranged between .20 and .33). All but two of the resulting correlations were statistically significant and were replicated in both units.

The results support the utility of the interactional approach to assessing a person's satisfaction with his environment. The strongest relationships were those between self–staff similarity and satisfaction with the staff and the institutional program. The magnitude of these relationships was considerably greater than those involving self–other resident or self–ideal self comparisons. The fact that these self–staff relationships hold for satisfaction with the orientation program and the group program indicates that the activities of the residents during the 10- to 14-day orientation program were almost totally staff-dominated. The residents' satisfaction with their opportunity for personal development in the program was more highly and consistently related to their perceived similarity to staff than to their perceived similarity to other residents. This underscores the importance of correctional staff in contributing to positive experiences within correctional programs.

An important aspect of this study relates to the use of the CIES as a measure of the similarity between the social climates of the two correctional units. Attempts to replicate psychological studies in different institutions are often unsuccessful, presumably in part because of important differences in the psychological environments or climates of the institutions studied. Measures that assess and compare these environments may provide information on the range of environmental variation within which replications of specific findings can reasonably be expected to occur.

Rule Breaking and Deviant Behavior. Do delinquents who break rules in a correctional program perceive that program deviantly? Our interest in this question was partly kindled by a general concern with the correlates of deviant perceptions and expectations, and by a study by Wood et al. (1966), who found that inmates labeled as "troublemakers" by institutional staff differed significantly from other inmates in the way they perceived their institutionalization. Wood identified groups of residents who varied in degree of troublemaking behavior. The subjects were 392 adolescent males, and three groups were formed as follows: the high-consensus troublemakers (HCT) consisted of those who were nominated by four or more staff members as troublemakers; the low-consensus troublemakers (LCT) consisted of those who received only one or two nominations; a control group (C) was established by random selection from residents who received no nominations as troublemakers.

The authors first showed that the three groups varied in actual troublemaking behavior (as recorded from disciplinary action records) exactly as would be expected from staff nominations. The high-consensus troublemakers saw less opportunity, less reasonable and sympathetic authority, and greater arbitrary unpredictability in the institutional situation than did the controls. In every comparison the HCT group defined the institutional situation in a significantly more "troublemaker-prone" manner than did the control group, and in every case the low-consensus troublemaker group fell in between. Thus residents whose definitions are positive or favorable are the ones who tend to adapt to the program, cooperate with its constraints and make most productive use of its resources.

Disciplinary Actions in Two Correctional Programs. An attempt was made to replicate the foregoing findings in the two juvenile correctional units used in the previous study. Regular disciplinary reports were made in each unit, and hearings that ended in specific dispositions of each case were held. A three-month record of all disciplinary infractions engaged in by all residents who participated in the earlier study was obtained. There was complete data on 171 residents, of which 132 broke no rules and 39 broke one or more institutional rules. The broken rules varied from "failure to clean living quarters" and "tearing a state T shirt," to "refusing to work," "disobeying the orders of staff," and "making derogatory remarks at staff and using profane language," to more disturbed behavior, ("urinating in the yard"), and more aggressive behavior, ("fighting in the dining room," "stealing other residents' property," "racial agitation," "breaking a window with fist in a state of enragement," "destroying library books," "carrying a razor blade in wallet," and so on).

The 39 rule breakers perceived the social environments of the two correctional units more negatively than did the 132 residents who did not break any rules. This was particularly true on Expressiveness, Practical Orientation, and Personal Problem Orientation. Do residents who are more serious and constant rule breakers (like the high-consensus troublemaking group of Wood et al.) view the social environment even more negatively? The 20 most serious and repeated rule breakers were compared with the 132 non-rule breakers. The more serious rule breakers perceived the social environments of the two correctional units much more negatively. In addition to the differences mentioned they also perceived less Support and Order and Organization, and not surprisingly, more Staff Control. Rule breakers also rate themselves as much less satisfied with the institution, as liking the staff less, as feeling that they have less chance to develop their abilities and self-confidence, and, interestingly, as being more likely to get into trouble in the institution. These results were even more strongly evident for the serious rule breakers. There may be considerable validity in these findings, since the serious rule breakers rated themselves as much less likely to "make it once you're back out on the streets."

Rule breakers also see themselves and the institutional staff much more negatively than do non-rule breakers. On the other hand, rule breakers see other residents much more positively than do non-rule breakers. Finally, rule breakers see themselves as more deviant from institutional staff, particularly from the housing unit officer and the disciplinary committee. To put it another way, the residents who do not break rules see themselves as more similar to other residents and to program staff than do residents who get into trouble.

It is, of course, unclear whether residents who have deviant perceptions are more likely to break rules and/or whether residents who break rules are more likely to experience the institution deviantly. Both processes probably occur. Chase's results (Chapter 8) suggest that residents who have deviant perceptions are more likely to abscond from the program. Thus there may be some value in identifying and counseling residents who initially develop particularly deviant perceptions of a correctional program.

Deviant Response Tendencies.   Are residents who perceive their program deviantly less likely to be satisfied and to believe that their program is helping them? Four measures of deviancy were used to provide information on these questions.

1. *Total Deviancy (Real)* is a measure of the absolute discrepancy between an individual resident's perception of his program and the average perceptions of the other residents.

2. *Total Deviancy (Ideal)* is the absolute discrepancy between an individual resident's concepts of an ideal program and the average ideal program conceptualizations of the other residents.

3. *Directional Deviancy* is an overall score reflecting the extent to which an individual resident sees his program as more or less positive than the other residents. High scores on the first eight subscales and a low score on Staff Control are considered to be in the "more positive" direction.

4. *Real–Ideal Discrepancy* is the squared differences between a resident's perception of his correctional milieu and his concepts of an ideal correctional milieu.

These four measures of deviancy were used earlier in studies of psychiatric treatment programs (Moos, 1974; Chapters 9 and 12). Basically, patients who saw their treatment milieu deviantly were less satisfied with the program, liked the staff less, and felt that what they were doing in the program was less likely to enhance their abilities and their self-esteem. They also tended to do somewhat more poorly at 6-month follow-up. The most consistent finding was that patients who perceived an environment more positively actually did better in that environment. Patients who perceived less real–ideal environment discrepancy were more satisfied with the program, liked the staff more, felt less anxious and felt that they could develop their personal abilities better.

The relationship between deviancy and patient reactions to the program and treatment outcome varied as a function of the characteristics of the treatment environment itself. The treatment milieu must be seen as a "moderator" variable, and deviancy must be thought of as an adaptive reaction in some environments. Patients who perceived their treatment program deviantly were more dissatisfied in programs that had more treatment-oriented milieus. In some programs with particularly undifferentiated "negative" or control-oriented milieus, however, deviancy was positively related to satisfaction and other positive reactions to the program. These findings indicate that results may sometimes not generalize from one program to another precisely because the programs have important differential characteristics.

A total of 29 correctional programs provided the data in an attempt to replicate these findings. Residents on the 29 units took both Form R and Form I of the CIES and also reported their general reactions to their units. The intercorrelations among the four deviancy scores were averaged over the 29 programs. The correlations were generally moderate; for example, Total Deviancy (Real) correlated positively with Total Deviancy (Ideal) and with Real–Ideal Discrepancy, whereas it correlated moderately negatively with Directional Deviancy. The results indicate that the four deviancy measures, although moderately related, assess somewhat different aspects of deviant perceptions.

Total Deviancy (Real and Ideal).   The two Total Deviancy scores (real and ideal) were correlated (over residents within each of the 29 units) with the residents' reactions to the program. The number of cases varied from unit to unit, but was usually between 25 and 45 residents. Negative correlations (the predicted direction) indicate that residents who show large Total Deviancy scores are less satisfied with the program, like the staff less, and feel that there are fewer opportunities for personal development. The predictions were not confirmed. The average within-program correlations were of only minimal magnitude (none was greater than .10) and were not significantly different from zero. Thus residents who perceive their programs (either real or ideal) in a deviant manner do not necessarily feel less satisfied, and so on.

However, there was great variability among programs in the magnitude and direction of the relationships between the deviancy scores and the resident's reactions to the program. For example, the within-unit correlations between Total Deviancy (real) and general satisfaction ranged from .52 to −.55, and the correlations between Total Deviancy (real) and the degree of personal growth the resident felt he could attain in the program ranged from .47 to −.56. Therefore, we performed a further analysis, similar to that done earlier on psychiatric programs. Seven of the 29 programs showed relatively high and consistently significant correlations between Total Deviancy (real) and the other variables. On the other hand, there was a group of three programs on which the relationships between Total Deviancy and general reactions to the program were in the reverse direction (i.e., they were consistently positive rather than negative).

Mean standard scores for the residents' perceptions of these two groups of units were calculated and the profiles for group A (the three programs on which the results were in the predicted direction) and group B (the seven programs on which the results were opposite to the predicted direction) are compared in Figure 9.1. The social environments of these two groups of correctional programs were dramatically different. The units on which deviant residents showed less satisfaction, and so on, have substantially higher scores on all three Relationship

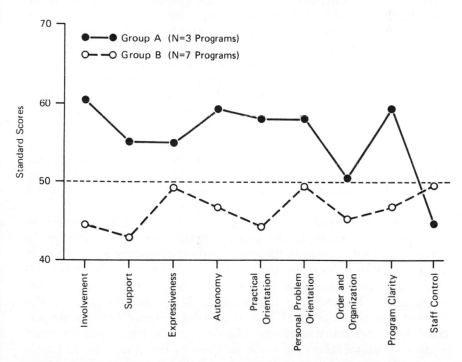

Figure 9.1 CIES Form R profiles for three group A programs and seven group B programs.

dimensions, all three Treatment Program dimensions, and the System Maintenance dimensions of Order and Organization and Program Clarity.

Psychiatric wards on which deviant patients showed less satisfaction had higher scores on the WAS Relationship dimensions of Involvement and Spontaneity and the Treatment Program dimensions of Practical Orientation and Personal Problem Orientation. Thus the two sets of results are almost identical. Deviancy is related to dissatisfaction only in those environments which have the most coherent and active treatment programs. Deviant perceptions of the environment are related to greater individual satisfaction and expectation of personal benefit when the environment itself is particularly negative and/or undifferentiated. The characteristics of a social environment are critical moderator variables that affect both the magnitude and direction of various hypothesized relationships.

Directional Deviancy and Real–Ideal Discrepancy. Similar within-unit correlations were calculated for each of the 29 units between both Directional Deviancy and Real–Ideal Discrepancy and the residents' reactions to the program. Table 9.2 summarizes the results, which are quite consistent. When residents perceive their programs more positively, they feel more satisfied with their program, like the staff more, and feel that the program gives them greater opportunities for personal growth. For example, 27 of the 29 within-unit correlations between Directional Deviancy and general satisfaction were in the right direction, and 17 of them were statistically significant. The results for Real–Ideal Discrepancy are generally similar (but reversed in sign), although not quite as strong. Since the results are quite consistent over the 29 units, they indicate that the relationships between these two deviancy scores and general reactions to the program do not vary substantially in different social environments.

These results were almost exact replications of the results in psychiatric programs; for example, the average correlation between Directional Deviancy and satisfaction in 23 hospital-based programs was .39. Other findings also show that individuals who perceive their environments more positively are more satisfied and actually perform better in those environments. For example, Kish et al. (1971) found that patients who obtained high scores on the Rotter Internal–External Control scale perceived their ward more positively. The authors also found that the mean length of hospitalization for small samples of Internals and Externals was significantly different, with the Internals having been hospitalized for a far shorter period. The Internals also perceived themselves as tak-

Table 9.2 Relationships Between Directional Deviancy and Real–Ideal Discrepancy and Resident Reactions

Reactions to Program	Directional Deviancy			Real–Ideal Discrepancy		
	Mean Correlation	Number in Predicted Direction (N = 29)	Number Significant (N = 29)	Mean Correlation	Number in Predicted Direction (N = 29)	Number Significant (N = 29)
General satisfaction	.36	27	17	−.21	24	11
Like staff	.30	25	17	−.09	18	8
Anxiety	−.11	20	5	.12	21	6
Personal development	.25	25	12	−.17	22	13

ing more initiatives in the areas of Involvement, Support, Practical Orientation, and Staff Control. Kish et al. note that the differences in perceptions of the treatment milieu may be realistic, since it is possible that the Internal patient is seen by staff as having greater potential for improvement and is thus treated in a more therapeutic fashion, while the External patient is relatively ignored and treated in a more custodial fashion. Thus people who perceive social milieus more positively may do so because these milieus are more positive for them.

Jesness (1968) has presented extensive data on the question of whether the resident's perception of treatment conditions is related to the extent of his change within the program. He gave residents an 81-item questionnaire, the Post-Opinion Poll, a portion of which measured their perceptions of the treatment environment on five subscales: Involvement, Permissiveness, Equalitarianism, Acceptance, and Fairness. Change scores were obtained for all residents on both the Jesness Inventory and on Behavior Check List factors as rated by staff. There were small but statistically significant relationships between the resident's perceptions of the five treatment dimensions and change scores on the Jesness Inventory. For example, residents who perceived more Trust, Permissiveness, and Fairness in the environment improved more on the Jesness Social Maladjustment, Value-Orientation, Autism, Alienation, Manifest Aggression, and Denial subscales. Interestingly, these relationships were strongest for the developmentally most mature residents. For these residents, the perception of Trust and Fairness in the environment was quite strongly related to positive changes on several of the Jesness Inventory scores. The relationships were considerably less clear and consistent for the less developmentally mature residents. Thus positive perception of the treatment environment may be most important for developmentally more mature higher ego strength residents. These residents are also probably the most amenable to treatment-oriented approaches.

In an interesting corroborative study, Ellsworth and Maroney (1972) examined the relationship between patients' perceptions of their ward and patient behavior. Staff rated the behavior of 75 patients on such variables as cooperation, ability to communicate with staff, and ability to plan realistically. Statistically significant relationships were found between patient behavior as rated by staff and perceptions of the treatment program. Those patients who saw their program and experiences in more positive terms were rated by staff as being more cooperative and communicative than those who reported negative experiences.

Walberg and Anderson (1968) have related measures of classroom climate and individual learning. They obtained measures of student perceptions of classroom climate on 18 subscales relevant to the classroom learning environment. They also acquired information on the affective, behavioral, and cognitive reactions of the students. The findings were complex, but Walberg and Anderson concluded that students with different perceptions of classroom climate changed in different ways during a physics course. For example, students who gained the most on physics achievement saw their classes as socially homogeneous, cohesive groups. Students who changed more in science understanding saw their classes as well-organized, with little friction between their fellow students. Students who reported greater enjoyment in laboratory work saw their classes as democratic in policy setting, as having a clear idea of class goals, and as being more satisfying. These results are quite intriguing, even though the analyses confounded individual differences in perceptions of classes with actual differences in the social climates of the classes. Thus the results may indicate that students who perceive classes as more democratic and clear on goals report enjoying their laboratory work more, and/or that classes that are actually more democratic and clear have students who enjoy their laboratory work more.

In a final relevant study Herr (1965) found that high school students categorized as high or middle achievers perceived more press for affiliation and dependence on others, for assistance and protection, for intense open emotional display, for detached impersonal thinking, and for problem-solving analysis and theorizing. The low achieving students perceived more press for self-depreciation and self-evaluation, for indifference or disregard for the feelings of others, for direct or indirect aggression, and for withholding friendship and support. Students who are better achievers perceive their high school environment more positively. These findings, which are very similar in studies on treatment environments, correctional environments, and educational environments, consistently demonstrate that individuals who see their environments more positively are more satisfied with and perform better in those environments.

However, the correlates of both deviant perceptions and expectations also depend on the characteristics of the social environment. In an earlier study, we used the COPES to assess the effect of the expectations of newly admitted members in four community-based programs. The hypothesis was that prospective members would make better use of a treatment program if their expectations of the social climate matched more closely with those of program participants. The initial expectations of those patients who later did well in a program were more realistic. The expectations of the patients who later did more poorly were unrealistically high, that is, they expected much greater emphasis on all three Relationship dimensions and all three Treatment Program dimensions than actually existed in the program.

The effects of deviant expectations depended on the characteristics of the program. When the social milieu of the program was generally negative and inconsistent, patients with unrealistically positive expectations did poorly and were more likely to prematurely drop out of the program. However, when the social milieu was generally positive and coherent, high expectations (which were now realistic) did not have those negative consequences. Members' program perceptions also became more accurate with experience in the program, particularly if their initial expectations were only moderately discrepant from actual program characteristics.

Role–Induction in Correctional Programs.   These results indicate that it might be worthwhile for staff to provide accurate information about their programs to incoming residents. Wood et al. (1966) point out that their results relating deviant perceptions and troublemaking behavior leave open the question of whether the deviant perceptions arise during the course of institutionalization or are brought to the institution by the resident. This is relevant to the intervention strategy that institutional staff might adopt. If the resident arrives at his perceptions mainly through his institutional experiences, personnel could concentrate on monitoring, regulating, or changing those experiences. If, on the other hand, individuals have initial negative expectations, change efforts might best be concentrated in the early period of commitment, with heavy emphasis on countering unfavorable views by structuring and interpreting the setting in as acceptable and meaningful a way as possible. Since an individual's adaptation is related to the way in which he perceives his environment, it is in the interest of an institution to see that its resources and objectives are not misinterpreted, at least in an overly negative manner.

Evidence indicates that providing systematic information about a new environment or a new experience helps to socialize an individual and increases the probability of positive outcome (Moos, 1974; Chapter 11). Giving people information about social environments (either before they enter or in their first few weeks in the environment) can enhance the accuracy of their perceptions and/or expectations, thus potentially reduce the incidence of maladaptation, runaway behavior, and so on. If an individual resident's very discrepant perceptions or expectations could be fed back to him in individual counseling sessions, he would learn that he perceived the social environment differently from others. He would thus be sensitized to the reasons for these differences and to the impact they might have on his overall functioning. Studies in both individual and group psychotherapy have shown that "role-reduction" or "socialization" interviews with prospective patients can enhance the therapeutic relationship and treatment outcome (e.g., Orne and Wender, 1968; Yalom et al., 1967).

Social climate scales like the CIES may be useful in helping to specify the psychosocial or perceived characteristics of different correctional programs. At a minimum, program descriptions should systematically describe the dimensions included in the Relationship, Treatment Program, and Systems Maintenance areas. Information about the social climate of an environment should help individuals more accurately select social environments that might be most beneficial to them. This logic is most likely to apply to correctional staff attempting to choose which correctional program to work on, and to prospective residents who might in the future be allowed to choose the kind of residential program (e.g., foster home, group home) they wish to participate in (see Chapter 10).

REFERENCES

Aichorn, A. *Wayward youth.* Viking Press, New York, 1935.

Brown, R. Models of attitude change. In T. M. Newcomb (Ed.), *New directions in psychology.* Holt, Rinehart & Winston, New York, 1962.

Burdock, E., Cheek, F., & Zubin, J. Predicting success in psychoanalytic training. In P. Hoch & J. Zubin (Eds.), *Current approaches to psychoanalysis.* Grune & Stratton, New York, 1960, pp. 176–191.

Clemmer, D. *The prison community.* Holt, Rinehart & Winston, New York, 1958.

Cook, T. The influence of client–counselor value similarity on change in meaning during brief counseling. *Journal of Counseling Psychology,* 13:77–81, 1966.

Ellsworth, R. & Maroney, R. Characteristics of psychiatric programs, and their effects on patients' adjustment. *Journal of Consulting and Clinical Psychology,* 39:436–447, 1972.

Eynon, T., Allen, H., & Reckless, W. Measuring the impact of juvenile correctional institution by perceptions of inmates and staff. *Journal of Research in Crime and Delinquency,* 8:93–107, 1971.

Glaser, D. *The effectiveness of a prison and parole system.* Bobbs-Merrill, Indianapolis, 1964.

Glueck, S. & Glueck, E. *Unraveling juvenile delinquency.* Harvard University Press, Cambridge, Mass., 1950.

Goldstein, A., Heller, K., & Sechrest, L. *Psychotherapy and the psychology of behavior change.* Wiley, New York, 1966.

Grusky, O. Role conflict in organization: A study of prison camp officials, *Administrative Science Quarterly,* 3:452–472, 1959.

Haggard, E. *Intraclass correlation and the analysis of variance.* Dryden Press, New York, 1958.

Herr, E. Differential perceptions of "Environmental press" by high school students. *Personnel and Guidance Journal,* 7:678–686, 1965.

Jesness, C. The Preston typology study. Unpublished manuscript, Institute for the Study of Crime and Delinquency, Sacramento, 1968.

Kish, G., Solber, K., & Uecker, A. Locus of control as a factor influencing patients' perceptions of ward atmosphere. *Journal of Clinical Psychology,* **27:**287–289, 1971.

Lott, A.G. & Lott, B.E. Group cohesiveness as interpersonal attraction. *Psychological Bulletin,* **64:**259–309, 1965.

Meltzoff, J. & Kornreich, M. *Research in psychotherapy.* Atherton Press, New York, 1970.

Moos, R. *Evaluating treatment environments: A social ecological approach.* Wiley, New York, 1974.

Orne, M. & Wender, P. Anticipatory socialization for psychotherapy: Method and rationale. *American Journal of Psychiatry,* **124:**1202–1212, 1968.

Pervin, L. A. A twenty-college study of student and college interaction using TAPE (transactional analysis of personality and environment): Rationale, reliability, and validity. *Journal of Educational Psychology,* **58:**290–303, 1967a.

Pervin, L. A. Satisfaction and perceived self-environment similarity: A semantic differential study of student–college interaction. *Journal of Personality,* **35:**623–634, 1967b.

Pervin, L. A. Performance and satisfaction as a function of individual–environment fit. *Psychological Bulletin,* **69:**56–68, 1968.

Piliavin, I. & Vadum, A. Reducing discrepancies in professional and custodial perspectives. *Journal of Research in Crime and Delinquency,* **5:**35–43, 1968.

Rogers, C., Gendlin, E., Kiesler, D. & Truax, C. *The therapeutic relationship and its impact.* University of Wisconsin Press, Madison, 1967.

Rosenthal, D. Changes in some moral values following psychotherapy. *Journal of Consulting Psychology,* **19:**431–436, 1955.

Stern, G. *People in context.* Wiley, New York, 1970.

Sutherland, E. & Cressey, D. *Principles of criminology,* 6th ed. Lippincott, Philadelphia, 1960, pp. 490–491.

Trickett, E. & Moos, R. Satisfaction with the correctional institution environment: An instance of perceived self-environment similarity. *Journal of Personality,* **40:**75–88, 1972.

Walberg, H. & Anderson, G. Classroom climate and individual learning. *Journal of Educational Psychology,* **59:**414–419, 1968.

Warren, M. Q. The case for differential treatment of delinquents. *Annals of the American Academy of Political and Social Science,* **381:**47–59, 1969.

Welkowitz, J., Cohen, J., & Ortmeyer, D. Value system similarity: Investigation of patient–therapist dyads. *Journal of Consulting Psychology,* **31:**48–55, 1967.

Wheeler, S. Socialization in correctional communities, *American Sociological Review,* **26:**697–712, 1961.

Wood, B., Wilson, G., Jessor, R., & Bogan, J. Troublemaking behavior in a correctional institution: Relationship to inmates' definition of their situation. *American Journal of Orthopsychiatry,* **36:**795–802, 1966.

Yalom, I., Houts, P., Newell, G., & Rand, K. Preparation of patients for group therapy. *Archives of General Psychiatry,* **17:**416–427, 1967.

PART FOUR

Applications to Community Settings

CHAPTER TEN

Community-Based
Correctional Programs

Corrections and the Community. Dissatisfaction with institutional correctional programs is at an all-time high. The case against the present system of institutionalization has been stated many times (e.g., Empey, 1967). The basic argument is twofold. First, there is no acceptable empirical evidence that incarceration deters crime or recidivism. Reducing the amount of time in an institution does not seem to significantly increase recidivism and may actually decrease it. Second, many studies have demonstrated the destructive impact of correctional institutions. For example, one of the recent government studies concluded that "life in many institutions is at best barren and futile, at worst unspeakably brutal and degrading . . . the conditions in which (inmates) live are the poorest possible preparation for their successful reentry into society and often merely reinforce in them a pattern of manipulation or destructiveness" (The Challenge of Crime in a Free Society, p. 159). Popular writers have strongly supported these conclusions (e.g., Mitford, 1973).

These considerations have fostered attempts to institute a wide range of community-based correctional alternatives. Burdman (1969) points out that more than 70% of all offenders can probably be treated in the community, although some may need short-term community-oriented confinement. The term "community treatment" means quite different things to different people. Alternatives to institutionalization include sentencing options such as suspended sentences, fines, and victim restitution programs; regular and enriched probation programs with low

233

caseload sizes; nonresidential work and/or group therapy programs, vocational, and academic educational programs; and a variety of prerelease and early release options such as work furlough programs and family visitation programs. There are also intensive nonresidential community programs such as halfway houses and daycare and out-patient clinics. Finally, there are community-based residential alternatives such as boarding homes, group homes, foster care, semi-institutional or "open" cottage living, forestry and work camps, and other "enriched" semi-institutional programs. Many programs combine one or more of the foregoing elements.

This chapter focuses on residential and intensive nonresidential (i.e., halfway houses, day care) community-based alternatives. We first examine some typical examples of programs that offer intensive intervention in lieu of institutionalization. We then deal more specifically with group homes, since they represent one major approach to community-oriented handling of delinquents who cannot remain in their family setting. A California project focusing on the development of group homes is discussed. An analysis indicating that there are six major types of intensive community-based program is presented. In the last section some guidelines for enhancing the accuracy and utility of published descriptions of community-based programs are discussed.

Residential and intensive nonresidential community programs have been used as supplements or alternatives to formal incarceration for juvenile and adult offenders for many years. The number and importance of these programs has greatly increased in the past decade. For example, Griggs and McCune (1972) report that at least 27 states and the District of Columbia have state-financed community treatment programs for adult offenders. Similar programs for juvenile offenders are considerably more prevalent (see Bradley, 1969; Community-based Correctional Programs, 1971; Warren, 1972). Some typical programs are discussed below.

Many of the original demonstration projects were patterned after the Highfields residential group center (see McCorkle, Elias, and Bixby, 1958). The Essexfields program was basically patterned after Highfields except that the boys returned to their homes every evening and also spent the weekend at home. Members arrived at Essexfields at 7:30 A.M. and were taken to a nearby county mental hospital for a full day of work (e.g., chopping wood, cutting grass, or removing snow). Lunch, dinner, and a small daily wage were provided at the hospital. After work the members were returned to Essexfields where they participate in guided group interaction sessions before returning to their homes in the late evening.

The Essexfields program attempts to reduce conformity to delinquent peer-determined norms and to encourage the development of new "pro-social" norms and behavior patterns. "The same pressure to conform which afflicts delinquents in the community through a delinquent peer group is applied at Essexfields by a peer group ascribing to conventional norms" (Pilnick, Elias, and Clapp, 1966, p. 113). Among the other out-standing features of the program are small size (which avoids bureaucrat-ic procedures and facilitates informal relations among members and staff), staggered admissions to and discharges from the program to en-sure continuity, maintenance of close community ties, and the ability of members to share administrative responsibilities and therapeutic roles with the staff.

The Provo experiment was a very similar nonresidential program fea-turing work in the community and the use of guided group interaction techniques (Empey and Erickson, 1972). Members of the experimental program were compared with two control groups of court wards in the Provo area: boys on regular probation and boys sent to the state training school. Two major findings stood out. First, when pre- and postprogram delinquency rates were compared, there were significant reductions in every program, including incarceration. Second, the reductions were greater for the boys who remained in the community than for those who were incarcerated. The experimental community program was asso-ciated with considerably less postprogram delinquency and adult crime than was incarceration. Empey and Erickson conclude that "efforts to improve correctional programs might be far more fruitful if they concen-trated upon the improvement of community rather than institutional designs" (p. 261).

Vasoli and Fahey (1970) described and evaluated a halfway house for parolees from a state reformatory for older juvenile offenders. The Notre Dame Youth Center was located in a residential hotel in Gary, Indiana. The center was the result of an unusual five-way collaboration involving a grant from the federal government, approval from the rele-vant state, city, and county agencies, supervision by a staff assembled and directed by a local university, and the development of job opportu-nities at a large local steel company. The primary focus of the project was vocational, although some counseling and supervision were provid-ed. Seventy-seven participants entered the halfway house, and 50 ob-tained jobs at the steel company. Alternative job placements were se-cured for the other 27 youths. Thus the vocational aspect of the program was regarded as highly successful. There were many problems because supervision was minimal; for example, several serious crimes were appar-ently plotted among parolees on Center premises. The authors conclude that halfway houses can serve an important function, although there are serious difficulties in placing groups of parolees in the same living setting.

Community residential programs have also been established for adult offenders. Generally these have been prerelease programs for individuals about to be paroled from prison. Euclid House, a therapeutic community halfway house for prisoners, uses group counseling and individual therapy to prepare inmates for their return to the community. Euclid House consists of two row houses in Washington, D.C., which hold up to 55 former inmates from a nearby state reformatory (Aledort and Jones, 1973). The house has a strong therapeutic community orientation and envisages a lengthy program of psychiatric treatment for it residents. Residents are encouraged to find full-time jobs but at the same time must participate in therapy sessions at the house. Supplementary training and service programs are planned (e.g., a training center for young lawyers and a day care center for working mothers).

Aledort and Jones point out that Euclid House differs significantly from the other correctional halfway houses in Washington. The primary task of the other houses is to effect the rapid reentry of wage earners into the community. As a result the major issues in these houses revolve around the former prisoners' ability or inability to handle vocational and work tasks. Very little if any psychotherapeutic work is done relevant to the other areas of the former prisoners' life (e.g., family and peer interactions). This type of house is similar to the Notre Dame Youth Center just described.

In distinction, Euclid House maximizes interactions by having house residents meet five times a week in one-hour team meetings. There are two one-hour community meetings per week and an open meeting in which members of the community can participate, as well as weekly family meetings, meetings for couples and singles groups, and home visits. A variety of issues are discussed in these meetings—responsibility and independence, authority roles and decision-making behavior, the open expressions of anxious and aggressive feelings, and so forth. Practical tasks such as negotiation with employers (and with staff) are also emphasized. Aledort and Jones present some evidence relevant to the success of the program; for example, there was a marked decrease in the number of escapes and the amount of recidivistic activity after the program had been in operation for 6 months.

Some adult rehabilitation programs offer a community alternative to incarceration in the regular jail and prison system. Ellsworth House represents one of the few such programs in which participants are randomly selected from the population of offenders already sentenced to a county jail for a term of 4 months or more (Lamb and Goertzel, 1974). Thus this program serves people who would otherwise be in the jail system, which in the county involved (San Mateo, California), includes a rural honor camp and a work furlough facility.

Ellsworth House can house 20 men. All residents must participate in some constructive full-time activity, such as employment, college, or a training program. The program at Ellsworth House has three phases in which residents obtain increasing autonomy and independence in return for which they are expected to assume increased responsibility. The climate of the house appears to be Relationship-oriented in that the men are encouraged to become involved in the house program and are given generous amounts of staff support. However, it is also high on System Maintenance dimensions in that it is clearly recognized that the men need careful structure and an organized program with firm and consistent limits. The emphasis is on the maintenance of personal growth and the development of both personal and vocations skills within a supportive and well-structured setting.

One-year follow-up of the Ellsworth House group and the regular jail program comparison group showed that the two groups had comparable recidivism rates (about 30% committed an offense that resulted in a jail sentence or revocation of probation within one year). However, slightly more of the Ellsworth House group (69%) than of the comparison group (56%) were regularly employed at the one-year follow-up. Although the results are preliminary, this is one of the first studies to empirically indicate (with a randomly selected control group) that a community alternative may work as well or better than a program of regular incarceration.

Keller and Alper (1971) and Grygier, Nease, and Anderson (1970) present general discussions detailing the strengths and weaknesses of various halfway house arrangements. Keller and Alper distinguish between two broad categories: (1) halfway in (i.e., houses that generally serve younger offenders on probation and may be residential or nonresidential), and (2) halfway out (i.e., houses that assist people who are ready to leave an institution and who are judged to be in need of help in readjusting to the community). Grygier et al. point out that halfway houses may offer financial security, vocational help, and general encouragement and moral support. However, they also allow for a concentration of offenders, which may reinforce rather than reduce criminal values and patterns of behavior. Other examples of community-oriented correctional programs are numerous. Adler (1971) discusses Relationship- and Treatment-oriented models; Mayer (1972) and Ziegler (1972) present various aspects of Therapeutic Community models;

Meyer, Odom, and Wax (1973) and Endres and Goke (1973) illustrate incentive and behavior modification models, and Maluccio and Marlow (1972) present a comprehensive overview of community-oriented residential treatment models for emotionally disturbed children. Post, Hicks, and Monfort (1968) describe a day care program for delinquents. McNeil (1967) discusses Genesee House, an informal, supportive type of halfway house program for young delinquents. Alper (1974) reviews a wide range of alternative correctional programs. One little-used alternative to institutionalization is restitution when a person has stolen or damaged something. Restitution is being used in Norway, Sweden, Argentina, and Colombia. Halfway houses and other open institutions have been established as alternatives or supplements to prison sentences in this country, in Europe, and in several Asian countries. Unusual programs such as maritime academies, ship construction training, and Outward Bound survival-training can give delinquents a sense of accomplishment, and may teach delinquents economically valuable skills that will ensure a steady income after release.

Group and Family Homes.   Group home and foster care programs have been developed mainly for those delinquents who do not need institutionalization but who cannot return to their family setting. Foster home programs are discussed in detail elsewhere (Community-based correctional programs, 1971). The group home differs from foster care in the following ways. The dwelling or house is often owned or rented by the social service agency; house parents and other staff are usually employed on a salaried, working week basis; there may be several unrelated adults providing services of varying degrees of intensity, and so forth (Gula, 1964; Herstein, 1964). It is important to distinguish between agency-operated group homes, which are generally staffed by employees of the agency responsible for placing youth in the program, and contract homes, which may be operated by a private organization (e.g., a church or civic group) or by private individuals (Rabinow, 1964).

There are many examples of experimental group home projects. The Silverlake Project is a part-time residential program based on the model of the Highfields and Essexfields programs. It also uses guided group interaction as its primary treatment modality. Residents live at Silverlake during the week but attend the local high school and return to their homes on weekends. Residents were randomly assigned to the program from a pool of male wards assigned to Boys Republic, a private institution in the Los Angeles area. Comparison of Boys Republic and Silverlake showed little advantage to either program in terms of the percentage of successful program completions or recidivism. However, since the average length of stay of Silverlake residents was only about half that of Boys Republic residents, Silverlake appears to have a considerable cost advantage (Empey and Lubeck, 1971).

Turner (1969) presents a lively and informative account of Norman House, which was started in 1954 as a small family home in a Victorian residence in London. Cilch (1971) discusses the Hillcrest project and Parolee House, a group home located in the business district of San Diego. The program is described as focusing on the positive interpersonal dynamics found in emotionally adequate homes and as attempting to establish a friendly, warm, trustful "homelike" climate. The development of a peer group subculture is fostered. In addition, "there was a purposeful lack of structure. The parole agent exercised no formal supervision in the house and rules came from the peer group and/or house manager" (p. 8). Thus Parolee House had the image of an almost totally permissive climate, although some structure did come from the peer group. There were only three areas of behavior restrictions (i.e., bringing girls, narcotics, or alcohol into the sleeping quarters), and the peer group culture admittedly never accepted even these restrictions. In addition, attendance at house group meetings was voluntary. This is an example of an almost purely relationship-centered treatment-oriented home.

Fixsen, Phillips, and Wolf (1973a) and Phillips et al. (1973) describe the setting and program of Achievement Place, a community-based family-style treatment home for male juvenile delinquents in Lawrence, Kansas. Residents are 12 to 16-year-old boys at the junior high school level who are referred to Achievement Place by the juvenile court. A behavior modification program using a point system and rewards such as snacks after school and before bedtime, television time, home time, and allowances, is used to motivate new and socially desirable behavior.

The goal of Achievement Place is to teach the boys appropriate social (manners and introductions), academic (study and homework behaviors), self-help (meal preparation and personal hygiene), and prevocational skills that may help them adjust successfully in the community. Further information about a typical day at Achievement Place and more specific details about how the behavior modification program operates are given by Fixsen et al. (1972) and Phillips et al. (1973).

One of the most important aspects of the Achievement Place program is its commitment to continual evaluation. The progress of each boy toward his individual behavior goals is continually being assessed in objective terms. When there are no signs of definite progress, the counselors or "teaching parents" can design new procedures and reevaluate their effectiveness. Achievement Place also uses procedure evaluations, which are concerned "with the carefully measured effects of a specific, well-described procedure on a specific, objectively defined behavior of a youth" (Fixsen et al. 1973; p. 109). In one example of procedure evaluation the authors assessed the impact of a self-government system on the participation of the boys in discussions of consequences for rule violations. The results indicated that the boys participated much more in the self-government system when they were given full responsibility for deciding the consequences for a peer who had violated a rule. This is an example of how new procedures can be behaviorally evaluated within the context of a specific correctional program.

Objective outcome criteria such as postrelease institutionalization, dropout rate, and school grades all point to the success of Achievement Place. For example, only 19% of the Achievement Place youths were institutionalized either during or after treatment (compared with 54% of a "probation" youth group). By the third semester after treatment, 90% of Achievement Place boys were attending public school, whereas only 37% of probation boys were still in school. More of the Achievement Place boys were passing their classes, and their average grades were higher. Phillips et al. argue that even comparable results of alternative community and regular institutional programs would strongly support the former, since "Such programs are more humane because the youths receive more individual care, remain in closer contact with their community, parents and friends and learn important social, family and community living skills. Second group homes are less expensive to operate . . ." (1973, p. 77).

The Community Treatment Program (CTP).   The Community Treatment Program (CTP) is one of the most comprehensive attempts to develop community-based treatment alternatives for juvenile offenders. One important conclusion to emerge from CTP is that residential alternatives may be a necessary component of any comprehensive correctional program. CTP's major initial purpose was to investigate the feasibility of substituting community programs for traditional institutional programs with a sample of delinquents committed to the California Youth Authority (CYA). Phase 1 of CTP lasted from 1961 to 1964. Phase 2 lasted from 1964 to 1969, and phase 3 lasted from 1969 to 1974. Recognition of the need for residential and other intensive alternatives has increased throughout the program.

In brief, the research procedure was organized along the following lines. An assessment of eligibility for the project was made first. Certain assaultive and other "dangerous" offenders were declared ineligible; for example, 35% of the males were placed in this category largely because of the type of offense they committed, such as armed robbery, assault with a deadly weapon, and forcible rape. However, 65% of the males and 83% of the females were found eligible and were then randomly assigned to either the experimental or the control program. These youths were also classified according to the maturity level (I level) diagnostic system (see Chapter 6). The overall results indicate that CTP is at least as effective, if not more effective, than traditional institutional programs (Palmer, 1971), although some important methodological issues have been raised regarding these findings (Beker and Heyman, 1972; Gibbons, 1970; Lerman, 1972; Moos, 1973).

The main concern here is with the treatment components actually utilized in the experimental community program. Specifically, to what extent were out-of-home residential placements necessary? In early reports (e.g., Warren, 1967) it was noted that the youths were seen by their parole agents two to five times weekly in individual, group, or family settings during the intensive stage of community treatment. Although most of the experimental youths resided in their own homes, partial- or full-day programming was often involved. In addition, if it appeared that a youth could not live in his or her own home and remain nondelinquent, a foster or group home placement was made. Although only 20 to 30% of the cases were in out-of-home placement at any one time, the proportion who were in one of these placements at some time during the project was striking: 65% of the boys and 90% of the girls who had been in the project for at least 12 months had had at least one paid out-of-home placement. There is some suggestion that this proportion may have decreased over time, but the exact figures are not available. However, at least in the early phases of the program, CTP parole agents were utilizing out-of-home placement considerably more frequently than were agents with regular caseloads.

The Group Home Project.   The need for out-of-home placements led to the "Differential Treatment Environments for Delinquents" or Group Home Project designed by CTP staff. The project established five types of group home, four for long-term care and one for temporary care. The type 1 or "protective" home was designed for immature and dependent delinquents whose family background involved neglect or violence. The home was to approximate normal nondisturbed family living as closely as possible. It was to emphasize involvement and support within a framework of clear and consistent rules and regulations. This type of home was initially designed for low maturity, unsocialized, passive, and immature conformist delinquents. Because of the small number of delinquents in these categories, however, it was mainly used by higher maturity neurotic anxious and neurotic acting-out subtypes.

The type 2 or "containment" home was designed for youths labeled as "defective characters," "psychopaths," and/or "culturally conforming" delinquents. This home was to provide clear structure and firm limits. It was to operate on a "nonfamily" basis and to emphasize concrete attainable demands for socially acceptable constructive behavior. Middle maturity manipulator and cultural conformist youths were to be served by this home.

The type 3 or "boarding" home was designed for more mature youths, presumably those who would soon be able to maintain themselves in an independent placement. This type of home, which was to provide a "YMCA hotel" atmosphere while still facilitating personal relationships among the youths, was designed primarily for higher maturity neurotic acting-out and neurotic anxious boys.

The type 4 or "temporary care" home was for youths who had a temporary placement need but for whom either temporary custody or independent living was currently viewed as inappropriate. These youths were allowed to continue their regular CTP program wherever possible (e.g., counseling, school work).

The planned type 5 or "short-term restriction" home was to be for boys in need of relatively restrictive behavioral controls, but it was never successfully established because no suitable group parents were located. However, an initially unplanned type 6 or "individualized" home designed to accommodate higher maturity level youths was established. This home was mainly for neurotic acting-out and neurotic anxious youths who were not yet ready to focus on the issues of physical and/or emotional independence (as were those placed in the type 3 boarding home), yet who were in need of a healthy "family life."

A CIES Observer Rating Form.   The social environments of seven group homes (there were two "protective" and two "containment" homes) were assessed by an adapted observer rating form of the CIES. Each content scale was rated in terms of a 4-point rating scale varying from "not at all characteristic" to "highly or markedly characteristic." Thirteen parole agents and two treatment supervisors made separate assessments of each home with which they were directly involved. In addition, the group home coordinator and researcher each rated several homes. There were 43 independent ratings in all (i.e., an average of 6 assessments of each of the 7 homes that were rated). Each home was rated by at least four staff members. Raters were instructed to focus on the home as a whole rather than simply on the group house mother and/or father. There was a high degree of interrater agreement: intraclass correlations were .94, .90, and .84, respectively, for three randomly selected raters within three randomly selected homes. Ninety-five percent of randomly selected independent ratings were not more than one scale point apart.

There was substantial variation among the group homes in social climate, although most did emphasize Support and Clarity. Homes with the highest Support and/or Clarity scores tended to last longer—at least one year or more. The two homes that had the greatest longevity were the type 3 boarding home (31 months) and a girls' group home (23 months), which is briefly described below. Both homes obtained scores of 3.0 or greater (on the 4-point rating scale) on all three Relationship dimensions and on the Treatment Program dimensions of Autonomy and Personal Problem Orientation. Both homes scored lowest on Order and Organization and Staff Control. Both homes were used primarily or exclusively for high maturity level (I₄ delinquents). One of the type 1 or "protective" homes lasted for a relatively long period and also showed high scores (average of 3.0 or greater) on the Involvement, Support, and Personal Problem Orientation subscales.

The type 2 or "containment" homes for middle maturity manipulator and immature conformist delinquents were quite different. They obtained their highest scores on Order and Organization (average rating 3.2) and Control (average rating 3.0). This was the exact reverse of the homes for higher maturity level delinquents, in which these two System Maintenance areas received the least emphasis. The "containment" homes were both terminated by CTP staff because they were functioning unsuccessfully. The home that was terminated most rapidly ranked first (in comparison to the other six homes) on Order and Organization and Staff Control, whereas it ranked no higher than fifth on any of the other dimensions. Most of the differences among the homes described were statistically significant. Thus there were important differences in the social climate of the more successful as opposed to the less successful homes. The differences in social climate and in relative success occurred partly because the homes had different types of residents, although the differences in "parents" may have been even more important.

The overall evaluation of the Group Home Project was generally positive, although many problems were noted (Palmer, 1972; Pearson, 1970). The boys provided very little positive feedback to the group home parents who reacted in turn by complaining and/or increasing restrictive controls. This increased the dissatisfaction of the parole agents, who reduced their support for the group home parents. Pearson concludes, as have many others, that group homes operated by the agency itself with salaried and professionally trained staff may provide better continuity of treatment and stability of atmosphere. Palmer (1972) presents a detailed and informative discussion of these and other issues relating to the group home project.

The importance of alternative residential components continues to be apparent during phase 3 of CTP, which involves the use of a differential treatment-oriented residential facility. CTP experience indicates that direct release into a community setting is not necessarily the most appropriate way of initiating the treatment process for all delinquents (Palmer, 1970). Some youngsters have little or no chance of undergoing successful community treatment, even in an intensive program like CTP. Thus one of the major hypotheses of CTP phase 3 is that certain groups of delinquents will derive greater benefit from a course of treatment initiated within a residential rather than a community setting.

Phase 3 uses two alternative initial treatment settings or strategies. One strategy is assignment to an intensive differential treatment-oriented residential program followed by assignment to the community program. The second strategy is direct release to an intensive program in the community as practiced in phases 1 and 2. The new residential component is housed in "dorm 3," one of the living units located at the Northern Reception Center Clinic, which in the past housed a regular institutional program (Turner, 1971). The dormitory provides short-term confinement when needed and gives CTP a greater degree of flexibility in the treatment of seriously delinquent and disturbed youths. A number of procedures are being used to evaluate this new residential component of CTP including the observer rating form of the CIES already discussed.

The main point is that CTP began as an intensive attempt to institute a community-based correctional program. As this program developed it became clear that available residential treatment alternatives (i.e., foster homes and group homes) were receiving substantial use. This led to the development of the Group Home Project. As CTP progressed the great difficulties in treating and controlling certain delinquent youngsters in a community setting became obvious. This finding led to phase 3 and the development of an additional residential component of the program. Thus a residential component may be a necessary part of any comprehensive set of community-based correctional services. Greenberg and Mayer (1972) and Mora et al. (1969) present informative examples of the use of group home care as a transitional stage between residential treatment and family placement.

The serious problems that may occur vis-à-vis the community in implementing new group homes cannot be ignored. Herstein (1964), in his discussion of McCormick House, identifies one type of problem associated with the larger community. McCormick House was located in a transitional community that accepted "fairly wide extremes of behavior" and tolerated very low requirements for school performance. It was thus "difficult to maintain a stable middle-class oriented structure at McCormick House" (p. 414). Herstein states that "we have been faced with a situation where the 'openness' of the community exerts severe pressure upon our ability to maintain stable expectations and values that stand in some contrast to many of the families and teenagers in this community" (p. 414). In addition, Palmer (1972) and Rabinow (1964) point out that many youths should not be placed into a group home setting, partly because they cannot tolerate the level of intimacy prevalent there. Group homes are clearly an important addition to the community-oriented handling of delinquent youth; however, they also present many unsolved problems of organizational structure, resident placement, and constructive community relationships.

Toward a Typology of Community Programs.   Our interest in differential treatment for different types of offenders (see Chapter 5) led us to attempt to construct a typology of community-based programs. The foregoing material has illustrated the wide variety of residential and group home community placements. Can the diversity of community programs be adequately characterized by a small number of basic types?

We had obtained data on the Community-Oriented Programs Environment Scale (COPES) from members of 78 American and British programs. The 58 American programs, which are described in more detail elsewhere (see Moos, 1974a; Chapter 10), included 2 rehabilitation workshops, 2 partial hospitalization programs, 11 halfway houses, 17 day care centers, 20 community care or foster homes, a patient-administered self-help program, and a small outpatient support group. Four alcoholism treatment programs were also included. The 20 British programs included 2 day hospitals in 2 major teaching centers in London and 18 halfway houses distributed across the United Kingdom. Three of these houses were administered by the London Council, whereas the remaining 15 houses, which were all relatively small and highly staffed, were administered by a privately endowed foundation.

The procedure was identical to that used in the cluster analyses reported in Chapter 5. The 10 members COPES standard scores for each of the 78 programs were used. Intraclass correlations were computed between each set of two programs to measure their similarity. This analysis produced a 78 × 78 correlation matrix that yielded a measure of the similarity of every program with every other program. The similarity matrix was subjected to the cluster analysis algorithm developed by Carlson (1972; see Chapter 5). Six types of community program, which closely resembled the types identified in institutional correctional and hospital-based psychiatric programs, were found.

The Therapeutic Community Program.   The first cluster consisted of 29 of the 78 programs. The average member COPES profile for these programs appears in Figure 10.1. These programs show elevations on all three Relationship and all four Treatment Program dimensions. They are average or below average in emphasis on all three System Maintenance dimensions. This profile is generally similar to the average patient profile for hospital-based therapeutic community programs, although the subscale elevations are not as high. This is probably because many of the programs were day care centers, thus could not easily develop as integrated and comprehensive a treatment program. Twenty of the programs were American, whereas nine were British. It is interesting to note that 14 of the 20 American programs were relatively heavily staffed day care or day treatment programs, but only three were community care homes. The Euclid House program described earlier would probably fall into the Therapeutic Community cluster.

The Relationship-Oriented Program.   Figure 10.1 also shows the average member COPES profile for the second cluster of 12 programs. These programs reveal considerably above-average emphasis on all three Relationship dimensions and on Order and Organization and Clarity. However, the programs do not particularly emphasize the Treatment Program dimensions. This profile is very similar to those for the correctional and psychiatric Relationship-oriented programs given in Chapter 5. Nine of the programs in this cluster were American, and six of these were either halfway houses or community care homes. The CTP "protective" homes, Parolee House and Essexfields, would probably fall into this cluster.

The Action-Oriented Program.   Figure 10.2 shows the average member standard score profile for the community programs in the Action-oriented cluster. Although there were only four programs in this cluster, they constitute a quite separate group. They are very similar to the hospital-based Action-oriented programs (see Figure 5.5). These programs strongly emphasize autonomy and independence and, to a some-

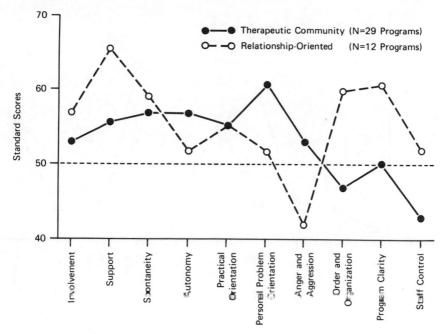

Figure 10.1 COPES Form R profiles for residents in Therapeutic Community and Relationship-oriented community programs.

what lesser extent, staff control. The Relationship dimensions and the other Treatment Program dimensions (except for Practical Orientation) are average or below average, as are both Order and Clarity. One of the programs in this cluster was a patient-administered "self help" program, located on an open ward on hospital grounds and completely run by a patient council. All administrative and behavior problems were handled by this elected patient group. Prospective members were screened and chosen by the group as a whole. All members had to either work, go to school, or attend a day treatment center. The program was specifically aimed at preparing men to live independently after a 6-month period. This is very similar to the Notre Dame Youth Center and the CTP type 3 "boarding" home described previously. The other three programs in this cluster were similarly designed to enhance planning for independent living.

The Insight-Oriented Program. Figure 10.2 also shows the average member COPES profile for the fourth cluster of eight Insight-oriented programs. These programs emphasize the open discussion of personal

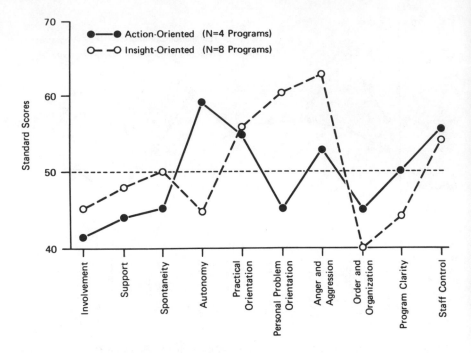

Figure 10.2   COPES Form R profiles for residents in Action-oriented and Insight-oriented community programs.

problems and feelings and, more specifically, the open expression of anger and aggression. They show average or below-average emphasis on all three Relationship dimensions, on Autonomy, and on Order and Organization and Clarity. They have slightly above-average emphasis on Practical Orientation and Staff Control. The Insight-oriented programs seem quite complementary to the Action-oriented programs. The former programs have their highest emphasis on Personal Problem Orientation and Anger and Aggression, but de-emphasize Autonomy; whereas the latter programs have their highest emphasis on Autonomy, but de-emphasize Personal Problem Orientation and Anger and Aggression. Both types of program are low on all three Relationship dimensions and on Order and Clarity. Both types are somewhat above average on Staff Control. The average member profile for the Insight-oriented cluster of community-based programs is virtually identical to the average profile for the hospital-based Insight-oriented programs (see Figure 5.5). Five of these eight programs were in the American sample; three were well-staffed day treatment centers, one was a mental health center, and one was a Treatment-oriented adolescent residential center.

The Control-Oriented Program. Surprisingly, 19 of the community programs fell into a Control-oriented cluster. Figure 10.3 gives the average member COPES profile for these programs. These programs indicate average or below-average emphasis on all dimensions except Order and Organization and Staff Control. This profile is strikingly similar to the average profile for the Control-oriented cluster in both the institutional correctional and the hospital-based samples (see Figures 5.3 and 5.6). Seventeen of the 19 community programs that were classified in this cluster were American; five of the programs were vocational and rehabilitation-oriented workshops (one of these was a British program). Eleven programs were community care homes for veterans, and two were VA-affiliated day care centers. Most of the programs dealt with somewhat older, more chronic patients who, even though they are functioning "in the community," need a relatively high degree of structure. The CTP "containment" home belongs in this cluster.

The Disturbed Behavior Program. The sixth and last cluster was composed of six programs, for which the average member COPES profile appears in Figure 10.3. These programs are well below average in all

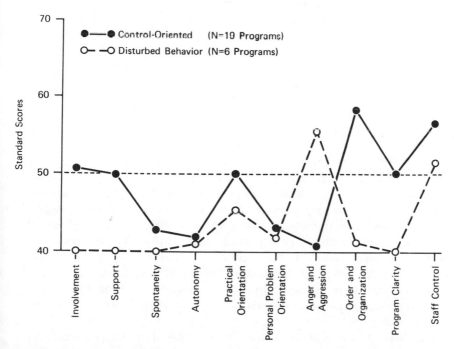

Figure 10.3 COPES Form R profiles for residents in Control-oriented and Disturbed Behavior community programs.

areas except Anger and Aggression and Staff Control. The profile is similar to that shown in Chapter 5 for hospital-based Disturbed Behavior programs, except that the hospital-based programs have somewhat more emphasis on Clarity and somewhat less on Staff Control. These six community-based programs were attempting to handle relatively acutely disturbed patients in an open community setting, thus needed to institute greater controls in comparison to other community programs.

Thus the three cluster analyses (i.e., one for institutional correctional programs, one for hospital-based psychiatric treatment programs, and one for community-oriented programs) show strikingly similar results. The three analyses have identified six similar program types. The categorization of correctional and psychiatric programs into Therapeutic Community, Relationship-oriented, Action-oriented, Insight-oriented, Control-oriented, and Disturbed Behavior programs may have considerable generality. It also seems to apply cross-culturally, at least to British programs, although more data are needed on this point. It must again be noted that there is substantial variation within each category. However, the categories do constitute a reasonable overall taxonomy of programs. They also represent programs that may be of differential utility for different delinquent types (see Chapter 5).

There is one especially notable aspect of these results. More than 30% of community-based programs have social environments that are not specifically treatment-oriented. Almost 25% of the programs (19 of 78) are Control-oriented (i.e., they do not emphasize any of the Relationship or the Treatment Program dimensions). These results, together with the results on the typology of correctional and psychiatric programs presented in Chapter 5, lead to the conclusion that some institutional programs may be "better" (at least in terms of their social climate characteristics) than some community-based programs.

Sarason (1974) has cautioned against uncritical enthusiasm about what community-based correctional and/or psychiatric settings can become. He feels that these settings may not be as different from regular institutional programs as the current literature suggests. For example, community-based programs usually rely on a traditional conception of professional responsibility rather than on an alternative conception of community responsibility. Sarason points out that most community programs are organized along hierarchical administrative lines very similar to those characteristic of institutional programs. He concludes that "there is little reason to expect that the adverse consequences will be discernibly less" (p. 188).

In a direct reversal of the usual line of reasoning, Sarason remarks that community programs may virtually guarantee the continued existence of institutional programs. He provides an example from the State of Connecticut in which the advent of community mental health centers appears to have resulted in a 400% increase in the state hospital readmission rate. There are fewer patients in the state hospitals and their stay is shorter; however, the number of times they come back to the hospital has dramatically increased. It is unclear whether this argument holds for corrections; however, Lerman (1972) has suggested that the Probation Subsidy program in California may have resulted in increased institutionalization in local county facilities. Thus one cannot assume that community programs will necessarily have more beneficial impacts than institutional programs.

On the whole, the movement toward community-based alternatives to regular institutional programs is clearly beneficial. However, it is impossible to classify community-based programs as "treatment-oriented" and institutional programs as "control-oriented." This analysis coincides closely with Lerman (1972), who has made an explicit distinction between treatment and control. He argues that the Community Treatment Program is more a control than a treatment program. This criticism is probably unreasonable, but it does correctly point out that community-based programs necessarily include a control component. Every community program must use some alternate mode of social control. In addition, as our analysis suggests, staff control may be the major component of a fairly large group of community programs.

The Need to Enhance Correctional Program Descriptions. The rapid proliferation of new community-based correctional programs has increased the need for more accurate and complete program descriptions. This is important for several reasons. First, professionals in the field are most often informed of new program developments by way of published program descriptions. Second, knowledge about a program is important for prospective residents and staff and for referring and other community agencies. Third, systematic information about community programs may engender more accurate expectations from residents and staff who enter the programs.

Fourth, preliminary evidence suggests that community programs may have greater *differential* impact than traditional programs. Greater differential impact for community programs is consistent with some of their special characteristics (e.g., smaller size and richer staffing, closeness to the community, thus to settings in which delinquents will need to function after release, greater variety in both physical and psychosocial characteristics, and residents who are potentially more amenable to beneficial staff influence).

The evidence on differential impact of community programs is sparse, but the following studies are of interest: Cunningham, Botwinik, Dolson, and Weickert (1969) did a 5-year study of community placement of mental patients released from a large Veterans Administration hospital. Among many findings they indicated that the size of the community placement home influenced patient success and failure. Surprisingly, patients in large homes (more than four patients) remained in the community about 20% longer than patients in small homes (four or fewer).

As discussed in Chapter 7, Clarke and Martin (1971) found several environmental factors related to differences in absconding rates from approved schools. Sinclair (1971) obtained similar findings in 46 community hostels. He found that the most successful hostels had wardens who favored a close relationship with residents, who were not overly permissive, and who agreed with their wives on attitudes toward discipline. Absconding, of course, is an "immediate" outcome measure. Have any studies suggested longer-term objective differential success rates of community programs?

Dunlop (1974) found that eight approved schools had significantly different success rates (as assessed by reconviction rates), even after differential intake was taken into account by ten "input" variables (e.g., number of previous court appearances, previous experience of institutional care, level of intelligence). She found that the more successful schools placed greater emphasis on work training. Schools that stressed leisure activities were less successful than other schools; however, these were also the schools lacking emphasis on work training. Schools that emphasized work also emphasized responsibility and maturity, had longer than average training periods, and had low rates of absconding and self-reported misbehavior.

Sinclair and Clarke (1973) have shown that absconding rates of approved schools are related to their success rates (as measured by the proportion of boys released on after-care who were not found guilty of an offense within 3 years of leaving) even when background factors (e.g., mean IQ and previous court appearances) were held constant. Thus there is some evidence that at least one type of community program—approved schools—may have rather substantial differential success rates.

Skeels (1966) has presented a remarkable study supporting the conclusion that a community-oriented intervention may have dramatic effects. He studied 13 mentally retarded children who experienced the effects of an early intervention consisting of a radical shift from one institutional environment to another. The major difference between the two institutions was in the amount of stimulation and the intensity of the relationships between the children and the adult caretakers. Eleven of the children were eventually placed in adoptive homes. In contrast, a control group of 12 similar children were exposed to a relatively nonstimulating orphanage environment over a prolonged period of time.

Over a period of 2 years the experimental group showed a substantial gain in functional intelligence (28.5 IQ points), whereas the control group showed a substantial loss (26.2 IQ points). Another follow-up was conducted 2½ years later. The 11 children who had been placed in adoptive homes increased their earlier gains in intelligence. The two not so placed had declined in their rate of mental growth. Skeels followed these children into adulthood. All 13 children in the experimental group were self supporting. None was in an institution. In the control group of 12 children, one had died in an institution and seven were still living in institutions.

Strikingly, the experimental group completed an average of 12 years of education and four completed some college work. The children in the control group completed an average of less than the third grade. These remarkable group differences also appeared in occupational achievement and income, in marital and family status, and in other areas. Skeels concluded that the difference between the two groups was due to the "program of nurturance and cognitive stimulation" which was "followed by placement in adoptive homes that provided love and affection and normal life experiences. ... It can be postulated that if the children in the contrast group had been placed in suitable adoptive homes, or given some other appropriate equivalent in early infancy, most or all of them would have achieved within the normal range of development . . ." (p. 56).

It is significant that community programs may have greater potential for differential impact on delinquents. Recent evidence on the outcome of psychotherapy suggests by analogy that this impact may be harmful as well as beneficial. The identification of the "deterioration effect" in psychotherapy has indicated that a small but important proportion of patients may grow significantly worse with treatment. It is likely that these findings are directly applicable to corrections. Thus we may expect both greater beneficial and greater harmful impact from community correctional programs. This differential impact will make it exceedingly important that placement strategies be more carefully worked out. In turn, this means that accurate systematic information about correctional programs will assume higher priority.

The program descriptions that have been written to fill these needs have depended primarily on observational techniques supplemented by questionnaires reporting type of staffing, resident characteristics, treatment and control techniques, physical setting, and so on. Many people feel that these published program descriptions "accentuate the positive," thus do not give a realistic account of program characteristics. For example, Jansen (1970) found that the published descriptions of halfway houses did not present an adequate picture of the programs she visited. Jansen says "but on visiting such houses I was struck by the discrepancy between write-ups and actual practices. This may well be caused by the complexity of community living where the real transactions are hard to put one's finger on" (p. 1499).

We used COPES to study the published descriptions of a sample of community programs to evaluate the information about the treatment milieu presented (Moos, 1974; Chapter 11). Descriptions were found for five community programs for which COPES test results of members and staff were also available. Ten "naive" judges were given copies of these articles and were asked to complete a COPES questionnaire on the basis of the information appearing in the article. The comparison of the results of the judges with those of the actual members and staff in the program indicated the extent to which the treatment milieu could be inferred from the article. Two of the published descriptions were relatively accurate and complete, whereas the other three tended to give judges an incorrect impression of the program. These results suggest that there are probably systematic distortions in many program descriptions.

Guidelines for Writing Correctional Program Descriptions.   Published descriptions of correctional programs should more adequately and systematically include information relevant to each of the major methods currently available for characterizing human environments. Each of the six dimension types, briefly mentioned in Chapter 1, is relevant in describing correctional programs.

1. Relevant *ecological* variables are those related to the architectural and physical design of the correctional facility. There is extensive evidence that the physical design characteristics of the location in which a correctional program is housed may have important attitudinal and behavioral consequences for program participants. For example, Gill (1962) has reviewed the connections between correctional philosophy and architecture and has suggested the need for four architecturally distinct types of correctional institution. Gill points out that the impact of correctional facilities in which men live in relatively small groups is quite different from that of the usual prison architecture, which houses several hundred men in a cell block and provides a single large dining room and recreation yard. The architectural characteristics of

the correctional facility may enhance or detract from treatment-oriented goals. Sommer (1971) has pointed out the possible architecturally induced effects of crowding, stimulus deprivation, and lack of privacy in correctional institutions (see also Gilbert, 1971 and Ricci, 1971).

For example, Turner (1969) has cogently illustrated the importance of the architectural and physical design characteristics of a group home. The Wilson home had three locations during 21 months. The first was in an older residential neighborhood that was centrally located. The home was a 12-bedroom, 5-bathroom structure in which each girl had her own room enjoying both privacy and a certain sense of autonomy. The living room, den, and library enabled girls to have visitors and entertain relatives and friends. The large dining room made it convenient to talk about problems around the dinner table and enhanced a cohesive family feeling. Turner points out that this was an ideal physical setting for a girls' group home because it "possessed a warm atmosphere and contained a great deal of room" (p. 28).

However, the home just described was sold by the owner, and the Wilson home moved to a residential area consisting mainly of college boarding homes, fraternity and sorority houses, and faculty housing. The temporary location was in a two-story brick home having five bedrooms, and a dining room that was converted into a sixth bedroom. This move had a negative impact on the girls. The layout made it difficult to provide a homelike atmosphere, and negative and insecure feelings were generated because it was rented on a temporary basis. Overcrowding was a serious problem. There was little or no privacy, and girls began using one another's belongings without permission. Anger and irritability increased, cosmetics and clothes were frequently missing, and the girls were continually accusing one another of stealing. In addition, the college community in which this house was located was not well suited for the girls. The girls were uncomfortable walking down the street. They felt embarrassed to walk by college youths, who purportedly stared at them with curiosity.

The Wilson home later moved to a third location, which was fairly new and modern in appearance. It contained eight bedrooms, a large family room, living room, a dining room, three bathrooms and a great deal of storage area. This home was located in a stable residential district, a feature that increased the girls' feelings of security. The home was to be permanent, and the girls' needs for both mutually supportive, cohesive interaction and privacy were more easily satisfied. Turner's informative account of these three group home locations illustrates the importance of each of the varied details that enter into the successful organization and structure of a group home, particularly its physical structure and architectural design.

Specific information in program descriptions might include the number of different types of room available in the facility, the size of the rooms, the number and size of bedrooms or dormitories, the type and general layout of furniture in the living room or common area, and the types of pictures and wall decorations and wall colors. Information about other physical facilities should also be included (e.g., the existence and size of a yard, recreation area, or gym, the size and layout of the cafeteria or dining room, and architectural aspects of surveillance and control facilities). This section of a program description does not need to be especially extensive; however, some information about the general physical settings helps to communicate a distinctive understanding of a program.

2. Some of the *behavior settings* that frequently occur in a correctional program (e.g., guided group interaction, community meetings, counseling sessions) are often mentioned in program descriptions. However, detailed descriptions of the settings in which vocational and educational training occurs are often forgotten. Since many residents feel that such experiences are the most important ones they have in a correctional program, this is a glaring oversight. In addition, the more informal settings (e.g., free time, meal time, recreational activities, visiting hours), which are often quite important in determining the social milieu, are seldom described at all. Since Barker (1968) and his colleagues have shown that the specific characteristics of behavior settings may have an important influence on the behavior and attitudes of their inhabitants, settings that occur relatively frequently should be carefully described.

3. *Organizational structure* dimensions are usually well covered in correctional program descriptions. The variables that fall into this category include the size of the program (number of residents), the resident–staff ratio, the basic cost of the program, and the number of types of staff. These are all important aspects of correctional programs. The failure of these organizational structure variables to correlate highly with perceived climate variables (see Chapter 3) indicates that they describe only one facet of a program. Organizational structure dimensions are necessary but not sufficient for describing correctional programs. On the other hand, simply knowing the size and staffing of a program can provide some important information about the social and interpersonal characteristics of that program.

4. Information about the *background characteristics* of the participants is usually included in program descriptions; however, this information is almost always much more complete for residents than for staff. Average age, length of incarceration, type of offense, number of previous arrests, and so on, are all variables commonly used and of obvious

importance in understanding the basic characteristics of the program. Much more information about the background characteristics of staff is desirable.

An example taken from a study of university student living groups may help clarify the importance of the fourth set of variables. A student's major field is a primary background characteristic. Brown (1968) manipulated the concentration of science or humanities students on different floors of a university residence hall. Two floors each had 44 science students and 11 humanities students, whereas two other floors each had 44 humanities students and 11 science students. The students who were majoring in fields similar to the majority of the other students on their floor were labeled the Majority group. Students who were majoring in fields dissimilar from the majority of the students on their floor were considered the Minority group.

What difference does it make whether a student is in a living group in which the majority of the other students have different background characteristics (i.e., college majors)? Brown identified several important differences between the Majority and the Minority groups. (1) A greater proportion of the Minority group changed their majors to fields similar to those of the Majority groups on their residence hall floor. (2) Of those who did not change their majors, significantly more of the Minority group became less certain of their vocational goal during the school year. (3) Significantly more of the Minority group had best friends who lived on other residence hall floors or in other residence halls. (4) Significantly more of the Minority group expressed dissatisfaction with residence hall life and with their total college experience. Brown concludes that the characteristics of the Majority group had an important impact on the Minority group.

Similar studies should be carried out in correctional programs. Do low maturity residents do better when they are housed with high maturity residents? Are younger residents more likely to be influenced in programs in which most residents are somewhat older? Do background characteristics such as the type of offense, ethnic origin, and violence potential, have differential impacts depending on whether a resident is in the majority or the minority? These questions suggest a new line of correctional research endeavors. In any case, group characteristics of residents and staff should be systematically included in correctional program descriptions.

5. *Psychosocial characteristics and social climate.* Methods like the CIES may be used to specify the psychosocial or perceived climate characteristics of the treatment milieu. Even if it is difficult or impossible to administer the entire CIES to all residents and staff, it may be possible to

administer the 40-item Short Form to a selected sample of residents or staff. In addition, outside observers can fill out the CIES on the basis of their observations of a program. Since most correctional programs have frequent visitors, it may be possible to have some of these individuals complete the CIES on the basis of their visits. Program descriptions should systematically describe each of the dimensions in the Relationship, Treatment Program, and System Maintenance areas.

6. Information about the kinds of behaviors and attitudes that tend to be reinforced (i.e., a *functional or reinforcement analysis* of the program) also needs to be acquired. Examples of functional analyses of correctional programs include the series of detailed descriptions of specific procedures at Achievement Place (Bailey et al. 1971; Fixsen, Phillips, and Wolf, 1972, 1973b; Phillips et al., 1971, 1973). Buehler, Patterson, and Furniss (1966) have also presented a detailed reinforcement analysis of behavior in correctional settings, as have Cohen and Filipczak (1971). Behavioral or functional analyses can identify the processes that maintain aggressive, hostile, and defiant behavior toward adults. These detailed analyses cannot be included in usual program descriptions; however, some observations are easy to obtain (e.g., a staff member or a resident can be taught to observe and identify the commonly used reinforcement sequences). Brief visits by an outside observer (e.g., a staff member from another correctional program, a visiting social worker) might also be used to obtain this information.

Ideally, descriptions of correctional programs should include information relevant to all six types of dimension. Each dimension gives a somewhat different perspective on a program. The use of all six should furnish relatively accurate and complete program descriptions. Aspects of program descriptions subject to individual perceptions (e.g., social climate) should make use of data-gathering methods that include a variety of individual perspectives; thus it will be possible to avoid overemphasizing specific biases. Residents and staff may have different views of program characteristics, and both perspectives should be included in program descriptions. Systematic inclusion of the views of an outside observer or interviewer is also helpful.

Different institutions usually know more about the individuals they are attempting to recruit or place than those individuals know about the institution. For example, colleges know more about the characteristics of entering students than entering students know about the colleges they plan to enter. Social workers, probation officers, and other program staff generally are better informed about the characteristics of the individual resident than about the program or programs into which they wish to place that resident. Furthermore, the prospective resident usually knows little or nothing about the salient program characteristics. Information about residential programs, especially those that are community-based, might be of some help in more adequately informing residents and staff about the characteristics of the program they are about to enter. Accurate, well-presented information about a program represents one important step in enhancing the adequacy of referral decisions, in raising resident and staff morale, and possibly in decreasing absconding and recidivism rates.

REFERENCES

Adler, J. Interpersonal relationships in residential treatment centers for disturbed children. *Child Welfare*, **50**:208–217, 1971.

Aledort, S. & Jones, M. The Euclid House: A therapeutic community halfway house for prisoners. *American Journal of Psychiatry*, **130**:286–289, 1973.

Alper, B. *Prisons inside-out: Alternatives in correctional reform.* Ballinger, Cambridge, Mass., 1974.

Bailey, J. S., Timbers, G. D., Phillips, E. L., & Wolf, M. M. Modification of articulation errors of pre-delinquents by their peers. *Journal of Applied Behavior Analysis*, **4**:265–281, 1971.

Barker, R. *Ecological psychology.* Stanford University Press, Stanford, Calif., 1968.

Beker, J. & Heyman, D. A critical appraisal of the California differential treatment typology of adolescent offenders. *Criminology*, **10**:3–59, 1972.

Bradley, H. B. Community-based treatment for young adult offenders. *Crime and Delinquency*, **15**:359–370, 1969.

Brown, R. D. Manipulation of environmental press in a college residence hall. *Personnel and Guidance Journal*, **46**:555–560, 1968.

Buehler, R., Patterson, G., & Furniss, J. The reinforcement of behavior in institutional settings. *Behavior Research and Therapy*, **4**:157–167, 1966.

Burdman, M. Realism in community-based correctional services. *Annals of the American Academy of Political and Social Science*, **381**:71–80, 1969.

Carlson, K. A method for identifying homogeneous classes. *Multivariate Behavioral Research*, **7**:483–488, 1972.

Cilch, K. Parolee House. *California Youth Authority Quarterly*, **24**:3–12, 1971.

Clarke, R. & Martin, D. *Absconding from approved schools.* Her Majesty's Stationery Office, London, 1971.

Cohen, H. & Filipczak, J. *A new learning environment.* Jossey-Bass, San Francisco, 1971.

Community-based correctional programs: Models and practices. Crime and Delinquency Topics Monograph, National Institute of Mental Health, Center for Studies of Crime and Delinquency, Rockville, Md., 1971.

Cunningham, M. K., Botwinik, W., Dolson, J., & Weickert, A. A. Community placement of released mental patients: A five-year study. *Social Work*, **14**:54–61, 1969.

Dunlop, A. Regime emphasis and school success. Home Office Research Report, London, 1974.

Empey, L. T. *Alternatives to incarceration.* Office of Juvenile Delinquency and Youth Development Studies in Delinquency, Government Printing Office, Washington, D.C., 1967.

Empey, L. T. & Erickson, M. L. *The Provo experiment: Evaluating community control of delinquency.* Lexington Books, Lexington, Mass., 1972.

Empey, L. T. & Lubeck, S. *The Silverlake experiment.* Aldine, Chicago, 1971.

Endres, V. J. & Goke, D. H. Time-out rooms in residential treatment centers. *Child Welfare,* **52:**359–366, 1973.

Fixsen, D. L., Philips, E. L. & Wolf, M. M. Achievement Place: The reliability of self-reporting and peer-reporting and their effects on behavior. *Journal of Applied Behavior Analysis,* **5:**19–30, 1972.

Fixsen, D. L., Phillips, E. L., & Wolf, M. M. The teaching–family model of group home treatment. In Y. Bakal (Ed.), *Closing correctional institutions: New strategies for youth services.* Lexington Books, Lexington, Mass., 1973a.

Fixsen, D. L., Phillips, E. L., & Wolf, M. M. Achievement Place: Experiments in self-government with pre-delinquents. *Journal of Applied Behavior Analysis,* **6:**31–47, 1973b.

Gibbons, D. Differential treatment of delinquents and interpersonal maturity levels theory: A critique. *Social Service Review,* **44:**22–33, 1970.

Gilbert, A. Observations about recent correctional architecture. In *New environments for the incarcerated,* U.S. Department of Justice, Law Enforcement Assistance Administration, National Institute of Law Enforcement and Criminal Justice, Washington, D.C., 1972, pp. 7–14.

Gill, H. B. Correctional philosophy and architecture. *Journal of Criminal Law, Criminology and Police Science,* **53:**312–322, 1962.

Greenberg, A. & Mayer, M. F. Group home care as an adjunct to residential treatment. *Child Welfare,* **51:**423–435, 1972.

Griggs, B. & McCune, G. Community-based correctional programs: A survey and analysis. *Federal Probation,* **36:**7–13, 1972.

Grygier, T., Nease, B., & Anderson, C. An exploratory study of halfway houses. *Crime and Delinquency,* **16:**280–291, 1970.

Gula, M. Group homes—New and differentiated tools in child welfare, delinquency, and mental health. *Child Welfare,* **43:**393–397, 1964.

Herstein, N. What is a group home? *Child Welfare,* **43:**403–414, 1964.

Jansen, E. The role of the halfway house in community mental health programs in the United Kingdom and America. *American Journal of Psychiatry,* **126:**142–148, 1970.

Keller, O. J. & Alper, B. S. *Halfway houses: Community-centered correction and treatment.* Lexington Books, Lexington, Mass., 1970.

Lamb, H. & Goertzel, V. Ellsworth House: A community alternative to jail. *American Journal of Psychiatry,* **131:**64–68, 1974.

Lerman, P. Community treatment, social control, and juvenile delinquency: Issues in correctional policy. Graduate School of Social Work, Rutgers University, New Brunswick, N. J., 1972.

Maluccio, A. N. & Marlow, W. D. Residential treatment of emotionally disturbed children: A review of the literature. *Social Service Review,* **46:**230–250, 1972.

Mayer, M. F. The group in residential treatment of adolescents. *Child Welfare,* **51:**482–493, 1972.

McCorkel, L. W., Elias, A., & Bixby, F. L. *The Highfields story.* Henry Holt, New York, 1958.

McNeil, F. A halfway-house program for delinquents. *Crime and Delinquency,* **13:**538–544, 1967.

Meyer, M., Odom, E., & Wax, B. Birth and life of an incentive system in a residential institution for adolescents. *Child Welfare,* **52:**503–509, 1973.

Mitford, J. *Kind and usual punishment: The prison business.* Knopf, New York, 1973.

Moos, R. Community-based correctional programs: A critical appraisal. Social Ecology Laboratory, Department of Psychiatry, Stanford University, Palo Alto, Calif., 1973.

Moos, R. *Evaluating treatment environments: A social ecological approach.* Wiley, New York, 1974.

Mora, G., Talmadge, M., Bryant, F., & Hayden, B. A residential treatment center moves toward the community mental health model. *Child Welfare,* **48:**585–590, 1969.

Palmer, T. The phase I, II and III experiments: Developments and progress. Community Treatment Project, Research Report No. 10, California Youth Authority, Sacramento, 1970.

Palmer, T. California's Community Treatment Program for delinquent adolescents. *Journal of Research in Crime and Delinquency,* **8:**74–92, 1971.

Palmer, T. The Group Home Project Final Report: Differential placement of delinquents in group homes. California Youth Authority, Sacramento, 1972.

Pearson, J. W. A differential use of group homes for delinquent boys. *Children,* **17:**143–148, 1970.

Phillips, E. L., Phillips, E. A., Fixsen, D. L., & Wolf, M. M. Achievement Place: Modification of the behaviors of pre-delinquent boys within a token economy. *Journal of Applied Behavior Analysis,* **4:**45–59, 1971.

Phillips, E. L., Phillips, E. A., Fixsen, D. L., & Wolf, M. M. Achievement Place: Behavior shaping works for delinquents, *Psychology Today,* **7:**74–79, 1973.

Pilnick, S., Elias, A., & Clapp, N. W. The Essexfields concept: A new approach to the social treatment of juvenile delinquents. *Journal of Applied Behavioral Science,* **2:**109–125, 1966.

Post, G. C., Hicks, R. A., & Monfort, M. F. Day care programs for delinquents: A new treatment approach. *Crime and Delinquency,* **14:**353–359, 1968.

Rabinow, I. Agency-operated group homes, *Child Welfare,* **43:**415–422, 1964.

Ricci, K. Using the building as a therapeutic tool in youth treatment. In *New environments for the incarcerated.* U.S. Department of Justice, Law Enforcement Assistance Administration, National Institute of Law Enforcement and Criminal Justice, Washington, D.C., 1972, pp. 22–32.

Sarason, S. B. *The psychological sense of community: Prospects for a community psychology.* Jossey-Bass, San Francisco, 1974.

Sinclair, I. *Hostels for probationers.* Her Majesty's Stationery Office, London, 1971.

Sinclair, I. & Clarke, R. Acting-out behavior and its significance for the residential treatment of delinquents. *Child Psychology and Psychiatry,* **14:**283–291, 1973.

Sommer, R. The social psychology of the cell environment. In *New environments for the incarcerated.* U.S. Department of Justice, Law Enforcement Administration, National

Institute of Law Enforcement and Criminal Justice, Washington, D.C., 1972, pp. 15–21.

Skeels, H. Adult status of children with contrasting early life experiences: A follow-up study. *Monograph of the Society for Research in Child Development,* **31,** 1966.

The challenge of crime in a free society: A report by the President's Commission on Law Enforcement and Administration of Justice, Government Printing Office, Washington, D.C., 1967.

Turner, E. A girls' group home: An approach to treating delinquent girls in the community. Community Treatment Project Report Series, No. 1, Department of the Youth Authority, Sacramento, 1969.

Turner, E. Community treatment's new residential component. *California Youth Authority Quarterly,* **24:**25–33, 1971.

Turner, M. The lessons of Norman House. *Annals of the American Academy of Political and Social Science,* **381:**39–46, 1969.

Vasoli, R. H. & Fahey, F. J. Halfway house for reformatory releases. *Crime and Delinquency,* **16:**292–304, 1970.

Warren, M. Q. The Community Treatment Project after 5 years. California Youth Authority, Sacramento, 1967.

Warren, M. Q. *Correctional treatment in community settings: A report of current research.* National Institute of Mental Health, Government Printing Office, Washington, D.C., 1972.

Ziegler, S. Residential treatment of emotionally disturbed children in Norway. *Child Welfare,* **51:**290–296, 1972.

CHAPTER ELEVEN

Families

RUDOLF H. MOOS AND BERNICE S. MOOS

Delinquency and the Family Environment. As correctional services become more integrated with community settings, it will become necessary to systematically assess the community settings that are important in determining the success of delinquency prevention and control. There are differential "risk factors" for delinquency in various kinds of community setting. The three most important types are probably the family environment, the work environment, and the peer group milieu. This chapter reviews some work on the relationship between delinquency and the family milieu, discusses studies that emphasize the importance of the family environment in influencing program outcome, and presents the development of a scale for the systematic assessment of 10 salient dimensions of family climates.

Interest in the relationship between the family environment and delinquency has a long tradition. Many studies have reinforced the widespread belief that delinquents often come from broken or inadequate homes. For example, Bandura and Walters (1959) compared 26 antisocial and aggressive boys, contacted through a probation department and a school guidance department, with 26 controls having no delinquency histories nor marked aggressive tendencies. Control and aggressive boys were matched closely by age and when possible by socioeconomic status. Both the boys and their parents were interviewed.

Parents of the aggressive boys discouraged emotional dependency of the adolescent sons. This was particularly true of the fathers, who were less warm and more rejecting as a whole than the control fathers. Aggression was handled inconsistently in the homes of the aggressive children. Both parents encouraged the boys' aggressiveness outside the home more often than the control parents. Aggression toward adults was generally punished, but aggression toward peers went unpunished.

McCord, McCord, and Zola (1959) reported findings on a group of men from the Cambridge–Somerville (Massachusetts) area whose behavior had been observed as young children. Boys who later became convicted delinquents more often came from broken homes or homes characterized as quarrelsome–neglecting than from cohesive or quarrelsome–affectionate homes. A cohesive home combined with a "love-oriented" style of discipline was associated with the lowest proportion of boys later convicted of crimes. Quarrelsome–neglecting homes with a lax or punitive style of discipline produced the highest proportion of delinquents.

McCord, McCord, and Howard (1963) followed up men who had been rated as aggressive as boys. Twenty-six of these aggressive boys later were convicted of crimes including larceny, breaking and entering, assault, and sex offenses. These men, called the antisocial aggressives, were compared against 26 aggressive boys who did not have any criminal records as adults. The latter group was called the socialized aggressives. The antisocial aggressives came from family environments characterized by more discord, neglect, and parental attacks on the children than the socialized aggressives. Mothers less often expressed approval, and fathers openly displayed their dislike of the antisocial aggressives. The family environments of socialized aggressives were distinguished by inconsistent discipline from the mothers, low expectations for the child, and little religious training.

McCord, McCord, and Howard (1961) compared the family environments of nondelinquent but aggressive boys with those of nonaggressive boys. Aggressive boys came from homes characterized by rejection, punitive and inconsistent discipline, little adequate supervision, and conflict between the parents. The parents themselves were often social deviants. Nonaggressive boys more often had affectionate relationships with their parents, adequate and firm supervision, and consistent, nonpunitive discipline. There was little conflict between the parents, who tended to be socially conformist.

Cortes and Gatti (1972) found that delinquents in the Boston area more often came from broken homes of low and middle socioeconomic status than did nondelinquents. The parents of delinquents were less religious, and the delinquent children less often felt inhibited by religious beliefs when participating in an illegal activity. The delinquents reported feeling less support and receiving less help from their fathers and mothers, and they were disciplined by their parents in a more physical, punitive, or vindictive manner.

These studies offer a clear contrast between the two types of families. One or both natural parents often are missing because of death, divorce, or separation, in delinquents' homes. When both parents are present, they tend to be overly harsh and punitive in their discipline of the child, often resorting to physical punishment. An important aspect of parental discipline is consistency over time and between parents. In homes with delinquent children discipline is more often inconsistent in both senses. Aggressive tendencies of children are encouraged in families that produce delinquents, especially if the aggression is directed toward the child's peers or other persons outside the home. Conflictual, rejecting, and unsupporting relationships are often found between family members in such families. The literature offers few clues to how some children of such families avoid delinquency, particularly why a delinquent may have law-abiding siblings. But many reasons are suggested for remaining away from home, aggressing against peers and adults, engaging in aggressive sexual relationships at an early age, and stealing from the more well to do.

Recidivism and the Family Setting.   Researchers working in correctional and psychiatric settings have noted that the social environment established in the prisoner's or patient's family is of great importance in understanding recidivism. In both types of setting it has been much easier to demonstrate program impact on inmates' and patients' behavior while in the institution than after release. Community environments, particularly the family environment, have long been known to affect the outcome of institutional releases. Several recent studies have demonstrated this relationship.

Davies (1969) and Davies and Sinclair (1971) emphasized the importance of the family environment of probationers. By comparing data on probationers living at home and other probationers assigned to hostels, the authors show that certain characteristics of the family and hostel environments are associated with better probation outcome. The reconviction rate of probationers living at home was examined at the end of 12 months of probation. Lower rates were found for boys from homes where the father was warm and affectionate toward the son but was a firm disciplinarian. Firm discipline from the mother was also beneficial, but only when the mother was supporting the father. Firm discipline from the mother was ineffective if the father was lax or erratic in his discipline.

Important differences in reconviction rates were found for two types of hostel resident. Some boys were committed to the hostels because their homes were thought to be prime causes of their delinquency. They were committed to give them a respite from the bad influences of their homes or to supply a period of discipline and training that was not available in their homes. Since most hostel releasees returned to their homes on release, one would expect the boys from problem homes to be reconvicted more often after release from the hostel than the remainder of the hostel residents. The 3-year reconviction rates for both groups of hostel residents was essentially the same, about 70%, but the boys from problem homes were more often reconvicted after their return home, whereas the other boys were more often reconvicted while they were still at the hostels.

The study also showed that support in the home environment (i.e., affection and positive attitudes toward the probationer) was associated with lower reconviction rates at one year following release from a hostel. Only 21% of the releasees living in highly supportive home environments had been reconvicted at 12 months, but 47% of the remainder, living in less supportive homes, were reconvicted in the first year after release.

Associated work in psychiatric settings points up the importance of family environments on released patients treated in the community. Manino and Shore (1974) found that released patients who lived with their conjugal families rather than with their parents or by themselves were rehospitalized less often. Rehospitalization was even less frequent if the former patient occupied a central and responsible position in the family (e.g., principal breadwinner). An aftercare program had good effects on unmarried patients living with their parents or alone, and on patients who occupied somewhat peripheral, not responsible, positions in their families.

Brown, Birley, and Wing (1972) reinforce these findings in their study of schizophrenic relapse. The degree of emotionality in the families of released schizophrenics was related to the frequency of relapses for patients released from two hospitals in England. A moderate level of expressions of warmth about the former patient was associated with fewer relapses. Negative emotional comments were rated in four areas: critical comments, hostile comments, indications of dissatisfaction with the patient, and overinvolvement with the patient. These ratings were highly intercorrelated, thus were combined into a single index of relatives' expressed emotion. A high rating on the expressed emotion index was associated with a high frequency of relapse. Very high levels of warmth were usually associated with overinvolvement with the patient, which explains the finding that only a moderate level of warmth was associated with lower relapse rates.

In this connection many residential programs have recognized the importance of the family and have therefore developed techniques for including the family in the treatment process. For example, Scott (1970) discusses the implementation of family group meetings in the Guided Group Interaction program at Boys Republic. Typical meetings consist of approximately five boys, their parents and, in certain cases, brothers and sisters. Realistic discharge planning is enhanced by these meetings. Kemp (1971) discusses the use of family treatment within the milieu of a residential treatment center. In this program the family agrees to spend a minimum of 6 hours a week in such activities as meals, special outings, conferences, and family therapy. This contact provides an opportunity for staff to understand the home environment, most important, it facilitates efforts to generalize learning from the center to the home and community. In this way the center is more likely to become an integral part of the life of the community. Considerable progress has recently been made in behavior modification techniques in which children and parents are observed in the "natural" home setting and parents are trained to function as "change agents" in relation to their delinquent and problem children (Patterson, 1971; Wiltz, 1973).

Maluccio and Marlow (1972) conclude their comprehensive review of residential treatment of disturbed children as follows:

> A child's post-institutional environment is a crucial influence in his functioning. The supports and services received by the child and his family following residential care seem more significantly related to eventual outcome than the degree or kind of emotional disturbance at the point of admission or discharge. Further work is needed to identify the specific factors in the post-institutional environment that lead to successful adaptation. (p. 242)

Assessing Family Environments.   Although everyone agrees that the family environment is crucial in shaping the child's potential for delinquency, relatively few attempts have been made to systematically assess the social climate of families. Pless and Satterwhite (1973) developed an instrument for assessing the overall adequacy of family functioning. A semistructured interview was administered to parents of 399 school children. About half the children were normal and the other half had some chronic disorder. A factor analysis of the responses resulted in five dimensions, labeled communication, togetherness, closeness, decision making, and child orientation. A single family functioning score was obtained by adding the responses to each question. Higher scores indicate more adequate family functioning.

   Two examples are given to show the differences between families with low and high family functioning scores. A family with a very high score of 34 consisted of the parents and three children who lived in a surburban home. Both parents had completed high school and both were employed. The parents felt that the family got along well together and was happier and closer than most families. The father spent a great deal of time with the children. Important family decisions were made jointly by husband and wife. In contrast, another surburban family consisting of parents and four children, had a family functioning score of just 7. The father believed in strict discipline but the mother did not. There was little communication between the parents, and the father spent little time with the children. The family did not often have activities together. Important decisions were usually made by the husband. The investigators note that measures of family functioning would be useful in program outcome studies because differences in family functioning levels may confound comparisons between treatment and control groups.

   Deykin (1972) has recently presented a model for assessing life functioning in families of delinquent or predelinquent boys. The technique provides for the quantification of six major areas of family life functioning: decision making, marital interaction, child rearing, emotional gratification, perception of and response to crisis, and perception of and response to community. These areas were measured in a sample of 33 families, and the results indicated that family scores in the six areas were relatively highly correlated, suggesting that one underlying dimension of family functioning is probably being assessed. The total score a family achieved was significantly related both to the type of antisocial behavior seen in the child and to the degree of change in the child after treatment. Families who obtained better functioning scores were more likely to have children who displayed passive antisocial behavior. Families who obtained poorer life functioning scores were more likely to have children who displayed aggressive antisocial behavior. The latter families were much more likely to have children who showed no change or even deterioration after intensive treatment. Deykin quite correctly points out that this "raises serious questions about the feasibility of treating the children without having a clear understanding of the family's needs and the means for meeting these needs" (p. 99). The family environment, then, may determine both the specific characteristics of the delinquency problem and the results that can be achieved by initiating treatment for that problem.

   Three examples may serve to clarify the manner in which the family environment may affect the development of delinquency. Many studies have shown that delinquency rates are higher in crowded neighborhoods. High population density conditions affect the pattern of social relationships in the family, and adolescents respond to the stressful social relationships that housing conditions have helped to create. These families are more likely to complain and to inhibit expressiveness, are often forced into close social relationships with neighboring families, show more conflict and strain, and so on (Mitchell, 1971). To reduce the consequences arising from high density, adolescent children are given greater freedom to leave the home, thereby reducing the density (at least temporarily). This weakens the control the family has over their children. This increase in conflict and decrease in support and control may facilitate the development of the kinds of delinquent problems that are characteristic of high density slum communities.

Another important aspect of the family environment is the attitude toward the institutionalized individual once he or she returns home. Lower-class families are usually more reluctant to accept a delinquent back after institutionalization. This indicates a lack of family support. An excellent example of the importance of family support comes from studies of posthospital adjustment after treatment for mental illness. Consider the following descriptions provided by Myers and Bean (1968) of the contrasting levels of support for two patients, both diagnosed schizophrenic.

> Mrs. S., (a) married woman with five children ranging in age from 1 to 12. . . . Mrs. S. and her husband . . . know more than a dozen neighbors and visit back and forth regularly . . . neither Mrs. S. nor her husband feel that they should hide the fact of her hospitalization . . . if the subject of mental illness arises they usually mention Mrs. S's successful treatment, (p. 188).
>
> Miss M. would like more friends but feels that people avoid her because she has "been up to the state mental hospital." She claims that the friends of her family have not treated her the same since her return. Her sister, with whom she lives, is embarrassed by the thought of the psychiatric hospitalization . . . family members are less willing to invite friends to their home and sometimes avoid their friends because they are embarrassed. (pp. 193–194)

In this connection, family expectations of the delinquent are of prime importance, since such expectations may be self-fulfilling. In homes in which family members have high expectations, (e.g., Achievement Orientation) delinquents may expect more of themselves. These greater pressures for success, for a return to normal living, and for the fulfillment of work and school functions are likely to be translated into better post-institutional performance.

Finally, Kohn (1972) was impressed with yet another aspect of the family environment that might contribute to unsuccessful coping behavior, role patterning, and socialization: "many lower class families transmit to their offspring an orientational system too limited and too rigid for dealing effectively with complex changing or stressful situations" (p. 300).

Specifically, Kohn suggests that lower-class families may transmit a somewhat conservative outlook that impairs resourceful adaptation, particularly in individuals "predisposed" to either mental illness or delinquency. Thus these brief examples suggest that aspects of the family environment such as cohesiveness, support, expressiveness, conflict, achievement expectations, and control may importantly influence the development and ultimate outcome of delinquent tendencies. Much more work needs to be done in this area.

The Family Environment Scale.   The foregoing considerations led to the development of a Family Environment Scale (FES), which assesses the social climate of families of all types. It focuses on the measurement and description of the interpersonal relationships among family members, on the directions of personal growth emphasized within the family, and on the basic organizational structure of the family. The rationale used for the development of the FES was again derived from the theoretical contributions of Henry Murray (1938) and his concept of environmental press (see Chapter 1). In this approach the consensus of individuals characterizing their environment constitutes a measure of environmental climate, and this environmental climate is thought to exert a directional influence on behavior. On the other hand, particularly in families, individual or highly deviant perceptions of the environment are also of critical importance.

Several methods were employed to gain a naturalistic understanding of family social environments and to obtain an initial pool of questionnaire items. Many individuals were interviewed to determine the characteristics of their families. Several people were involved in writing a large range of potential items. Possible press dimensions and additional items were adapted from the other Social Climate scales. Several initial forms were developed on which preliminary pretest information was gathered. These procedures resulted in an initial 200-item form of the FES that assessed 12 dimensions we thought would differentiate among families. These dimensions were: Involvement–Cohesion, Support, Expressiveness, Conflict, Independence, Achievement Orientation, Intellectual–Cultural Orientation, Active Recreational Orientation, Moral–Religious Emphasis, Order and Organization, Clarity, and Control.

The exact choice and wording of items was again guided by the formulation of environmental press. Each item had to identify characteristics of an environment that would exert a press toward Cohesion or Academic Achievement or Moral–Religious emphasis. For example, a press toward Cohesion is inferred from the following kinds of item: "Family members really help and support one another," and "There is a feeling of unity and cohesion in our family." A press toward Achievement Orientation is inferred from these items: "We feel it is important to be the best at whatever you do," and "Getting ahead in life is very important in our family." A press toward Moral–Religious emphasis is inferred from items like these: "Family members attend church, synagogue, or Sunday School fairly often," and "The Bible is a very important book in our home."

The initial 200-item form of the FES was administered to more than 1000 individuals in a sample of 285 families. The data were collected from a wide range of families to ensure that the resulting scale would be applicable to the broadest possible variety of family situations. This was accomplished by sampling families from several diverse sources. First, families were recruited from three different church groups, from a newspaper advertisement, and through students at a local high school. Second, an ethnic minority sample was recruited from sources just named and partly by having black and Mexican-American research assistants obtain data from samples of black and Mexican-American families. Third, a disturbed or "clinic" family sample was collected from two different sources—a psychiatrically oriented family clinic and a probation and parole department affiliated with a local correctional facility.

The data from these three samples were used to develop a revised 90-item, 10-subscale Form R (real) of the FES. In brief, various psychometric test construction criteria were used for selecting items to be included in the final Form R.

1. The overall item split should be as close to 50–50 as possible, to avoid items characteristic only of extreme families.

2. Items should correlate more highly with their own than with any other subscale. All the final 90 items met this criterion, and only 4 items correlated below .40 with their own subscale.

3. Each subscale should have an approximately equal number of items scored true and scored false to control for acquiescence response set.

4. The final subscales should be only moderately intercorrelated.

5. Each item (and each subscale) had to maximally discriminate among families.

Basically, each of these psychometric criteria had to be met in all three samples of families. Using these criteria, two pairs of subscales (Cohesion and Support, and Order and Organization and Clarity) were collapsed because their items were highly intercorrelated. Many items with relatively low item–subscale correlations or extreme item splits were eliminated. The final 10 subscales of the Family Environment Scale (FES) are listed and briefly defined in Table 11.1. The complete Form R and its scoring key are given in Appendix B.

Table 11.1 Family Environment Scale Subscale Descriptions

	Relationship Dimensions	
1.	*Cohesion*	The extent to which family members are concerned and committed to the family and the degree to which family members are helpful and supportive of each other.
2.	*Expressiveness*	The extent to which family members are allowed and encouraged to act openly and to express their feelings directly.
3.	*Conflict*	The extent to which the open expression of anger and aggression and generally conflictual interactions are characteristic of the family.
	Personal Growth Dimensions	
4.	*Independence*	The extent to which family members are encouraged to be assertive, self-sufficient, to make their own decisions and to think things out for themselves.
5.	*Achievement Orientation*	The extent to which different types of activities (i.e., school and work) are cast into an achievement oriented or competitive framework.
6.	*Intellectual– Cultural Orientation*	The extent to which the family is concerned about political, social, intellectual, and cultural activities.
7.	*Active Recreational Orientation*	The extent to which the family participates actively in various recreational and sporting activities.

8. *Moral–
   Religious
   Emphasis*   The extent to which the family actively dis-
                                  cusses and emphasizes ethical and religious is-
                                  sues and values.

System Maintenance Dimensions

9. *Organization*   Measures how important order and organi-
                                  zation are in the family in terms of structuring
                                  the family activities, financial planning and the
                                  explicitness and clarity in regard to family
                                  rules and responsibilities.

10. *Control*   Assesses the extent to which the family is or-
                                  ganized in a hierarchical manner, the rigidity
                                  of family rules and procedures and the extent
                                  to which family members order each other
                                  around.

The basic psychometric test construction data for the FES are given in the Preliminary Manual (Moos, 1974a). In brief, the subscale internal consistencies (Kuder-Richardson Formula 20) were all in an acceptable range, varying from a low of .64 for Independence to a high of .79 for Moral–Religious Emphasis. The average item–subscale correlations varied from moderate (.45 for Independence) to substantial (.58 for Cohesiveness). The test–retest reliabilities of individual scores on the FES subscales were calculated for 47 family members in 9 families who took the FES twice, with approximately 8 weeks between testings. The test–retest reliabilities were all quite acceptable, varying from a low of .68 for Independence to a high of .86 for Cohesiveness. The 10 subscale scores were intercorrelated for a sample 814 family members in 240 families. The average subscale intercorrelations were around .20, indicating that the subscales measure quite distinct although somewhat related aspects of family social environments.

Three additional forms of the Family Environment Scale have also been developed. A 40-item Short Form (Form S) of the FES was developed to permit relatively rapid assessments of either large families and/or groups of families. The logic and procedures used were identical to those used in deriving the Short Form of the CIES (see Chapter 2). The similarity of profiles obtained using only four items from each subscale (Form S), as compared to using the complete nine items (Form R), was investigated by calculating intraclass correlations (Haggard, 1958) between 11 family profiles obtained using the two different forms.

It should be noted that these were all large families, that is, families with five or more family members all of whom adequately completed the FES. Ten of these correlations were above .90 and the other was above .80. Thus preliminary data indicate that the use of Form S results in a family profile highly similar to that obtained using Form R, at least for relatively large families. The first 40 items on the regular Form R are the Short Form items, as shown by an asterisk on the scoring key in Appendix B.

The Form R items have also been reworded so that family members can answer them in terms of the type of family environment they would ideally like. This form was developed to measure the goals and value orientations of family members. What kinds of family environment do they consider ideal? In what areas are mother's and father's goals similar? In what areas do children agree with parents? In what areas do they basically disagree? To what extent do personal growth goals vary from family to family? To what extent do parents in high socioeconomic level families have different views of ideal families? To what extent do ethnic minority families have different goals and value orientations with regard to family climate?

The Form R items and instructions have also been reworded to permit individuals to answer them in terms of what they expect a family climate to be like. This form may be useful in premarital counseling, to facilitate prospective marital partners' discussions of what they expect their family milieu to be like. It may also help in identifying the expectations of foster children when they are about to enter a new family, and individuals who have been divorced and/or widowed may use the form in discussing their expected family milieu with a prospective husband or wife. The items and instructions for both the Ideal family form (Form I) and the Expectations form (Form E) are given in the FES preliminary manual (Moos, 1974).

Clinical Interpretation of Family Profiles. As explained previously, the items on the FES are grouped into 10 subscales: three assess Relationship dimensions (Cohesion, Expressiveness, Conflict), five assess Personal Growth or Personal Development dimensions (Achievement Orientation, Intellectual–Cultural Orientation, Active Recreational Orientation, Moral–Religious Emphasis), and the other two assess System Maintenance dimensions (Organization and Control). Some primary uses for the FES are the derivation of detailed descriptions of the social environments of families, the comparison of parent and child perceptions, the assessment of changes in family environments over time, and the contrasting of different families with one another. Four illustrative profile interpretations are presented here, in which the family as a whole is the central object of the study, analogous to the individual patient in a clinical case description.

Family 142: High Relationship and Low Control.   Figure 11.1 is the FES profile for family 142 compared with the average score obtained by all the families in the overall normative group. This family was one of the few in the sample in which there were no children. The 33-year-old husband was a student and the 26-year-old wife was working in a university community. As the profile indicates, the couple feel quite positively about the social environment they have established. They obtained substantially above-average scores on the Relationship dimensions of Cohesion and Expressiveness and a substantially below-average score on Conflict. Husband and wife agreed with items like the following: "We put a lot of energy into what we do at home," "There is a feeling of togetherness in our family," "We really get along well with each

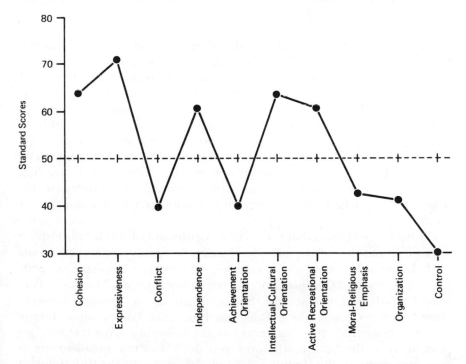

Figure 11.1   FES Form R profiles for family 142.

other," "We say anything we want to around home," "We tell each other about our personal problems," and "Money and paying bills is openly talked about in our family."

There is moderately above-average emphasis on three of the Personal Growth dimensions in this family—namely, Independence, Intellectual–Cultural Orientation, and Active Recreational Orientation. The husband and wife answer "true" to items like: "We think things out for ourselves in our family," "We come and go as we want to in our family," "We often talk about political and social problems," "Learning about new and different things is very important in our family," "We often go to movies, sports events, camping, etc.," and "Friends often come over for dinner or to visit." On the other hand, the degree of Achievement Orientation and Moral-Religious Emphasis was moderately below average in this family. In addition there was little emphasis on either Organization or Control. Importantly, the husband and wife responded almost identically to the items on the three Relationship and the five Personal Growth dimensions. They showed slight disagreement on the System Maintenance dimensions, with the wife perceiving somewhat more Organization and Control than the husband, but their degree of agreement was relatively high.

Family 338: An Achievement-Oriented Family. Figure 11.2 shows the profile for a somewhat different family, composed of four members. The father, aged 60, was born in a Central American country and had managed to obtain only a partial high school education. The mother, aged 55, was born in the United States and had completed her high school education. The family was strongly upwardly mobile, and both the 24-year-old daughter and the 23-year-old-son had finished college. The family was relatively stable (they had lived in their current home for more than 5 years) and quite well off, the nine-room house had four bedrooms, a living room, and separate dining and laundry rooms. The family was Catholic and attended religious services about once a week.

Figure 11.2 indicates that the social environment of this family is quite different from that of the previous family. In family 338 the emphasis on Cohesiveness is only about average, whereas the emphasis on both Expressiveness and Conflict is moderately below average. The major Personal Growth characteristics of this family are in the areas of Achievement Orientation and Moral–Religious Emphasis. For example, family members answered "true" to items like the following: "We feel it is important to be the best at whatever you do," "Getting ahead in life is very important in our family," "We always strive to do things just a

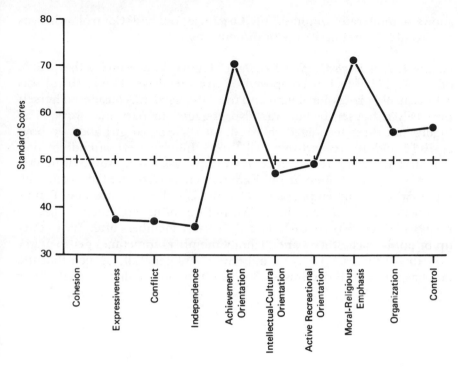

Figure 11.2   FES Form R profile for family 338.

little better the next time," "We believe in competition and may the best man win." Items on the Moral–Religious Emphasis scale on which the members in family 338 agreed include: "Family members attend church, synagogue, or Sunday school fairly often," "Family members have strict ideas about what is right and wrong," "We believe there are some things you just have to take on faith," and "The Bible is a very important book in our home." In terms of the System Maintenance dimensions, family members perceive their family as being slightly above average.

Thus Figures 11.1 and 11.2 illustrate two quite different family social environments. In family 142, the emphasis on Cohesion and Expressiveness is fairly high. This family tends to emphasize Independence, Intellectual–Cultural Orientation, and Active Recreational Orientation. Family 338, on the other hand, does not emphasize these dimensions. Instead, the latter family strongly emphasizes the Personal Growth dimensions of Achievement Orientation and Moral–Religious Emphasis, which are both de-emphasized in family 142. Furthermore, family 338 shows a moderate emphasis on Organization and Control, whereas family 142 de-emphasizes both dimensions.

Family 171: A High Conflict Family.   Figure 11.3 presents the profile of family 171, which is composed of five members. The husband was a 43-year-old professional man and the wife, aged 42, considered herself primarily a housewife but was also engaged in part-time work. The family had three teen-aged children: an 18-year-old girl and two boys aged 15 and 16, respectively. All three children were attending high school. The profile reveals that this family was having some difficulty. The emphasis on Cohesion and Expressiveness is substantially below average, whereas the emphasis on Conflict is well above average. Family members agreed to items like: "We fight a lot in our family," "Family members often criticize each other," "Family members often try to one-up or outdo each other," and "Family members sometimes get so angry they throw things." All five family members generally agreed that the emphasis on Expressiveness was low and that on Conflict was high. Four

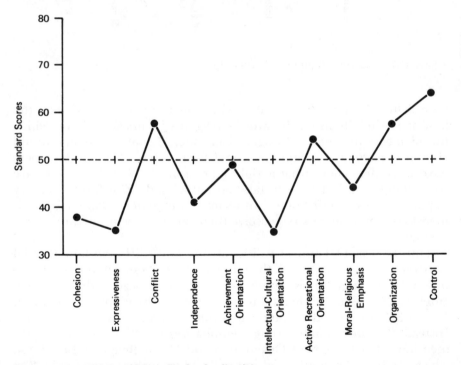

Figure 11.3   FES Form R profile for family 171.

members agreed that the emphasis on Cohesion was low; only the father felt that the family was moderately cohesive.

The profile also indicates little emphasis on any of the Personal Growth dimensions. It is almost as if the family lacked specific direction. On the other hand, the family was held together by a relatively high emphasis on both Organization and Control. Family members agreed with items like: "Activities in our family are pretty carefully planned," "We are generally very neat and orderly," "Family members make sure their rooms are neat," "There are set ways of doing things at home," "There is a strong emphasis on following rules in our family," and "Rules are pretty inflexible in our household." Thus this profile illustrates yet another family social environment.

Family 377: Parent–Child Discrepancies.   The last example demonstrates how the information obtained by the FES can be used to identify the similarities and differences in the perceptions of the different members of one family. Figure 11.4 separately shows the FES subscale means of the parents and children in family 377, selected from our clinic subsample. The father was a 65-year-old man with a high school education. The mother was 61 years old and had had 2 years of college. The 17-year-old son was currently in the twelfth grade, and the 16-year-old daughter was in the eleventh grade. The family lived in a suburban residential community and was active in various clubs and organizations (e.g., Parent–Teacher Association and the local homeowners' association). They indicated no current religious preference and that they never attended religious services. They had contacted the clinic because the 17-year-old boy had been arrested for an offense involving marijuana. He had been institutionalized for several months but was presently on probation and was making relatively good progress. The 16-year-old daughter had recently decided to press criminal charges against an older man who had been having sexual relations with her for some time. She was described as being relatively immature and as the "dumb one" in the family.

The profiles for the parents and children illustrate the similarities and differences in the way in which they perceive the social environment of their family. Parents and children basically agree in their perceptions of all three Relationship dimensions. However, the parents perceive much more emphasis on Independence and Intellectual–Cultural Orientation than do the children. These differences, which are on the order of 3 to 4 mean raw score points, are substantial. The family members agree quite closely on the degree of emphasis on the other three Personal Growth dimensions. They also agree on the amount of emphasis on

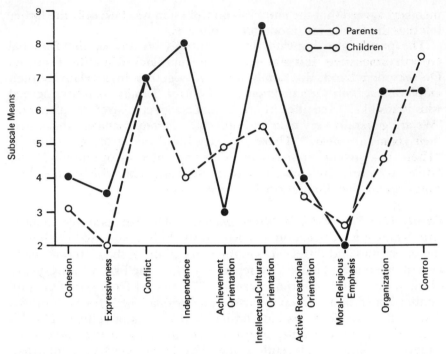

Figure 11.4 FES Form R profiles for parents and children in family 377.

Control; however, the parents see considerably more emphasis on Organization than do the children. Overall, the children perceive the family environment somewhat more negatively than do their parents.

Profiles such as those in Figure 11.4 can also be drawn for individual family members. The FES results can be summarized for an entire family, and the family can be compared with a selected normative sample, as shown in the first three examples. On the other hand, the perceptions of parents or children, or the perceptions of each individual family member, can be compared and contrasted.

Correlates of Family Climates. We have acquired relatively few additional data to which the FES can be related. A family background form is being developed to systematically obtain a broad variety of information about each family. Preliminary analyses have been completed on five specific issues.

First, are there consistent sex differences in the way in which family social environments are perceived? To study this question, 80 four-person families (mother, father, one son, and one daughter) were selected. Do mothers and fathers show systematic differences in the way they perceive the social environment of their families? Do sons and daughters show systematic differences? The only statistically significant difference that appeared in these comparisons was a tendency for mothers to perceive a somewhat higher emphasis on Active Recreational Orientation than did fathers. Mothers also perceived somewhat more emphasis on both Intellectual–Cultural Orientation and Moral–Religious Emphasis than did fathers, but neither of these differences attained significance. There were no significant differences between sons and daughters. Thus the general conclusion is that there are no consistent sex differences in perceptions of family social environments. This does not mean, of course, that there may not be important differences within specific families.

Second, are there consistent parent–child differences in the way in which families are perceived? Mothers $(N = 267)$ and fathers $(N = 236)$ were combined because there were no consistent sex differences in perceptions of family climate. Sons and daughters (total $N = 550$) were combined for the same reason. There are small but systematic differences in the ways in which parents and children perceive their family environments. On the average, children see less emphasis on Cohesion and Expressiveness and more emphasis on Conflict than do parents. Children also see somewhat less Independence, Intellectual–Cultural Orientation, and Moral–Religious Emphasis, and somewhat more Achievement Orientation and Active Recreational Orientation. The extent of agreement or disagreement with regard to family climate varies considerably from family to family. Parents and children in some families show very high agreement; whereas in others there is considerable disagreement. The extent of agreement displayed by family members in this regard is itself an important family characteristic.

Third, family size was related to the FES subscales. There were 46 three-member, 67 four-member, 68 five-member, and 47 six-member families, as well as 35 families with seven or more members. There is a general tendency for Cohesiveness and Expressiveness to decrease and for Conflict to increase with increasing family size. This is particularly striking in comparing three- and four-member families with families in which there are seven or more family members. For example, the average score on Cohesion was about one point higher for three-member families than for families with seven or more members. On the other hand, the average Conflict score for three-member families was over 1.5 points lower than that for families with seven or more members. Both these differences were statistically significant.

There is also a tendency for the emphasis on Independence to decline somewhat with family size, although this is not strongly evident until we examine the largest families. Moral–Religious Emphasis tends to increase with family size. This is also particularly evident with the largest families. Finally, as might be expected, the emphasis on Control tends to exhibit a linear and rather substantial increase with family size. Thus the general tendency is for Cohesion, Expressiveness, and Independence to decrease with family size, whereas Conflict, Control, and Moral–Religious Emphasis increase with family size. The other four dimensions did not change significantly in relation to family size.

Fourth, we obtained some information on the drinking habits of a sample of families. Families were asked how often they drank wine, beer, and hard liquor. They responded to each of these items on a 4-point scale ranging from never to often. The family beer, wine, and hard liquor scores were combined, and the 32 families who obtained the lowest scores were then compared with the 36 families who obtained the highest scores. Essentially, the 32 families in the first group hardly ever drank wine, beer, or hard liqour, whereas the 36 families in the second group drank wine, beer, and hard liquor fairly often. Moral–Religious Emphasis was the only subscale to differentiate among these two groups of families, with the families who drank rarely or never obtaining a significantly higher score.

Some further analyses were undertaken to see whether there were consistent differences in the way in which different family members perceived the two groups of families. Thus fathers', mothers', and children's FES subscale scores in the two groups of families were compared. All family members agreed that Moral–Religious Emphasis was higher in the low drinking than in the high drinking families. Some other suggestive differences also emerged. Fathers in the high drinking families perceived more emphasis on Expressiveness than fathers in the low drinking families. However, mothers in the high drinking families perceived less emphasis on Cohesion and more on Conflict than mothers in the low drinking families. In addition, the mothers in the high drinking families perceived less emphasis on Achievement Orientation and on family Organization. Thus the mothers in the high drinking families saw their family social environment somewhat more negatively than the mothers in the low drinking families.

The same conclusions held for children—for example, the children in the low drinking families perceived more emphasis on Cohesion, Expressiveness, Achievement Orientation, and family Organization than did the children in the high drinking families. On the other hand, the latter children reported more emphasis on Intellectual–Cultural Orientation. These results are preliminary (and they are based on families with drinking patterns within the normal range); however, they support the notion that family drinking patterns may affect family members in very different ways. The results are consistent with the clinical impression that mothers and children are affected more than the father, who usually does the most drinking.

Fifth, a comparison was made between 42 clinic families and 42 matched normal families. The 42 clinic families had been included in one of our clinic samples. The 42 normal families were closely matched with the clinic families on a one-to-one basis in terms of family size and composition. The clinic families obtained significantly lower scores on Cohesion, on Intellectual–Cultural Orientation, and on Active Recreational Orientation. They obtained higher scores on both Conflict and Control, but these differences were not quite statistically significant. The clinic families also obtained lower scores on Expressiveness and Independence and higher scores on Achievement Orientation, but again these differences did not quite reach significance. In general, however, the differences between the clinic and matched normal families are consistent with expectations and provide some initial support for the construct validity of the FES.

We have also recently completed the development of a Work Environment Scale (WES), which measures 10 dimensions of the social climates of work milieus (Moos and Insel, 1974), and of a Group Environment Scale (GES), which measures 10 dimensions of the social environments of social, task-oriented, and therapeutic or self-help groups (Moos 1974b). Our aim is to develop additional ways of conceptualizing social environments to identify the salient dimensions of the community settings in which delinquents must function. Adequate outcome studies need techniques by which both institutional environments and more naturalistically occurring community settings can be assessed (see Chapter 7). The development of these methods should make it possible to predict criteria of program outcome from characteristics of community environments as well as from characteristics of correctional programs.

The clinical utility of different methods of measuring both program and community environments of delinquents needs to be systematically investigated. This should be done in a case-oriented manner, that is, by developing case descriptions that include various types of information about the individual's relevant ecological niche. The inclusion of information about the environmental characteristics with which each individual must cope will make for far richer, more meaningful clinical case descriptions (see Chapter 11 for an example). In addition, this information should help to more meaningfully organize individual treatment

programs around the delinquents' community settings. There is currently increased emphasis on keeping delinquents out of institutions and
returning them to their home communitites. The identification of the
psychosocial environmental factors that favor successful individual outcome would constitute a valuable clinical contribution.

Toward Enhancing Individual–Community Congruence.   Systematic
research aimed at identifying basic categories of naturally occurring community settings in which people function is now underway. For example,
Price and Bouffard (1974) have grouped situations in terms of appropriateness of certain behaviors in those situations. Price and Blashfield
(1973) examined the entire population of behavior settings ($N = 455$),
which were assessed by 43 variables in a small midwestern town. The
variables used for assessment included the authority system to which
the setting belongs (i.e., church, school, government agency), the action
patterns likely to occur in the setting (i.e., business, education, physical
health, recreation), the age and sex characteristics of various classes of
individuals participating in the settings, the size of the setting, and the
duration and frequency of occurrence of the setting.

A cluster analyses of the 455 settings yielded 12 distinct clusters or
behavior setting types. For example, cluster one was labeled "youth performance settings" and was distinguished from the other clusters by a
preponderance of very young performers. Typical examples of behavior
settings in this cluster were Christmas programs, Scout banquets, and
amateur talent shows. Other clusters were labeled as follows: religious
settings (church-sponsored activities, fellowship meetings), women's organizational settings (sewing clubs, garden clubs, ladies' aid societies),
elementary school settings, high school settings, fund-raising settings,
men's organization settings (church deacon meetings, Kiwanis club meetings, athletic banquets), local business settings (banks, service stations,
grocery stores, laundries), large membership settings (refreshment
stands, street fairs, machinery exhibitions, parades), audience event settings (school assemblies, graduation exercises, class plays), and government settings (township board meetings, elections and polling places,
city council meetings).

This analysis identifies the overall behavior setting structure of an
entire community. The results make it possible to begin to characterize
the ecological environment of an individual by identifying the basic
properties of the types of behavior setting he or she characteristically
frequents. It also might enable one to individually structure an ecological
environment that is varied and stimulating, yet unlikely to promote de-

linquent activity. Correctional practitioners will need to know more about the overall structure and dynamics of the community settings in which they work. The methods used by Price and Blashfield should eventually help supply more systematic information about the specific adaptation and coping skills needed to participate in community settings of various types. Price and Blashfield also point out that their results might be of utility for diagnosing entire communities for their potential pathogenic and health-promoting characteristics.

A number of authors have commented on the importance of person–environment fit or compatibility (e.g., Pervin, 1968; Sells, 1963; Stern, 1964). Wicker (1972) has comprehensively discussed the events that shape behavior to be compatible with the immediate environment. He describes person–environment congruence in terms of various theoretical positions such as operant learning, observation learning, behavior settng theory, and social exchange theory. He also points out that few behaviors are consistently followed by positive or negative reinforcers, regardless of the situation. In fact, many behaviors that are rewarded in one situation are punished in another. For example, loud and raucous behavior may be rewarded in settings such as taverns, parties, and football games but punished in other settings, such as churches, funeral chapels, and golf tournaments. Wicker suggests that available information sources may contribute to behavior–environment congruence by directing people into settings appropriate for the behaviors they wish to enact.

Importantly, Wicker notes that recent research has indicated that individuals' judgments about how they would respond in hypothetical situations are consistently better predictors of actual behavior than are traditional measures of attitude. Thus may one obtain substantial information about how an individual will adapt in a new group home or work milieu simply by asking the individual how he would react to the setting.

Holland (1966) has contributed a particularly interesting theory of model personality types and model environments. He believes that vocational satisfaction and performance depend "on the congruency between one's personality and the environment (composed largely of other people) in which one works" (p. 6). He proposes six model environments, each one dominated by a given type of personality and typified by physical settings posing special problems and stresses. The six model environments are labeled as follows: Realistic, Intellectual, Social, Conventional, Enterprising, and Artistic. For example, the Realistic environment is characterized by the necessity to complete specific concrete tasks. It is populated by people such as airplane mechanics, construction inspectors, electricians, and filling station attendants. The tasks usually necessitate tools and machines and demand carefulness, close attention, speed, and persistence. Close interpersonal relationships are of minimal importance. This type of environment is conceptually similar to our Action-oriented type of treatment program.

In distinction, Holland's Social environment features problems that require the ability to interpret and modify human behavior and special knowledge in caring for and communicating with other people. Example occupations include clinical psychologist, welfare agency employee, high school teacher, and counselor. Frequent prolonged personal relationships with others are necessary. A high degree of social sensitivity and skill is demanded, and there may be emotional "work hazards" because of the necessity of relatively close personal relationships with students, employees, and/or patients. This kind of environment seems quite similar to our Relationship-oriented treatment program.

Holland proposes six analogous personality types (i.e., Realistic, Intellectual, Social, Conventional, Enterprising, and Artistic), who presumably perform better and are more satisfied in the specific environment in which they are most congruent. The notion of enhancing person–environment congruence underlies the potential importance of our model of six types of correctional, psychiatric hospital, and community treatment programs. It might be most useful for correctional programs to model themselves after certain kinds of community setting, since delinquents could then be trained to function adequately in settings very similar to those in which they will later participate.

REFERENCES

Bandura, A. & Walters, R. H. *Adolescent aggression: A study of the influence of child-training practices and family interrelationships.* Ronald Press, New York, 1959.

Brown, G. W., Birley, J. L. T. & Wing, J. K. Influence of family life on the course of schizophrenic disorders: A replication. *British Journal of Psychiatry,* **121:**241–258, 1972.

Cortes, J. B. & Gatti, F. M. *Delinquency and crime: A biopsychosocial approach.* Seminar Press, New York, 1972.

Davies, M. *Probationers in their social environment.* Her Majesty's Stationery Office, London, 1969.

Davies, M. & Sinclair, I. Families, hostels and delinquents: An attempt to assess cause and effect. *British Journal of Criminology,* **11:**213–229, 1971.

Deykin, E. Life functioning in families of delinquent boys: An assessment model. *Social Service Review,* **46:**90–102, 1972.

Haggard, E. *Intraclass correlation and the analysis of variance.* Dryden Press, New York, 1958.

Holland, J. L. *The psychology of vocational choice: A theory of personality types and model environments.* Blaisdell, Waltham, Mass., 1966.

Kemp, C. J. Family treatment within the milieu of a residential treatment center. *Child Welfare*, **50:**229–235, 1971.

Kohn, M. Class, family, and schizophrehia: A reformulation. *Social Forces*, **50:**295–304, 1972.

Maluccio, A. N. & Marlow, W. D. Residential treatment of emotionally disturbed children: A review of the literature. *Social Service Review*, **46:**230–250, 1972.

Manino, F. V. & Shore, M. F. Family structure, aftercare, and post-hospital adjustment. *American Journal of Orthopsychiatry*, **44:**76–85, 1974.

McCord, W., McCord, J., & Zola, I. *Origins of crime*. Columbia Univeristy Press, New York, 1959.

McCord, W., McCord, J., & Howard, A. Familial correlates of aggression in nondelinquent male children. *Journal of Abnormal and Social Psychology*, **62:**79–93, 1961.

McCord, J., McCord, W., & Howard, A. Family interaction as antecedent to the direction of male aggressiveness. *Journal of Abnormal and Social Psychology*, **66:**239–242, 1963.

Mitchell, R. Some social implications of high density housing. *American Sociological Review*, **36:**18–29, 1971.

Moos, R. *Family Environment Scale Preliminary Manual*. Consulting Psychologists Press, Palo Alto, Calif., 1974a.

Moos, R. *Group Environment Scale Preliminary Manual*. Consulting Psychologists Press, Palo Alto, Calif., 1974b.

Moos, R. & Insel, P. *Work Environment Scale Preliminary Manual*. Consulting Psychologists Press, Palo Alto, Calif., 1974.

Murray, H. *Explorations in personality*. Oxford University Press, New York, 1938.

Myers, J. K. & Bean, L. L. *A decade later: A follow-up of social class and mental illness*. Wiley, New York, 1968.

Patterson, G. *Families in treatment*. Research Press, Champaign-Urbana, Ill., 1971.

Pervin, L. A. Performance and satisfaction as a function of individual–environment fit. *Psychological Bulletin*, **69:**56–68, 1968.

Pless, I. B. & Satterwhite, B. A measure of family functioning and its application. *Social Science and Medicine*, **7:**613–621, 1973.

Price, R. & Blashfield, R. Explorations in the taxonomy of behavior settings: Analysis of dimensions and classification of settings. *American Journal of Community Psychology*, in press, 1975.

Price, R. H. & Bouffard, D. L. Behavioral appropriateness and situational constraint as dimensions of social behavior. *Journal of Personality and Social Psychology*, **30:** 579–586, 1974.

Scott, M. L. Small groups—An effective treatment approach in residential programs for adolescents. *Child Welfare*, **49:**161–164, 1970.

Sells, S. B. An interactionist looks at the environment. *American Psychologist*, **18:**696–702, 1963.

Stern, G. G. $B = f(P, E)$. *Journal of Personality Assessment*, **28:**161–168, 1964.

Wicker, A. W. Processes which mediate behavior–environment congruence. *Behavioral Science*, **17:**265–277, 1972.

Wiltz, N. A. Behavioral therapy techniques in treatment of emotionally disturbed children and their families. *Child Welfare*, **52:**483–492, 1973.

CHAPTER TWELVE

Military Companies

Measuring Military Company Environments. This chapter discusses the application of the measurement of social climate to a different setting—military companies. This work is included for three reasons. First, the work in military companies represents an extension of the logic of our approach to a different yet related "type of environment." According to Lang (1965), the military is a "total institution" as Erving Goffman defined that term. Second, the military is an important environment for a large group of young men and (increasingly) women. Many young men who have spent time in correctional facilities later spend time in the service, and vice versa.

Third, we had a unique opportunity to obtain objective test performance and sick call data and to relate these to the social climate of military companies. Social climate is clearly related to morale, satisfaction, self-esteem, and so on. But to what extent is social climate related to more objective outcome measures? Does the weak relationship between correctional climates and parole outcome indicate that the social milieu does not affect more objective outcome measures? Or is it perhaps too much to expect a closer relationship, given the impact of current community settings, the long delay between supposed "impact" and "outcome," discretionary police decision making, and other variables? The data from military companies provided an opportunity to determine how closely social climate is related to "immediate" objective outcome measures (e.g., test performance at the end of training). The general logic and approach used in military companies are directly analogous to those used in correctional settings (Chapter 7).

Marlowe (1959) and Bourne (1967) have described the process of basic training and have emphasized some of the social and psychological factors involved in individual adaptations to this process. Marlowe discussed the importance of unclear expectations, of the establishment of a "buddy-ship relation," of the sense of tenuousness experienced by the recruit, of the importance of group spirit and company morale, and of the rising sense of anger and frustration often felt by individual recruits. Bourne stresses similar issues and also discusses the importance of the "status stripping process," through which the outward signs of the recruit's previous civilian identity are moved.

In this connection, Datel and Lifrak (1969) found differences among military units at Fort Ord and Fort Dix both in the initial levels and in the changes of negative affect scores during basic training. These data show that the social environments of military training companies are quite different and that the differences probably result in considerably different experiences (and levels of distress) for recruits. Other relevant literature indicates that factors we would label "social climate" (e.g., morale, leadership, discipline) are of critical importance in determining enlisted men's adjustment to the military milieu in both combat and noncombat situations (e.g., Appel, 1966; Glass et al., 1961). These were some of the considerations that led us to construct an inventory by which to systematically assess the social environments of military companies.

The Military Company Environment Inventory (MCEI).   The logic underlying the development of the MCEI was similar to that used for the CIES. The details are given in the MCEI Manual (Moos, 1973). In brief, an 84-item MCEI was derived from a random sample of 509 subjects taken from 13 companies. A factor analysis was performed on an initial group of 146 items, intercorrelated over the sample of 509 subjects. Seven factor dimensions were sufficient to describe the basic characteristics of military company environments. Items were selected for inclusion by several criteria. First, each item had to correlate more highly with its own than with any other subscale score. Second, the item should discriminate significantly among military companies—more than 90% of the final 84 items did so. Third, an attempt was made to select items that had been answered in one direction by no more than 75% of subjects. Again, more than 90% of the items selected met this criterion.

The use of these criteria resulted in an 84-item Form R (Real) of the MCEI. Table 12.1 lists the seven final subscales and briefly defines each. The full 84-item Scale and scoring key are given in the Manual (Moos, 1973).

Table 12.1   Military Company Environment Inventory (Form R)

1.	*Involvement*	how actively enlisted men participate and take interest in the functions of their company.
2.	*Peer Cohesion*	measures the social and interpersonal relationships that develop among the enlisted men and their tendency to stick together and help one another.
3.	*Officer Support*	the degree of friendship and communication between officers and enlisted men, and how much officers attempt to help and encourage enlisted men.
4.	*Personal Status*	the extent that individual differences among enlisted men are recognized and respected, and the emphasis on enlisted men assuming responsibility for running the barracks and company.
5.	*Order and Organization*	the emphasis on organization and following a daily schedule and the emphasis on physical neatness in the barracks.
6.	*Clarity*	how clearly the regulations and line of authority of the company are understood by the enlisted men, and to what extent they know what is expected of them and what will be the consequence of not meeting these expectations.
7.	*Officer Control*	the extent to which officers use commands, close supervision, ridicule, rewards, and punishment (threatened or real) to keep enlisted men under necessary controls.

The Involvement, Peer Cohesion, and Officer Support subscales measure Relationship dimensions. These subscales assess the extent to which the men are involved in the company, the extent to which the enlisted men support and help one another, the extent to which the officers support and help the enlisted men, and the degree of spontaneous and free and open expression within these relationships.

The next subscale, Personal Status, is a Personal Development or personal growth dimension. The last three subscales of Order and Organization, Clarity, and Officer Control are designed to assess System Maintenance dimensions, which are conceptually identical to those we obtained in correctional and treatment environments. Thus the military environment is similar to other environments in terms of the Relationship and System Maintenance dimensions, but differs from these other environments in that only one Personal Growth dimension was identified.

The average item-subscale correlations and internal consistencies of the subscales are all in an acceptable range. The subscale intercorrelations are generally low to moderate, with only three of the correlations being above .45. Further psychometric details about the MCEI are given in the Manual (Moos, 1973), which also tells how we developed the 28-item Short Form, Form E (which assesses expectations of military companies), and Form I (which assesses concepts of ideal military companies).

Although enlisted men generally agree on certain aspects of the climate of military companies, there are substantial differences among companies. Two profile interpretations are presented here, to illustrate some of the primary uses of the MCEI—deriving detailed descriptions of company environments, comparing the perceptions of officers and enlisted men, assessing the changes in company environments over time, contrasting different companies and performing other evaluations.

Figure 12.1 presents the MCEI profiles of two companies at the fourth week of basic training. The companies show moderate but not substantial differences. Company 39 has average scores on most of the dimensions, although there is well below-average emphasis on Officer Support and well above-average emphasis on Officer Control. Company 45, on the other hand, has several scores that are slightly above average and two scores (Involvement and Personal Status) that are moderately above average. Peer Cohesion is below average in Company 45, whereas it is somewhat above average in Company 39.

Some specific items give a concrete idea of the differences between these two companies. For example, more of the men in Company 45 agreed with Involvement subscale items such as: "A lot of interesting things go on in this company," "The enlisted men are proud of the company," and "Enlisted men here really try to improve and learn." On the other hand, more of the men in Company 39 agreed with Peer Cohesion items such as: "Enlisted men around here care about each other," and "Enlisted men often do things together during off-duty hours." The men in Company 45 agreed more strongly with several of the Officer Support items including: "The NCOs and officers act on enlisted men's suggestions," "In this company enlisted men can talk freely with their NCOs," "NCOs tell enlisted men when they do a good job," and "NCOs and officers go out of their way to help enlisted men."

Figure 12.2 shows the contrasting MCEI profiles of two other companies, having substantially different social environments. These profiles were picked to more fully illustrate the range of variation that occurs

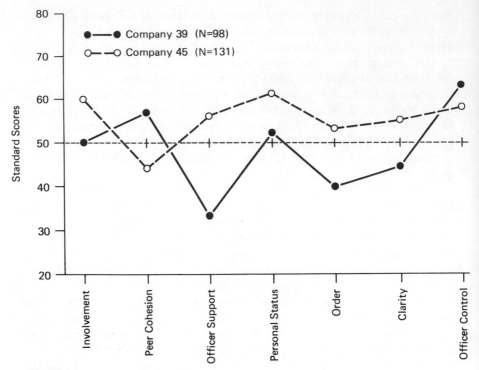

Figure 12.1   MCEI profiles for companies 39 and 45.

in MCEI results. Company 10 is 1 standard deviation above the mean on the Involvement, Peer Cohesion, Order and Organization, and Clarity subscales. Company 15, on the other hand, is 2 standard deviations above the mean on Officer Support, but between 1 and 2 standard deviations below the mean on Involvement, Peer Cohesion, Order and Organization, Clarity, and Officer Control.

Some of the same Relationship dimension items that differentiated between Companies 39 and 45 also differentiate between Companies 10 and 15, but the differences between the latter companies are considerably larger. The men in Company 10 were far more likely to answer "true" to items like "Enlisted men put a lot of energy into what they do around here," "Enlisted men here really try to improve and learn," and "The more effective enlisted men help the less effective ones." A high emphasis on System Maintenance (as evidenced by high scores on Order and Organization, Clarity, and Officer Control) is compatible with high company morale (as evidenced by high scores on Involvement and Peer Cohesion).

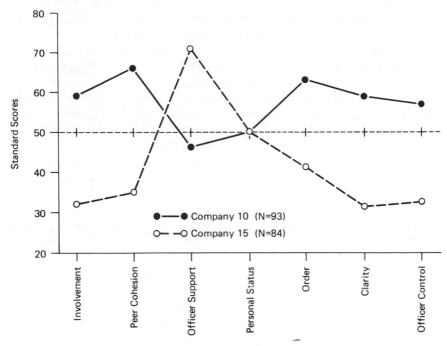

Figure 12.2 MCEI profiles for companies 10 and 15.

For example, the men in Company 10 were more likely to answer "true" to many of the items on the System Maintenance dimensions, including: "This company is very strict about enlisted men leaving the company area without saying where they are going" (99%), "It is clear how the skills being learned will help the enlisted men to be good soldiers" (88%), "Enlisted men who break minor company regulations are punished for it" (95%), and "The company gives passes easily" (98% false). These items illustrate that Company 10 has a higher emphasis on Clarity and Officer Control than Company 15. Thus there are seen to be quite diverse social environments in military companies. Different types of men are more likely to function well in one type of company than in another. Military command needs to facilitate a variety of company environments, rather than pushing for a monolithic model.

Stress in Military Environments. Military companies can be described in terms of seven salient dimensions of the social environment. In this section we try to determine the extent to which the social environment of military companies can lessen the stress of basic training. We are aware of no previous studies that have directly related the social environments of military companies to indices of company performance. However, there is some literature on the effects of certain dimensions of social environments (mainly cohesion) on the performance of work-related tasks in training companies and in experimental or actual field conditions (e.g., Shils and Janowitz, 1948; George, 1971; Little, 1964).

For example, Goodacre (1951) used a sociometric test of group cohesion based on buddy choices and compared the resultant cohesion index to the performance of jeep reconnaissance squads on a field test. The field problem consisted of 12 tactical situations (e.g., an air attack, the outposting of a road junction, and a troop withdrawal), which were constructed to closely represent battlefield conditions. The 12 six-man squads tested varied substantially on the cohesion index and on field problem total performance scores. The rank-order correlation between the two scores across the 12 squads was .77, indicating a very strong relationship between group cohesion and group performance.

Nelson and Berry (1963) studied group cohesion in 24 marine basic training platoons. The cohesion index, constructed on the basis of friendship choices, was positively related to the homogeneity of background characteristics (e.g., age, education, geographical region of origin) of the men in the platoons. There was no correlation between group cohesion and individual performance, but platoons above the median on cohesion had much more favorable attitudes toward the Marine Corps. Adams (1954) related equalitarian attitudes measured by a sentence completion instrument to the overall performance of 11-man bomber crews as rated in the squadron training report. High-performance crews clustered in the upper middle of the equalitarianism scale, implying that too much equalitarianism (high personal status?) may result in lower performance.

Lott and Lott (1965) have presented a comprehensive review of the literature on the cohesiveness of small groups and its correlates. Cohesiveness is much more clearly related to attitudes (e.g., positive evaluations of the group and its members) than to task performance, although several studies indicating solid relationships between group cohesiveness and group performance measures are presented. But other relevant variables, such as situational demands and personal characteristics of group members, have often been ignored. Even more important, such other characteristics of the social environment as Support, Personal Status, Clarity, and Control, have rarely if ever been measured. These social environmental dimensions may themselves have an independent impact on group performance.

Eight basic combat training companies were studied with the MCEI and the Manifest Affect Adjective Check List (MAACL) during the fourth week of training. Specific indices of company performance were compiled from records. These indices were: number of sick calls, firing scores (BRM), physical training scores (PCPT), graded test scores, and both AWOL rates and number of article 15s (disciplinary infractions). A total of 1432 men were involved in the study; the number in each company varied from 112 to 224.

The MAACL is a self-administered test that provides measures of three clinically relevant negative affects: Anxiety, Depression, and Hostility. The subject is instructed to mark words that describe his feelings during a certain time period. A high score on the Anxiety Scale is obtained by checking anxiety-laden words like afraid, frightened, nervous, and tense and by not checking more pleasurable words such as calm, cheerful, contented, and happy. A high score on the Depression Scale is made by checking items like alone, discouraged, gloomy, and hopeless and by not checking items like active, enthusiastic, healthy, and strong. Finally, a high score on the Hostility Scale is obtained by checking items like angry, bitter, disgusted, and offended and by not checking agreeable, cooperative, friendly, sympathetic, and similar items. Extensive normative and other data on the MAACL is available (Zuckerman and Lubin, 1965).

Company Climate and Negative Affect.   All seven MCEI subscales significantly differentiated among the eight companies. Thus the social environments of the eight companies showed substantial differences. Rank-order correlations were computed over companies ($N = 8$) between the MCEI and the MAACL scores. The results indicated the following: (1) men experience significantly more anxiety in companies with high Officer Control (.79) and low Personal Status (−.67); (2) men experience more depression in companies with high Officer Control (.79) and low Peer Cohesion (−.86), and Personal Status (−.60); (3) men experience more hostility in companies with high Officer Control (.69), low Clarity (−.86), and low scores on all three Relationship dimensions of Involvement (−.67), Peer Cohesion (−.63), and Officer Support (−.95). Although these relationships are not mutually independent, since the MAACL scales are relatively highly interrelated and the MCEI scales are moderately interrelated, the number and magnitude of statistically significant correlations is striking.

The data indicate that men experience less anxiety, depression and hostility in companies that strongly emphasize Involvement, Peer Cohesion, and Officer Support. This is a particularly important finding since, as Datel and Lifrak (1969) indicate, the rise in hostility exhibited by enlisted men over the 8 weeks of basic training is greater than the rise in either anxiety or depression. Datel points out that upon entering the military the typical recruit is moderately insecure and fearful, but he is also open, receptive, cooperative, and nonhostile. At the conclusion of training the insecurity and fearfulness are maintained, but the levels of sadness and anger have increased substantially. Our data show that high levels of hostility are also less likely to occur in companies that emphasize Clarity and de-emphasize Officer Control.

The men feel much less depressed in companies that place high emphasis on Peer Cohesion. In addition, they feel less anxious, depressed, and angry in companies that emphasize Personal Status. The dimension of Officer Control shows the highest and most consistent relationship to negative affect. Men feel much more anxious, depressed, and angry in companies in which officers harshly command and in which close supervision, ridicule, and threatened or real punishments are used to keep enlisted men under strict control. Thus there are substantial relationships between the social environment of a company and the mood of the men in that company.

Company Climate, Test Performance, and Sick Call.   As described previously, data on AWOL and article 15 disciplinary actions, on sick call and on test scores (firing scores, physical training scores, and graded test scores) were obtained for each of the eight companies. The scores on the three test performance measures were each rank-ordered and the companies were given an overall rank order based on their total test performance scores. The companies were separately rank-ordered on the number of sick calls they reported. Unfortunately, there were not enough AWOLs and article 15 disciplinary actions (and their variations from company to company were too limited) to permit further analysis. The test scores varied significantly among companies. The number of sick calls reported showed substantial differences among companies—from a low of 172 during the 8-week basic training cycle in one company to a high of 576 in another.

Rank-order correlations between the MCEI subscale means and the sick call and test performance criteria were computed. The only significant relationship was one of .58 between Peer Cohesion and test performance, indicating that men tested better in companies that strongly emphasized Peer Cohesion. Since several of the correlations between the MCEI and the sick call and test score performance criteria were of at least moderate magnitude (although not quite statistically significant), a further analysis was conducted.

Each of the MCEI items are answered either true or false. First, the percentage true was calculated for each item for each of the eight companies. Next, each of the 84 items was correlated with the two-company outcome criteria. These were rank-order correlations in which the companies were rank-ordered on each of the two performance criteria and on the percentage of men who answered each item in the true direction. Many items showed moderate to high correlations with two performance criteria (e.g., 26 of the 84 items correlated .40 or greater with the performance criterion, and 24 corelated .40 or greater with the sick call criterion). The surprising finding was that there was relatively little overlap in the specific items relating to these two criteria. It was thus possible to contruct two nonoverlapping 15-item MCEI subscales that were highly related to the two outcome criteria.

The 15 items on the Test Performance Scale (see Table 12.2) were chosen because of their high individual correlations with the test score performance criterion. The total scores on these 15 items correlates .83 with the actual test scores performance of the eight companies. The content of the items is instructive. Almost half the items (i.e., the first seven items) are from the Peer Cohesion subscale. These items indicate that high Peer Cohesion is probably the most important characteristic of high-performance companies. More effective men in these companies help less effective ones. The men talk to one another about their personal problems. The expression of feelings is relatively open and spontaneous. The men feel that they get to know one another relatively well. They often do things together during off-duty hours.

The next six items fall into the areas of Officer Support and Clarity. The men understand how the skills they are learning will help them to be good soldiers. The men try to improve and learn. They feel that the officers know what they (the men) want. The officers do not argue and disagree openly in front of the men. The men see the officers as setting an example of orderliness and neatness. The last two items indicate that Autonomy and Personal Status may be slightly suppressed in high-performance companies. The men feel that they are not encouraged to learn new ways of doing things and that they are not strongly encouraged to think and act for themselves. These items give a fairly clear picture of the basic characteristics of high-performing basic training companies. Peer Cohesion is high. Certain aspects of Officer Support and Clarity are high, but autonomy and independence are not strongly emphasized. It was not possible to cross-validate with an additional sample of basic training companies. However, we did look at another sample of 16 companies to determine whether the 15 items in the Test Performance Scale discriminated between high- and low-performance companies (as rated by the brigade commander) in a direction consistent with

Table 12.2 Test Performance Subscale Items and Scoring Key

Scoring Direction	Item
T	The more effective enlisted men (EM) help the less effective ones.
T	EM tell each other about their personal problems.
T	Personal problems are openly talked about.
F	EM tend to hide their feelings from one another.
F	In this company, it's hard to tell how EM are feeling.
F	It takes a long time for EM to get to know one another in this company.
T	EM often do things together during off-duty hours.
T	It is clear how the skills being learned will help EM to be good soldiers.
T	EM here really try to improve and learn.
T	The non-commissioned officers (NCOs) and officers know what the EM want.
F	NCOs sometimes argue among themselves.
F	NCOs get chewed out in front of their men.
T	The NCOs and officers set the example for neatness and orderliness.
F	EM are encouraged to learn new ways to do things.
F	EM are encouraged to think and act for themselves.

the results just given. Thirteen of the items did discriminate in the correct direction in this sample. Thus there is some evidence that the characteristics tapped by these 15 items may generally be related to high company performance, although more careful and more complete cross-validation is clearly necessary.

The 15 items on the Sick Call Scale (Table 12.3) present a picture of a very different kind of company. The first seven items indicate that more men go on sick call in companies that have a relatively high emphasis on Order and Organization. Six of the first seven items are on the Order and Organization scale, and the seventh item is on the Clarity scale. Men in high sick call companies see the company as being very strict about following the daily schedule and about the men reporting where they are going. The men feel they are kept relatively busy and that the company is relatively well-organized (e.g., the day room is not messy, there is little turnover of officers, the men know when the commander will be inspecting the company).

Table 12.3 Sick Call Subscale Items and Scoring Key

Scoring Direction	Item
T	This company is very strict about EM following the daily schedule.
T	The company is strict about EM leaving the company area without saying where they're going.
T	EM are pretty busy all of the time.
F	The day room is often messy.
F	Things are sometimes very disorganized around here.
F	There is frequent turnover of NCOs and officers in this unit.
T	EM know when the commander will be inspecting the company.
T	Men in this unit seem bored most of the time.
T	The work here is repetitious and boring.
F	It's O.K. to act a little different around here.
F	EM are expected to take leadership in this company.
T	NCOs are constantly checking on the men and supervise them very closely.
T	Men are ridiculed in front of others.
T	EM never know when an officer will ask to see them.
F	NCOs and officers help new men to get oriented to the company.

The next four items show that the men have very low Personal Status and are bored. The men feel that their work is repetitious and boring, that they cannot act somewhat differently if they want to, and that they are not expected or encouraged to take leadership in the company. The last four items indicate that all this occurs in a company with relatively high emphasis on Officer Control. For example, the men feel that the officers are constantly checking up on them and supervising them very closely. The men feel that they are ridiculed in front of their peers, that the officers do not help them to get oriented to the company, and that they never know when an officer will ask to see them.

The characteristics of high sick call companies are thus quite clear. Order and Organization is high and borders on extreme restrictiveness. The men are kept busy, but they perceive the tasks to be repetitious and boring. Various aspects of relatively strict Officer Control are emphasized, whereas the men's Personal Status is de-emphasized. No wonder these men go on sick call more often! Since we have no separate data on sick call from the other 16 companies, the results could not be cross-validated. Although the results make good sense, cross-validation is clearly necessary.

The Impact of Military Milieus.   The findings indicate substantial relationships between company environment and affect, test perform-ance, and sick call. Men feel less anxious, depressed, and hostile in companies that emphasize the Relationship dimensions of Involvement, Peer Cohesion, and Officer Support, and the Personal Growth dimen-sion of Personal Status. Men also feel less affective distress in companies that de-emphasize Officer Control. Men feel less hostile in companies that are high in Clarity. Companies that are most successful in reducing affective distress are not necessarily most successful on test performance criteria.

Companies that were high on the test performance criterion empha-sized Peer Cohesion, Officer Support, and Clarity, but also slightly de-emphasized Personal Status. High-performance companies were not rig-id and restrictive, but neither did they heavily stress the men's autonomy and independence. Companies in which sick call was high were some-what different: they had very high emphasis on both Order and Organi-zation and Officer Control and very low emphasis on Involvement and Personal Status.

The Relationship dimensions are of particular importance since they are strongly related to all three outcome criteria. Emphasis on Peer Cohesion (i.e., close "buddy" relationships) was quite important, espe-cially in test performance. This corroborates Goodacre's (1951) finding that cohesive groups show better task performance. In another study Goodacre (1953) was interested in the differences in group characteris-tics between good and poor performing rifle squads. The criterion con-sisted of ratings of squad performance on a 6-hour firing field problem that called on nine-man squads to perform most of the duties found in a "normal" combat situation. The men in the high-performance squads reported much more "buddying around" together on the post after duty hours (Peer Cohesion). They were more likely to give orders to other men during the field problem without the explicit authority to do so (Personal Status). The men in the high-scoring squads reported greater satisfaction with how their squad leader ran the field problem, more satisfaction with their present position in the squad, and greater pride in their squad. They also felt that their squad was one that other men would like to join if given the chance. Thus Involvement and Peer Cohesion were clearly higher in the better performing squads.

The finding that Personal Status is slightly suppressed in high-performance companies is similar to Adams' finding that high-performance bomber crews clustered in the upper middle of an equalitarianism scale. Fiedler (1960) has presented a number of studies indicating that psychologically distant leaders may be more effective in promoting task productivity than leaders who are psychologically closer to their group members. He reported studies of basketball teams, surveying teams, B-29 crews, tank crews, and consumer cooperatives. In each case the leaders in the better performing groups perceived greater distance between themselves and their co-workers than did the leaders in the groups who performed more poorly. Leaders who saw themselves as psychologically distant were generally more effective than leaders who tended toward warmer, psychologically closer interpersonal relations with their subordinates. Thus a certain amount of interpersonal distance and formal role orientation may be necessary for high productivity in some task-oriented groups.

Jones, Hornick, and Sells (1972) have studied the organizational characteristics of naval ships in the context of a social systems model. They conceived of organizational climate as including those common orientations and perceptions of crew members which reflect environmental factors. They developed an Organization Climate Questionnaire (OCQ) from a sample of individual respondents taken from four ships. Three clusters of items emerged from a factor analysis of the OCQ. The first cluster, a measure of the individual's perspective of the military way of life, included such items as the man's image of the Navy, his perceptions of the opportunities for advancement, and his identification with his job. The second factor assessed general orientation toward the support and fostering of the individual within the organizational context. Variables such as encouragement of individual responsibility, friendliness and warmth of the work environment, the extent of support from superiors, and the degree of trust in the social milieu, were included. The third factor reflected specific demands and characteristics related to the work milieu (e.g., internal cooperation among departments, tolerance of change, group cohesiveness, degree of downward communication, standards of quality, and accuracy).

There were systematic differences in the ways in which the crew members perceived the organizational characteristics of the four ships. The ship that was picked by the flotilla commander as the best performing and most efficient of the four, also had the highest scores on all three clusters. The crew members on this ship were much more likely to recommend the Navy to a prospective recruit and much less likely to report that they would definitely not join the Navy again. Thus these results show some important relationships between the organizational climate of Navy ships and both performance and attitudinal criteria.

The similarity between these results on the impact of military environ-ments, and findings on the impact of social environments in other insti-tutions is discussed in Chapter 13. Evidence that certain dimensions of the social environment may have distinctive influences on psychosomatic and psychophysiological processes, thus on sick call rates, is also dis-cussed in Chapter 13.

Positive Perceptions and Expectations.   The influence of expectations was assessed by studying the social environments of three contrasting basic combat training companies. Men in each of the companies were given the MCEI and the MAACL at the end of the second, fourth, sixth, and eighth weeks of training. In addition, a subsample of men in each company were given an expectations form (Form E) of both tests when they arrived at the reception station. The men were given Form E of the MCEI and were asked what they expected the social environment of the company to be like. On the MAACL the men were asked to describe the feelings "you expect to have midway through basic training." How did the men's expectations accord with the actual charac-teristics of their companies? The overall degree of accuracy of the sub-jects' expectations varied widely among the three companies—mainly be-cause the three companies developed quite different social environ-ments.

During the second week of basic training the men saw Company A as about average on all the MCEI subscales except Officer Control, which was seen as moderately above average. The company environment be-came much more positive over time (e.g., Officer Support and Personal Status increased between the second and fourth weeks of training). By the eighth week Company A was above average on Involvement, Peer Cohesion, Personal Status, and Officer Support. The company also showed decreases in all three System Maintenance dimensions.

The men in Company B had quite negative perceptions of their social environment during the second week of training; for example, their scores on Peer Cohesion and Officer Support were about average, whereas their scores on Officer Control were well above average. The social environment of Company B showed relatively little change over the 8-week basic training cycle. The MCEI profiles obtained during the sixth and eighth weeks were quite similar to those obtained during the second and fourth weeks. Company B remained highly stable over time and showed no other outstanding characteristics.

The social environment in Company C was initially similar to that in Company B. The milieu of this company, however, became more negative over time. In the sixth week Company C had about average scores on five of the dimensions and below-average scores on Peer Cohesion and Order and Organization. Company C ended with well below-average scores on six of the seven MCEI dimensions, particularly Peer Cohesion and Order and Organization.

In summary, the social environments of the three companies studied developed quite differently. The men in Company A expected a more negative environment than actually developed. Company A finished with an above-average emphasis on Officer Support and Personal Status. Company B ended being average on all dimensions except Officer Control, which was substantially above average. Company C never developed a cohesive social environment and finished with average or below-average scores on all MCEI dimensions. The actual company environment was considerably more negative than the men had expected. Thus Company A was mainly held together by Officer Support and Company B mainly by Officer Control; Company C was a socially disorganized environment.

The three companies differed predictably in their MAACL subscale scores. There were no differences among them in the men's initial expectations of the amount of distress they would feel during the training process. But there were substantial differences in the amount of distress the men actually did feel. The men in Company A experienced the least Anxiety, Depression, and Hostility. In addition, they reported considerably less Anxiety and Depression than they had expected. Since the men in all three companies expected almost exactly the same degree of negative affect, this finding indicates that the specific characteristics of the social environment of a company (particularly high levels of Officer Support and Personal Status) may serve to mitigate the distressful affect that usually occurs during basic training.

The men in companies B and C experienced approximately the same amount of Anxiety, but those in Company C experienced more Depression and Hostility. In addition, the decreases in negative affect between the sixth and eighth week of training were greater for the men in Company B. Thus the men in Company C had higher levels of Depression and Hostility in the eighth week of training than did the men in Company B. These feelings were far more intense than the men in Company C had initially anticipated.

The sick call results were exactly as expected: the mean number of sick calls per man was 1.90 in Company A, 2.16 in Company B, and 2.90 in Company C. Company A also had considerably higher than average performance on firing, physical training, and graded tests than did either of the other companies. These results again illustrate the variations in the social environments of different military companies. They also indicate that these variations are not necessarily apparent during the second week of basic training. Social environments seem to "jell" or "not jell" after about two weeks. In any case, the overall distress, sick leave, and performance scores of the three companies were exactly as would be predicted on the basis of the results described earlier.

These results indicate that different social environments develop in different ways over time. Every social environment must be viewed as a "unique organism" in that it has a unique developmental history. Why did Company A develop differently from Company C? Was it because of the men's initial expectations? Was it because of some particularly strict officers in one company? Was it because of the specific mix of men who happen to be assigned to each company? Presumably, any of these and a multitude of other factors can be influential in shaping the development of a military training company. Since company environments have differential impacts on mood and behavior, it is important to identify and foster the development of social environmental factors that facilitate the achievement of high morale and effective task performance.

The Correlates of Positive Perceptions and Expectations.   Are an individual's expectations of the social environment of his company related to his mood or performance during basic training? There were very large individual differences in both negative affect scores and performance indices among the men in each of the three companies. For example, in Company A at the fourth week of training, the mean Anxiety score was 10.0, with a range from 2 to 19. The mean Depression score was 19.1, but the range was from 5 to 39; the mean Hostility scores was 12.7, and the range was from 3 to 23. Thus the amount of individual variation in negative affect is considerable.

To determine the extent to which differences in initial expectations would relate to this individual variation, we performed the following analyses. Two deviancy scores were obtained for each man at the eighth week of training. The first score assessed the discrepancy between a man's initial expectations of his company and what the company was actually like. The second measured the discrepancy between a man's perception of his company and the average perception of the other enlisted men in the company. These deviancy scores measure the extent of a man's positive expectations and/or perceptions of his company.

Table 12.4 shows the relationships between positive perceptions and expectations and a man's moods at the end of training. Initially having positive expectations made a greater difference in both companies A and B than it did in Company C. Men who had more positive expectations in Company A felt considerably less anxious, depressed, and hostile at the eighth week. These correlations are quite substantial. Similar but much weaker results were obtained in Company B; however, the results for Company C were quite different. There were no relationships between positive expectations and negative affect at the eighth week.

The results show that positive expectations of a social climate are adaptive when that social climate turns out to be as good or better than the individual initially expected. But when the environment is worse than expected, positive expectations have no particular adaptive value, at least in relation to the experience of negative affect. However, there were no significant relationships between positive expectations and either test performance scores or sick call rates. The correlations between expectations and graded test performance were consistently positive, and those between expectations and sick call rates were consistently negative, but none were statistically significant.

The results for positive perceptions are very similar to those for positive expectations (see Table 12.4). Men in Company A who perceive the social environment more positively display considerably less negative affect. However, there is little or no relationship between positive perceptions of the company and negative affect in companies B and C.

Table 12.4 Relationship Between Positive Perceptions and Expectations and MAACL Scores for Three Companies

Company	Correlates of Positive Expectations		
	Anxiety	Depression	Hostility
A (N = 43)	−.50**	−.39**	−.53**
B (N = 53)	−.16	−.30*	−.24
C (N = 54)	.07	.02	.00
	Correlates of Positive Perceptions		
	Anxiety	Depression	Hostility
A (N = 43)	−.54**	−.42**	−.55**
B (N = 53)	−.24	−.21	−.09
C (N = 54)	.03	−.13	−.16

*$p < .05$.
**$p < .01$.

The relationships between positive perceptions and sick call were low but consistently negative, indicating that men who perceive the company more positively tend to report for sick call less frequently. There were positive correlations between positive perceptions and the three performance criteria, but the correlations were generally low and not statistically significant.

Thus men who have positive expectations and/or perceptions of basic training companies show considerably less negative affect during basic training. They also have a slight tendency toward a decreased sick call rate. However, they do not perform any better, at least as measured by firing, physical training, and graded test scores. These findings hold mainly for Company A, in which the social milieu is relatively positive and also at least as positive as the men initially expected it to be. For Company C, on the other hand, there were no relationships between positive expectations or perceptions and negative affect, sick call rate, or test performance. Positive expectations and perceptions are not particularly helpful when the social environment is itself relatively negative.

Contrasting Clinical Case Histories.   These results can be illustrated with specific clinical case examples of two men in Company A. John L. came from a white, lower-middle-class Southern family of four children. He enlisted in the Army because he felt he could obtain excellent vocational electronics training that would be useful to him regardless of whether or not he later chose an Army career. He expected his company environment to be more positive than it actually was, and more positive than he himself actually saw it at both the fourth and eighth weeks of training. Importantly, John both expected and perceived a high amount of Peer Cohesion, much more than the other men in the company. This indicates that John was able to establish close relationships in a particular subgroup within the company. John agreed with 10 of the 12 items on the Peer Cohesion subscale, whereas the company mean was 7.5.

John was able to function considerably better than average. His MAACL negative affect scores were about at the average of the company at the fourth week. At that time he complained of moderate anxiety (calling himself fearful, frightened, tense, and nervous), of moderate depression (calling himself blue, suffering, and unhappy), and of moderate hostility (describing himself as angry, irritated, and offended). His scores on Anxiety (9), Depression (19), and Hostility (14) were all very close to average in Company A.

However, the situation had dramatically changed by the eighth week.

John now had remarkably lower MAACL scores (3 on Anxiety, 11 on Depression, and 4 on Hostility). Thus John was feeling much better than most of the men in the company at this time. It is interesting to note that John had expected to experience rather negative feelings when he first entered the company. His expectations about the amount of negative affect he would feel were quite realistic, particularly for Anxiety and Depression. For example, on the expectation form of the MAACL he obtained a score of 13 on Anxiety and 26 on Depression. During the second week of basic training he had scores of 11 on Anxiety and 28 on Depression. His scores on these negative affect dimensions then fell drastically during the last 6 weeks of basic training.

Did John perform better than average? He went to sick call twice during the 8 weeks of basic training, which was exactly average for his company. However, he was in the top 10% of the company on both the firing test and the physical training test, and he was in the top 20% on the graded test criterion. John expected a generally positive social environment, and he felt that Company A was generally positive in that respect. He was quite accurate in predicting the amount of distress he would feel during the initial weeks of basic training. He was able to develop relatively close and cohesive relationships with a group of his peers. His distress declined sharply over the course of basic training. Finally, he performed better than average on all three Army basic training performance criteria. Importantly, he accomplished this in a company that had a relatively positive social environment.

Sam S., who was also in Company A, presents a striking contrast. Sam came from a middle-class Midwestern farming family of seven children. He had considerable trouble adjusting to high school, even though his intellectual capacity was about average. He joined the Army to escape from a difficult school situation, and he and his family hoped that the Army routine and training would be beneficial. Sam's expectations were slightly more negative than both his own and the other men's perceptions of the actual company environment. Sam was one of a small group of men in Company A (about 10 in all) who had extremely deviant expectations and perceptions. For example, he anticipated considerably less Involvement, Officer Support, Personal Status, Order and Organization, and Clarity than did the other men, scoring in the lowest 5% on four of these five subscales. On the other hand, Sam expected considerably more Peer Cohesion and Officer Control than the other men did. Sam also perceived the company environment quite deviantly. For example, at the fourth week he perceived much more emphasis on Involvement and Peer Cohesion and much less emphasis on Officer Support, Personal Status, Clarity, and Officer Control than did the other men.

His perceptions were similar at week eight. There is one important point of similarity between John L. and Sam S.—they both expected and perceived relatively high amounts of Peer Cohesion.

How did Sam feel and perform? When he entered the Army, seriously frightened and debilitated, he expected the absolute worst. Sam expected to feel seriously anxious (e.g., desperate, panicky, and terrified), extremely depressed (discouraged, hopeless, miserable, and terrible) and quite hostile (angry, bitter, furious, outraged). Interestingly, Sam was quite accurate in predicting how he actually felt during the initial weeks of basic training. He was indeed seriously anxious, very depressed, and angry by the second week of training. Things temporarily went better for Sam between the second and the fourth weeks. He was able to establish some relationships with other men and thought that he was making a reasonable adjustment to Army life. His Anxiety, Depression, and Hostility scores dropped temporarily.

Unfortunately, Sam was too "deviant" to sustain the buddy relationships he had tentatively developed. Thus whereas John had shown substantial decreases in negative affect between the fourth and eighth weeks, Sam displayed substantial increases, particularly on Depression and Hostility. The trend in negative affect scores for Sam was directly opposite to the trend for the company as a whole. Sam only attended sick call once during the 8 weeks. This was below the company average of 1.9. However, his performance on all three test criteria was below the fifteenth percentile in his company.

Information and Expectation.   The results indicate that positive expectations and perceptions are strongly related to men's moods under certain conditions. Positive perceptions and expectations are related to less affective distress in companies that have generally positive (or better than expected) social environments. When the social environment of the company is undifferentiated and negative (or worse than expected), there is little or no relationship between the men's expectations and perceptions and their mood or performance. The case histories of the two men in Company A graphically illustrate these findings. John L., who had very positive perceptions and expectations, performed considerably better than average and showed low affective distress. Sam S. had very negative perceptions and expectations; his performance was well below average, and he showed very high affective distress.

The correlates of deviant perceptions and expectations are discussed in Chapter 9. Again, the most important finding is that the effects of deviant perceptions and expectations depend on the characteristics of the social environment. This finding has now been replicated in four social environments: hospital-based treatment programs, community-based treatment programs, juvenile correctional institutions, and military training companies. In addition, we have recent evidence that students who actively wish to change their university living group (i.e., have filled out an application in the housing office to move from one dormitory to another) perceive the emotional support in their living group to be much lower than the other students perceive it. They also see other aspects of the social environment of the living group more negatively than do their peers. These findings indicate that investigators who wish to study deviant perceptions and expectations must take into account the characteristics of the social environment in which the research is done.

Many investigators have shown that initial expectations may be crucial in determining various important outcomes (e.g., Rosenthal, 1968; Rosenthal and Jacobson, 1968). Goldstein (1962) has presented a review of this area, focusing on psychotherapy. He points out that both initial expectancies and the later confirmation or nonconfirmation of the expectancies are important. The degree of mutuality or compatibility of patient and therapist role expectations appears to be critical. Evidence on the importance of deviant expectations and perceptions indicates that information-giving procedures could be helpful in enhancing enlisted men's adaptation to military companies (see Chapter 10).

Facilitating Social Change in Military Milieus.   Developing methods of assessing social environments and making these assessments useful to participants through feedback has been motivated by our desire to facilitate planned change in social settings. The basic rationale underlying the use of the Social Climate Scales in these procedures has been previously reviewed (Moos, 1974; see especially Chapters 4 and 11). Chapter 4 discusses this rationale as it applies to correctional institutions. This social change methodology should be applicable to current concerns of making the military environment more satisfactory, positive, and growth-enhancing for recruits.

Bey (1970) and Bourne (1970) consider the importance of "organizational diagnosis" of military units, particularly in relation to the prevention of psychiatric disorder. Bey points out that "in order to carry out prevention at these levels the psychiatrist must have information about the personnel, functioning and dynamics of the various units within the community" (p. 230). In a later paper Bey and Smith (1971) describe a method of consultation with combat units that employs a participant observer. They found that consultation made the units' problems legitimate ones for discussion, provided an opportunity for the open expression of feelings, opened lines of communication between different individuals, and increased unit morale.

Parrish and Morgan (1965) present a case in which the "patient–organism" was an entire military unit. The company in question had a sick call rate double that of comparable companies, and there had been one suicide and three divorces reported in the recent past. Observation indicated that the company commander, who was from Iowa, showed "prodigious energy and extreme meticulousness about details" (p. 467). He drove his men mercilessly and always seemed discontent with their performance. This attitude engendered a great deal of passive resistance among the men. When the commander stated that he had never "had trouble with a man from Iowa," the men inspired the only enlisted man in the company who was from Iowa to become "happily drunk" and to "desecrate the commander's picture" (p. 468). Consultation with the commander was effective in getting him to change both his attitude and his leadership style, with a resultant decrease in organizational stress.

There have been some cogent critiques of this approach. For example, serious objections are raised by Daniels (1969) in an extremely thoughtful paper. She points out that "psychiatrists in the military perform their service primarily for the organization rather than for the particular patient they examine . . . the organization becomes the patient and individuals within it are treated from that perspective" (p. 255). She concludes that the psychiatrist may often perform as an agent of the organization, to control deviance within the system. Given this situation, conflicts between professional and organizational values may easily be resolved in favor of the organization. Friedman (1972) also questions the organizational approach. He feels that accurate assessment of individual psychopathology is as important as understanding the structure of a social community, such as a military unit. He basically agrees with Daniels and states that "the thrust of the community approach will be to serve organizational purposes while seriously ignoring professional values. . . . The psychiatrist . . . is the overseer of a system of social control which is distinctly nonmedical in its character" (p. 122).

Our methodology may overcome some of these objections, primarily because each individual in the company is asked to present his views of the company's social milieu. Given the radical changes now occurring in military organizations, it is not too farfetched to suppose that the opinions and attitudes of the individual enlisted man will become far more significant. The use of our methods might help enlisted men achieve a new sense of competence—a sense of being able to change and control their own social environment. Satisfaction and morale in the military service might thus be enhanced.

REFERENCES

Adams, S. Social climate and productivity in small military groups. *American Sociological Review,* **19:**421–425, 1954.

Appel, J. Preventive psychiatry. In *Neuropsychiatry in World War II,* Medical Department, U.S. Army, Office of the Surgeon General, Washington, D.C., 1966.

Bey, D. Division psychiatry in Viet Nam. *American Journal of Psychiatry,* **127:**228–232, 1970.

Bey, D. & Smith, W. Organizational consultation in a combat unit. *American Journal of Psychiatry,* **128:**401–406, 1971.

Bourne, P. Some observations on the psychosocial phenomena seen in basic training. *Psychiatry,* **30:**187–196, 1967.

Bourne, P. Military psychiatry and the Viet Nam experience. *American Journal of Psychiatry,* **127:**481–488, 1970.

Daniels, A. The captive professional: Bureaucratic limitations in the practice of military psychiatry. *Journal of Health and Social Behavior,* **10:**255–265, 1969.

Datel, W. & Lifrak, S. Expectations, affect change, and military performance in the Army recruit. *Psychological Reports,* **24:**855–879, 1969.

Fiedler, F. The leader's psychological distance and group effectiveness. In D. Cartwright & A. Zander (Eds.), *Group dynamics: Research and theory,* Harper & Row, New York, 1960.

Friedman, H. Military psychiatry. *Archives of General Psychiatry,* **26:**118–123, 1972.

George, A. L. Primary groups, organization and military performance. In R. W. Little (Ed.), *Handbook of military institutions.* Sage Publications, Beverly Hills, Calif., 1971.

Glass, A., Artiss, K., Gibbs, J., & Sweeney, V. The current status of Army psychiatry. *American Journal of Psychiatry,* **117:**673–683, 1961.

Goldstein, A. *Therapist–patient expectancies in psychotherapy.* Pergamon Press, New York, 1962.

Goodacre, D. M. The use of a sociometric test as a predictor of combat unit effectiveness. *Sociometry,* **14:**148–152, 1951.

Goodacre, D. M. Group characteristics of good and poor performing combat units. *Sociometry,* **16:**168–179, 1953.

Jones, A., Hornick, C., & Sells, S. A social systems analysis of the naval organization: Organizational characteristics and effectiveness of naval ships. Institute of Behavioral Research, Texas Christian University, 1972.

Lang, K. Military organizations. In J. March (Ed.), *Handbook of Organizations.* Rand McNally, Skokie, Ill., 1965.

Little, R. W. Buddy relations and combat performance. In M. Janowitz (Ed.), *The new military: Changing patterns of organization.* Russell Sage Foundation, New York, 1964.

Lott, A. J. & Lott, B. E. Group cohesiveness as interpersonal attraction: A review of relationships with antecedent and consequent variables. *Psychological Bulletin,* **64:**259–309, 1965.

Marlowe, D. H. The basic training process. In K. Artiss (Ed.), *The symptom as communication in schizophrenia*. Grune & Stratton, New York, 1959.

Moos, R. Military Company Environment Inventory Manual. Social Ecology Laboratory, Department of Psychiatry, Stanford University, Palo Alto, Calif., 1973.

Moos, R. *Evaluating treatment environments: A social ecological approach*. Wiley, New York, 1974.

Nelson, P. & Berry, N. Cohesion in Marine recruit platoons. *Journal of Psychology*, **68:**61–71, 1963.

Parrish, M. & Morgan, R. The problem of being from Iowa. *Medical Bulletin of the U.S. Army, Europe*, **22:**467–468, 1965.

Rosenthal, R. *Experimenter effects in behavioral research*. Appleton-Century-Crofts, New York, 1968.

Rosenthal, R. & Jacobson, L. *Pygmalion in the classroom*. Holt, Rinehart & Winston, New York, 1968.

Shils, E. A. & Janowitz, M. Cohesion and disintegration in the Wehrmacht in World War II. *Public Opinion Quarterly*, **12:**280–315, 1948.

Zuckerman, M. & Lubin, B. The Multiple Affect Adjective Check List. Educational & Industrial Testing Service, San Diego, Calif., 1965.

CHAPTER THIRTEEN

Implications and Applications

Overview of Results. In this chapter we review the empirical results, discuss the impact of social climate on attitudinal, performance, and health-related criteria, and consider some relevant methodological and conceptual issues.

In the first chapter, we illustrated the concept of social climate. Many people believe that the social climate or atmosphere importantly affects people's experience and functioning. Empirical evidence relating to the variability of individual behavior across natural social settings was presented. Most investigators agree that the proportion of variance in behavior attributable to the impact of environmental or social setting variables is usually statistically significant and practically important. The fact that people do vary their behavior considerably from setting to setting supports the notion that the social climate of a setting may have an important impact.

Developing the Social Climate Scales. We discussed the development of Social Climate Scales to measure the characteristics of three different types of environment: correctional programs (Chapter 2), families (Chapter 11), and military companies (Chapter 12). The three scales measure the characteristics of their respective social environments by asking the individuals functioning in the environment about the characteristics of the milieu. We wanted to provide simple methods by which individuals can easily assess their social climates. We wanted to develop techniques that would be useful in ongoing efforts to change and improve people's living and working settings. We also hoped that the techniques would be useful in periodic assessments of social environments and that they might identify particularly dysfunctional environments (e.g., those with high dropout or illness rates).

The Correctional Institutions Environment Scale (CIES) was thus developed to measure the social climates of correctional programs as perceived by residents and staff. The choice of items was guided by the concept of environmental press, that is, the characteristic demands or features of the environment as seen by those who live in it. We derived a 90-item 10-subscale form of the CIES from samples of normative data gathered from more than 100 juvenile and 90 audit correctional programs. The Family Environment Scale (FES) and the Military Company Environment Inventory (MCEI) were derived using a similar conceptual approach and similar psychometric techniques.

The data presented in Chapter 2 indicate that the CIES subscales have adequate psychometric characteristics. The social environments of programs having a consistent treatment philosophy are extremely stable over relatively long periods of time (e.g., up to 2 years). The CIES profile is basically stable when the program is stable, but it is sensitive to program change when change occurs. Resident and staff perceptions of correctional programs are only minimally related either to their background characteristics or to their tendency to answer items about themselves in socially desirable directions. The role position of an individual in an environment (e.g., resident or staff) affects his perception of that environment much more than do his background characteristics. These results are virtually identical to those obtained earlier with the WAS and COPES (Moos, 1974a, Chapters 2 and 10).

Perhaps most important is the idea that vastly different social environments can be characterized by common or similar dimensions. The Social Climate Scales for correctional, family, and military environments assess three major types of dimensions: Relationship, Personal Development, and System Maintenance and System Change dimensions. As described in Chapter 1, Relationship dimensions are generally similar across different environments. They identify the nature and intensity of personal relationships within those environments. The basic dimensions are Involvement, Cohesion, and/or Support and Expressiveness, although a dimension measuring the degree of interpersonal conflict is also found in families. System Maintenance and System Change dimensions are also relatively similar across environments. They assess the extent to which the environment is orderly, clear in its expectations, able to maintain control, and responsive to change. The basic dimensions are Order and Organization, Clarity, and Control.

Personal Development dimensions vary a good deal among environments. In correctional institutions these dimensions (Autonomy, Practical Orientation, Personal Problem Orientation) assess the major directions treatment programs may take. In families these dimensions (e.g., Independence, Achievement Orientation, Moral–Religious Emphasis) indicate the directions in which families may wish their members to develop. In military companies only one relevant dimension, which assesses the amount of personal status allowed enlisted men in the company, was identified. The overall conceptualization may ultimately be useful in understanding and predicting behavior stability and change from one setting to another.

The Diversity of Correctional Programs.   Contrary to the overly uniform descriptions of many correctional programs, we found great diversity. Almost every conceivable kind of social climate seemed to exist in some correctional program. Illustrative case studies of several different programs were presented (Chapter 4). Correctional programs vary along at least nine identifiable dimensions of social climate, and each dimension should be taken into account in an accurate and complete description of a program.

However, given this diversity, there are certain basic characteristics which describe many correctional programs. Pervasive negative social conditions currently characterize many correctional institutions. Our data may represent the first large sample of opinions about correctional programs gathered directly from the residents themselves. More than 7300 residents (3651 residents in juvenile institutions and 3703 residents in adult institutions) answered the CIES items. A substantial proportion of these residents agreed that their programs were characterized by few social activities, lack of group spirit or cohesion, fearfulness of staff, and generally unclear expectations. Staff are often perceived as rigidly controlling the environment, as not helping and supporting residents, and as not encouraging resident autonomy, independence, or leadership. These basic conditions have been described by many others.

The negative social conditions which exist in many adult and juvenile correctional programs are not necessary. The variability of current conditions, and existing examples of cohesive treatment-oriented programs, illustrate the potential for beneficial change in the system. We also found that juvenile programs were perceived more positively than were adult programs. There were general differences among different types of juvenile programs; for example, ranches and camps were perceived as considerably more Relationship- and Treatment-Oriented than were juvenile hall programs. Most of the evidence indicates that these differences are not primarily a function of differences in resident background characteristics but of the type of program staff attempt to maintain.

This point is illustrated in the evaluation study comparing a behavior modification and a transactional analysis program (Chapter 6). The training schools using these divergent treatment approaches developed different social climates even though the background characteristics of the residents assigned to the programs were virtually identical. The specific type of resident in a program does not necessarily determine the social climate of that program. There were also large variations in the social climates of treatment programs that were presumably using the "same" overall treatment strategy. The CIES, a useful technique for characterizing the social environments of correctional programs, provided data that were in some respects convergent with and in other respects divergent from the information yielded by other methods of describing the behavior modification and transactional analysis programs. These results are consistent with other evidence that Social Climate Scales obtain information beyond that which is obtained by either naturalistic descriptive or objective organizational methods for describing correctional and other social environments.

We supplied information about the relationship between the social climate of a correctional program and other more objective organizational characteristics of that program, primarily size and staffing. As the size of a correctional program increases, the emphasis on Support and Expressiveness decreases, as does the emphasis on Autonomy, Personal Problem Orientation, and Clarity. The results for staff—resident ratio are almost exactly identical, although of course, they are in the opposite direction. These results are basically similar to those found earlier in treatment environments (Moos, 1974a, Chapters 6 and 12), but the magnitude of the relationships was higher in the correctional than in the psychiatric sample. Chapter 3 deals with the mechanisms by which size and staffing may have an impact on social climate, and some ways in which these effects may be partially alleviated.

Types of Correctional and Community Programs. Perhaps the most significant new concept presented here is the notion that there are six basic program types, which are identified in correctional institutions, in psychiatric hospitals, and in community programs. The six types are described in Chapters 5 and 10. In brief, there are four types of Treatment-oriented programs. The Therapeutic Community program strongly emphasizes the Relationship (Involvement, Cohesion, and Expressiveness) dimensions and all Treatment Program areas (i.e., the programs foster autonomy and independence, have a practical task orientation, and emphasize the expression of personal problems and feelings). These characteristics are found in a context that is relatively well structured in the institutional correctional setting but not in the psychiatric hospital or community settings. The Relationship-oriented program emphasizes Involvement and Cohesion on the one hand, and a high degree of organization and clarity of expectations, on the other. However, there is relatively little emphasis on the Treatment Program dimensions. These programs could be called "warm and clear," but we have labeled them Relationship-oriented because their basic therapeutic ingredients are most likely their strongly supportive and cohesive interpersonal relationships.

The third type of Treatment-oriented program, the Action-oriented program, is clearly differentiated from the first two types. The emphasis on Relationship dimensions and cohesiveness is average or below average, as is the emphasis on organization and clarity. This is in sharp contrast to the first two Treatment-oriented program types. The Action-oriented programs are primarily characterized by above-average emphasis on resident autonomy and independent responsibility. The community Action-oriented programs also emphasize a practical or task orientation, as do the institutional correctional programs. In addition, the institutional correctional Action-oriented programs show two characteristics not shared by the Action-oriented programs in the other two samples, namely, above-average emphasis on Expressiveness and below-average emphasis on Staff Control. Thus the Action-oriented programs are generally similar in the three samples, although there are some differences.

The Insight-oriented programs in all three samples emphasize the open expression of feelings and the discussion of personal problems. However, the Insight-oriented programs in the institutional correctional sample also exhibited moderate emphasis on the Relationship and the other Treatment Program dimensions, whereas this was not the case in either the psychiatric hospital or the community samples. Thus at least in the latter two samples, the Insight-oriented programs emphasize the open expression of personal problems, but in an environment lacking in Support or Cohesion. Attempting to express one's personal feelings in such an environment must be quite different from the experience of making the same attempt in a Therapeutic Community or Relationship-oriented milieu.

The other two clusters of programs were identified as Control-oriented and as Disturbed Behavior programs. The Control-oriented or custodial programs emphasize organization and control. They show below-average emphasis on all other dimensions. The Disturbed Behavior programs, which mainly handle deeply disturbed and/or violence-prone individuals, reveal below-average emphasis on most dimensions. The expression of anger and aggression is relatively high in such programs, however, and the staff attempt to handle the problem through increasing control (in the institutional correctional and community samples) and program clarity (in the psychiatric hospital sample).

Thus although there are some differences, the essential characteristics of the six program types are similar in the three samples. This indicates that there is considerable range and diversity of program characteristics in correctional institutions, in psychiatric hospitals, and in community-based programs. Control-oriented or custodial programs are identified in all three samples. The proportion of Control-oriented programs was actually greater in the psychiatric than in the correctional sample. However, this was probably an artifact of our sampling procedures, since it is easier to obtain data from patients in custodial psychiatric settings than from residents in custodial correctional settings. On the other hand, some community settings are also mainly Control-oriented or custodial.

The obvious conclusion is that one cannot identify the characteristics of a program simply by identifying its institutional affiliation or location. Some community-oriented programs are more Control-oriented than some institutional programs; conversely, some institutional programs are more Treatment-oriented than some community programs. One must be cautious about making assumptions about the characteristics of a program's social environment if that environment has not been systematically assessed. The relevance of a typology of treatment programs in relation to a typology of offenders and to differential treatment prescriptions and person–program congruence is discussed in Chapters 5 and 10.

Resident and Staff Congruence. The average differences between the perceptions of residents and staff regarding the social environments of their programs are very large. This conclusion holds for both the juvenile and the adult samples. Staff members perceive the conditions in correctional programs considerably more positively than do residents in the same programs. These results are consistent with our findings in hospital-based psychiatric programs, although the resident–staff differences in correctional programs are considerably larger than the patient–staff differences in psychiatric programs.

The average resident–staff profile correlation for the sample of 78 correctional programs was not significantly different from zero. Residents and staff show no overall agreement whatever on the characteristics of their programs! This is in sharp contrast to the results on three samples of psychiatric programs, in which the average resident–staff congruence was relatively high. The processes responsible for increasing congruence in psychiatric programs do not necessarily occur in correctional programs. Residents and staff do not necessarily share a "mutual reality of events." Discussions of value orientations about the program and about changes in the program are less likely to occur. Residents who do not share the dominant value orientations of correctional programs cannot easily leave these programs, although this may become increasingly possible with community-based programs.

The overall degree of resident–staff congruence does vary substantially among correctional programs. For example, resident–staff congruence is higher in Treatment-oriented programs, particularly Therapeutic Community and Relationship-oriented programs, than it is in Control-oriented programs. The problem for correctional staff is determining how to induce progressive conformity with staff rather than with resident values. Residents who are opposed to staff values are much more likely to publicly express their values than are residents who are supportive of staff values (e.g., Glaser, 1964). The evidence that increased resident–staff contact leads to increased resident–staff perception and value congruence and greater staff influence on residents is substantial. As Glaser has pointed out, "inmates are most influenced by staff who treat them with fairness and predictability" (1964, p. 133). There is no inherent reason for residents and staff in custodial or Control-oriented programs to be unable to communicate as well with each other, thus to show as high a degree of perception and value congruence, as residents and staff in Treatment-oriented programs.

One of the important issues here is size and staffing, since there is more disagreement among residents and among staff in larger and/or more poorly staffed programs. This tendency is found in both correctional and psychiatric settings. Greatly increasing the staffing in correctional programs could help to enhance resident–staff communication and congruence, thus the degree of "pro-social" normative influence exerted by staff on delinquents.

Deviant Perceptions and Expectations. When residents perceive their programs more positively, they feel more satisfied, like the staff more, and feel that the program gives them greater opportunities for personal growth. Other investigators have also found that individuals who perceive their environments more positively are more satisfied and actually perform better in those environments. There is some suggestion that positive perceptions may be more important for higher maturity level delinquents, perhaps because such individuals are more readily influenced by the social environment, but this finding needs further corroboration (Chapter 9).

The correlates of deviant perceptions varied depending on the social milieu of the program. Deviancy was related to dissatisfaction only in environments having the most coherent and active treatment programs. Deviant perceptions were related to greater individual satisfaction and expectation of personal benefit when the environment itself was negative and/or undifferentiated. The social milieu is a "moderator" variable; deviancy is an adaptive reaction in some environments. These findings suggest that experimental research may sometimes fail to generalize across settings precisely because the settings have important differential characteristics.

Residents who perceive themselves most similarly to staff and other residents are more satisfied with the staff and the institutional program. This underscores the salience of staff in contributing to positive experiences within correctional programs. Finally, we found that delinquents who broke rules in a correctional program perceived that program more deviantly. Rule breakers rate themselves as much less satisfied with the institution, as liking the staff less, as feeling that they have less chance to develop their abilities and self-confidence and, importantly, as being more likely to get into trouble in the institution. Rule breakers see themselves and the institutional staff much more negatively than do non-rule breakers, but they see other residents much more positively.

Accurate and complete prior information about new social environments can enhance the accuracy of a person's perceptions and expectations and, hopefully, his successful adaptation. Descriptions of correctional programs should include some information relevant to each of the major ways in which human environments have been characterized. Information about the social climate of an environment should help individuals more accurately select the social environments that might be most beneficial to them. This logic applies to staff, choosing which correctional program to work in, and to residents, who may some day be allowed to choose the kind of community-based program they wish to participate in.

The results just summarized were corroborated in the work in military companies. Men who had positive expectations and/or perceptions of their companies displayed less negative affect during basic training. They also had a slight tendency to show a decreased sick call rate; however, they did not actually perform better. These findings held only for the two companies in which the social milieu was relatively positive, and also at least as positive as the men initially expected it to be. There were no relationships between positive expectations or perceptions and any of the criteria for the third company. Positive expectations of a social climate are adaptive when that climate turns out to be as good or better than the individual initially expected. Positive expectations and perceptions are not particularly helpful when the social environment is itself relatively negative (see also Moos, 1974a, Chapter 12).

Practical Utility. We have always been especially concerned about the clinical and practical utility of our measurement techniques. We carried out three demonstration studies in which the treatment environments of different psychiatric programs were successfully changed using information and feedback on Social Climate Scale results (see Moos, 1974a; Chapters 4 and 11). These studies indicated that systematic information about programs aids staff in articulating their concerns. Staff who infrequently verbalize their opinions are able to think of salient issues in terms of the Social Climate Scale dimensions. Program changes may then take place within a generally consistent treatment ideology. Feedback and discussion sessions using social climate data often make practical applications out of ongoing teaching and research.

The majority of staff felt that the CIES profiles portrayed their program environments relatively accurately and completely. They also felt that definite changes were suggested by the evaluation. The CIES allows staff to more accurately define the type of program they currently have, in terms of their own perceptions, as well as those of the residents. An example of the use of the CIES in the process of institutional consultation is presented in Chapter 4. The CIES may assist staff in developing a more differentiated cognitive framework for understanding their programs and problems. It provides accurate, up-to-date information about how different programs in an institution are perceived, and it encourages staff to become program designers and planners rather than simply passive participants. We also found that the "reputation" or image of a program may differ from the actual characteristics of the program, at least as perceived by its own residents and staff. Although we cannot say from our data whether the reputation or the program participants' perceptions are the most accurate, it is important to know when considerable differences exist between them. Correctional administrators often react to the reputation or image of a program rather than to its actual characteristics.

The further development of techniques whereby Social Climate Scale and other information about delinquents' environments can be systematically used in clinical case descriptions and in treatment planning is of

utmost importance. Developing additional techniques relevant to measuring family, work, and group environments will make it possible to
describe institutional and community-based treatment environments, as
well as naturally occurring community settings, on generally commensur-
ate dimensions. Program staff should be able to use information about
a delinquent's work and family environment to more rationally plan
his treatment.

The practical utility of the Social Climate Scales and other environmental assessment methods has been discussed in detail elsewhere (Moos,
1947b). Several major uses can be identified for the scales:

1. The scales can be used to describe in detail how various participants
in a social environment view that environment. Some related uses are
to compare the perceptions of different groups of program participants
and to monitor fluctuations in the social climate of an environment over
time. The degree of agreement between different groups about what
their social environment is like is itself a descriptive characteristic of
that environment. A more complete description of an environment may
be obtained when the Ideal Form of the relevant Social Climate Scale
is used, since the goals and value orientations of different program participants are also assessed.

2. The Social Climate Scales can be filled out by observers or other
individuals who are not directly participating in a particular environment. For example, observers can complete the CIES on the basis of
their observations of specific correctional programs. This raises the possibility of comparing resident and/or staff perceptions of the social environments of their programs with the perceptions of outside observers.

3. Another major use of the scales is in comparisons among different
social environments. We have illustrated this use with correctional programs, but it also applies to other social environments. For example,
how do families of different socioeconomic levels compare with one
another? In what ways do the social environments of broken families
differ from those of intact families? Does the prolonged absence of one
family member have a demonstrable impact on family social environment?

In addition, there is currently growing judicial and social concern
with the issues of "right to treatment" and "adequacy of treatment."
Thus far the questions are typically answered with vague and unreliable
testimony from self-proclaimed "expert witnesses." The scales might be
used to furnish more systematic assessment of changes in psychiatric,
correctional, and other facilities. These assessments would be in addition
to the usual data about staff–patient ratios, cost per patient, and so

on. For example, repeated assessment with the CIES might help supply very useful information about the changes that have resulted following court-ordered improvement in correctional facilities.

4. The impact of environmental change may be evaluated. This has been illustrated for correctional programs, but it also applies to other environments. For example, to what extent does individual or group psychotherapy change the social environment of a family? To what extent does a job promotion or demotion (or the prolonged unemployment of the family wage earner) change family social environment?

5. The Social Climate Scales can be related to different kinds of outcome criteria—subjective criteria, such as morale and satisfaction, various mood states, and self-esteem; objective or performance criteria, such as behavioral changes and other indices of program outcome; and health-related criteria, such as complaints of physical and mental symptoms and the incidence of major illnesses.

6. The scales can be related to other ways of describing environments. For example, what is the relation between a program's social environment and the average resident background characteristics, or the size and staffing of the program? What is the relation between the family environment and certain background characteristics of family members? Does the social environment of a program (or of a family) depend on the physical and architectural characteristics of its location?

7. Information about the social climate can be fed back to the participants in a social environment, to motivate people in the environment to seek to change it. The scales allow respondents in an environment to define more accurately the type of social environment they have and as a result of detailed feedback, to identify and implement specific changes that might improve their milieu.

8. The completeness and accuracy of descriptions of environments can be enhanced if information about psychosocial characteristics and social climate is systematically included. Available descriptions of social environments generally characterize the environment as it is seen by a very small and unrepresentative sample (e.g., the head of a correctional program). The Social Climate Scales are useful in specifying the psychosocial or perceived climate characteristics of different social environments. Giving people information about social environments can enhance the accuracy of their perceptions and/or expectations, thus can potentially reduce the incidence of maladaptation. This means that the information provided by the scales may help people select and transcend their social environments. The scales may also be useful in finding social environments in which people feel congruent (e.g., selecting specific group homes for delinquents).

9. The type of information obtained by the scales should also make for richer and more meaningful case descriptions. Consider the enormous gain in information if one could describe the basic "ecological niche" in which an individual functions. Suppose an individual resident is released from a correctional program: predictions of his ultimate success might be much better if we had information about the characteristics of the work, group, and family milieus in which he must function. The use of the Social Climate Scales for clinical case descriptions can be a first step in building the kind of detailed descriptions of specific social environments that are necessary to understand individual functioning in its natural complexity.

10. Finally, the scales provide relevant and meaningful dimensions along which social environments in different countries may be compared. The basic dimensions measured by the scales are clearly relevant in Western European countries and could probably be used to assess the social environments of institutions in the developing countries.

The Impact of Social Environments.   As was pointed out earlier, social environments are active and directed with respect to their inhabitants. Environments have programs that organize and shape the behavior of the people in them. One of the major reasons for the need to measure environments is the differential impacts they have on the people who live and function in them. Some current evidence regarding such impacts is examined here. The review is necessarily selective and draws heavily on the work conducted in our Laboratory. Three related categories of outcome criteria are considered. First, we deal with subjective criteria, such as satisfaction and morale, and personal feelings (anxiety, depression, anger). Second, we examine evidence about more objective criteria, such as the outcome of correctional and psychiatric programs and achievement levels in high school and college. Third, we focus on health-related criteria, briefly examining evidence that physical and/or mental symptoms may occur more frequently in certain social environments.

Correctional Settings.   The results of our studies in juvenile correctional institutions were quite clear-cut (see Chapter 7). As the emphasis on the Relationship and Personal Development dimensions increases, residents like each other and the staff more and feel that they have greater opportunities for personal growth. They report taking more initiatives in the areas of affiliation, self-revealing, autonomy, and submission. In addition, in a dynamically oriented treatment setting, they show greater increases in independence and calmness and greater decreases in withdrawal and social anxiety. Exactly the reverse results hold for the dimension of Staff Control; for example, as Staff Control increases, residents like each other and the staff less and feel that they have less to gain from the program. There is a tendency for general satisfaction to increase as the emphasis on the Relationship and Personal Development dimensions increases, but this tendency is relatively weak.

We present some preliminary evidence indicating that certain correctional climates may have a small beneficial influence on parole performance. Residents in programs with high community tenure rates, in comparison with residents in programs with low community tenure rates, are more likely to report that: (1) staff punish residents by restricting them; (2) residents will get into trouble if they argue with one another; (3) residents cannot call staff by their first names; (4) residents are expected to share their personal problems with one another; (5) things are sometimes very disorganized, and staff sometimes argue openly; (6) staff do not discourage talking about sexual matters; (7) counselors and other staff have time to encourage residents; (8) certain things that happen in the program are involving; (9) staff do not encourage group activities among residents; and (10) residents are not trying very hard to improve and get better. These responses suggest that high community tenure programs are characterized by a moderate degree of staff control, moderate interpersonal communication, resident–staff openness, and staff support, and moderate emphasis on involvement. There is an emphasis on staff control, but it is not rigid and strict enough to discourage openness and expressiveness.

The notion that the social climate of a correctional program is related to the way residents and staff react to that program has been corroborated by many studies (reviewed in Chapter 7). The basic finding is that treatment-oriented programs have a positive "in-house" impact on residents' morale and behavior, but there is little or no "spillover" into their postrelease attitudes or behavior. Our results raise the possibility that the programs in which residents show maximum "in-house" improvement may not be the same programs that achieve maximum results on community functioning criteria such as parole performance.

There is evidence that absconder rates vary substantially from program to program (Chapter 8). This is partly a result of opportunity factors, peer group pressures, the amount of early program orientation, the degree of tolerance for deviancy, and the overall social climate of the program. Chase showed that youths who rate their programs as low on Expressiveness and high on Personal Problem Orientation and Staff Control, and have high Manifest Aggression scores, are more likely to abscond than other youths. She also showed that some camps have considerably higher absconding rates than other camps. Personality and background variables alone do not account for these differences. Sinclair (1971) found that a warm and kind attitude by the warden and his wife accompanied by strict and consistent discipline were most likely to result in a low proportion of boys absconding. This is the type of program that would probably fall into our Relationship-oriented category.

Military Settings.   Enlisted men generally feel less anxious, depressed, and hostile in companies that emphasize Involvement, Peer Cohesion, Officer Support, and Personal Status. There was some suggestion of a specificity of relationships between certain dimensions of the social environment and certain moods. Enlisted men were most likely to feel depressed in companies in which Peer Cohesion was low. The degree of Officer Control had an important impact on the men's moods; that is, enlisted men felt significantly more anxious, depressed, and hostile in companies in which Officer Control was high.

Dimensions of company environments are also related to objective indices of test performance at the end of basic training. Peer Cohesion, Officer Support, and Clarity (of expectations) are the three most important characteristics of high-performance companies. Autonomy and Independence are not strongly emphasized. Evidence from other studies that the Relationship dimensions, particularly Peer Cohesion and Officer Support, are related to performance indices in both combat and non-combat situations, is reviewed in Chapter 12.

Psychiatric Settings.   Our studies in hospital and community programs found that when Relationship and Treatment Program dimensions (except for Anger and Aggression) are emphasized, morale is generally high, patients feel more satisfied, like each other and the staff more, and are more hopeful about treatment. Emphasis on Staff Control is usually negatively related to each of these variables.

We also found that programs with high dropout rates have little emphasis in either the Relationship or the System Maintenance areas. Programs with high release rates are relatively strong in the System Maintenance areas and in the Personal Development area of Practical Orientation. Programs that keep patients out of the hospital longest emphasize the Relationship and System Maintenance dimensions and the Personal Development dimensions, particularly Autonomy and Practical Orientation. Other studies of psychiatric treatment outcome show generally similar findings (Ellsworth et al., 1971; Spiegel and Younger, 1972; see Moos, 1974a, Chapter 8).

Similar work in individual and group psychotherapy has focused almost exclusively on Relationship dimensions. Certain important therapist qualities appear to be relevant to almost all types of psychotherapy. The evidence indicates that when the therapist qualities of authenticity, genuineness, warmth, and empathic understanding are present in a relationship, positive personality change is likely to follow (Truax and Mitchell, 1971). Negative change or personality deterioration is likely to occur when they are absent. These dimensions are clearly what we have termed Relationship dimensions. Empathy, warmth, and genuineness assess the overall quality of the relationship between the patient and therapist exactly as Involvement, Support, and Expressiveness assess the general quality of the relationships among individuals in a social milieu.

Educational Settings.   Pace (1969) presents a number of relationships between the College and University Environment Scale (CUES) subscale scores and student attitudes and activities. Colleges high on CUES Community and Awareness subscales (Relationship dimensions) have a high proportion of students who feel a strong emotional attachment to the college. In addition, it is rare for students to report not having participated in any extracurricular activities in college environments high on CUES Community. Petersen et al. (1970) relate the subscales of the Institutional Functioning Inventory (IFI) to seven factors of student protest in a sample of 50 institutions. A number of relationships are presented, but most interestingly student radicalism as a protest factor was highly related to the IFI subscales of Human Diversity and Concern for Improvement of Society (Personal Development dimensions). The other relationships found were generally predictable ones—the absence of senior faculty and the quality of instruction were protest issues in institutions with a low emphasis on undergraduate learning. Classified research was a protest issue in institutions with a high emphasis on concern for advancing knowledge.

We have completed a study linking students' satisfaction and moods to the social environments of their high school classrooms. Students expressed greater satisfaction in classrooms characterized by high student involvement, by a personal student–teacher relationship, by innovative teaching methods, and by clarity of rules for classroom behavior (Trickett and Moos, 1974). Classroom social environment was also related to students' moods. Students felt more secure and interested in classrooms that emphasized the Relationship dimensions of Involvement, Affiliation, and Teacher Support. Students reported feeling angrier in classrooms that were low in Teacher Support and Order and Organization.

Classrooms in which students felt that much material was learned were both similar to and different from "satisfying" classrooms. Involvement,

Teacher Support, and Rule Clarity were highly emphasized. But this kind of classroom also emphasized Competition and Order and Organization. Thus the picture of the classroom in which students report a great deal of content learning combines an affective concern with students as people (Relationship dimensions) with an emphasis on students working hard for academic rewards (Competition) within a coherent, organized context (Order and Organization and Rule Clarity).

Walberg (1969) has used his Learning Environment Inventory (LEI) to show that classroom social environment may mediate classroom learning. Data were collected from approximately 3700 students in 144 high school physics classes. Both cognitive and noncognitive learning criteria were measured. The cognitive criteria included a test on understanding science, a test covering the assumptions, activities, products, and ethics of science, and a test of general physics knowledge. The noncognitive criteria included measures of interest in physics. The results were extremely intriguing. Students who were in classes characterized by high Satisfaction and low Friction, Cliqueness, and Apathy gained significantly more on all three noncognitive learning criteria. Students who were in classes characterized by high Difficulty gained significantly more on all three cognitive learning criteria. Thus classes seen as more difficult and competitive (Personal Development dimensions) gained more on physics achievement and science understanding, whereas classes seen as more satisfying and as having less Friction, Apathy, and Cliqueness (Relationship dimensions) gained more on reported science interest and activities.

Walberg's study and our study support each other. Students express greater satisfaction, show more interest in their course material, and actually engage in more course-relevant activities in classes that are high on Relationship dimensions. Students feel they learn more, and actually do learn more, in classrooms that are competitive and intellectually challenging. In some further work we found that teachers who establish socially cohesive classrooms (high on Relationship dimensions) tend to give higher average grades, whereas teachers in classrooms high on Teacher Control tend to give lower average grades. Perhaps it is no wonder that students feel more secure, interested, and satisfied in the former type of classroom!

Physical Health and Well-Being.   A physician advises a harried executive with high blood pressure to spend a week in the country. A pediatrician recommends that an underdeveloped, neglected child be sent to a foster home. An allergist encourages an asthmatic patient to find a job with more human contact. A heart specialist urges an overworked administrator to delegate some of his responsibilities to others. Each of these health professionals is responding to the belief that the social environment has an important impact on health. Space permits only brief examples here. Some of the relevant work has been reviewed elsewhere (Kiritz and Moos, 1974).

There is abundant evidence that one dimension of the social environment—that is, work pressure—is importantly related to health. Rosenman and Friedman have identified a behavior pattern which they believe is associated with high risk of coronary artery disease (Friedman, 1969). The coronary-prone behavior pattern designated type A, as distinguished from the low-risk type B, is characterized by extreme aggressiveness, competitiveness, and ambition, along with feelings of restlessness and in particular a profound sense of time urgency. Rosenman and Friedman believe that the contemporary Western environment encourages development of this pattern. They also believe that the pattern represents the interaction of environmental influences and individuals' susceptibilities, arguing that the pattern may not occur if a type A individual is removed to a type B setting.

Caffrey (1968) has shown that it is possible to rank environments according to the degree to which their "atmospheres" encourage type A behavior. He had three physicians rate 14 Benedictine and 11 Trappist monasteries using paired comparison methods. The individual monks were also rated by their abbots and by their peers. Caffrey then showed that groups of monks having a higher proportion of type A's living in type A environments and taking a high-fat diet had the highest prevalence rates of coronary disease.

The association of work pressure and coronary disease gains support elsewhere in the literature. For example, French and Caplan (1973) studied 22 white collar males at NASA over a 3-day period. They telemetered heart rate, measured serum cholesterol, and had observers rate behavior. "Quantitative work overload" as indexed by the observers' ratings was positively correlated with serum cholesterol. Subjective indices of work overload were correlated with both physiological measures. Other studies demonstrate relationships between work pressure and physiological changes. Froberg and his associates (1971) studied 12 young female invoicing clerks performing their usual work in their usual environment, during 4 consecutive days. On the first experimental day, piece wages were added to the subjects' salaries. Urine samples taken three times a day were assayed for adrenalin and noradrenalin. During the salaried control days the work output was very close to normal. On the piecework days, which the girls described as hurried and tiring, the mean adrenalin and noradrenalin excretion rose by 40 and 27% respectively. One additional finding supports the hypothesis that responsibility and work pressure may have accumulative noxious effect. Air traffic controllers who work under extreme time pressure, bearing the responsibility for hundreds of lives, have higher risk and earlier onset of hypertension and peptic ulcer than a control group of second-class airmen (Cobb and Rose, 1973).

We have completed two studies in this area. One study related the social environments of eight military basic training companies to their sick call rates (Chapter 12). Men in high sick call companies perceived the company to be very strict about following the daily schedule and about the men reporting where they were going. The men felt that they were kept very busy and that the company was relatively well organized. Other items indicated that the men felt that they had particularly low personal status and also that they were bored. The men believed the work they were doing was repetitious and boring, they could not act different if they wanted to, and that they were not encouraged to take leadership in the company. Additional items indicated that all this occurred in a company that highly emphasized Officer Control. For example, the men felt that the noncommissioned officers were constantly checking on them and supervising them very closely. They felt that they were ridiculed in front of the other men, that the officers did not help orient them to the company, and that they never quite knew when an officer would ask to see them. Thus the characteristics of high sick call companies include an emphasis on Order and Organization bordering on extreme restrictiveness; the men are kept busy, but with tasks they perceive to be repetitious and boring. Relatively strict officer control is emphasized and the enlisted man's personal status is de-emphasized. One obvious way to adapt to this kind of noxious social environment is to become ill.

These findings were nicely supported in a study of nine high school classrooms. The social environment of the classrooms was assessed and careful absentee records were kept. Student absences were divided into those that occurred for medical and nonmedical reasons, respectively. The results were striking. Classrooms high in student medical absences were characterized by a lack of emphasis on the Relationship dimensions of Involvement and Teacher Support and the System Change dimension of Innovation. They also exhibited a high degree of emphasis on the Personal Development dimensions of Task Orientation and Competition and the System Maintenance dimension of Teacher Control. The findings were basically similar for nonmedical absences. Thus, perhaps not surprisingly, students stay away from classes they perceive to be restrictive and difficult even if they feel that they learn more, and actually do learn more, in these classes.

What do all these studies tell us about the impacts of social environments? People are more satisfied and tend to perform better when the relationship areas are emphasized. They are also less likely to drop out, be absent, and report that they are sick. People also tend to do better in environments that emphasize the Personal Growth dimensions, but some personal costs may be involved. Students learn more but are absent more often in classrooms that emphasize competition and difficulty. Patients do better in treatment programs that emphasize Autonomy and Practical Orientation. Students learn more in universities that emphasize independent study, high standards, criticism, and breadth of interests. But greater responsibility and greater work pressure may have certain negative physiological concomitants—greater arousal and increased probability of cardiac dysfunction. Such effects probably also occur in patients who are pushed out of hospitals and in students who are pushed to the limits of their performance capacities.

Order and clarity generally appear to have a weak but positive impact on satisfaction, moods, and performance. Control generally has a negative impact; however, this appears to depend in part on the rigidity of the control and in part on the age and developmental maturity of the people involved. Rigid control is less palatable with advancing maturity.

Future research will need to assess the effects of more relationship-oriented "benevolent" control on different individuals in different institutions. For example, there is evidence that autistic children tend to react more favorably to high structure situations (Schopler et al., 1971). In addition, autistic children who are functioning on a higher developmental level were better able to utilize relative lack of structure than were those functioning on a lower developmental level. Thus high control may be necessary and beneficial for certain individuals. The clearest conclusion is that satisfying human relationships in all social environments studied to date facilitate personal growth and development. However we know that "love is not enough"; thus the effects of Personal Development and System Maintenance dimensions merit further study.

Social climate may provide the general context within which more specific training procedures may or may not have their intended effect. Vocational skills must be taught in vocational training programs; reading, arithmetic, and other academic skills must be taught in settings specifically geared to enhancing these skills, and so on. However, two teachers who are objectively teaching almost identical course material to similar types of students may achieve drastically different results. The social climate within which more specific intervention or teaching procedures occur may help to determine the effectiveness of these procedures.

Some Conceptual and Methodological Issues.   Some important issues which have been raised in relation to the concept and measurement of social climate are discussed here.

1.   Is not the social climate of an environment adequately explained or accounted for by other readily available, more objective environmental dimensions?

We have related each of the Social Climate Scales to organizational structure dimensions (e.g., size and staffing) and/or to the average background characteristics of the individuals in the environment (e.g., age, education, chronicity). Social Climate Scales show moderate but not substantial correlations with these other sets of variables. Pace (1969) concluded that data about perceived environmental characteristics give information that is congruent with, but in substantial addition to, information presented by more objective institutional variables. This is consistent with findings reported by others on the relationships between social climate data and more objective indices differentiating among universities (Astin, 1968; Centra, 1970; Stern, 1970). Thus different methods of assessing institutional environments should be used in conjunction whenever possible. Data about the social climate adds some unique information about an environment.

2.   Is not the social climate of an environment mainly dependent on the types of people in that environment? After all, certain people tend to establish certain social environments.

We suggest that the average background characteristics of the people in an environment (i.e., the types of people) is one major way of characterizing social settings. Certain groups, or types of people, have a tendency to establish certain kinds of social environment, particularly if they form stable relationships over long periods of time. In these situations there are moderate correlations between the average background characteristics of the people and the characteristics of the social milieu. On the other hand, we found quite different social climates in two psychiatric programs with essentially identical types of patient (Moos, 1974a; Chapter 5). Quite different social climates developed in two correctional schools with virtually identical resident populations but divergent treatment programs (Chapter 6).

Thus the average background characteristics of the inhabitants of an environment may at times be moderately correlated with the social climate of that environment. However, this relationship is usually not substantial. Furthermore, the background characteristics of residents in correctional programs (and of patients in psychiatric programs) do not necessarily determine the characteristics of the program's social climate. This, of course, is exactly what correctional reformers argue. Their major point is that the people who are in correctional institutions would behave quite differently in a different social and physical milieu. This assumes that one could develop a different social climate given the same residents. We believe that this point of view is essentially correct.

3. *Do social climate indices actually discriminate among environments? If so what proportion of the variance is related to differences among environments?*

Social environments differ greatly from one another. Basically every Social Climate Scale discriminates significantly among the relevant environmental units. We calculated the average proportion of the total subscale variance accounted for by differences among environmental subunits for several of our scales. Differences among psychiatric programs accounted for between 20 and 30% of the subscale variance. The results were similar in correctional programs. In a sample of 38 classrooms we found that the Classroom Environment Scale subscales accounted for 48% of the variance for Innovation and 47% for Task Orientation but only 21% for Affiliation.

Centra (1970) found that the proportion of total factor variance attributable to differences among institutions on his Questionnaire on Student and College Characteristics ranged from 21 to 68% with a mean of 35% for the eight factor scales and from 3 to 75% with a mean of 21% for the 77 items. Thus no single answer can be given to this question. The proportion of variance that is accounted for by environmental differences obviously depends on the sample of environments being studied. Our general conclusion is that the proportion of variance attributable to differences among environments is usually quite substantial. Interestingly, it is very similar to the proportion of variance usually accounted for by individual difference measures of personality traits (Mischel, 1968). Social Climate Scales discriminate among environments about as well as personality tests discriminate among people.

4. *Are not measures of social climate highly unstable? After all, social environments can and do change very rapidly.*

The social environments of psychiatric and correctional programs may remain highly stable over relatively long periods of time (up to 2 to 3 years), assuming that the program retains a reasonably consistent over-

all treatment philosophy. For example, profile stabilities average around
.75 with 9-month test–retest intervals. We found profile stabilities of
over .90 in 2-week test–retest administrations of the Classroom Environment Scale and stabilities averaging over .90 in 1-month test–retest administrations of the University Residence Environment Scale. Thus the
underlying characteristics of social environments may remain highly stable. On the other hand, Social Climate Scales are usually sensitive to
environmental change when environmental change occurs.

5. *Is not a person's perception of an environment really a function of his*
    personality characteristics? To the extent that this is so, indices of perceived
    climate do not really measure environmental characteristics at all; rather,
    they measure personality characteristics.

There is substantial empirical evidence on this question, most of it
indicating that individual personality characteristics are only minimally
related to environmental perceptions. McFee (1961) studied the relationship between student perception of the college environment and student
personality needs. She failed to find any correlations between environmental perceptions and personality needs. Items about conditions the
student was unlikely to have encountered (e.g., those low in "exposure
value") produced less agreement and were somewhat more influenced
by need than were items about widely shared experiences. Pace (1969)
came to similar conclusions, since the responses to the items on the
College and University Environment Scales were also not influenced by
the personal characteristics of the students.

However, different individuals often perceive the "same" social environment differently (e.g., see Herr, 1965; Jansen, 1967). Thus there
are some relationships between individual personality and/or background characteristics of subjects and their perceptions of the environment, but these relationships are not usually very substantial. It is also
unclear how well they reflect differences in the subenvironments experienced by individuals. It does seem quite reasonable that under high
environmental uncertainty and high need, an individual will answer an
environmental item in a way that is congruent with his particular need
structure. Most important, an individual's role position in an environment (e.g., teacher or student, supervisor or worker) may also have a
major impact on his perceptions of that environment. Personality and
background variables may thus be related to environmental perceptions
through the mediating effects of role positions.

6. *Are there not subenvironments within larger environments which differ in*
    social climate?

Some environments show large variations in social climate, particularly in institutions that are organized into smaller subunits (e.g., hospitals, prisons, high schools, and colleges). The social climate may vary extensively from one correctional program to another in the same institution or from one classroom to another in the same high school. University students who major in different fields and/or who live in different dormitories are often operating in quite different social climates even though they are in the same university. This is one of the reasons we have focused on relatively small environmental units (i.e., correctional cottages, psychiatric treatment programs, classrooms, and student living groups). We believe that many applications of the social climate concept make somewhat more sense in these smaller environments in which individual inhabitants usually have direct face-to-face contact with one another.

7. *The social climate methodology is much too subjective. Either more specific questions with concrete behavioral referents and/or more objective outside observers should be used to provide data on social environments.*

These are very reasonable cautions, although there is very little evidence clearly pointing to the superiority of a more objective methodology. We simply do not know whether judgments of social climate dimensions by objective observers relate more highly to a relevant outcome criteria than do the perceptions of environmental participants themselves. Social climate dimensions can easily be observed and rated by outsiders, as can specific behaviors that are considered to be relevant indicators of each dimension.

There is some evidence that global perceptions may relate more highly to relevant outcome criteria than do specific behaviors. Schneider (1973) found that bank customers decide to switch their bank accounts on the basis of generalized perceptions they have of the bank. Items descriptive of employee behavior had the highest correlations (negative) with customer intention to switch. For example, "the bank employees bend over backwards to provide good service," and "the atmosphere in my bank is warm and friendly." The important additional finding was that these general impressions (which must be based on specific events and experiences of bank customers, such as waiting time and procedure for queuing customers) were more strongly related to switching intentions than were the specific events and experiences themselves. Many more data are needed on these questions. Subjective global perceptions of social climate may fare relatively well, since it is these global impressions which individuals remember and take into account in making major decisions about their lives.

8. *The three major categories of social climate dimensions are important, but they are clearly not sufficient. One can easily identify many other relevant dimensions.*

This is certainly correct. Since Relationship, Personal Development, and System Maintenance and System Change dimensions occur in all environments studied to date, these must be assessed if one wishes to have a reasonably complete picture of a social environment. However, additional dimensions and/or other conceptual schemes need to be developed. Other dimensions may be most useful in certain specific prediction situations. For example, we are currently involved in an outcome study of alcohol treatment programs. We feel that the "alcohologenic" properties of the community environment (e.g., how heavily does the spouse drink? how many of the person's friends drink?) may predict alcohol treatment outcome better than any other social climate dimension.

9. *Throughout this book it is implied that social climate has an "impact"; that is, that social climate "causes" certain results. Strictly speaking, correlations have been demonstrated between social climate and some outcome criteria. These are correlations and must be treated as such. It is not legitimate to infer causation from these data.*

This criticism is basically correct, although the evidence for the "impact" of social climate is becoming somewhat stronger. The findings relating morale and self-esteem to social climate in correctional and psychiatric programs are clearly correlational. The findings on pre–post changes on personality and behavioral rating measures support the conclusion (albeit weakly) that the social climate of a program may differentially "influence" change. The analyses relating the social climates of psychiatric and correctional programs to objective indices of treatment outcome, particularly postinstitutional treatment outcome, and those relating company test performance and sick call rates to company climates, are less amenable to this criticism. However, there are many viable alternative explanations; for example, it is still possible that "better" patients and/or residents were somehow selected into the better community tenure programs. Perhaps the best current conclusion is that the social climates of various environments have been fairly consistently and pervasively related to a variety of outcome criteria. Our own point of view is that the social climate does influence these criteria. But the foregoing criticism is well taken, and caution must be exercised in interpreting the results presented here.

10. *Some investigators have argued that certain dimensions of the social envi-
     ronment are positive or growth-producing, whereas other dimensions are
     negative or growth-inhibiting. Is it not too soon to make this kind of global
     conclusion, particularly since the impacts of social environments depend
     on so many different variables? They may also differ from one individual
     to another.*

This is an important caution. There is some evidence that Relationship
and Personal Development dimensions are growth-producing and that
the System Maintenance dimension of Control is growth-inhibiting. On
the other hand, strong emphasis on certain Personal Development dimensions (e.g., Competition) may relate to increased dropout and absenteeism rates, and strong emphasis on other Personal Development dimensions (e.g., Autonomy and Responsibility) may relate to maladaptive
physiological arousal and/or physical and mental symptoms. Also, some
people react positively to control, and some social environments need
high control to function adequately. We must make value judgments
in arranging new and changing old social environments, but we must
be careful not to confuse these value judgments with dependable empirical data indicating what the differential impacts of social environments
on different outcome criteria actually are.

11. *Since the social climate of an environment does not constitute a stimulus
     (or a set of stimuli), it cannot affect behavior. Only stimuli can affect
     behavior.*

This criticism has been raised by Astin (1968), who illustrates his point
by an example from the College Characteristics Index: "Many students
drive sports cars." Astin points out that the item simply reflects the impression of the observer and that the observer's judgment is not itself
a stimulus that can affect other students. Astin suggests an alternative
method of phrasing the question: "Did you drive a sports car at college
during the past year?" The measure of the environment would then
consist of the proportion of students at a college who responded positively. Driving a sports car represents a stimulus that can (and does) have
an impact on the behavior and attitudes of other students.
    Although Astin's distinction is an important one, he is picking a rela-
tively easy example to illustrate his point. First, many items in his Inventory of College Activities (ICA) do not constitute stimuli for most other
students—for example, "Had psychotherapy or personal counseling,"
"Ate lunch or dinner alone," "Violated college rules or regulations without getting caught." Second, the ICA itself does not follow Astin's "stim-

ulus" logic, presumably because much of the relevant information about environments is judgmental. Astin includes such items as asking the student whether the instructor in his courses was "exceptionally well-grounded in the course subject matter," whether the instructor was "enthusiastic," "had a good sense of humor," "was often sarcastic," and "was often dull and uninteresting." These items are clearly judgmental and subjective. Third, as pointed out earlier, some of the most important information about social environments probably relates to people's overall global impressions of those environments.

However, one should include information about potential stimuli (in our terms, the average behavioral characteristics of the inhabitants of the environment) in any differentiated analysis of the social milieu. The extent to which these behavioral stimulus characteristics relate to more global impressions, and the extent to which each relates to important outcomes, then becomes an empirical question. We are currently involved in such an investigation of the differential impacts of university student living groups.

12. *Environments have differential impacts on people; however, is this not mainly because people select environments that are likely to have certain impacts. The evidence presented for environmental impact is really evidence that people differentially choose the environments that have the impact they desire.*

This important issue has recently been raised by Bowers (1973) and Wachtel (1973). For example, Wachtel points out that:

> The understanding of any one person's behavior in an interpersonal situation solely in terms of the stimuli *presented to* him gives only a partial and misleading picture, for to a very large extent these stimuli are *created* by him. They are responses to his own behaviors, events he has played a role in bringing about, rather than occurrences independent of who he is and over which he has no control. The seductive hysterical woman who is annoyed at having to face the aggressive amorous advances of numbers of men has much to learn about the origin of the stimuli she complains she must cope with. So, too, does the man who complains about the problems in dealing with his wife's nagging but fails to understand how this situation which presents itself to him derives in turn from his own procrastinating, unresponsible behavior." (p. 330)

Wachtel says that much of a person's social environment is engendered by his own behavior. Thus people create certain social environments, which then "reciprocate" by fostering certain behaviors and attitudes.

Human behavior is both chosen and caused. People actively select and create their own environments. However, environments also actively select and create their own people. In addition, people do not usually have adequate power to change the environmental conditions other people have created. This is particularly true for young children and for the aged, but it is also generally the case in any environment in which there is an imbalance of power. Residents in most correctional facilities have limited power to change their sociophysical environment. This is also true of patients in most psychiatric programs, of students in most junior high and high school classrooms, of employees in most work situations, and even of individual members in many families. Although man is not passively molded by his environments, neither are his environments passively molded by him.

Certain environments are particularly powerful "molders" of human behavior. Wolins (1969) has discussed the differential impact of group care settings in Austria, Israel, Poland, and Yugoslavia, noting that these settings have a powerful impact on the children within them. For example, the children's values change differentially in line with the expectations of the particular group care setting. Wolins points out that the more intensive, committed, cohesive, and socially integrated the setting, the greater its impact.

Bloom (1964) has presented cogent evidence that the environment is a determiner of the extent and kind of change that takes place in different human characteristics. He concludes that there is a strong relationship between the magnitude of change in a characteristic (e.g., IQ score, school achievement) and the environment in which the individual is functioning. Most characteristics are affected more powerfully during the period of their most rapid development. In addition, very powerful environments have more pervasive effects. Bloom notes that: "Perhaps the major point to be made about such environments is their pervasiveness, that is the individual is completely engulfed in a situation which presses him from every angle toward a particular type of development or outcome. It is the extent to which a particular solution is overdetermined that makes for a powerful environment" (p. 212). Thus one cannot underemphasize the extent to which human environments shape their inhabitants. As Winston Churchill said: "We shape our buildings, and afterwards our buildings shape us."

REFERENCES

Astin, A. *The college environment.* American Council on Education, Washington, D.C., 1968.

Bloom, B. S. *Stability and change in human characteristics.* Wiley, New York, 1964.

Bowers, B. S. Situationism in psychology: An analysis and a critique. *Psychological Review,* **80**: 307–336, 1973.

Caffrey, B. Reliability and validity of personality and behavioral measures in a study of coronary heart disease. *Journal of Chronic Disease,* **21:** 191–204, 1968.

Centra, J. The college environment revisited: Current descriptions and a comparison of three methods of assessment. Research Memorandum 70-44. Educational Testing Service, Princeton, N.J., 1970.

Cobb, S. & Rose, R. Hypertension, peptic ulcer and diabetes in air traffic controllers. *Journal of the American Medical Association,* **224:** 489–492, 1973.

Ellsworth, R., Maroney, R., Klett, W., Gordon, H. & Gunn, R. Milieu characteristics of successful psychiatric treatment programs. *American Journal of Orthopsychiatry,* **41:**427–441, 1971.

French, J. & Caplan, R. Organizational stress and individual strain. In *The failure of success,* A. Marrow, (Ed.). AMACOM (a division of The American Management Association), New York, 1973.

Friedman, M. *Pathogenesis of coronary artery disease.* McGraw-Hill, New York, 1969.

Froberg, J., Karlsson, C., Levi, L., & Lidberg, L. Physiological and biochemical stress reactions induced by psychosocial stimuli. In *Society, stress and disease,* Vol. 1, L. Levi (Ed.) Oxford University Press, London, 1971.

Glaser, D. *The effectiveness of a prison parole system.* Bobbs-Merrill, Indianapolis, 1964.

Herr, E. Differential perceptions of "Environmental press" by high school students. *Personnel and Guidance Journal,* **7:**678–686, 1965.

Jansen, D. Characteristics of student leaders. Doctoral dissertation, Indiana University. *Dissertation Abstracts,* **28:**3768A, 1967.

Kiritz, S. & Moos, R. Physiological effects of social environments. *Psychosomatic Medicine,* **36:**96–114, 1974.

McFee, A. The relation of students' needs to their perceptions of a college environment. *Journal of Educational Psychology,* **52:**25–29, 1961.

Mischel, W. *Personality and assessment.* Wiley, New York, 1968.

Moos, R. *Evaluating treatment environments: A social ecological approach.* Wiley, New York, 1974a.

Moos, R. *The Social Climate Scales: An overview.* Consulting Psychologists Press, Palo Alto, Calif., 1974b.

Pace, R. *College and University Environment Scales.* Technical Manual, 2nd ed. Educational Testing Service, Princeton, N.J., 1969.

Peterson, R., Centra, J., Hartnett, R. & Linn, R. *Institutional Functioning Inventory: Preliminary Technical Manual.* Educational Testing Service, Princeton, N.J., 1970.

Schneider, B. The perception of organizational climate: The customer's view. *Journal of Applied Psychology,* **57:**248–256, 1973.

Schopler, E., Brehm, S., Kinsbourne, M., & Reichler, R. Effect of treatment structure on development in autistic children. *Archives of General Psychiatry,* **24:**415–421, 1971.

Sinclair, I. *Hostels for probationers.* Her Majesty's Stationery Office, London, 1971.

Spiegel, D. & Younger, J. Ward climate and community stay of psychiatric patients. *Journal of Consulting and Clinical Psychology,* **39:**62–69, 1972.

Stern, G. *People in context: Measuring person–environment congruence in education and industry*, Wiley, New York, 1970.

Trickett, E. & Moos, R. Personal correlates of contrasting environments: Student satisfaction in high school classrooms. *American Journal of Community Psychology*, **2:**1–12, 1974.

Truax, C. B. & Mitchell, K. M. Research on certain therapist interpersonal skills in relation to process and outcome. In A. Bergin & S. Garfield (Eds.), *Handbook of psychotherapy and behavior change: An empirical analysis.* Wiley, New York, 1971.

Wachtel, P. L. Psychodynamics, behavior therapy, and the implacable experimenter: An inquiry into the consistency of personality. *Journal of Abnormal Psychology*, **82:**324–334, 1973.

Walberg, H. Social environment as a mediator of classroom learning. *Journal of Educational Psychology*, **60:**443–448, 1969.

Wolins, M. Group care: Friend or foe? *Social Work*, **14:**35–53, 1969.

APPENDIX A

Correctional
Institutions
Environment Scale
Scoring Key

APPENDIX B

Family Environment
Scale Scoring Key

Correctional Institutions Environment Scale Scoring Key

Below is the scoring key for the subscales of the different forms of the Correctional Institutions Environment Scale. The Real program (Form R), Ideal program (Form I), and Expectation forms (Form E) are directly parallel, and all items are scored in the same direction on all three forms. The 36 items included in the Short Form are marked with an asterisk. An item listed as "true" (T) is scored 1 point if marked "true" by the individual taking the scale, and an item listed as "false" (F) is scored 1 point if marked "false." The total subscale score is simply the number of items answered in the scored direction.

The Correctional Institutions Environment Scale and Manual have been published and are available for interested users (Moos, 1974a). Users of the previous 86-item Form C of the CIES should note that slight changes have been made in the instrument as presented in the Manual (and in the scoring key in this Appendix) to increase its utility: *(a)* four items (numbers 84, 85, 87, and 90, unscored) were added to make the CIES an even 90 items; *(b)* the items were reordered both to facilitate hand-scoring and to make the first 36 items the Short Form (Form S) items.

INVOLVEMENT

Real, Ideal and Expectation Form Item Number	Scoring Direction	
1*	T	The residents are proud of this unit.
10	T	Residents here really try to improve and get better.
19*	T	Residents on this unit care about each other.
28*	F	There is very little group spirit on this unit.
37	T	Residents put a lot of energy into what they do around here.
46	F	The unit has very few social activities.
55	F	Very few things around here ever get people excited.
64	T	Discussions are pretty interesting on this unit.
73	F	Residents don't do anything around here unless the staff ask them to.
82	T	This is a friendly unit.

SUPPORT

Real, Ideal, and Expectation Form Item Number	Scoring Direction	
2*	F	Staff have very little time to encourage residents.
11*	T	Staff are interested in following up residents once they leave.
20*	T	The staff help new residents get acquainted on the unit.
29*	T	The more mature residents on this unit help take care of the less mature ones.
38	F	Residents rarely help each other.
47	T	Staff go out of their way to help residents.
56	T	Staff are involved in resident activities.
65	F	Counselors have very little time to encourage residents.
74	T	Staff encourage group activities among residents.
83	T	The staff know what the residents want.

EXPRESSIVENESS

Real, Ideal, and Expectation Form Item Number	Scoring Direction	
3*	T	Residents are encouraged to show their feelings.
12*	F	Residents tend to hide their feelings from the staff.
21*	T	Staff and residents say how they feel about each other.
30*	T	People say what they really think around here.
39	T	Residents say anything they want to the counselors.
48	F	Residents are careful about what they say when staff are around.
57	F	When residents disagree with each other, they keep it to themselves.
66	F	It is hard to tell how residents are feeling on this unit.
75	T	On this unit staff think it is a healthy thing to argue.
84	(filler item)	Residents on this unit rarely argue.

AUTONOMY

Real, Ideal, and Expectation Form Item Number	Scoring Direction	
4*	T	The staff act on residents' suggestions.
13*	T	Residents are expected to take leadership on the unit.
22*	F	The staff give residents very little responsibility.
31*	T	Residents have a say about what goes on here.
40	F	The staff discourage criticism.
49	T	Staff encourage residents to start their own activities.
58	F	Staff rarely give in to resident pressure.
67	T	Residents here are encouraged to be independent.
76	F	There is no resident government on this unit.
85	(filler item)	Residents are encouraged to make their own decisions.

PRACTICAL ORIENTATION

Real, Ideal, and Expectation Form Item Number	Scoring Direction	
5*	F	There is very little emphasis on making plans for getting out of here.
14*	T	Residents are encouraged to plan for the future.
23*	T	Residents are encouraged to learn new ways of doing things.
32*	F	There is very little emphasis on what residents will be doing after they leave the unit.
41	F	Staff care more about how residents feel than about their practical problems.
50	T	This unit emphasizes training for new kinds of jobs.
59	T	Residents here are expected to work toward their goals.
68	T	New treatment approaches are often tried on this unit.
77	T	Residents must make plans before leaving the unit.
86	F	There is very little emphasis on making residents more practical.

PERSONAL PROBLEM ORIENTATION

Real, Ideal, and Expectation Form Item Number	Scoring Direction	
6*	T	Residents are expected to share their personal problems with each other.
15*	F	Residents rarely talk about their personal problems with other residents.
24*	T	Personal problems are openly talked about.
33*	T	Discussions on the unit emphasize understanding personal problems.
42	T	Staff are mainly interested in learning about residents' feelings.
51	F	Residents are rarely asked personal questions by the staff.
60	F	The staff discourage talking about sex.
69	T	Staff try to help residents understand themselves.
78	F	Residents hardly ever discuss their sexual lives.
87	(filler item)	Residents cannot openly discuss their personal problems here.

ORDER AND ORGANIZATION

Real, Ideal, and Expectation Form Item Number	Scoring Direction	
7*	T	The staff make sure that the unit is always neat.
16*	F	The day room is often messy.
25*	F	The unit usually looks a little messy.
34*	T	This is a very well organized unit.
43	F	Things are sometimes very disorganized around here.
52	F	Many residents look messy.
61	T	Residents' activities are carefully planned.
70	F	Counselors sometimes don't show up for their appointments with residents.
79	T	The staff set an example for neatness and orderliness.
88	T	Residents are rarely kept waiting when they have appointments with the staff.

CLARITY

Real, Ideal, and Expectation Form Item Number	Scoring Direction	
8*	F	Staff sometimes argue with each other.
17*	T	If a resident's program is changed, someone on the staff always tells him why.
26*	T	When residents first arrive on the unit, someone shows them around and explains how the unit operates.
35*	F	Staff are always changing their minds here.
44	T	Staff tell residents when they're doing well.
53	T	If a resident breaks a rule, he knows what will happen to him.
62	F	Residents are always changing their minds here.
71	F	Residents never know when a counselor will ask to see them.
80	F	Residents never know when they will be transferred from this unit.
89	T	The residents know when counselors will be on the unit.

STAFF CONTROL

Real, Ideal, and Expectation Form Item Number	Scoring Direction	
9*	T	Once a schedule is arranged for a resident, he must follow it.
18*	F	Residents may criticize staff members to their faces.
27*	T	Residents will be transferred from this unit if they don't obey the rules.
36*	T	All decisions about the unit are made by the staff and not by the residents.
45	F	The staff very rarely punish residents by restricting them.
54	F	Staff don't order the residents around.
63	T	If one resident argues with another, he will get into trouble with the staff.
72	T	The unit staff regularly check up on the residents.
81	F	Residents can call staff by their first names.
90	(filler item)	The staff do not tolerate sexual behavior by residents.

Family Environment Scale
Scoring Key

Below is the scoring key for the subscales of the different forms of the Family Environment Scale. The Real family (Form R), Ideal family (Form I), and Expectation forms (Form E) are directly parallel, and all items are scored in the same direction on all three forms. The 40 items included in the Short Form are marked with an asterisk. An item listed as "true" (T) is scored 1 point if marked "true" by the individual taking the scale, and an item listed as "false" (F) is scored 1 point if marked "false." The total subscale score is simply the number of items answered in the scored direction.

The Family Environment Scale and Manual have been published and are available for interested users (Moos, 1974b).

COHESION

Real, Ideal, and Expectation Form Item Number	Scoring Direction	
1*	T	Family members really help and support one another.
11*	F	We often seem to be killing time at home.
21*	T	We put a lot of energy into what we do at home.
31*	T	There is a feeling of togetherness in our family.
41	F	We rarely volunteer when something has to be done at home.
51	T	Family members really back each other up.
61	F	There is very little group spirit in our family.
71	T	We really get along well with each other.
81	T	There is plenty of time and attention for everyone in our family.

EXPRESSIVENESS

Real, Ideal, and Expectation Form Item Number	Scoring Direction	
2*	F	Family members often keep their feelings to themselves.
12*	T	We say anything we want to around home.
22*	F	It's hard to "blow off steam" at home without upsetting somebody.
32*	T	We tell each other about our personal problems.
42	T	If we feel like doing something on the spur of the moment we often just pick up and go.
52	F	Someone usually gets upset if you complain in our family.
62	T	Money and paying bills is openly talked about in our family.
72	F	We are usually careful about what we say to each other.
82	T	There are a lot of spontaneous discussions in our family.

CONFLICT

Real, Ideal, and Expectation Form Item Number	Scoring Direction	
3*	T	We fight a lot in our family.
13*	F	Family members rarely become openly angry.
23*	T	Family members sometimes get so angry they throw things.
33*	F	Family members hardly ever lose their tempers.
43	T	Family members often criticize each other.
53	T	Family members sometimes hit each other.
63	F	If there's a disagreement in our family, we try hard to smooth things over and keep the peace.
73	T	Family members often try to one up or outdo each other.
83	F	In our family, we believe you don't ever get anywhere by raising your voice.

INDEPENDENCE

Real, Ideal, and Expectation Form Item Number	Scoring Direction	
4*	F	We don't do things on our own very often in our family.
14*	T	In our family, we are strongly encouraged to be independent.
24*	T	We think things out for ourselves in our family.
34*	T	We come and go as we want to in our family.
44	F	There is very little privacy in our family.
54	T	Family members almost always rely on themselves when a problem comes up.
64	T	Family members strongly encourage each other to stand up for their rights.
74	F	It's hard to be by yourself without hurting someone's feelings in our household.
84	F	We are not really encouraged to speak up for ourselves in our family.

ACHIEVEMENT ORIENTATION

Real, Ideal, and Expectation Form Item Number	Scoring Direction	
5*	T	We feel it is important to be the best at whatever you do.
15*	T	Getting ahead in life is very important in our family.
25*	F	How much money a person makes is not very important to us.
35*	T	We believe in competition and "may the best man win."
45	T	We always strive to do things just a little better the next time.
55	F	Family members rarely worry about job promotions, school grades, etc.
65	F	In our family, we don't try that hard to succeed.
75	T	"Work before play" is the rule in our family.
85	T	Family members are often compared with others as to how well they are doing at work or school.

INTELLECTUAL—CULTURAL ORIENTATION

Real, Ideal, and Expectation Form Item Number	Scoring Direction	
6*	T	We often talk about political and social problems.
16*	F	We rarely go to lectures, plays, or concerts.
26*	T	Learning about new and different things is very important in our family.
36*	F	We are not that interested in cultural activities.
46	F	We rarely have intellectual discussions.
56	T	Someone in our family plays a musical instrument.
66	T	Family members often go to the library.
76	F	Watching TV is more important than reading in our family.
86	T	Family members really like music, art, and literature.

ACTIVE RECREATIONAL ORIENTATION

Real, Ideal, and Expectation Form Item Number	Scoring Direction	
7*	F	We spend most weekends and evenings at home.
17*	T	Friends often come over for dinner or to visit.
27*	F	Nobody in our family is active in sports, Little League, bowling, etc.
37*	T	We often go to movies, sports events, camping, etc.
47	T	Everyone in our family has a hobby or two.
57	F	Family members are not very involved in recreational activities outside work or school.
67	T	Family members sometimes attend courses or take lessons for some hobby or interest (outside of school).
77	T	Family members go out a lot.
87	F	Our main form of entertainment is watching TV or listening to the radio.

Real, Ideal, and Expectation Form Item Number	Scoring Direction	
8*	T	Family members attend church, synagogue, or Sunday School fairly often.
18*	F	We don't say prayers in our family.
28*	T	We often talk about the religious meaning of Christmas, Passover, or other holidays.
38*	F	We don't believe in heaven or hell.
48	T	Family members have strict ideas about what is right and wrong.
58	T	We believe there are some things you just have to take on faith.
68	F	In our family, each person has different ideas about what is right and wrong.
78	T	The Bible is a very important book in our home.
88	T	Family members believe that if you sin you will be punished.

ORGANIZATION

Real, Ideal, and Expectation Form Item Number	Scoring Direction	
9*	T	Activities in our family are pretty carefully planned.
19*	T	We are generally very neat and orderly.
29*	F	It's often hard to find things when you need them in our household.
39*	T	Being on time is very important in our family.
49	F	People change their minds often in our family.
59	T	Family members make sure their rooms are neat.
69	T	Each person's duties are clearly defined in our family.
79	F	Money is not handled very carefully in our family.
89	T	Dishes are usually done immediately after eating.

CONTROL

Real, Ideal, and Expectation Form Item Number	Scoring Direction	
10*	F	Family members are rarely ordered around.
20*	F	There are very few rules to follow in our family.
30*	T	There is one family member who makes most of the decisions.
40*	T	There are set ways of doing things at home.
50	T	There is a strong emphasis on following rules in our family.
60	F	Everyone has an equal say in family decisions.
70	F	We can do whatever we want to in our family.
80	T	Rules are pretty inflexible in our household.
90	T	You can't get away with much in our family.

REFERENCES

Moos, R. Correctional Institutions Environment Scale Manual. Consulting Psychologists Press, Palo Alto, Calif., 1974a.

Moos, R. Family Environment Scale Preliminary Manual. Consulting Psychologists Press, Palo Alto, Calif., 1974b.

Author Index

Subject Index